ADVANCE PRAISE FOR

learning in places

"*Learning in Places: The Informal Education Reader* may sound at first a bit ambitious. In fact, not only is there nothing else like it in 'the field,' but it is indeed canonical—in its quality, in its range of interests, and, appropriately, in its description and analysis of the variegated nature of the settings or 'places' in which learning occurs."

Philip Wexler, Professor of Sociology of Education,
School of Education, Hebrew University, Jerusalem

learning in places

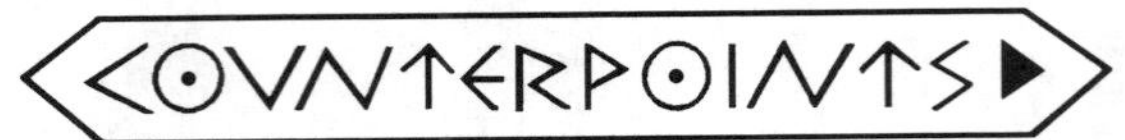

Studies in the Postmodern Theory of Education

Joe L. Kincheloe and Shirley R. Steinberg
General Editors

Vol. 249

PETER LANG
New York • Washington, D.C./Baltimore • Bern
Frankfurt am Main • Berlin • Brussels • Vienna • Oxford

learning in places

THE INFORMAL EDUCATION READER

EDITED BY

ZVI BEKERMAN,

NICHOLAS C. BURBULES,

DIANA SILBERMAN KELLER

PETER LANG

New York • Washington, D.C./Baltimore • Bern

Frankfurt am Main • Berlin • Brussels • Vienna • Oxford

Library of Congress Cataloging-in-Publication Data

Learning in places: the informal education reader/ edited by Zvi Bekerman, Nicholas C. Burbules, Diana Silberman-Keller.
p. cm. — (Counterpoints; vol. 249)
Includes bibliographical references and index.
1. Non-formal education. 2. Self-culture. 3. Continuing education.
I. Bekerman, Zvi. II. Burbules, Nicholas C. III. Silberman-Keller, Diana. IV. Series: Counterpoints (New York, N.Y.); v. 249.
LC45.3.L43 371.38—dc22 2003025194
ISBN 978-0-8204-6786-3
ISSN 1058-1634

Bibliographic information published by **Die Deutsche Bibliothek**.
Die Deutsche Bibliothek lists this publication in the "Deutsche Nationalbibliografie"; detailed bibliographic data is available on the Internet at http://dnb.ddb.de/.

Cover design by Sophie Boorsch Appel

The paper in this book meets the guidelines for permanence and durability of the Committee on Production Guidelines for Book Longevity of the Council of Library Resources.

29 Broadway, 18th floor, New York, NY 10006
www.peterlang.com

Printed in the United States of America

CONTENTS

INTRODUCTION

ZVI BEKERMAN, NICHOLAS C. BURBULES, AND DIANA SILBERMAN-KELLER

Any new book on a widely published topic, especially a rather large book, must explain and justify itself as yet another addition to the literature: Why another book on informal learning? We believe that *Learning in Places: The Informal Education Reader* fills an important gap in the literature and approaches the problem of formal and informal education in a distinctive way. "Learning in places" suggests that an emphasis on learning "loci" can yield a perspective through which questions regarding formality and informality in education are viewed in relation to the increasing variety of learning sites: the home; the workplace; libraries; museums; popular culture; the media; the streetcorner, the mall, and other "public" spaces; and, most recently, the Internet. Hence we seek to free up the study of learning from constraining assumptions about traditional institutional arrangements and hegemonic definitions of what counts as "learning." This book recounts teaching and learning processes in a variety of sites and under a range of circumstances.

Moreover, referring to the second part of our title, an "informal education reader," this can be read with two meanings: a reader on informal education, or a reader organized in a more informal way. Indeed, it is both. While every essay in this collection is a serious piece of original scholarship on informal education, rigorously reviewed and revised by the editors, the constellation of perspectives here is "informal" in the sense that we have not tried to impose a uniform theoretical perspective, style, or format on the pieces, in order to preserve their character as a polyphonically voiced and internationally representative conversation about the changing meanings and contexts that shape formal and informal education today; indeed, some of the pieces raise fundamental questions on ways in which that very distinction may need to be rethought.

Accordingly, this volume charts what we regard as a transformation in educational thinking, shining light on teaching and learning activities normally on the periphery of study within the field of education. Formal education has long been the preferred daughter of educational theorizing while nonformal education has been relegated to the position of an exotic or poor relative. For the most part, policymakers who approach the subject regard much of non-formal education as supplemental, marginal, or recreational—i.e., not centrally important. Even the rhetoric adopted by those who practice it often seems to assume this position, defining the nonformal in negative terms, as education which is not formal. The full educational potential of nonformal education in a positive sense, as an important and unique domain that is not just a substitute for, or a supplement to, "real" education, is seldom recognized.

Sporadically in the past decades, academicians have approached this subject from a variety of theoretical and methodological perspectives. Anthropologists, philosophers, psychologists, and sociologists of education have begun to recognize the need to attend to spheres and sites other than schools, where education takes place. More recently, attempts have been made to discuss the possible *contribution of* nonformal educational approaches to more formal activities.

High modernity and globalization have raised old and new questions about a variety of educational problems in and out of school. Citizenship instruction, multicultural tensions, distance education, workplace training, and the improvement of school pedagogies are only a few of the challenges confronting education around the world today. In all of these areas, nonformal education has taken on a greater role; yet no concerted effort has been undertaken to create a resource book that can introduce academic, professional, and lay readers to a field which, while not yet fully shaped, is becoming more and more central. Our interest in putting together a collection of papers relevant to nonformal education follows from this situation. Accordingly, we aim to present some of the most promising theoretical advances in the field; to analyze a variety of social, cultural, political, historical, and economic contexts within which nonformal education has developed (as well as those in which it is hidden, erased, or unappropriated); and to probe into the views of knowledge which nourish the development of nonformal learning contexts and the practices through which nonformal learning is implemented.

These theoretical and methodological choices express our intention to treat *learning* as something that happens in a variety of places and to think of these *places* as sites that generate learning in a variety of forms, which should force us to reconsider the meaning of "a good education." Even the informal/formal dichotomy is questioned here, and many of the papers in this volume adopt an overall approach that emphasizes the (possible) *relation* between these two domains.

Opening this volume, Smith examines some aspects of the renewed interest in informal education and explores the possibilities for learning that flows from associational life (*la vie associative*) in schools. Smith argues that informal education is, essentially, a noncurriculum form that can make a significant contribution to the development of a more convivial public life. It is especially important today, in light of the increasing tendency of neoliberal economic regimes to marketize social services, among them public education, thereby transforming their purposes and functions in ways that have had a deleterious impact on public life. This shift has reconfigured these services so that they can be priced and sold; it has induced people to see them as something to be purchased (if they can afford them), rather than simply as a right they can expect as citizens; it has transformed the workforce from one working for collective aims, with a public service ethic, to one working to produce profits for owners of capital.

Smith characterizes informal education as being based on conversational practices. While he looks positively at the possibility of incorporating informal education into schools, he points out the dilemmas inherent in the idea of "formalizing" informal education, which could undermine the very purpose of ameliorating some of the shortcomings of formal education through including informal learning at schools. Amongst these dilemmas he includes tendencies in the formal system such as the increased use of coursework; the need to address mandated curriculum requirements; and an increased emphasis upon monitoring and bureaucratic activity. By contrast, informal education emphasizes confidentiality; personal discipline; learning about sensitive issues; and the uniqueness of its targets. Smith concludes that alternating the two approaches to education and learning strategies within schools could moderate the impact of neoliberal attitudes in formal education, if policymakers will come to appreciate that the learning involved in associational activity is of fundamental importance to the well-being of society.

The next two articles in this volume approach the home and parents as educators. Ash and Wells and Goldman examine the "forgotten" role of parents, since the development of formal education, as mediating early learning processes. Applying activity theory to the analysis of two different, yet complementary, dialogically-based episodes of artifact-mediated joint activity—one in a museum, the second in a classroom—Ash and Wells argue that the characteristics of productive learning activities are remarkably similar in the two settings. They conclude that those responsible for the design of learning and teaching environments must create conditions that will closely match the principles laid out in the article, where the practice of dialogue improves the possibilities of learning.

Goldman has worked with a team of parents, teachers, researchers, and materials developers on a project called PRIMES, dedicated to finding ways to reconnect parents of middle grades students with the school math enterprise. Their assumption was that helping to make visible the mathematics that people do in their lives and showing how it is connected to the school math of their children would begin to lay a foundation for more productive parental involvement in school math. The work they report on here makes the case for parents' continued role in the learning process especially after their children leave elementary schools, and shows that parents have a knowledge base for being truly helpful. Goldman's basic conclusions are that:

- Parents use math successfully in their everyday lives, whether they label it as "math" or not; and
- Once invited to do so, parents can use these everyday competencies to support their children in their math achievements.

The growing presence of after-school programs in the U.S.A. offered an opportunity for Hull and Greeno to reexamine and challenge two common assumptions within the field of education. The first is that the ways people learn and develop differ, of necessity, depending on whether the context for learning is formal or informal, within school settings or outside them. The second assumption examines and challenges the hierarchical relationship that is commonly assumed between school and nonschool: that learning out-of-school—through participation in after-school programs, for example—should be *supplemental* to learning in school. They argue for a reversal of this relationship: *that school should be understood as being supplementary to students' out-of-school worlds.* Hull and Greeno present their arguments through an examination of cases of mathematics and literacy learning in classrooms, after-school programs, and workplaces. In some instances, powerful learning takes place at school, and in such cases the best relationship to an after-school program is one of seamless continuation. But in other instances—and Hull and Greeno suggest that these might be in the majority—school is organized in less than optimal ways, and children have less than optimal chances to develop relationships with teachers and with subject matter that support their learning. In such instances, learning in other contexts is not helped by close association with school activities.

In discussing the construct of identity, the centerpiece of their analysis, Hull and Greeno review different ways of theorizing identity and agency, principally the idea of identity and agency as positional (in respect to interactions and to subject matter) and as connected to entering a discourse. In the course of their analysis, they challenge common misconceptions related to formal learning (usually associated with the institution of school) and informal learning (usually associated with nonschool worlds), especially learning in after-school or out-of-school programs.

Nocon and Cole "steer" between two theoretical interpretations of the function of schooling: one seeing it as a tool for access to participation in a democratic society for future citizens and workers; and the other seeing it as a means of colonizing immigrants and the poor by the state and industry in a process of rationalized distribution of access to wealth and power. Nocon and Cole focus on after-school programs and ask whether they are invaded by school and hence also play a role in these processes of colonization and restricted access. They describe the Fifth Dimension, a model (Cole, 1996) used to create systems of mixed activities: Children come to play (and learn); adult students come to learn (and play); researchers and community members come to work (and play and learn). The authors' general argument, which moves between the evaluation and the revision of this after-school educational model, is that while potentially "semicolonizing," after-school programs complement formal schooling as valuable sites of informal education because they provide low income and immigrant children with access to social development and learning without failure.

Continuing the line that links a conceptual consideration of formal and informal learning settings, Callanan and Braswell's research concludes that parents have a unique perspective on their children's learning in both informal and formal settings. They reach these conclusions by studying children's interactions with the Alice's Wonderland exhibit in the San Jose Children's Discovery Museum; interactions that were enhanced when parents accompanied the children. An analysis of parent-child conversations related to science concepts suggests that these conversations greatly improved the chances that children would link their museum experiences to abstract scientific concepts. From this perspective, Callanan and Braswell found that parents' participation in informal education activities with their children supports and strengthens formal learning

In their paper Maynard and Greenfield show how formal schooling as well as exposure to television and commercial activities transform the ways in which learners respond to informal learning in traditional settings. Maynard and Greenfield present historical research that diachronically and synchronically explores the nature and development of cultural teaching and learning in traditional communities in Mexico. Cultural teaching adapts to changing ecocultural circumstances; parents and siblings socialize children in accordance with a changing world. Cultures develop fairly general models of cultural teaching that are the foundation for further adaptation to environmental change. Maynard and Greenfield stress the connection between the adaptive modes of cultural teaching and particular emphases in cognitive development. From an evolutionary perspective, adaptation of informal education to a changing environment is connected to cognitive ontogeny. Active participation in learning in a particular domain leads to cognitive development in that domain. Further experience with a given cognitive skill in a new domain can lead to cross-domain generalizations of the skill in question. At the same time, cultural teaching conceptualized as the ability to teach according to a particular cultural model with techniques and tools adapted to the developmental level of the learner also respects the constraints of cognitive maturation.

Schugurensky's article reflects on the political and social landscape of Latin America and examines the informal civic and political learning that occurs in local processes of deliberation and decision making. His article has two main sections. The first advances a conceptual discussion of informal learning; the second draws upon theories of situated learning and of participatory democracy, as well as other current research, to analyze the pedagogical dimensions of the participatory budget of Porto Alegre, Brazil, an experiment in local democracy that has been in place since 1989.

Dichotomizing not between formal and informal learning places but between the social and cultural contours of informal learning places, Duensing's article examines case studies of science and technology museums and science centers as cultural creations and cultural institutions. Duensing argues that like formal education institutions, informal education institutions reflect the cultural contexts in which they exist. In their exhibits and educational programs these centers develop and disseminate images and understandings concerning both the content and process of science and of learning. Different museums and centers do this in different ways, but they are all embedded in sociocultural contexts of museum practice, science, and public education as well as national and local cultural milieus that influence the form and content of their presentations. This chapter examines different ways in which exhibits and programs have been designed and adapted by museum staff to fit particular cultural contexts in science centers in a variety of different countries. Duensing's discussion centers on ways in which these adaptations perpetuate certain cultural norms, thought, and practices, and she explores the kinds of learning experiences the museum creates for its visitors, which can then lead to issues of access and potential connections to formal classroom practice, as discussed in other chapters of this book.

Informal learning in advanced industrial societies has grown in quantity, quality, and thematic subjects, and it is in this context that Livingstone's article offers a broad picture of this situation. Livingstone examines different conceptions of informal learning, summarizes and critically assesses the empirical research to date on the extent of informal learning in advanced industrial societies, and offers suggestions for future research on informal learning practices with a particular focus on survey research.

Hanchaia is the Hebrew word for group working (facilitating), and its use in Israel (a society where traditional and modern tendencies of development and conservation interweave) offers some insights that might possibly be used by the large number of NGOs dealing with education toward values.

Values education is a strategy that stresses the function of values as adaptation facilitators that, through values clarification, alleviate the need to face basic existential dilemmas in daily life. Bekerman's article examines group work as a pedagogical approach implemented in informal educational settings, and he questions the types of goals it achieves in areas related to values education. He assumes that new identities are not built solely on the basis of a rejection of traditional views or by simply buying into critical perspectives but, rather, by formulating and offering symbolic and concrete alternatives to the ones under suspicion. He thus questions the extent to which the pedagogy under examination ultimately serves to challenge or support hegemonic modes of thought. Through the analysis of in-depth interviews, he uncovers mediating hegemonic cultural strategies that dwell in the practices of this pedagogy. His paper cautions theoreticians and educators about supporting uncritically any pedagogical strategy whatsoever—whether informal or other.

Envisioning the possibility of theorizing about the common characteristics of the principles and practices that generate modern informal education, Silberman-Keller aims to arrive at a characterization of "nonformal pedagogy." The underlying assumption of Silberman-Keller's essay is that any given pedagogy, whether humanistic, conservative, liberal, or critical, creates and reflects a narrative that includes its ideal vision of educators, learners, and teaching and learning processes. Images of time and place are created and shaped within the exclusive narrative framework of every type of pedagogy. Her essay introduces the concept of "nonformal pedagogy" and interprets one of its characteristic practices as the active creation and reflection of images of place and time. She assumes that images of place and time configure and are configured by specific practices performed during educational activities in nonformal educational settings. Although the research that has fed her essay draws from a variety of representative educational institutions that comprise a "non-formal educational system" (including community centers, youth movements, and historical, art, and science museums that run educational activities, advocatory and interest educational organizations and local government units dealing with nonformal education activities), Silberman-Keller believes that similar images of place and time characterize nonformal educational practices as a social and cultural phenomena across contexts. On the basis of this assumption, it might be possible to state that nonformal pedagogy interprets the term "education" in a specific and special way.

Burbules focuses on what he calls "self-educating communities," groups engaged in formal, informal, or nonformal teaching and learning activities amongst themselves. His primary interest is with online self-educating communities, those using the Internet as an educational medium. The first section of his paper offers a typology of the kinds of online networks that are formed with such coeducation in mind. His second section discusses the internal practices and norms that allow these networks to act successfully as self-educating communities and the areas in which these practices and norms can run into conflict with one another. His third section situates the discussion against the background of different conceptions of formal, informal, nonformal, and lifelong learning.

Completely blurring differences between formal and informal settings, McDermott's critical article concludes that theories of ingenious or disabled learning have been treated as if they were a resource in the explanation of different kinds of children and different kinds of learning. McDermott claims that learning theories are not in our lives just to help us explain differential learning. Rather they are a part of what must be explained, taken into account, and confronted. They and the institutional demands to which they answer are part of what must be changed. We do not need new theories of learning as much as new institutions for their emergence and application; we need not change our theories of learning as much as we need to change ourselves.

In closing but not concluding this introduction, it is worthwhile to think of Cortazar's novel *Hopscotch,* in which he presents various possibilities of reading a novel and/or, by extension, every book. He proposes a linear order and alternatively an order that allows "jumping"—like playing hopscotch—from chapter to chapter according to a delineated and alternative plan of order of the chapters. It is in this sense that the order of chapters presented in this introduction reflects one way of reading the thematic relations between them. But we are aware that there are many more interrelations that can be drawn. The reader is thus invited to create his/her own pattern of reading and cross-reading the insights of *Learning in Places.*

BEYOND THE CURRICULUM

FOSTERING ASSOCIATIONAL LIFE IN SCHOOLS

MARK K. SMITH

There has been a significant growth in the numbers of specialist informal educators working within schools in a number of countries. In Britain, for example, political pressures to raise educational standards have led to narrowing of the focus of classroom teachers. It has entailed increased workloads; the implementation of a national curriculum; and an emphasis on ensuring that school life is marked by reasonable behavior and is attractive to potential students and their parents. One result has been a range of government and local programs to introduce informal educators and support workers into schools. The *Excellence in Cities* (DfEE, 1999) initiative introduced learning mentors into many English schools; the *Connexions* strategy (DfEE, 2000) personal advisers; and the Scottish *New Community Schools* program (Scottish Office, 1999) youth workers. Alongside this there has been a growing orientation among policymakers to learning beyond the classroom and its contribution to formal educational achievement, and the deepening of the skill base seen as necessary for economic competitiveness (e.g., Bentley, 1998; Leadbeater, 2000). An aspect of this has been the use of problematic notions such as lifelong learning (Field, 2000). In the United States, we have seen a parallel growth in interest in full-service schooling (Dryfoos, 1994); a concern with "helping in the hallways" (Hazler, 1998); and a growing interest in after-school programs (Halpern, 2003). Similarly, those schools that have tried to grapple with the notion of multiple intelligences have had to look at creating a variety of environments for learning—many of which embrace the informal.

Unfortunately, increasing the number of informal educators has not necessarily enhanced the quality of informal education in schools. They, like their teacher colleagues, often find themselves running prepackaged programs and constrained by inappropriate targets. Worryingly, a number have chosen or absorbed ways of thinking and being that approach education as a commodity. They have lost touch with informal education as a noncurriculum form and the possibilities for learning that flow from associational life (*la vie associative*). In this chapter, I explore some key aspects of the current situation—drawing heavily on UK experience. I suggest that it is still possible to cultivate a "vocabulary of hope" (Halpin, 2003) within schooling—and that informal education with its emphasis on conversation and association can make a significant contribution to the development of a more convivial public life. However, there are particular areas of tension that must be addressed if space is to be carved out by classroom teachers and informal educators for engaged and critical practice.

GLOBALIZATION, PROFESSIONALIZATION, AND COMMODIFICATION IN EDUCATION

The increased use of specialist informal educators within schools has to be set in the context of broader movements. In the last quarter of the twentieth century, and particularly in those countries where neoliberal economic policies dominated, there was strong pressure to "roll-back" local state regulation, and to transform non-market and "social" spheres such as public health and education services into arenas of commercial activity. Such marketization was, and is, increasingly difficult to disentangle from the intensification of globalization (Giroux, 2000, p. 6). We saw attempts within many education and welfare systems to:

- Reconfigure services so that they can be priced and sold.
- Induce people to want to buy them rather than simply have the right to expect them as citizens.
- Transform the workforce from one working for collective aims with a service ethic to one working to produce profits for owners of capital and subject to market discipline.
- Underwrite risks to capital by the state. (Leys, 2001; p. 4)

In other words, there was a process of commodification—and the attempt to standardize "products" and to find economies of scale. While being linked to an intensification of globalization, this process was also part of a long-running growth in institutionalization and reliance on "expertise." In his influential exploration and critique of these movements, Ivan Illich (1973, 1977) argues that they contribute to dehumanization. "[I]nstitutions create the needs and control their satisfaction, and, by so doing, turn the human being and her or his creativity into objects" (Finger and Asún, 2001, p. 10). There has been a reconfiguration of what it meant to be "professional." In more recent years, within many education systems, this has been expressed as a shift away from a concern with connoisseurship and criticism (Eisner, 1985, 1998) and a wish to work well within a community of practice (Wenger, 1999). In their place has come a much stronger focus on rule-following, correct procedure, and management.

The opening up of education systems within the United Kingdom to corporate activity required major intervention by national government. By the end of the twentieth century, the United Kingdom had moved from having one of the most decentralized schooling systems in the world to one of the most tightly controlled and state regulated (Alexander, 2000, p. 122). The corporate need for efficiency, calculability, predictability, and control (the qualities that Ritzer [1993] used to define the "McDonaldization process") required government action.

During the 1980s and early 1990s this project was partly carried forward by the rise of managerialism in many "Western" education systems. Both frontline educators and those in authority were encouraged and trained to see themselves as managers, and to reframe the problems of education as exercises in delivering the right outcomes. The language and disposition of management also quickly moved into the classroom via initiatives such as the UK national curriculum. In many systems, there was also a wholesale strengthening of the market. Schools had to compete for students, for example, in order to sustain and extend their funding. This, in turn, meant that they have had to market their activities and to develop their own "brands." They had to sell "the learning experience" and the particular qualities of their institution. To do this, complex processes had to be reduced to easily identified packages; philosophies to sound-bites; and students and their parents become "consumers" (see, for example, Wolf, 2002). We have seen a growing focus on outcome and an associated intensification of testing and accrediting learning. As Stewart (1992, p. 27) demonstrated some time ago there is a fundamental problem with the way that such business models have been applied: "The real danger is that unthinking adoption of the private sector model prevents the development of an approach to management in the public services in general or to the social services in particular based on their distinctive purposes, conditions and tasks." The result was a drive toward the achievement of specified outcomes and the adoption of standardized teaching models. The emphasis was less on community and equity, and rather more on individual advancement and the need to satisfy investors and influential consumers. Education had come to resemble a private, rather than public, good.

As a result of these processes, schooling is now viewed as offering lucrative market opportunities. Giroux (2000, p. 85) reports that in the United States the for-profit education market represented around $600 billion in revenue for transnational, corporate interests. Over 1,000 state schools have been contracted out to private companies (Monbiot, 2000, p. 336). In Britain, education management "looks like it is about to become big business" (op. cit.). Educational Action Zones (beginning in 1998) have had significant corporate involvement. The Lambeth Zone is run by Shell, for example, not the local education authority. In Southwark, the education service was contracted out to W. S. Atkins (unsuccessfully as it turned out), and Kings Manor School, Guildford, became the first state school to have its administration handed to a private company in 1999. Kenway and Bullen (2001) have charted similar shifts in the marketization of Australian schooling.

Learning has increasingly been portrayed as a commodity or as investment, rather than as a way of exploring what might make for the good life or human flourishing. Teachers' and educators' ability to ask critical questions about the world in which they live has been compromised. The market ideologies they have assimilated (along with others in these societies), the direction of the curricula they are required to "deliver," and the readiness of the colleges, schools, and agencies in which they operate to embrace corporate sponsorship and intervention have combined to degrade their work to such an extent as to question whether what they are engaged in can be rightfully be called education (MacIntrye, 2002). In a very real sense, they are engaged in furthering what Erich Fromm described as alienation. People become treated as commodities, and experience their "life forces" as an investment that must bring them "the maximum profit obtainable under existing market conditions" (Fromm, 1957, p. 67). It is a form of education that looks to "having" rather than "being" (Fromm, 1976).

ASSOCIATIONAL LIFE AND THE PUBLIC INTEREST

To counter the effects of commodification and institutionalization, we need to step outside the current, dominant discourses within schooling systems. We need, for example, to adopt ways of thinking and acting that have at their core an informed commitment to human flourishing in its fullest sense (Marples, 1999). We also need to reassert the public domain and to police the boundaries between it and the market sector with some vigilance (Leys, 2001, p. 222). Furthermore, we need, as educators, to be able to do what is right rather than what is "correct" (Jeffs & Smith, 1990, pp. 1–23). But how is all this to be achieved within societies and systems conditioned by globalization and neoliberalism and in which there are asymmetrical relations of power? The answer, of course, is that progress will always be partial. But we can, at least, offer alternatives and seek to undermine the narrowing and demeaning processes that pass under the name of education in many systems. Ways of educating that look to well-being and participation in the common life have been well articulated. However, accounts of such work, and exploration of the vision that runs through it, are sometimes dismissed as "utopian." Yet without that appreciation of what could be, and a critique of the present, there can be little hope for education. As David Halpin (2003, p. 44) has argued, the challenge for schooling today is "not to learn without utopias, but rather to seek to delineate new ones which help to fuel fresh conceptions of what might contribute to the creation of schools of positive consequence for all that attend them."

Of particular relevancy is working for a recovery of approaches to educating that embrace democracy and association. Alexis de Tocqueville made the case long ago (in the 1830s) that "the strength of free peoples resides in the local community" and that local institutions have considerable educative power: "they put [liberty] within the people's reach; they teach people to appreciate its peaceful enjoyment and accustom them to make use of it" (1994, pp. 63–64). Local institutions such as churches, tenants groups, and community organizations involve people in freely combining together in order to further some agreed purpose, and are part of larger political processes. They also usually carry within them some valuing of cooperation and a commitment to those in memberships, and may be thought of as mutual aid organizations (Bishop & Hoggett, 1986, p. 33; Smith, 1994, pp. 151–53). The democratic potential of such associations; the way in which they foster dialogue, relationship, and friendship; and the extent to which the reciprocity and cooperation involved offer a counterbalance to the individualization and commodification of neoliberalism provide us with an obvious and important starting point. As Freire (1974, p. 36) once put it, people learn social and political responsibility "only by *experiencing* that responsibility."

Association—joining together in companionship or to undertake some task, and the educative power of playing one's part in a group or association (Doyle & Smith, 1999, p. 44)—was a defining feature, for example, of youth work in the United Kingdom for most of the twentieth century and was strongly advocated in the Albemarle Report (Ministry of Education, 1960). It has also been a key aspect of the community association and center movement (Broady et al., 1990; Fisher, 1994) and an important strand within community work and "community education" (Elsdon et al., 1995; Galbraith, 1990). However, "association" has been less of an explicit focus for exploration and practice in recent years in the United Kingdom. At one level, this is hardly surprising, given the pressure toward commodification and market individualism outlined earlier. While associational activity remains significant, there are indications that there has been a significant decline since the 1960s (paralleling that charted by Putnam [2000] in the United States). Alongside this, Putnam argues, has come a growing social distance among neighbors, friends, and the extended family. The result, he contends, is a significant decline in social capital—social networks and the associated norms of reciprocity.

THE NATURE AND POTENTIAL OF INFORMAL EDUCATION

It is in this context that we have to make sense of "informal education." Within schooling discourses the term has usually been associated with the flourishing of particular approaches to primary school practice in the United Kingdom in the late 1960s and early 1970s. As Alexander (1988, p. 148) has commented:

> Certain words have acquired a peculiar potency in primary education, and few more so than "informal." Never properly defined, yet ever suggestive of ideas and practices which were indisputably right, "informal" was the flagship of the semantic armada of 1960s Primaryspeak . . . spontaneity, flexibility, naturalness, growth, needs, interests, freedom . . . self-expression, discovery and many more.

In more recent years, the most consistent usage with regard to primary schooling appears to be the noun "informality," rather than the adjective "informal." Thus, instead of informal education, we might talk of informality in pedagogy, in curriculum, in organization, in evaluation, and in personal style (Blyth, 1988).

In other practice settings, there has been a tradition of more sustained attention to the principles and practice of informal education. This includes the work of Malcolm Knowles (1950) and others within adult education (drawing on traditions of thinking articulated by an earlier generation of educators such as Eduard Lindeman [1926] and Basil Yeaxlee [1929]), and Josephine Macalister Brew (1946) within youth work. Significantly, such thinkers have explicitly linked informal education to the cultivation of associational and group life.

Much of the subsequent discussion of informal education has tended to flow from an administrative perspective. Perhaps the best-known approach is to separate formal, nonformal, and informal education (after Coombs et al.,

1973). Within this categorization, informal education is the lifelong process in which people learn from everyday experience, and nonformal education is organized activity outside formal systems. Formal education is linked with schools and training institutions; nonformal education with community groups and nongovernmental organizations; and informal education covers what is left (Jeffs & Smith, 1999a, p. 118). There is an important point for policy in this distinction—as the recent interest in what has been termed "informal learning" within UK discussions has shown (see, for example, Colley et al., 2002; Coffield, 2000). If schools and colleges have only a limited place in the learning that occurs in a society, questions must be asked about the focus on such institutions. Would funding be better deployed elsewhere? Does the current obsession with accreditation have any merit? Should researchers explore learning in everyday life in more depth? However, once this point is noted, there is little conceptual mileage in this particular division of education (or, indeed, learning—see Billett, 2001).

The main problem with regard to theoretical development is that as soon as we begin to look at the characteristics of learning activities within "dedicated" and nondedicated learning environments, we find a striking mix of educational and learning processes in each (Smith, 1988, pp. 125–26). For example, as Henze (1992) and others have shown, people teach and organize educational events as part of their everyday experience. A grandfather might show a child how to use a key to unlock a door; a mother may work with her daughter around reading—and so on. These educational events would not be defined administratively as "formal"—yet in their essence they may be little different to what happens in a classroom. Both grandfather and mother may set out to teach particular skills. For this reason, discussion of informal and formal learning, or informal and formal education, must move beyond a simple focus on context or setting, and look to the processes and experiences involved in each. In the case of the latter, it can be argued that informal education is largely driven by conversation (and has formal interludes), while formal education is curriculum-driven (and has informal interludes) (Jeffs & Smith, 1990, 1999a). In other words, formal education entails a plan of action and defined content. It also involves creating a particular social and, often, physical setting—the most familiar example being a classroom. In contrast, informal education is shaped by conversation. It is not tied to particular environments. However, whether we are identified as formal or informal educator we will use a mix of the formal and informal. What sets the two apart is the relative emphasis placed upon curricula and conversation, and the range of settings in which they may work. Different settings will offer a novel mix of resources and opportunities for learning and will have contrasting expectations associated with them (Jeffs & Smith, 1990, pp. 1–23).

Informal education tends to be unpredictable—practitioners do not know where it might lead. In conversation they have to catch the moment where they can say or do something to deepen people's thinking or to put others in touch with their feelings (Jeffs & Smith, 1999b, pp. 209–10). This "going with the flow" opens up considerable possibility and the opportunity to get into rewarding areas. There is the chance, for example, to connect with the questions, issues, and feelings that are significant to people, rather than what they think might be important. "Catching the moment" can quickly take conversations into the realms of feelings, experiences, and relationships. In informal education we respond to situations, to experiences.

Thus far, we can see that when viewed as a process, informal education works through, and is driven by, conversation; involves exploring and enlarging experience; and can take place in any setting. Not having recourse to a curriculum, informal educators have to discern what might be the appropriate response. To do this with integrity, they have to develop with others some sense of what might make for human flourishing. It could be argued that all educators should develop this if they are to act in an informed and committed way. However, without the prop of curriculum, it is revealed as a fundamental necessity for informal educators. Although some might want to avoid its implications, they cannot. The medium they work through—conversation—is a relation they enter into; they can be caught up in it and sometimes carried away by it (Burbules, 1993, p. xii). It involves particular commitments and dispositions. Unlike many of those working in formal settings, relationships with informal educators take place on a voluntary basis. People are rarely under any obligation to talk to an informal educator (Jeffs & Smith, 1999a, p. 84). It is for these reasons that informal education has a particular place in the process of working so that people may share in a common life (Dewey's famous [1916] focus for education). The sorts of values and behaviors needed for conversation to take place are exactly what are required if democracy and "fraternity" are to flourish.

Not having a curriculum also removes a hiding place for educators. Instead of seeking to transmit information, they have to engage with situations and with people—and this inevitably throws their character into the spotlight. Their behavior, attitudes, and values are scrutinized. If they do not "practice what they preach," or are not fair, truthful, or unselfish in their conduct, they will not be heard or heeded. This also applies to formal educators. If we are to believe Parker J. Palmer (1998, p. 10), good teaching cannot be reduced to technique, but flows from "the identity and integrity of the teacher." It entails self-knowledge.

> When I do not know myself, I cannot know who my students are. I will see them through a glass darkly, in the shadows of my unexamined life—and when I cannot see them clearly, I cannot teach them well. When I do not know myself, I cannot know my subject . . . I will know it only abstractly, from a distance, a congeries of concepts as far removed from the world as I am from personal truth. (Palmer, 1998, p. 2)

However, it is easy in many education systems with their focus on the "delivery" of prepackaged programs, testing, and the achievement of externally set targets and outcomes for educators to become technicians and to lose their sense of agency. In the United Kingdom, following government interventions in teacher training, teachers now learn little about the social context of teaching and educational philosophy, and there is little attempt to develop Eisner's (1998) twin orientations of connoisseurship and criticism. The training of informal educators such as youth workers has lagged behind such regulation, and has retained some emphasis on self-knowledge, critique, and social awareness—although this is disappearing as the impact of the broader forces of commodification, globalization, and institutionalization is felt—and government policies (especially in England) around youth work shift toward a more overt focus on targeted intervention and accreditation (Smith, 2003).

THE DECLINE IN CLASSROOM TEACHERS' INVOLVEMENT IN INFORMAL EDUCATION—AND THE RISE OF THE SPECIALIST

Not unexpectedly, given the commodification and institutionalization of education, one of the significant long-term movements within schooling and further education in the United Kingdom has been a decrease in the amount of time that classroom teachers have been able, or prepared, to give to informal education—both in terms of extracurricular activity and free-ranging conversation within the classroom. The formal side of their work has increased markedly. Their average working week has risen significantly since the mid-1980s (to somewhere around 56 hours during term time). Four particular things have been significant here:

The Increased Use of Coursework

The use of coursework as a form of assessment has grown markedly since the early 1970s. It began, in part, as a means of accrediting those students who experienced difficulties in doing exams. Subsequently, the ability to assess longer term and more substantial pieces of work has appealed, as has its relative success in keeping students working. Coursework has meant a significant increase in the marking load of teachers and lecturers, and a corresponding decline in time available for extracurricular activities.

The Need to Address Curriculum Requirements

With the introduction of the national curriculum (and the associated regime of testing and inspection), there appears to have been a marked change in the orientation of teachers within classrooms. There has been considerably less freedom for teachers and students to explore ideas and phenomenon outside its detailed specifications—and to take time on those areas that excite them. A process of standardization has taken place. Teachers are under pressure to complete programs and to raise and sustain student performance in assessed subjects. This tendency has been further strengthened with the introduction of literacy and numeracy strategies in the second half of the 1990s. Moreover, the way national curriculum was framed placed students in a "more passive and conformist role" (Alexander, 2000, p. 565). Space for conversation and the freedom to "go with the flow" was severely constrained. The tone and direction of school inspections added to these movements—and help to sustain a climate of conformity. Failure to address the requirements of the national curriculum and other government initiatives has important consequences for schools.

An Increased Emphasis upon Monitoring and Bureaucratic Activity

The expansion of coursework and the operation of a national curriculum have contributed to a significant growth in bureaucratic activity—coursework has to be recorded and organized; and the progress of students monitored and evaluated. The activities of teachers, too, have to be checked. Other factors also have been at work here to increase the amount of time that teachers have to spend in writing reports and keeping records, and in taking part in meetings. Two key elements here have been changing policies around students with special educational needs and the impact of child protection legislation.

A Focus on Teachers as Managers

As has already been noted, the vocabulary of management has become part of the everyday experience of teachers and educators within schools. Not only are they encouraged to frame curricula activity in managerial terms, they also have to organize the activities of classroom assistants and others. A number of things flow from this. One of the most significant features is the impact on the way they conceptualize their role and their relationship with learners. As managers of learning situations, they are less likely to join with students in the search for meaning and understanding. Significantly, there is less talk of teaching being a calling. There is now a strong appeal to the technical in which plans have to be followed, skills employed, and outcomes monitored. Schooling and education are seen as productive activities rather than an invitation to engage in the formation of practical judgment (to use Aristotle's distinction).

The overall impact has been a decline in the amount of time and freedom that classroom teachers have to engage with their students in conversation and open-ended activities. They are also less disposed to such engagement. There has also been a growth in the numbers of specialist and ancillary workers involved in schools and colleges. The biggest increase has been in classroom assistants, but there also has been a significant expansion in England in the number of youth workers, learning mentors (largely as part of the *Excellence in Cities* Initiative), and personal advisers (as part of the Connexions Service). The rationale is clear. As the Department for Education and Skills has stated in respect of learning mentors,

> . . . they take some of the burden off teachers, who often feel as though they should be helping pupils to overcome problems inside and outside school. Having a Learning Mentor to help pupils tackle these problems free[s] teachers to teach. . . . [and] to concentrate and focus on delivering the national curriculum. (DfES, 2002a)

While there has been some room for interpretation in the learning mentor role, this is now being eroded and there are strong central expectations associated with it. It is hard to escape the conclusion that we have seen Taylorism in action. Schools and colleges have come to more strongly resemble production lines: the educational task has been subdivided, workers operate in their particular areas to a centrally defined plan, and their products dispatched to the market.

THE EXTENSION OF CURRICULAR ACTIVITY AND A FOCUS ON OUTCOME

Alongside growing constraints upon the activities of classroom teachers and others within schools and colleges there has been a growing appreciation in policy debates of the significance of relationships and learning beyond the formality of the classroom. This appears to have been picked up earlier in the United States, where there has been a sustained tradition of participation in student government and sports and arts clubs (Fashola, 2001). However, there has been a developing body of research in both Britain and the United States demonstrating links between involvement by children and young people in organized activities and associational life and educational achievement (as well as there being broader benefits in terms of building social capital) (reviewed in NFER, 1999; see also MacBeath, 1999), and around creating the right environment within the family and local networks (discussed in Hughes et al., 1994; Munn, 1993).

One of the most significant developments in the United Kingdom has been around "out of school learning." With the operation of organizations such as Education Extra in the United Kingdom—and the development of government policies around raising educational achievement, lifelong learning, and social inclusion—there has been a growing interest in out of school hours learning (OSHL). Michael Barber, for example, has written that, "however much schools improve, inspiration and motivation to learn are much more likely to come from children who benefit from involvement in out of school activities as well as formal schooling" (1997, p. 257). Government-funded studies demonstrated a link between what were considered successful schools and the amount of extracurricular activity and homework (Barber et al., 1997). Significantly, these researchers looked to both the traditional sphere of clubs and societies (what they called "curriculum enrichment") and additional study support provided through the medium of homework clubs and extra tuition (so-called curriculum extension). Government and other monies (e.g., from the National Lottery New Opportunities Fund and the Princes Trust) began to flow into schools and colleges (especially those in areas of significant educational disadvantage) and to other settings such as libraries to develop the work. Unfortunately, the focus has been on curriculum extension.

The employment of informal educators such as youth workers and learning mentors has been a significant feature of these developments. Sometimes working alongside teachers and lecturers, sometimes working on their own, informal educators classically offer the opportunity to develop more associational and conversational environments for learning. There is often a tension here, particularly with regard to homework clubs, and it mainly comes from two directions. The first concerns the informality and noisiness of the work (and the contrast it provides with the other activities that usually happen around study in schools and libraries). The second involves worries that many informal educators are putting broader educational aims above the more specific curriculum objectives linked to the completion of homework.

This last tension highlights a worrying trend. One of the key features of the current interest in out of school (and college) hours learning is that the more liberal notion of extracurricular activity has been replaced by curricular-focused activity. This has certainly been a feature of government policies in England around the "transformation" of youth work (DfEE, 2001; DfES, 2002b). Out of school hours learning looks to extend and enrich the curriculum, to tie such learning more closely to government and schooling objectives. It is not necessarily about the interests and enthusiasms of students. In this respect it is interesting to contrast this with the development of informal science education in the United States. Often linked to museum and science center activity,

> . . . informal education consists of learning activities that are voluntary and self-directed, life-long, and motivated mainly by intrinsic interests, curiosity, exploration, manipulation, fantasy, task completion, and social interaction. Informal learning occurs in an out-of-school setting and can be linear or non-linear and often is self-paced and visual- or object-oriented. It provides an experiential base and motivation for further activity and learning. The outcomes of informal learning experiences in science, mathematics, and technology include a sense of fun and wonder in addition to a better understanding of concepts, topics, processes of thinking in scientific and technical disciplines, and an increased knowledge about career opportunities in these fields. (National Science Foundation, 1997)

Unfortunately, the current obsession with targets and the completion of prescribed coursework rather works against the sense of fun and wonder that the National Science Foundation values. It is also a further example of the movement toward institutionalization that Ivan Illich discussed some 30 years ago. The extension of schooling (and other forms of institutionalization) undermines people, he argued. "It diminishes their confidence in themselves, and in their capacity to solve problems . . . It kills convivial relationships. Finally it colonizes life like a parasite or a cancer that kills creativity" (Finger & Asún, 2001, p. 10). We can see that informal education can offer an alternative—but it does depend on its practitioners developing strategies to distance their work (and their thinking) from the sorts of packaged and prescribed activities that are the normal fare of schools and colleges and holding on to the notion of extracurricular activity rather than falling into the trap of curriculum extension. It also entails them working with lecturers, classroom teachers, and managers to deepen their appreciation of educational forms that value process and conversation—and to demonstrate that there are ways of evaluating the work other than an obsession with measurable changes in the individuals they are working with.

INDIVIDUALIZATION AND THE MOVE TO CASE MANAGEMENT

Within UK government policy generally, there has been an increasing focus upon targeting interventions at identified individuals. Perhaps the clearest expression of the move toward individual targeting can be found in UK government initiatives to insert learning mentors and personal advisers into schools and colleges. People are identified who are in need of intervention so that they may reenter education, training, or work. Individual action programs are devised and implemented. Programs are then assessed on whether these named individuals return to learning or enter work—rather than on any contribution made to the quality of civic life, personal flourishing, or social relationships that arise out of the process. Essentially, a form of case management is seen as the dominant way of working (see Jeffs & Smith, 2002).

The work of learning mentors is a good indication of the direction work has taken. Some schools in England did not initially adopt a case-management approach. They preferred instead to focus more strongly on what they might be doing to cause or exacerbate problems with students. For them, learning mentors offered an opportunity to open up a dialogue with students and to see how the school might alter to better accommodate their needs. While still having to "deliver" the objectives set by the government, there did appear to be some freedom in how these may be approached around the role of the mentor. However, learning mentor posts are funded directly by central government—and they each have to undertake a common training. As a result, there has been pressure to focus on one-to-one mentoring and support and to take on many of the information, assessment, and coordinating and accessing roles associated with personal advisers. According to the Department for Education and Skills in England, their task is to work alongside teaching and pastoral staff in order to, "assess, identify and work with those pupils who need extra help to overcome barriers to learning inside and outside school" (DfES, 2002a). Their focus on the individual is clear. A central task is to provide "one-to-one mentoring and support." They are expected:

> To draw up and implement an action plan for each child who needs particular support (except where the child is already subject to an individually-tailored plan, in which case, to contribute to reviews and work towards objectives in the plan). To maintain regular contact with families/carers of children receiving support, and to encourage positive family involvement in the child's learning. (DfES, 2002a)

Learning mentors are also expected to "work closely with parents to help them provide an environment at home which is conducive to learning" (op. cit.).

The model involved is very close to the notion of case management within social work. It stands in direct contrast with the traditional orientation within youth work and informal education to the group and its life. Part of the issue facing informal educators here is that there has been a loss of faith in the educative power of group and associational life within some key sectors—most noticeably within youth work and community work. In the former, the demise of the youth center as vibrant work environment in many UK youth services (in large part an outcome of wider social forces and the need to satisfy government funding agendas) has contributed to a turning away from associational ways of working such as the club work. In the 1980s we witnessed a move to more focused and targeted work, often with individuals, often in the form of short-term projects. Thus, when the government accelerated their push toward more individualized forms of intervention in the late 1990s, they were pushing at an open door. Many youth workers and their managers had lost sight of what lay at the heart of their work. "To encourage young people to come together into groups of their own choosing is the fundamental task of the Service," the Albemarle Report famously declared in 1960 (Ministry of Education, 1960, p. 52). That is not what current strategy involves in England (DfEE, 2001; DfES, 2002a). Instead, youth services are being pushed into adopting an individualized model of work bearing a close resemblance to traditional North American approaches to youth development (Smith, 2003).

CONFLICTING FRAMEWORKS

The major danger facing informal educators in the light of the above is that they get incorporated into activities that work against their core commitments. Given the dominance of curricular-thinking, individualization, and the orientation to control, ways of working that stress conversation, association, and relationship are not likely to be easily understood or appreciated. Indeed, this has become an area of fundamental concern. UK government services and funding, for example, have tightened their foci and targets, and implemented much stronger regimes of monitoring, inspection, and evaluation. For those informal educators who have worked to stay true to their craft, there are four key flashpoints when functioning within schools.

Confidentiality

The status of the information that informal educators gain about the lives and situations of the people they are working with in schools and colleges and how they are expected to handle it is one of the most problematic areas. What is right from the perspective of informal educators is not necessarily what is correct in terms of school and college policies and procedures. The problem here is usually that workers are expected to pass on information about students. If a young woman comes to an informal educator to talk about her worries that she might be pregnant, then this conversation will normally be expected to be reported to the relevant person in the pastoral system, and so on. That young woman might not want the school or college authorities to know about this aspect of her personal life—and may just want space to explore matters. This can put the informal educator in a difficult position if she or he is employed by the school or college. One way of creating some room for this sort of conversation has been to ensure that the informal educator works for an external agency, and that there are clear, agreed boundaries with regard to disclosures (e.g., as is the case in many of the new community school initiatives in Scotland). However, similar issues are now arising within UK state-run and -sponsored youth services, especially in England. The requirement to track individual progress via a national database within the Connexions strategy and an emphasis on multiagency working has led to a diminution of the ability of young people to limit the spread of personal information about their lives and experiences.

Discipline

On the whole, informal educators have a more relaxed orientation to questions of discipline. If they are looking to association and relationship, then their fundamental concern is to work so that the group can take responsibility and look to its tasks. They may make very firm interventions—for example—where there are issues of safety and justice. However, for much of the time informal educators look to help build environments where conversation and engagement can happen. This tends to mean that there is more noise and playfulness in the settings where they are working than is usually associated with educators in schools and colleges. Inevitably tensions arise with other teachers and with managers. For example, informal educators working in hallways in colleges may well be comfortable with boisterous behavior, but the lecturers in adjoining classrooms could well find it disruptive.

Learning about Sensitive Issues

The approach that informal educators may take to the discussion, for example, of sexual behavior or drug usage has, historically, been more open and direct than that usually associated with schools. Indeed, what is taught in schools (and, to some extent, colleges) is more closely circumscribed by law and the threat of external intervention. The cautious approach adopted by many schools leads to "a reliance on pre-packed teaching materials and presentational styles which focus on information giving, both of which predictably thwart dialogue" (Jeffs & Smith, 1999b, p. 207). Informal educators generally offer an alternative way of working with their attention to experience, open conversation, and relationship—but can hit real difficulties, especially if they are directly employed by the school or college.

Targets

Success may well be measured in very different ways by schools and colleges, and informal educators. The former are more likely to look to academic achievement, attendance, and "good" behavior as indicators of success; historically informal educators are more likely to be concerned with the quality of the life of the group, the learning involved, and the all-round flourishing of individuals. The "problem" facing informal educators is that their work cannot be honestly evaluated by the sorts of crude outcomes usually employed by schools, government inspectors, and even their own agencies. In truth, the same argument can also be made about schools and colleges, but it does pose a particular problem for informal educators as they do not have the same recourse to familiar indicators such as exam success. One result of the pressure to demonstrate outcome has been a misguided turn to schemes that accredit experience and learning by some informal educators—a trend accelerated in England by government policies around youth services (Smith, 2003).

This is not an exhaustive list of the sorts of issues that arise—but it does bring out some of the key dimensions. There are bound to be conflicts when educators and workers from different practice traditions have to work together—but informal educators in schools and colleges start with an obvious disadvantage. Their orientation and approach is, generally, significantly out of step with the ways of working that dominate schooling. The fundamental tension lies in their commitment to conversation (and what flows from it), and to practical reasoning. They have to work out what might be right for each situation and relate this to what might make for human flourishing. The result is a concern for process, relationship, and praxis—informed, committed action. It was for this reason that the McNair Report (Board of Education, 1944, p. 103) described the role of youth worker as "guide, philosopher and friend to young people." When working with colleagues and in systems oriented to targets and outcomes, submission to externally designed curricula, and to hierarchy there will always be tensions—and the possibility of taking on ways of working at odds with the central concerns of informal education.

CONCLUSION: WHAT FUTURE FOR INFORMAL EDUCATION WITHIN SCHOOLS?

From this survey, we can see that the expanding numbers of workers within schools and colleges in the United Kingdom who are not classroom teachers has meant that a number of informal educators have found themselves walking through school and college gates. Some have been able to develop innovative work that looks to relationship and association. Others have experienced a constant and disheartening struggle. The dominant tides of surveillance, curricular expansion, and individualization have sometimes proved too much for them. The values and practices of informal education do not fit easily into the current schooling paradigm—but its practitioners have a duty to work within institutions such as schools and colleges so that they may be more convivial for learning. As Ivan Illich wrote, "[W]e must find more ways to learn and teach: the educational qualities of all institutions must increase again" (Illich, 1973, p. 30). Unfortunately, the political context and orientation of many education systems is such that it is all too easy for informal educators to lose their way and to take on ways of thinking and working that fail those they work with. In addition, they are often employed on programs that relate to specific government targets or policy aims—and this can seriously compromise the quality of the encounters they have with learners. If they enter into conversation with a strong agenda formed outside the situation they are in constant danger of hijacking and ultimately sabotaging the exchange.

It is perhaps a sign of the times that in recent years one of the strongest arguments for the need to examine the learning potential of institutions has come from those like Peter Senge (1990) who have sought to alter the character of business organizations (creating so-called learning organizations). While some of these writers have had a concern with dialogue and organizational forms that are more just, many have not had the sorts of interests and commitments that Ivan Illich described as "convivial." Within education there has been much talk of lifelong learning, but it has only impacted on schools and colleges in the most instrumental ways. Sadly, Illich's analysis of schooling has increased resonance today:

> Many students, especially those who are poor, intuitively know what the schools do for them. They school them to confuse process and substance. Once these become blurred, a new logic is assumed: the more treatment there is, the better are the results; or, escalation leads to success. The pupil is thereby "schooled" to confuse teaching with learning, grade advancement with education, a diploma with competence, and fluency with the ability to say something new. His imagination is "schooled" to accept service in place of value. (Illich, 1973, p. 9)

So how might progress be made?

First, it is important that specialist informal educators with children and young people recognize that they are engaged in an activity that is in the "middle territory" between social work and classroom teaching (Kornbeck, 2002, p. 49). They have to resist attempts to bring their activities more into the mainstream of schooling and other welfare services. In England, for example, there has been a concerted attempt to transform state sponsored and run youth work into "youth development." The result has been a significant turn to individualized from associational endeavor, an increased emphasis on formal and planned activity; and a focus on outcomes that can be accredited. In other words, there has been a shift from informal to formal education and training (Smith, 2003). Within schools specialist informal educators need to work in the "in-between" spaces on the margins of systems and groups. When informal educators are drawn into the center of systems, two things tend to happen. On the one hand, they fall prey to the very things they need to be counteracting—institutionalization, commodification, and individualization—and in so doing lose their distinctive identity. On the other hand, they tend to function in a way that centralizes their role and diminishes the agency of learners. By working on the margins of systems and groups, informal educators can focus on helping to create environments where others can take responsibility and build relationships that are mutually satisfying.

Second, it is crucial that informal educators keep trying to encourage people to recognize and experience the power of association. As Josephine Macalister Brew (1946) argued some years ago, the central vehicle for informal educators to cultivate a commitment to community, citizenship, and cooperation is the voluntary association of members—the club or group. Brew saw in the "club" a means by which people could freely identify with one another and gain the skills, disposition, and knowledge necessary for citizenship. In some respects, the current interest in social capital (most significantly expressed in the work of Robert Putnam, 2000) provide a hopeful discourse for informal educators. The significant gains in happiness, health, and welfare in those communities where there is a strong associational life provides a strong rationale for informal education. In this respect, specialist informal educators have a role in schools and colleges. Working so that people may join groups—whether they are organized around enthusiasms and interests, social activity, or economic and political aims—and can make a considerable contribution to welfare in itself. Putnam also demonstrates that educational achievement is likely to rise significantly, and the quality of day-to-day interaction is likely to be enhanced by a much greater emphasis on the cultivation of extracurricula activity involving groups and teams.

Third, it is necessary to keep on making the case against seeing curriculum as a central, defining feature of education. Currently dominant appreciations of curriculum theory and practice emerged in the school and in relation to other schooling ideas such as subject and lesson. Informal educators work with purpose and intent—and manage without resort to a curriculum for most of the time. It is only in the interludes where they need to facilitate more formal explorations that it becomes a possible reference point. Alongside the imposition of national or external curricula on schools, one of the more disturbing phenomena in a number of education systems in recent years has been the colonization of a range of extracurricular activities and encounters through the means of curriculum "enrichment" and "extension." The extension of curriculum thinking and practice inevitably leads to the formalization of encounters, the limitation of journeys of understanding generated by conversation and dialogue, and the subverting of associational spaces. Unfortunately, this process hasn't only happened within schools. Within the United Kingdom, for example, there was been growing adoption of curriculum theory and practice by youth workers. In part this arose out of a concern to demonstrate their worth—and the use of notions such as curriculum appeared to make it easier to gain recognition. The result was a slide into accreditation and growing dictation from the center with regard to the direction, content, and organization of the work.

Fourth, we have to recognize that while specialist informal educators can contribute to educational renewal in schools, it is in the realm of the classroom teacher that fundamental movement has to happen. Informal educators when they are able to embrace their role as guides, philosophers, and friends provide a glimpse of what a renewal of teaching might involve. When space is made for association, relationship, and conversation, people are able to learn in a deeper way about themselves, being with others, and being in the world. Limiting the role of curriculum allows us to attend to experience. It also enables us to approach students as whole people.

In addition, the way in which informal educators have to develop and engage an appreciation of what might make for human flourishing to inform their involvement in the lives of others is of fundamental significance to classroom practice. It helps us to see how we can strengthen the moral dimension of teaching (and connect it more strongly with the essence of education). As D. P. Liston (2000) has argued, we need to place an understanding of the "Good" and an orientation to love at the heart of teaching. This, in turn, entails recognizing that the character, orientation, and integrity of educators are of deep importance. It is no accident that the training of informal education normally involves significant attention to the self—and it needs also to do so for classroom teaching.

> [K]nowing my students and my subject depends heavily on self-knowledge. When I do not know myself, I cannot know who my students are. I will see them through a glass darkly, in the shadows of my unexamined life—and when I cannot see them clearly, I cannot teach them well. When I do not know myself, I cannot know my subject—not at the deepest levels of embodied, personal meaning. I will know it only abstractly, from a distance, a congeries of concepts as far removed from the world as I am from personal truth. (Palmer, 1998, p. 2)

Specialist informal educators can only do so much. They, like classroom teachers, have been constrained, and to some extent overtaken, by institutionalization and commodification. However, we can still see how much classroom teachers can learn from informal educators' concern with association, relationship, and conversation.

Last, it is important to place the above within a historical and political context. Some may well suggest that the idea that schools and classrooms can be changed so they foster association, relationship, and conversation is a utopian dream. Yet such a "vocabulary of hope" is an essential feature of education. As David Halpin (2003, p. 30) has argued, teaching is premised on hope—on the possibility that it will foster improvement. Being hopeful as a teacher, he maintains, "facilitates innovation and an earnestness to do well in one's work." He also contends that hope is a relational construct "which in the education context requires teachers to look for and build up 'Good' in their students." Viewed historically, the current obsession with outcomes, curriculum, and testing is a strand of thinking and practice that ebbs and flows. It gains ground and is then found wanting (see, for example, Kliebart, 1987). We also know that the "more overtly and more directly politicians attempt to organize education for economic ends, the higher the likelihood of waste and disappointment" (Wolf, 2002, p. xiii). Furthermore, we can appreciate that the dominance of one set of ideas can never be complete, and that power is never stable and so cannot be monolithic (Gramsci, 1971, pp. 323–33). In complex systems such as schooling there are usually gaps and spaces that can be inhabited by those who engage in a "vocabulary of hope." It might well be that the room for maneuver is constrained at times, but things can change quickly. Within any system there are moments of crisis and dysfunction that can be utilized by those who seek educational renewal along the lines discussed here (Smith, 1994, pp. 151–67).

This chapter draws upon research reported in Smith (2002).

REFERENCES

Alexander, R. (1988). Garden or jungle? Teacher development and informal primary education, in A. Blyth (ed.), *Informal Primary Education Today.* Lewes: Falmer Press.

Alexander, R. (2000). *Culture and pedagogy: International comparisons in primary education.* Oxford: Blackwell.

Barber, M. (1997). *The learning game: Arguments for an educational revolution.* London: Indigo Press.

Barber, M., et al. (1997). *School performance and extracurricular provision.* London: Department for Education and Employment.

Bentley, T. (1998). *Learning beyond the classroom: Education for a changing world.* London: Routledge.

Billett, S. (2001). Participation and continuity at work: A critique of current workplace learning discourses. *Context, power and perspective: Confronting the challenges to improving attainment in learning at work.* Joint Network/SKOPE/TLRP International workshop 8–10 November 2001, Sunley Management Centre, University College of Northampton. Available in *the informal education archives:* <http://www.infed.org/archives/e-texts/billett_workplace_learning>.

Bishop, J., & Hoggett, P. (1986) *Organizing around enthusiasms. Mutual aid in leisure.* London: Comedia.

Blyth, A. (ed.). (1988). *Informal primary education today: Essays and studies.* Lewes: Falmer.

Board of Education. (1944). *Teachers and youth leaders: Report of the committee appointed by the President of the Board of Education to consider the supply, recruitment and training of teachers and youth leaders.* London: HMSO. Part 2 is reproduced in *the informal education archives:* <http://www.infed.org/archives/e-texts/mcnair_part_two.htm>.

Brew, J. M. (1946). *Informal education: Adventures and reflections.* London: Faber.

Broady, M., Clarke, R., Marks, H., Mills, R., Sims, E., Smith, M., & White, L. (1990). *Enterprising neighbours: The development of the community association in Britain.* London: National Federation of Community Organisations.

Burbules, N. (1993). *Dialogue in teaching. Theory and practice.* New York: Teachers College Press.

Burbules, N. C., & Torres, C. A. (2000). *Globalization and education: Critical perspectives.* London: Routledge.

Coffield, F. (ed.). (2000). The necessity of lifelong learning. Bristol: Policy Press.

Colley, H., Hodkinson, P., & Malcolm, J. (2002). *Nonformal learning: Mapping the conceptual terrain. A consultation report.* Leeds: University of Leeds Lifelong Learning Institute. Also available in *the informal education archives:* <http://www.infed.org/archives/e-texts/colley_informal_learning.htm>.

Coombs, P. H., with Prosser, C., & Ahmed, M. (1973). *New paths to learning for rural children and youth.* New York: International Council for Educational Development.

Department for Education and Employment. (1999). *Excellence in cities.* London: DfEE. <http://www.standards.dfee.gov.uk/library/publications/excellence/additional/EicLeaMent/>.

Department for Education and Employment. (2000). *Connexions: The best start in life for every young person.* London: DfEE. <http://www.connexions.gov.uk/strategy.htm>.

DfEE. (2001). *Transforming youth work.* London: Department for Education and Employment. <http://www.connexions.gov.uk/publi.htm>.

Department for Education and Skills/National Youth Agency. (2001). *Youth work and study support framework: Key policy and practice issues.* Leicester: National Youth Agency.

Department for Education and Skills. (2002a). Learning mentors. *The Standards Site:* <http://www.standards.dfes.gov.uk/excellence/policies/Mentors/?template=pub&articleid=3917>.

Department for Education and Skills. (2002b). *Transforming youth work—resourcing excellent youth services.* London: Department for Education and Skills/Connexions.

Dewey, J. (1916). *Democracy and education* (1965 ed.). New York: Macmillan.

Doyle, M. E., & Smith, M. K. (1999). Born and bred: Leadership, heart and informal education. London: YMCA George Williams College/Rank Foundation.

Dryfoos, J. (1994).s *Full-service schools. A revolution in health and social services for children, youth and families.* San Francisco: Jossey-Bass.

Eisner, E. W. (1985). *The art of educational evaluation. A personal view.* Barcombe: Falmer.

Eisner, E. (1998). *The enlightened eye: Qualitative inquiry and the enhancement of educational practice.* Upper Saddle River, NJ: Merrill.

Elsdon, K. T., with Reynolds, J., & Stewart, S. (1995). *Voluntary organizations: Citizenship, learning and change.* Leicester: National Institute of Adult Continuing Education.

Fashola, O. (2001). *Building effective afterschool programs.* Thousand Oaks, CA: Corwin Press.

Field, J. (2000). *Lifelong learning and the new educational order.* Stoke on Trent: Trentham Books.

Finger, M., & Asún, J. M. (2001). *Adult education at the crossroads: Learning our way out.* London: Zed Books.

Fisher, R. (1994). *Let the people decide: Neighborhood organizing in America* (2nd ed.). New York: Twayne Publishers.

Freire, P. (1974). *Education: The practice of freedom.* London: Readers and Writers Publishing Cooperative.

Fromm, E. (1957). *The art of loving* (1995 ed.). London: Thorsons.

Fromm, E. (1976). *To have or to be* (1979 ed.). London: Abacus.

Galbraith, M. W. (ed.). (1990). *Education through community organizations.* San Francisco: Jossey-Bass.

Giroux, H. A. (2000). *Stealing innocence: Corporate culture's war on children.* New York: Palgrave.

Gramsci, A. (1971). *Selections from prison notebooks.* London: Lawrence and Wishart.

Gray, J. (1999). *False dawn: The delusions of global capitalism.* London: Granta.

Grundy, S. (1987). *Curriculum: Product or praxis?* Lewes: Falmer Press.

Halpern, R. (2003). *Making play work: The promise of after-school programs for low income children.* New York: Teachers College Press.

Halpin, D. (2003). *Hope and education: The role of the utopian imagination.* London: Routledge.

Hazler, R. J. (1998). *Helping in the hallways: Advanced strategies for enhancing school relationships.* Thousand Oaks, CA: Corwin Books.

Henze, R. C. (1992). *Informal teaching and learning: A study of everyday cognition in a Greek community.* Hillsdale, NJ: Lawrence Erlbaum Associates.

Hirst, P. (1994). *Associative democracy: New forms of economic and social governance.* Cambridge: Polity.

Hughes, M., Wikely, F., & Nash, T. (1994). *Parents and their children's schools.* Oxford: Blackwell.

Illich, I. (1973). *Deschooling society.* Harmondsworth: Penguin.

Illich, Ivan, et al. (1977). *Disabling professions.* London: Marion Boyars.

Jeffs, T., & Smith, M. (eds.). (1990). *Using informal education.* Milton Keynes: Open University Press. Available in *the informal education archives:* <http://www.infed.org/archives/usinginformaleducation/default.htm>.

Jeffs, T., & Smith, M. K. (1999a). *Informal education: Conversation, democracy and learning.* Ticknall: Education Now.

Jeffs, T., & Smith, M. K. (1999b). Informal education and health promotion, in E. R. Perkins, I. Simnett, & L. Wright (eds.), *Evidence-based health promotion.* London: John Wiley.

Jeffs, T., & Smith, M. K. (2002). Individualization and youth work. *Youth and Policy* 76: 39–65.

Kenway, J., & Bullen, E. (2001). *Consuming children. Education-entertainment-advertising.* Buckingham: Open University Press.

Kliebard, H. M. (1987). *The struggle for the American curriculum, 1893–1958.* New York: Routledge.

Knowles, M. S. (1950). *Informal adult education.* New York: Association Press.

Kornbeck, J. (2002). Fælles Kerne verus national kontekst? Socialpædagogikken på europakortet. *Tidsskrift for Socialpædagogik* 10: 42–55.

Leadbeater, C. (2000). *Living on thin air.* London: Penguin.

Leys, C. (2001). *Market-driven politics: Neoliberal democracy and the public interest.* London: Verso Books.

Lindeman, E. C. (1926). *The meaning of adult education.* New York: New Republic.

Liston, D. P. (2000). Love and despair in teaching. *Educational Theory* 50(1): 81–102.

MacBeath, J. (1999). *Study support in Scottish schools.* Edinburgh: The Scottish Office.

MacIntyre, A. (2002). Alasdair MacIntyre on education: In dialogue with Joseph Dunne. *Journal of Philosophy of Education* 36(1): 1–19.

Marples, R. (1999). Well-being as an aim of education, in R. Marples (ed.), *The aims of education.* London: Routledge.

Ministry of Education. (1960). The youth service in England and Wales (The Albemarle Report). London: HMSO. Key chapters available in *the informal education archives:* <http://www.infed.org/archives/albemarle_report/index.htm>.

Monbiot, G. (2000). *Captive state: The corporate takeover of Britain.* London: Pan.

Munn, P. (ed.). (1993). *Parents and schools: Customers, managers or partners?* London: Routledge.

National Science Foundation. (1997). *Informal science education: Supplements to Active Research Awards.* <http://www.nsf.gov/pubs/1997/nsf9770/isesupl.htm>.

NFER. (1999). *The benefits of study support: A review of opinion and research.* Slough: NFER.

Palmer, P. J. (1998). *The courage to teach: Exploring the inner landscape of a teacher's life.* San Francisco: Jossey-Bass.

Putnam, R. D. (2000). *Bowling alone: The collapse and revival of American community.* New York: Simon and Schuster.

Ritzer, G. (1993). *The McDonaldization of society.* Thousand Oaks, CA: Pine Forge Press.

Scottish Office. (1999). *New community schools: The prospectus.* Edinburgh: The Scottish Office.

Senge, P. M. (1990). *The fifth discipline: The art and practice of the learning organization.* London: Random House.

Smith, M. (1988). *Developing youth work: Informal education, mutual aid and popular practice.* Milton Keynes: Open University Press.

Smith, M. K. (1994). *Local education: Community, conversation, action.* Buckingham: Open University Press.

Smith, M. K. (2000). Association, la vie associative and lifelong learning. *The Encyclopedia of Informal Education.* <http://www.infed.org/association/b-assoc.htm>. Last updated: July 2002.

Smith, M. K. (2002). Informal education in schools and colleges. *The Encyclopedia of Informal Education.* <http://www.infed.org/schooling/inf-sch.htm>. Last updated: September 2002.

Smith, M. K. (2003). From youth work to youth development: The new government framework for English youth services. *Youth and Policy* 79: 46–59.

Stewart, J. (1992). Guidelines for public service management: Lessons not to be learnt from the private sector, in P. Carter et al. (eds.), *Changing social work and welfare.* Buckingham: Open University Press.

Tocqueville, A. de. (1994). *Deomcracy in America* [ed. by J. P. Mayer]. London: Fontana Press.

Wenger, E. (1999). *Communities of practice: Learning, meaning and identity.* Cambridge: Cambridge University Press.

Wolf, A. (2002). *Does education matter? Myths about education and economic growth.* London: Penguin.

Yeaxlee, B. (1929). *Lifelong education: A sketch of the range and significance of the adult education movement.* London: Cassell and Company.

DIALOGIC INQUIRY IN CLASSROOM AND MUSEUM

ACTIONS, TOOLS, AND TALK

DORIS ASH AND GORDON WELLS

INTRODUCTION

While many researchers have examined learners' dialogic interactions in the classroom (Mercer, 2002; Nassaji & Wells, 2000; Nystrand, 1997), it is only recently that learning dialogues in museum settings have begun to be explored (Ash, 2003; Leinhardt, Crowley, & Knutson, 2002). In this chapter, we compare and contrast dialogic inquiry interactions in museum and classroom settings in order to uncover common principles of learning. In the past few years researchers have begun applying learning theory, based on classroom work, to informal environments (Paris & Ash, 2002); conversely, research on participation in informal settings has advanced our understanding of the science of learning (Rogoff, 1994; 1998). Part of the power of the combined research perspective offered in this chapter is that it deals even-handedly with both formal and informal environments, assuming that each has much to offer the other, theoretically and practically. We know that one setting is not better than another; in fact, in this paper we uncover the characteristics and learning principles that cut across both contexts, and that must be taken into account in all informal education.

Following ideas originated by Vygotsky and Dewey, we propose that education, whether formal or informal, should have at its heart the practice of dialogic inquiry. We take the notion of inquiry from constructivism (Piaget,

1952), which noted that learners build on their existing understandings and make sense of the world through material and symbolic actions and interactions. By engaging with materials, ideas, and utterances, learners are active agents, constructing knowledge rather than passively receiving it.

Inquiry is an active, process-driven, problem-oriented approach to knowledge building that invites active participation in tool-mediated action. As originally conceived under the influence of Piaget, inquiry focused on individuals making sense of physical or intellectual phenomena. However, treating learning as occurring in social isolation is now seen as "conceptually unsatisfying and ecologically deficient" (Salomon & Perkins, 1998, p. 1). Instead, the focus can be on multiple individuals, interacting with both one another and a culturally rich, socially situated environment. Vygotsky (1987) argued that knowledge is created and appropriated in joint activities, in which participants utilize tools that embody the past discoveries and achievements of their culture to address current problems, and to achieve goals that will shape their future as well as their present. Taking place in the classroom, or museum, or during a field trip, collaborative goal-oriented activity transforms the current situation, and even the tools employed, making them available for further use in new ways. Most important, joint activity brings about transformations in participants' knowledge, skills, and self-identities (Penuel & Wertsch, 1995).

Today, the terms "sociocultural" and "social constructivist" are frequently used to describe Vygotskian theories, which have become a major influence on our understanding and design of complex learning and teaching environments (Brown & Campione, 1996; Bereiter & Scardamalia, 1996; Wells, 1999). The use of collaborative communities of knowledge building in classroom settings to exemplify the rich elaborations of sociocultural learning theory abound (Brown et al., 1993; Warren, Ballenger, Ogonowski, Rosebery, & Hudicourt-Barnes, 2000; Wells, 1999). There are, however, very fewer such studies outside the classroom (Calabrese-Barton, 1998; Rogoff, 1994). Museum examples of sociocultural learning are only now becoming available (Leinhardt, Crowley, & Knutson, 2002; Paris, 2002). Some of this new research specifically explores dialogic inquiry in informal settings (Ash, 2003), although no one to date has explored the interrelated roles of dialogue, inquiry, object, and outcome, nor have they based their underlying generalizations across learning environments on cultural historical activity theoretical (CHAT) perspectives.

Our aim in this chapter is to do exactly this, by exploring the similarities and differences in dialogic inquiry in formal and informal settings. We analyze examples of dialogic inquiry in both classroom and museum, with theoretical underpinnings from Dewey, Piaget, and Vygotsky that apply to both settings. Ultimately we believe that this will result in a more generalized learning theory, applicable equally across all learning contexts.

ACTIVITY IN THE ZONE OF PROXIMAL DEVELOPMENT (ZPD)

Vygotsky suggested that all human activity is mediated by artifacts that are used as tools in acting on objects to produce desired outcomes. Artifacts can be of three kinds: primary artifacts, such as hammers, fax machines, computer simulations, or texts; secondary artifacts, or "representations of primary artifacts" (Cole, 1996, p. 121); and tertiary artifacts, that describe or theorize about the relationships among actions, artifacts and the actors using them (Wartofsky, 1979). The object of the activity can be material (a physical object) or symbolic (e.g., a conversation, or a thought experiment), or both (Cole, 1996). The outcome is the result of the artifact-mediated action on the object.

Leont'ev (1981) deepened our understanding of the central role of mediation in activity by including the cultural and historical context within which the activity is situated. Building on this fundamental insight, Engeström (1993) uses a more complex structure to capture how action is embedded in the context of cultural activity, as shown in Figure 1.

While Engeström's activity model represents greater complexity, it is still unidirectional in its portrayal of subjects acting on objects. Yet dialogic activities, such as learning and teaching, are fundamentally multidirectional and relational, and they are precisely the activity systems and environments that learning theory wishes to elucidate. For this reason, it has become crucial to

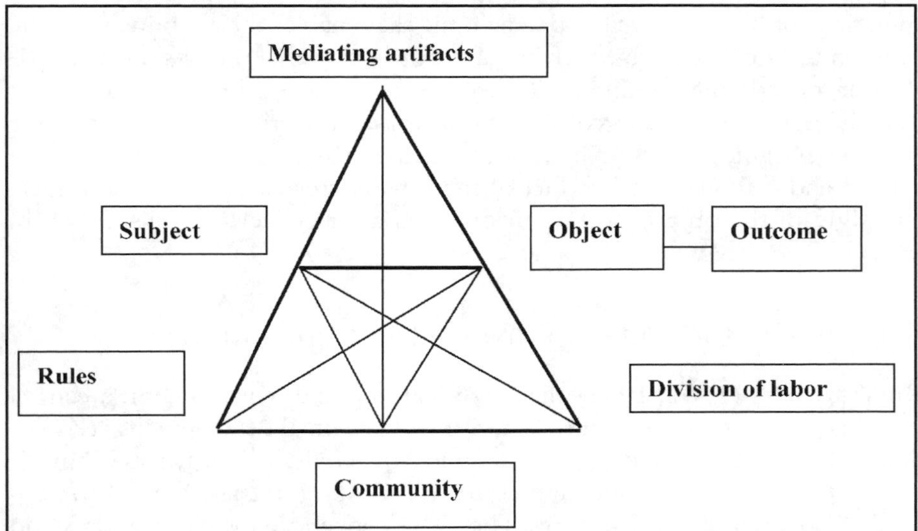

Figure 1: Engeström's model of an activity system

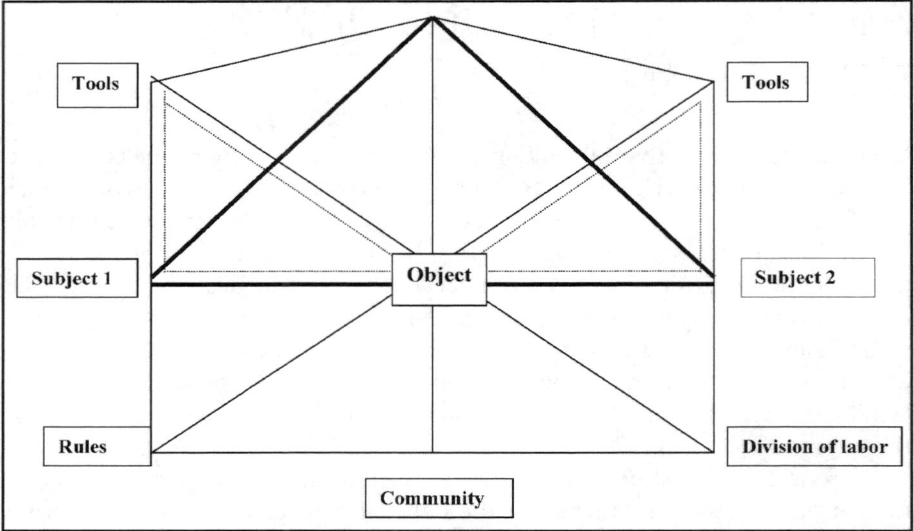

Figure 2: Dialogue in joint activity from Wells (2002, p. 59)

understand and represent dialogue as being reciprocal, with talk being simultaneously tool, object, and outcome in collaborative activities.

In order to integrate dialogue into representations of activity, Wells (2002) has designed the activity triangle in Figure 2. This model incorporates multiple subjects (people), multidirectionality, and multiple tools (material and symbolic), which together produce a variety of outcomes, such as buildings or books, as well as the dialogue that enables their production. The outcomes of collaborative activity have both a material dimension (the artifact produced) and a symbolic dimension (the meaning of the artifact). The dialogue, which facilitates collaboration, is also a material/symbolic outcome in its own right. The interplay between dialogue as a means for acting on the object and dialogue as a product of the activity creates an "enriched understanding of the object, both individually and collectively" (Wells, 2002, p. 50).

Dialogue in the Zone of Proximal Development

In Vygotsky's (1981; 1987) theory of learning and development, a central place is given to the concept of "the zone of proximal development" (ZPD). The ZPD has been defined as "the region of activity that learners can navigate with aid from a supporting context, including but not limited to people" (Brown et al., 1993, p. 5). The ZPD concept helps us to understand the myriad ways an individual's development can be assisted by other learners, both face-to-face and through interaction with the artifacts that others have designed. In Vygotsky's account of the social origins of mind, language is recognized as the most powerful medium for negotiating meaning in the ZPD. It is thus the preeminent tool for learning-and-teaching, as learners use words and the concepts that they embody in dialogic collaboration.

We adopt here an expanded concept of the ZPD, recognizing dialogue as one of a variety of mediational tools, including signs, displays, books, videos, other learners in collaborative activities, and the designated "teacher." Using this expanded definition, we analyze episodes of dialogue observed in museums and classrooms. In both settings, we find participants contributing according to their current ability to do so, while simultaneously providing support for others as they achieve their individual and collective goals.

Dialogic Content

Regarding dialogic content Bereiter (1994, p. 7) suggested that conversations allow "participants [to] recognize [the understanding gained] as superior to their previous understandings." Wells (1999) insisted that students need to have productive curricular activities that are both personally and socially significant. In the Fostering a Community of Learners (FCL) project, Brown et al. (1993) argued that classrooms require intellectually honest materials that move understanding toward the big ideas of science. In prior research in science classrooms (Ash & Brown, 1996), children investigated thematic areas and advanced their understanding of biological principles. Thematic areas, such as feeding and reproduction were tracked over time and across different content areas. In recent research at life sciences museums (Ash, 2003), family members, individually and collectively, engaged with the same themes, which provided entry into the deepest principles of life sciences, such as adaptation.

Yet, interesting themes are not enough to ensure that dialogic inquiry occurs. Much depends on how activities are pursued and on the "division of labor" (Engeström, 1993) between the participants undertaking them. Family dialogue in museums typically involves a limited number of participants and a distribution of prior knowledge among them, all of which can be conducive to dialogic inquiry. By contrast, classrooms are often constrained by time limits, class size, prescribed curricula, and high-stakes assessment demands. However, despite such challenges, many teachers recognize the efficacy of dialogic inquiry. The classroom vignette below shows some of the same features that can be observed in the museum vignette and in other out-of-school settings (Brown & Cole, 2002).

A number of key features characterize successful collaborative groups in either classroom or museum setting. Effective collaborative activities encourage participants to have fun and to contribute at the appropriate level for their current ability; they also allow room for diverse interests and ways to learn from and with shared "objects," either material or symbolic. Most important, they provide strong motivation for participants to work together productively (Scardamalia et al., 1994).

Two Vignettes

We present the following vignettes to exemplify how key features of dialogic inquiry with the ZPD occur in both informal and formal contexts. They illustrate that understanding

1. is jointly mediated with others involved in both doing (gestures, pushing buttons, etc.) and talking;
2. is situated in a discourse in which each individual's contribution both responds to what preceded and anticipates further dialogue;
3. incorporates a variety of artifacts;
4. involves outcomes that are continually transformed; and
5. moved learners toward interesting and intellectually honest ideas.

We present each vignette by summarizing the key features of the setting, presenting the data, and then briefly analyzing the features of the activities.

Museum Vignette

The Life through Time: The Evidence for Evolution exhibition represented the sequential story of evolution from the first evidence of life to the present, exposing learners to biological principles such as adaptation and natural selection. It included live animals, such as horseshoe crabs, and realistic dioramas progressing from the earliest ocean life, through dinosaurs, to the first mammals. There were computer interactive displays (CID) throughout the exhibition, one of which was the context for this vignette.

The family was one of many selected on the basis of age, number of children, availability, and interest over time. All family conversations at exhibits, and pre- and post-visit family interviews were videotaped and/or audiotaped. This particular CID, with video screen and touch choice buttons, called for decisions that would permit the survival of FISHO, an imaginary evolving fish. The goal was to teach principles of survival in a changing world. The choices involved characteristics, such as habitat, reproductive patterns, feeding, and protection from predators. The dialogue began with the younger son and the father; later the older son and mother joined them.

There were three levels of dialogue: first, written, pictorial, and oral computer language, which prompted evolutionary choices; second, the dialogue of the parents and children, an ongoing and dynamic process; and, finally, the dialogue of the outcome, that is the meaning built by the family as the dialogue progressed. The first decision that the display required was to decide (in response to visual and verbal prompts) where FISHO would live: stay in the water or move onto land. In the language of activity theory, the material artifact (CID) is a complex mediating tool for the subjects (the family). The object is the set of choices from which one must be selected, and the outcome (depending on the choice made) is the survival or extinction of FISHO. In the segment below, the CID prompts are indicated in CAPITALS, the **family dialogue is in bold print**; *additional explanatory comments are in italics;* and [. . .] indicates deleted segments. Segments of dialogue are set in a box.

Partial CID text
THIS IS WHERE OUR STORY BEGINS . . . FISHO THE AMAZING HAS GILLS FOR BREATHING IN WATER . . . IT IS TIME FOR YOU TO DECIDE FISHO'S FATE. SHOULD SHE CONTINUE TO TRY TO LIVE IN WATER OR LAND?
DAD: You have a choice. You can choose between land or water. Do you want to see what happens when the fish tries to live on land?
Boy (seven): ***gestures land***
DAD: All right. "ACT ONE, LAND HO."
(Father reads the CID text)

The father interpreted the first question for his son, thus easing the boy's entry to the game. The CID provided pictures, explanatory text, time limits, and choices for possible evolutionary outcomes. The father and the boy interacted collaboratively, yet the father and CID provided support for the son. The material was intellectually challenging for both father and son.

WELL, YOU HAVE DECIDED TO PACK YOUR BAGS FOR DRY LAND . . . IT IS FAMILY TIME. YOU WILL WANT TO PROVIDE A SAFE PLACE TO LAY YOUR EGGS . . .
(The choice is between fish eggs or lizard eggs
BOY (seven): Lizard eggs.
DAD: Yeah.
(Father affirms son's choice)

The CID next prompted consideration of reproduction. It had become apparent that the underlying biological design framework was to promote reasoning about adaptation and natural selection, with an emphasis on balancing the resulting benefits and liabilities. The father and CID led.

. . . MORE OFFSPRING. ACT TWO ASKS THE QUESTION, WHERE TO LAY YOUR EGGS, LAND OR WATER? CLICK YOUR CHOICE, YOU HAVE TEN SECONDS TO DECIDE THE FATE OF GENERATIONS TO COME.
BOY (seven): "EGGS OVER LAND."
(The boy read)
DAD: "WATER OVER EASY, EGGS OVER LAND"—Your choice.
(The father read and gave the choice to the son.
The boy chose water)
DAD: "ACT TWO. EGGS WATER SIDE UP."
(The father read)

With this prompt, the boy chose eggs in the water. He had already placed FISHO on land with lizard eggs; so this was a poor choice. He didn't understand the advantages and disadvantages, yet the father did not tell him the answer. They were genuinely collaborating; partly because neither one knew the answer, or how the CID would guide them.

. . . SINCE YOU GAVE UP YOUR GILLS, YOU HAVE LIMITED UNDERWATER TIME TO SUPERVISE THE KIDS. LESS OFFSPRING, YOU STAY AS YOU ARE. IT ALSO MEANS THE END OF THE PLAY. TO SEE HOW YOU CAN EVOLVE ON, CLICK EGGS OVER LAND . . .
(The CID models reasoning about the advantages and disadvantages of adaptations; land lizards can't protect eggs in the water so they will die. The CID gives players a second chance)
DAD: Is it disappointing that you couldn't evolve to something else? . . . It says "PLEASE WAIT, EVOLVING TAKES TIME."
(A clever message from the CID designers regarding the time it takes to evolve)

By asking if it was disappointing, the father invited his son to reflect on possible choices, rather than saying his decision was wrong. He modeled thinking about multiple outcomes of natural selection. Then the CID allowed them to reconsider, and to pick eggs on land, suggesting that survival for the future depends on having babies survive, explaining that if you are a land, air-breathing animal, it is not possible to care for water-living young. This is a potent example of reasoning about advantages and disadvantages. Over the next few minutes, the CID marched steadily through a series of survival adaptations, including feeding and metabolic rates. At the food decision point, the son selected insects.

. . . BUGS ARE PRETTY EMPTY CALORIES AND THEY DON'T GIVE YOU MUCH ENERGY WHEN YOU NEED IT, AND YOU NEED IT TO GET TO ACT 3. SO WHAT IS YOUR CHOICE? CONTINUE WITH BUGS OR MOVE ON TO BIGGER FOOD.
(The CID provided direct teaching, prompting players to change their mind)
DAD: Go for bigger food.
(The father directs)
BOY (seven): Bigger food, yes.
DAD: "HOLD ON. I AM INVOLVED IN EVOLVING. MOVE ON TO A BIGGER FOOD . . ."

Next they are asked to decide how to defend themselves, through fighting or escaping; the boy chooses escaping.

DAD: Do you want to defend yourself or head for the hills?
DO YOU DEFEND YOURSELF OR ESCAPE?
BOY (seven): Escape.
(The son chose)
DAD: Good choice.
(Father praises)
A WISE CHOICE. THAT ONE HAS ITS ADVANTAGES AND THE MAIN ONE IS THAT YOU ARE STILL ALIVE. THERE IS ONE PROBLEM HERE THOUGH, MOST LIZARDS ARE NOT BUILT TO RUN AND BREATHE AND THAT MEANS A LOT OF REST STOPS AND AS YOU CAN SEE, SITTING AROUND REFUELING IS NOT SO HEALTHY.
(CID prompts revision)

The son made this decision, with support from both the father and the CID.

DAD: Lunchtime, uh oh. He changes.
THERE IS A WAY OUT THOUGH. STEP UP AND CLICK DINO DOOR OR MAMMAL DOOR, BECAUSE DINOSAURS OR MAMMALS CAN BREATHE WHILE RUNNING. I KNOW YOU ARE TIRED.
DAD: Mammals.
(The father directs)
WHOA, LOOKS LIKE A CHANGE HAS COME OVER YOU. THE HAIR, THE FLOPPY EARS, AND RUBBERY NOSE . . . CHANGE MUST HAVE MADE YOU PRETTY HUNGRY, LET'S EAT. IT HAS ON ITS MENU, PLANTS OR MEATS, SO WHAT DO YOU HAVE A HANKERING FOR?

The father made this decision, as the content had become more complex, and the time limit of 10 seconds approached.

DAD: Carnivore or ?
(The father prompts an answer)
BOY (seven): I know which one it is.
(The boy is ready to choose)
DAD: I don't think either one is necessarily right. It gives you ten seconds . . .
(The game times out)

Time ran out and the game ended, just as the older son and mother joined the father and younger son. The entire family started the game again, this time with the older son choosing. As he did so, the younger son was by his side and the mother and father stood slightly behind, talking and smiling. The younger son coached the older son, exactly as the father had coached him five minutes earlier.

MOM: Press the red button.
(Mother coaches)
DAD: You get to make evolutionary choices for these guys.
(Father coaches)
BOY (seven): I made it go on land.
(Younger son coaches)
(Older boy picks land)
MOM: That is a good choice.
(Mother praises)
BOY (seven): I know, we got turned into a lizard.
(Younger son prompts)

Everyone coached the older son, as the decision making became collaborative among four people and the CID.

MOM: That is the way it happened, isn't it?
(Mother suggests that the CID reflects real evolution)
BOY (seven): Evolving takes time"
(The younger son repeats what his father had said five minutes before)

This vignette illustrates how collaborative conversations are simultaneously process and product and have multiple purposes of having fun, learning new ideas; and solving problems. This dialogue was co-constructed among the family members and the CID, and meaning was shared across all five participants. Each player influenced the dialogue; the dialogue built on itself smoothly from start to finish.

In this analysis, we focus on two points that relate directly to the activity model in Figure 2. The first tracks the changing nature of the mediation offered by all four participants and by the CID. The second discusses the outcomes.

Mediation in collaborative dialogue helps generate topics, and keeps learners involved. In this example, the CID was the primary mediator (the teacher); it set the rules, agenda, and time frame. The first collaborators were the boy (seven) and the father. The father mediated the son's activities by reading and repeating text, by providing prompts, and by making decisions for him. Later, four subjects collaborated. The mutual interdependence of speakers and mediating artifact illustrates effectively the need for a complex activity representation, such as Figure 2, in order to represent more than one subject, multiple directionality, and changing outcomes over time.

The CID designers mediated the humans' dialogue and actions while teaching about survival, natural selection, and adaptation, turning these principles into two levels of rules: operating the mechanical CID; and operating with the concepts. These latter conceptual rules included the advantages and disadvantages for particular survival adaptations, and the need for time in the process of evolution. The zone of proximal development for this example contained the CID and all four family members. Family members brought different expertise levels to the dialogic activity; their use of complex biological material traversed differences of experience, age, and ability to communicate They were mutually challenged by complex biological principles, thus reflecting the bi-directional nature of the appropriation process within the ZPD. As the CID carried the didactic load, the parents were free to collaborate with the boys in making the required choices. The biological themes of breeding, feeding, and so on required all members to mediate dialogically for each other; at several points there was a relatively evenly balanced collaboration, at other times the father or the younger son led. The idea that evolving takes time is a sophisticated biological principle. The father read the CID message on the evolving process at the beginning; by the end the younger son was able to repeat it. These survival themes provide the necessary antecedents for more complex biological thinking (Ash, 1995, 2002), for both adults and children, making the CID an excellent "teacher" for this family.

Two outcomes of this vignette are important here, enjoyment and learning. At the preinterview, the mother said she wanted to "have fun as a family." After the activity, all family members stated that they had enjoyed the problem-solving. The father and younger son remained at the CID for over 10 minutes, actively playing, watching, or prompting others; the mother, although least involved, watched, prompted, smiled, and listened.

Family members also learned quite a bit, as evidenced by their recall of the CID dialogue. While watching the video at a post-visit interview, one year later, the father said: "I think we are looking at this video about evolution. You pick the dinosaur and then figure out what it evolved into. You can make decisions along the way. I thought that after going through the exhibit, because of the stuff we had read, we were able to pick ones that we knew would survive, because we knew how they were connected." Both sons used terms such as "carnivore," "herbivore," "reptile," and "mammals" in describing the activity. The older son said he learned how to play the game by watching the younger son play.

Classroom Vignette

Unlike the museum with its interactive displays, school classrooms rarely provide opportunities for true dialogue. (Nystrand, 1997).[1] Indeed, the majority of the talk that occurs, at least when the teacher is working with the whole class, is governed by what Tharp and Gallimore (1988) called the "recitation script." Typically, this takes the form of a series of three-turn exchanges, in each of which the teacher asks a question, a student responds, and the teacher evaluates the student's answer. From a social constructivist perspective, however, this form of interaction is both ineffective and inappropriate. As students frequently report, although they may be able to pass the test, they do not construct any personal understanding of the topics taught; furthermore, the recitation script severely constrains the opportunity for students to express their own ideas or to comment on, extend, or challenge those of other participants. Yet, as we have argued earlier, it is through collaborative knowledge building that both individual and group understanding is developed and extended.

However, a more dialogic mode of interaction is very definitely possible, even when guided by the teacher's curricular goals. This can be seen very clearly in the following vignette, which is taken from a lesson taught by one of a group of teachers who were exploring how to make inquiry the dominant approach to curricular topics and to create collaborative knowledge-building communities in their classrooms.[2]

When there is one teacher and 25 to 35 students, it is essential that the interaction be managed in such a way that all students have opportunity and encouragement to contribute and to have their ideas and points of view listened to respectfully and responded to in a constructive as well as a critical manner. Thus, most sequences of talk are initiated by the teacher, and often with the posing of a question. However, there are some important distinctions between different types of question, notably in terms of who is treated as "knowing" the information requested and in the discretion available to the respondent in deciding on the content and scope of the answer (Haneda, 2004; Nassaji & Wells, 2000; Nystrand, 1997). So, although the teacher may ask the initiating question, she can choose whether to request information that she knows and the student is expected to know (a test or "display" question) or to ask a "genuine" question that solicits information or opinions from students in order to engage in a collaborative exploration of a topic or issue. In this latter case, it is the student rather than the teacher who has the role of "primary knower" (Berry, 1981). In addition, in forming the question, the teacher can make it "open-ended," or constrain the answer to a phrase or simply a "yes" or "no" rejoinder.

In the vignette that follows, the teacher is clearly managing the interaction, but the questions asked—despite their form on some occasions—are designed to elicit the students' thoughts and opinions about the topics under discussion. Furthermore, although the teacher frequently takes the third turn in the exchange, the follow-up move serves either to acknowledge the student contribution in a positive manner or to invite further exploration of the topic.

Estimating, Predicting, and Guessing

This extract comes from a lesson in a unit on mass in a class of eight- and nine-year-olds. The overall goal of the unit was for students to understand that mass remains constant even when matter changes state. In the previous lesson, it had become apparent that a number of groups had failed to predict the outcome prior to experimenting with the different materials. At that time, the teacher had emphasized the importance of making a prediction because, in order to predict the outcome, one needs to consider what one already knows about the situation and how the experimental intervention is likely to change it. She had also drawn attention to the need to take account of the contributions of previous speakers in framing one's own contribution to discussion.

In the following extract, the teacher revisits the issue of predicting by asking the class to consider the relationship among "predicting," "estimating," and "guessing." Only the first thirty turns of the discussion are included below; however, it continued for some 30 minutes, as different students introduced a variety of scenarios in their attempts to clarify the differences and similarities.[3] By the end, as the teacher commented later, there was really nothing further for her to add; among them, the students had made all the distinctions that were found when they subsequently consulted the Concise Oxford Dictionary.

(Note. In the transcript, participants are identified by the initial letter of their name; T = Teacher, and S = Unidentified Student. CAPS indicate emphasis, * indicates an inaudible word, and < > enclose passages where what was said is uncertain.)

1 T	When I say "estimate" and "predict" or "predict, don't bother to estimate," what am I saying? Are they two different activities—mental activities that you have to do? Are they two different mental activities? How many people think they're two different mental activities?	T's question, although phrased as asking for a Yes/No response, functions to invite students' opinions.
	[Most children put up their hands]	
2 T	How many people think they're NOT two different mental activities?	P takes a "No Difference" position. His answer provides a starting point for discussion.
	[Philips raises his hand]	
3 T	Why not, Philips?	
4 P	Cos like they're more—more or less the same.	
5 T	How are they the same?	
6 P	"Estimate" is like—sort of like guess and "predict" is like um—guess—yes, guess too . . . ** (drowned by next speaker)	
7 T	OK. You heard somebody who says they're not the same. Now there's a whole bunch of people who say they're two different mental activities. What do YOU think, Emily?	
8 E	I think that they are two different things because "predict" is sort of like guess what will happen and then "estimate" is like you estimate the mass using a form of weight, centimeters and it's not just with mass, you estimate other things.	E disagrees and struggles to find a way of explaining the difference.
9 T	OK	
10 A	I don't agree with Philips either because "predict" sort of means like what WILL happen and "estimate" is the—er—do it—estimating something that's already there, but taking it further.	A introduces the idea of the future orientation of "predict."
11 T	Now, listen to both answers. None of the answers are right or wrong. Will someone make a distinction?—Auritro has made a little—even a more—greater distinction. OK?	T makes clear that all answers are acceptable.
12 J	I don't agree with Philips (laughs) because he said that "estimate" is guessing and "predicting" is ALSO guessing but um—actually guessing is also different from those two because when you guess you don't have very much information about the object or the thing (T: uh-huh) and so you're just making a—like a wild guess but when you predict you're—you're actually you're maybe doing an experiment and you are trying—using the information, you are trying to find out what would happen—	J introduces the importance of the information base in using the terms.
13 T	Mm	
14 J	—and estimating is um different from guess because you have um certain information, for instance if you estimate the mass, you get the object in your hand and you and you have the weights in the other hand and you can sort of like estimate the mass, so it's not guessing	
	8 turns omitted	
22 M	Well, I . . . I don't agree with Philips because "estimating" is like you look at the object and you think about how much it weighs or how tall it is and "predicting" is like you predict if it'll be—like predicting is like—you predict whether you can say it like what we did yester—the other day when we predicted whether it'll change or not change or it'll be the same . . .	

Figure 3: Classroom Vignette *(continues)*

23 T	OK. Emily?	
24 E	I'd really like to <revise it> a little but I started by <changing a little> and discuss everything so we get a little information and then you go further see what will happen next. I think it's true and for estimating we also like—<for anything> you look at the object and then you guess—well you DON'T guess but then you try to—like you have a—some weights and then you like try to feel the um—see what it weighs or that's how I <think it is . . .> (trailing off)	In stating that she is revising her first attempt, E draws attention to the progressive nature of the ongoing discussion.
25 T	OK. Wilson?	
26W	I don't agree with um . . . Philips because . . . um in our math book it says "estimate to the nearest tenth" but it didn't—it doesn't say "PREDICT to the nearest tenth"	W adds a new idea: estimating involves measurement.
27 T	That's right. So what's the distinction? Good, you're using—<you're> using experience in math .to help you make a distinction and do you ever see in your science that I ask you to predict? . . .	
	[One or two children nod in agreement]	
28 T	In your science activity it also asks you to estimate. So the very fact that sometimes for certain things you use the word "predict" and for certain you will have to use "estimate," therefore you think there's a distinction? Just from usage, OK? Any more?	
29 C	Well, um—in—and another one is—because I also with Wilson—I agree with Wilson—because another way of predicting like—it's a totally different thing from estimating cos um . . . in our-—in our math books, like Wilson said, um . . . estimate is—they say estimate to the nearest hundred or <nearest> thousand, but predict um . . . it's not as accurate . . .	C restates W's argument about measurement.
30 T	OK. So you're beginning to say "estimate" is a mathematical thing and "predict" is a—not tied to math . That's one distinction. There are other distinctions made <and> we're going to recap to that. OK, let Philips have a say since everybody says, "I disagree with Philips," poor Philips!	T summarizes so far and then invites P to respond to those who disagreed with him.

Figure 3—*continued*

This discussion shows students "thinking aloud" as they struggle with words to express their understanding of the relationship among the three terms ("predicting," "estimating." and "guessing"). They anchor their positions in relation to Philips's (unacceptable) claim that the three terms are essentially synonymous. However, as the discussion develops, other students' contributions provide building blocks for the collaborative attempt to refine the distinction. For example, having listened to Frances, Emily sees the issue they are considering in a new light and, without waiting to be nominated, she initiates a new sequence:

> I sort of agree with Frances that, before, I would have estimated, it would have been ABOUT the object, like, for example, the ball—about the ball—but then "predict" is like what will HAPpen if you do something to the ball, so I will now use "predict."

This episode is an example of collaborative knowledge building. It also builds upon students' prior practical work experimenting with the effects of changing the state of different materials. Even though there is a clear temporal separation between the materially and symbolically oriented activities, it is evident that the children bring to the discussion a fund of experiential meaning for the terms being contrasted.

The teacher has orchestrated the sequencing of the activities and managed the discussion. Although she initiates many of the sequences and frequently contributes a follow-up move, she does so with the purpose of eliciting students' ideas and highlighting the interconnections among them. Clearly, although "working in the zone of proximal development," she does not see the providing of assistance to be her sole prerogative. Rather, she acts on the explicit assumption that knowledge and expertise are widely distributed among the members of the class as a whole and among the artifacts—journal entries, tables of results, information books, etc.—that they had drawn on in their previous activities. While clearly the manager of the activity, she does not act as the sole source and arbiter of knowledge but seeks to elicit many points of view while at the same time helping individual students to express their contributions in ways that will advance the collaborative discussion.

These two features—clear demarcation of different types of activity and explicit assignment of roles and speaking turns—have a great deal to do with the logistical problems of organizing joint activity when large numbers are involved. However, formal learning does not have to be transmissionary. For what we see here is a teacher and her students functioning as a knowledge-building community in which it is assumed that (a) the outcome of the discussion is not known in advance but is the object of joint inquiry, (b) all points of view will be given thoughtful consideration, and (c) progress is made by building on previous contributions, whether by exemplifying, extending, or disagreeing with them.

Discussion

These two vignettes differed in the number of participants, kind of setting, type of mediation, disciplinary content, allotted time, and other surface features. We have noted, however, that the same principles characterized effective opportunities for learning in each context. Even though the time ranged from a few minutes in the museum to several days in the classroom, effective and lasting knowledge building took place between and among people and mediating artifacts in both settings. In each case the "improvable object" (1) was jointly mediated with others involved in both doing (gestures, pushing buttons) and talking; (2) was situated in a discourse in which each individual's contribution both responded to what had preceded and anticipated further dialogue; (3) incorporated a variety of artifacts; (4) involved outcomes that were gradually and continually transformed; and (5) moved learners toward interesting and intellectually honest ideas. In short, the object of their activities, both intended and unintended, was to advance understanding.

Each vignette involved material tools, such as texts, experimental materials, chalkboards, and computers; each also included intellectual or symbolic tools, such as "scripts" for tasks, iconic representations (e.g., computer drawings of animals), and explicit goals presented by the "teacher." Different participants brought different mediational forces to bear over time. Each dialogic segment included evidence of both the participants' current understanding and some understanding of the role of possible artifacts, whether material or symbolic, to use in moving toward an outcome.

In both vignettes, the participants actively engaged with important content and attempted to progress toward the mutually agreed outcome. Often this is not true, because content is typically controlled by a standardized curriculum. However, in classrooms that are organized as communities of inquiry learning, as in museum settings (Ash, 2002), content can be jointly negotiated. In both vignettes, negotiation of meaning occurred in relation to interesting and important disciplinary content, influenced by the learners as well as the "teacher."

All learning settings require participants' effort to listen responsively to others' ideas. However, in these vignettes, as participants collaborated in knowledge building, they both added to meaning jointly and simultaneously moved toward greater individual understanding through the ongoing challenge of responding to other speakers. For example, the younger son at the museum offered the comment that "evolving takes time," an idea he had heard just five minutes before, while in the discussion of predicting and estimating, as they picked up and developed each others' ideas, the children were quite evidently clarifying and extending their own understandings.

A further common feature of both vignettes is that the development of understanding occurred cumulatively, over time, and involved a number of related activities. As one activity finished, another began, based, at least in part, on the outcome of the first activity. Thus, outcomes became the mediating tool for the next activity. In this respect, dialogue is similar to activity involving material tools, for the meanings made as the product of one interaction become the foundation for the next. Thus, like material action, dialogue moves from being a process to being a product. On the small scale of family or classroom community, as on the larger scale of historical time, knowledge and material artifacts that are created in one activity become part of the community's resources for use as tools on future occasions.

CONCLUSION

We have provided an account of Vygotsky's theory of learning and development and of the related theory of activity. We have applied these theories to analyses of joint activity episodes in both museum and classroom. We highlighted their common features by focusing on the core concept of artifact-mediated joint activity. Based on our findings, we argue that both classroom and museum contexts can demonstrate similar characteristics of collaborative knowledge building, mediated by artifacts and dialogue, where the "answer" is not determined in advance, and where expertise is distributed. These vignettes analyzed according to a sociocultural theoretical framework are clear representations of the fact that a social constructivist inquiry approach is both valuable and feasible in "informal" and "formal" settings, even though each setting reflects different social, cultural, and historical roots.

These two educational settings, classroom and museum, have seldom been considered jointly in this way. Yet, when we do, it becomes apparent that the characteristics of productive learning activities are remarkably similar across the two settings. There are also important differences in organization between classrooms and museums, in particular the need for deliberate structuring and sequencing of component activities with a large number of learners. The differences in organization, however, are not related to the formality or informality of the setting; rather, they are responses to the constraints of the contexts within which learning occurs.

There are, in our view, important implications to be drawn from this work. First, in designing learning environments, whatever the setting, those responsible for learning and teaching contexts must create conditions that will most closely match the principles of learning suggested by sociocultural and activity theory. Second, we believe that the research presented here, together with the theoretical perspective from which it is taken, will help deepen our understanding of learning, either in museums or in classrooms. By investigating dialogic inquiry in both museums and classrooms, and by focusing on the ways in which participants work to provide mutual assistance in the zone of proximal development, we hope to have made a contribution to this endeavor.

NOTES

1. Based on a large corpus of recorded observations in middle and high school classrooms, Nystrand and his colleagues calculated that what they call "dialogic spells" occurred in no more than 6% of the observed lessons.
2. The Developing Inquiring Communities in Education Project, supported by grants from the Spencer Foundation, is a group of teachers in public schools in Metro Toronto and faculty and graduate students from OISE/University of Toronto. More information about the group and their publications can be found on their Web page at: <http://www.oise.utoronto.ca/~ctd/DICEP>.
3. This whole science unit is discussed in more detail in Wells (1999, Ch. 6).

REFERENCES

Ash, D. (2003). Dialogic inquiry of family groups in a science museum. *Journal of Research in Science Teaching, 40* (2): 138–62.

Ash, D. (2002). Negotiation of thematic conversations about biology. In G. Leinhardt, K. Crowley, & K. Knutson (Eds.), *Learning conversations in museums.* (pp. 357–400). Mahwah, NJ: Lawrence Erlbaum Associates.

Ash, D. (1995). *From functional reasoning to an adaptationist stance: Children's transition toward deep biology.* Unpublished thesis. University of California, Berkeley.

Ash, D., & Brown, A. L. (1996, April). *Thematic continuities guide shifts in biological reasoning: Children's transition towards deep principles of evolution.* Paper presented at the annual meeting of American Educational Research Association, New York.

Bakhtin, M. (Eds. Holquist, M., & Emerson, C.) (1986). *Speech genres and other late essays* (1st ed.). Austin: University of Texas Press.

Bereiter, C. (1994). Implications of postmodernism for science, or, science as progressive discourse. *Educational Psychologist, 29*(1): 3–12.

Bereiter, C., & Scardamalia, M. (1996). Rethinking learning. In D. Olson & N. Torrance (Eds.), *The handbook of education and human development.* (pp. 485–513). Cambridge, MA: Blackwell.

Berry, M. (1981). Systemic linguistics and discourse analysis: A multi-layered approach to exchange structure. In M. Coulthard & M. Montgomery (Eds.), *Studies in discourse analysis.* London: Routledge and Kegan Paul.

Brown, A. L. (1992). Design experiments: Theoretical and methodical challenges in creating complex interventions in classroom settings. *The Journal of Learning Sciences, 2*(2): 141–78.

Brown, A. L., & Campione, J. C. (1996). Psychological theory and the design of learning environments: On procedures, principles and systems. In L. Schauble and R. Glaser (Eds.), *Innovations in learning: New environments for education.* (pp. 289–325). Mahwah, NJ: Lawrence Erlbaum Associates.

Brown, A. L., & Campione, J. C. (1994). Guided discovery in a community of learners. In K. McGilly (Ed.), *Classroom lessons: Integrating cognitive theory and classroom practice.* (pp. 229–70). Cambridge, MA: MIT Press.

Brown, A. L., Ash, D., Rutherford, M., Nakagawa, K., Gordon A., & Campione, J. C. (1993). Distributed expertise in the classroom. In G. Salomon (Ed.), *Distributed cognitions: Psychological and educational considerations.* (pp. 188–228). New York: Cambridge University Press.

Brown, K., & Cole, M. (2002). Cultural historical activity theory and the expansion of opportunities for learning after school. In G. Wells & G. Claxton (Eds.), *Learning for life in the 21st century: Sociocultural perspectives on the future of education.* (pp. 225–38). Oxford: Blackwell.

Calabrese-Barton, A. C. (1998). Teaching science with homeless children: Pedagogy, representation, and identity. *Journal of Research in Science Teaching, 35*(4): 379–94.

Cole, M. (1996). *Cultural psychology: A once and future discipline.* Cambridge, MA: The Bellknap Press of Harvard University Press.

Engeström, Y. (1993). *Learning, working, imagining: Twelve studies in activity theory.* Helsinki: Orienta-Konsultit.

Halliday, M. A. K. (1993). Towards a language-based theory of learning. *Linguistics and Education, 5:* 93–116.

Haneda, M. (2004). The joint construction of meaning in writing conferences. *Applied Linguistics, 25:* 178–219.

Leinhardt, G., Crowley, K., & Knutson, K. (2002). *Learning conversations: Explanation and identity in museums.* Mahwah, NJ: Lawrence Erlbaum Associates.

Leont'ev, A. N. (1981). The problem of activity in psychology. In J. V. Wertsch (Ed.), *The concept of activity in Soviet psychology.* (pp. 37–71). Armonk, NY: Sharpe Press.

Mercer, N. (2002). Developing dialogues. In G. Wells & G. Claxton (Eds.), *Learning for life in the 21st century: Sociocultural perspectives on the future of education* (pp. 141–53). Oxford: Blackwell.

Nassaji, H., & Wells, G. (2000). What's the use of triadic dialogue? An investigation of teacher-student interaction. *Applied Linguistics, 21*(3): 376–406.

Nystrand, M. (1997). *Opening dialogue: Understanding the dynamics of language and learning in the English classroom.* New York: Teachers College Press.

Piaget, J. (1952). *The Origins of Intelligence in Children,* M. Cook trans. New York: International University Press.

Paris, S. G., & Ash, D. (2002). Reciprocal theory building inside and outside museums. *Curator, 43* (3): 199–210.

Penuel, W., & Wertsch, J. V. (1995). Vygotsky and identity formation: A sociocultural approach. *Educational Psychologist, 30(2):* 83–92.

Rogoff, B. (1994). Developing understanding of the idea of communities of learners. Scribner Award address, American Educational Research Asscociation, New Orleans, April (Published in *Mind, Culture and Activity, 1(4)*: 209–29.

Salomon, J., & Perkins, D. (1998). Individual and social aspects of learning. *Review of Research in Education, 23:* 1–12.

Scardamalia, M., Bereiter, C., & Lamon, M. (1994). The CSILE project: Trying to bring the classroom into World 3. In K. McGilley (Ed.), *Classroom lessons: Integrating cognitive theory and classroom practice,* (pp. 201–28). Cambridge, MA: MIT Press.

Tharp, R. G., & Gallimore, R. (1988). *Rousing minds to life: Teaching, learning, and schooling in social context.* Cambridge: Cambridge University Press.

Vygotsky, L. S. (1981). The genesis of higher mental functions. In J. V. Wertsch (Ed.), *The concept of activity in Soviet Psychology.* (pp. 144–88). Armonk, NY: Sharpe.

Vygotsky, L. S. (1978). *Mind in society: The development of higher psychological processes.* Cambridge, MA: Harvard University Press.

Vygotsky, L. S. (1934/1987). Thinking and speech. In R. W. Rieber & A. S. Carton (Eds.), *The collected works of L. S. Vygotsky, Volume 1: Problems of general psychology.* New York: Plenum.

Warren, B., Ballenger, C., Ogonowski, M., Hudicourt-Barnes, J., & Rosebery, A. S. (2000). Re-thinking diversity in learning science: The logic of everyday languages. *Journal of Research in Science Teaching, 38(5): 529–52.*

Wartofsky, M. (1979). *Models, representation and scientific understanding.* Boston: Reidel.

Wells, G. (2002). Dialogue in activity theory. *Mind, Culture and Activity.*

Wells, G. (1999). *Dialogic inquiry: Towards a sociocultural practice and theory of education.* New York: Cambridge University Press.

Wertsch, J. (1991). *Voices of the mind: A sociocultural approach to mediated action.* Cambridge, MA: Harvard University Press.

A NEW ANGLE ON FAMILIES

CONNECTING THE MATHEMATICS OF LIFE WITH SCHOOL MATHEMATICS

SHELLEY GOLDMAN

There is widespread recognition in the field of education that parents are the first, primary, and most persistent educators of their children. Few question the centrality of parents as the first educators. Babies learn to sit, walk, talk, and interact in complex social arrangements during their first few years. Parents are their primary guides, and most do the job wonderfully. Children are amazingly accomplished learners in their early years, soaking up the world and constantly developing. Then comes school.

From the first day of kindergarten (or day care if family members work), parents begin handing over responsibilityto the school for what is to be learned. Parents stay partners in the process, although the school coopts more and more of the cognitive learning goals of children with every year. Research shows that parents of elementary school students spend time at both school and home working on school-related activities. They take their children to school, attend school meetings and functions, join the parent-teacher groups, help in the classroom, read with their children at home, and help with homework and school projects. As students progress up the years in school, the partnership weakens and more and more of what is to be learned is left in the hands of teachers. By the time children reach the middle school years (grades 6–8), the coopting of the learning responsibilities by the school has become severe and highly formalized. For a parent, this can feel extreme. At the start of sixth grade, my daughter's school sent letters home advising parents not to come to school with their children. The school gave two reasons: so traffic near the school could be alleviated and the children might learn to be more independent. From that "welcome" letter on, correspondence from the school referred to our daughter as "your student," symbolically placing her and the responsibility for her learning in the institutional life of the school as opposed to the life of the family. Entrance to middle school finds parents stripped of subject area responsibilities as well. What is to be learned is highly formalized—it's been decontextualized, outlined, jargonized, standardized, and made accountable to institutional demands. This is especially true in mathematics where most parents abdicate responsibility for the learning to the school, and usually without question. Once children get past multiplication and division facts and into operations with fractions and decimals, parents have difficulty connecting to school mathematics and put their stock in schools and teachers being more able.

Alienation from the school for parents creates an unfortunate loss. Research shows that family involvement is more important to student success than family income or education, and that this is true for children from preschool to the upper grades (Coleman, 1966; Epstein, 1995; de Kanter, Ginsburg, & Milne, 1987; Henderson & Berla, 1994; Keith & Keith, 1993; Jencks, 1972; Liontos, 1992; McLaughlin & Shields, 1986; Stevenson & Baker, 1987). The studies bear out what educators have known for quite some time: parents are the primary and most committed educators of their children, and children will succeed in school learning when parents are informed and involved (AAUW, 1996; AAUW, 1995; NRC, 1989; California Department of Education, 1999). While educators are aware of the need to involve parents, and a few success stories are inspiring, most schools have not found meaningful ways to keep parents involved (Moles, 1996). The relationship between schools and parents is extremely complex, and even the best circumstances still leave gaps in parents' connection to school subjects such as mathematics. If parents participate, usually they are asked to do so only as "helpers on the side" (Medrich et al., 1982; McDermott, Goldman, & Varenne, 1984).

The alienation runs deep and even the best intentions for partnerships are difficult to realize. This is definitely the case for school mathematics, which is burdened with high dropout rates. Failure at school math seems to have a lasting impact on people that is strong enough, even years later, to define their confidence in their abilities to help their children. Interestingly, adults seem to remember two types of problems in their mathematics classrooms: the first is about the mathematics itself, which was often difficult, boring, and irrelevant; the second is about their moments of failure when they felt "stupid," lost confidence, failed, or stopped taking math classes. For most parents, the connection to school math is assumed to be broken. We recognize that there are many steps along the road to fixing this alienated school/family relationship.

I worked with a team of parents, teachers, researchers, and materials developers on a project called PRIMES (Parents Rediscovering and Interacting with Math and Engaging Schools) to find ways to reconnect parents of middle grades students with the math they do at home and the math done at school. Our hunch was that helping to make visible the mathematics that people do in their lives and showing how it is connected to the school math of their children would begin to lay a foundation for more productive parental math involvement. The work reported makes the case for parents staying active in the learning process especially after their children leave elementary school. The work shows parents have a knowledge base for connecting with the formal agenda of school math. It also makes the case for more reciprocity between the informal math of home and the more formal math of the school.

These connections are revealed in the following ways. First, a family with children in middle school and high school is shadowed as the family members enjoy activities that also involve them in mathematics. After we see the family in action, the mathematics is extracted from the context of the family activity, highlighted, and its connections to the math that students are asked to solve at school are explained. Finally, the case is used as a representative example to discuss the steps that can be taken for more parents to appreciate their math knowledge and for that knowledge to come into play with more formal school mathematics.

The PRIMES project aimed to increase parental confidence and participation with the school around mathematics. PRIMES was rooted in a national call to improve the quality of parent partnership in the education of children. A 1994 national report, *Strong Families, Strong Schools,* emphasized that "more sustained attention needs to be paid to that most vital of links—the promise and potential of parents and other family members as the most important teachers of their children" (Shields, 1994). One month later, the US Secretary of Education added, "Thirty years of research tells us that the starting point of American education is parent expectations and parental involvement with their children's education. This consistent finding applies to every family regardless of the parents' station in life, their income, or their educational background" (Riley, 1994).

PRIMES sought to encourage more parent and school partnerships by building on a different, competence-based view of parents and math. In particular, we hypothesized that:

- parents use math successfully in their everyday lives, whether they label it as math or not; and,
- once invited to do so, parents can use their everyday math competencies as a base for supporting their children's school math success.

Our first goal was to improve parents' knowledge of school math topics by helping them see the connection between school math and the math they used in everyday life. We set about working with parents, teachers, and community educators to develop materials that help all uncover, discover, and try to create links based on the informal math of daily life. Our strategy was to start with real-life, engaging contexts for mathematical work and then to use the accomplishments from the family realities to show how everyday math was topically related to and engaged the math concepts, symbols, and representations of the middle school curriculum. For example, with one set of materials, parents and teachers might use math skills for making decisions about automobile purchasing, financing, and insurance, and our job was to show them how their skills relate to the school math topics such as algebra.

Our second goal was to foster parents' understanding of, and relationship with, middle-school math policy and infrastructure through creating materials for workshops on school policies and parents' rights. These advocacy materials, like the math-based materials described earlier, help foster an understanding that school math success is dependent on many factors that involve parents, ones that are quite independent of their understanding of classroom math. Our workshops were designed to help parents understand that they can help simply by being knowledgeable of school programs, policies, and opportunities for support. A topic taken up in one set of materials, for example, is, "When does the school offer algebra and how do you find out if your child is ready?" Another topics is, "Who to go to in the school for help?"

PRIMES developed and relied on a design consortium to help us plan for, construct, and field test parent math and advocacy materials. The consortium consisted of four partner teams from different San Francisco Bay Area cities. With two school district--based teams and two community center–based teams that all had parent members, we had a working group that reflected state and national demographics in terms of ethnic and economic diversity. Most important, the teams represented a good mix of parents and educators. Ultimately, the teams designed with us a series of nine workshops based on everyday life problems, a television special about families and math called *The Family Angle,* and a booklet called *Middle School Math: What Every Parent Should Know and Can Do.*

We searched for everyday life contexts that involved mathematical practices by brainstorming many situations and by asking people to report to us the occasions on which they did math. Some contexts came easily into the discussions, such as doubling recipes, or grocery shopping for the best buy on different brand items, or dealing with interest. Others were less obvious, such as optimizing travel times based on city bus routes or making crafts and sewing. Nevertheless, we identified many everyday life contexts that were rich with mathematics, examined the different ways that design team members said they approached them, and teased out the mathematics content of their experiences.

A huge question that needed to be answered was whether the informal math of the families could connect productively with the formal math of the school. A first question was stated this way, "What kinds of mathematical work do families accomplish in the course of everyday living, and is it related at all to the math worked on in school?" The answer to the first part of the question was complicated because we found that even though family members accomplish math in the context of their lives, they do not define it as such. Parents do not see what they do as mathematics; they see what they do as "getting by." That made answering the second part of the question more difficult. If there was math being accomplished in the course of family activities, it was going to be our job to see how it connected to school math and to determine whether or not any connections could be made productive for either context. We found that the wisdom of parents prevails and that their messages about math have profound implications for how connections between the informal math context of the home can be connected to the formal math learning context of the school.

This paper is about these complex questions and answers. The versions of math that parents and their children accomplished were vastly different from those that school required. Family versions used shortcuts and workarounds. They rarely applied formulas or even thought of them. And they hardly ever used formal mathematical terms such as "similarity," "proportionality," or "function," even when they employed their operational equivalents to figure out sewing, purchasing problems, or baseball statistics. Ultimately, these findings defined the nature of our work. We saw ourselves as helping to place a mirror up for parents, children, and teachers so they could all see that the very powers they possess to get by in life are related to the mathematics their children were accountable to in school. Our workshops, videos, and advocacy materials developed into vehicles for showing people how they already do math in their lives and for helping them discover ways to use that math with children at home and at school. Our idea was to bring informal and formal versions of mathematics into alignment and show that they do not have to be treated as if they are mutually exclusive.

The next section illustrates compelling examples of how people use math in their family lives and how the math they do to "get by" is actually related to the math students are asked to do at school. We meet one family as its members prepare to send their high schooler to the prom, and we examine the mathematics in practice. In the final section, some thoughts are offered about how connections between the regular, informal mathematical work and the more formal mathematics of the school might be elucidated, reinforced, and used for the benefit of all.

RESEARCH ON MATHEMATICS IN DAILY CONTEXTS

Why believe in the applicability of the everyday connections to the more formal math of the school? Over the past 20 years, researchers have developed a body of findings about *intuitive understanding* of mathematics and other formal conceptual systems. One part of this work has dealt with mathematics in out-of-school settings. Research by Lave (1988), Nunes, Schliemann, and Carraher (1993), Saxe (1990), and others has shown that success in many ordinary work practices depends on reasoning that requires a significant understanding of mathematical concepts and principles. From the use of fractions by people on Weight Watchers' diets to the strategies used to make a profit by Brazilian children selling candy, math is all around us. An inescapable conclusion of this work is that abilities to reason mathematically in practical situations are widespread. Much mathematical reasoning goes unrecognized if attention is limited to reasoning that uses standard symbolic forms or school-laden procedures, formulas, and algorithms. In fact, several of the studies have shown that many people who reason successfully with mathematical principles in daily life activities are not as successful when given tasks involving standard school versions.

Other projects have focused attention on family education and mathematics. The Algebra Project, for example, has organized communities to make algebra accessible to middle-school students regardless of prior skill or achievement. The project believes that gaining skills in algebra allows students to participate in high school science and math classes, which are gateways for college entrance. Three aspects characterize the project: the centrality of families to the work of organizing for success; the recruitment of grassroots people for leadership; and the principle of organizing in the context in which one lives, and working with the issues in that context (Moses, 2002). Family Math, taking a different tack, has children and parents attend courses together where they learn math games they can play at home. The locus can be the home, the community, or the school and can be about organizing locally to empower people with math or with advocacy activities.

The prior research on cognition in daily contexts and parental involvement establishes the potential of finding ways to connect out-of-school cognition with school learning in ways that build on everyone's knowledge and skills and increases mathematics capabilities. Evidence was accumulating that shows people's inherent abilities to reason in accord with these principles is much stronger than usually believed. In PRIMES, we wanted to mobilize the parents' intuitive understandings and actual practices with mathematics in an effort to provide a confidence builder that could promote parent support of their children with new levels of confidence. Because we were able to develop community-based design teams to help us with our work, we had the opportunity to work intensely with six families, who we visited in their homes, and videotaped as they engaged in family activities. This enabled us to learn more about how, when, and where mathematics was practiced in their everyday lives. We kept field notes and videotaped all our meetings and visits. Our process was participatory in nature, keyed to the interests and engagements of the families, and truly based on a mandate of research in action. Our research goal was to find out how families engaged with math in the context of their out-of-school lives and to test the possibilities for connections to school math.

MATHEMATICS IN THE FAMILY

The six families we visited at home were open enough to let us snoop around their lives. They were committed to what we would learn from the project. Still, most of them doubted we were going to find them doing any math in their daily activities. Our first meetings with each family involved observing the family members as they moved through their days and interviewing them about their interests, hobbies, family activities, and special events. Parents were able to identify math they did as part of their jobs, and almost all identified budgeting as math work. Interestingly, most people thought they only did arithmetic in their daily lives, even when it involved complicated personal finances or three-dimensional building projects. The children had quite a bit to say about the math they did in school, but basically all of the parents and children saw school math, with the exception of homework, as separate from their family lives. Very early on we learned that if the families did nonschool mathematical work together, they rarely thought of it as mathematics. We ruled out instances of homework on the grounds that homework was an example of school math brought into the home setting (McDermott et al., 1984), then took a careful look at what family members said they did together. We observed that some of the activities, such as building shelves, participating in sports, fundraising, sewing, dancing, planning and taking family trips, and cooking, were all rich contexts for mathematics. So we asked the family members to bear with us and let us follow them in some of their activities. They were not believers; they agreed to us following them with cameras running because they were nice people.

They actually agreed to a lot. They not only had to schedule events with their families, they had to schedule them with us and our film crew. Scheduling is serious business in families and was its own mathematical activity. Adding our team increased scheduling demands exponentially, but the families persisted. We also had to contact the commercial sites such as restaurants, amusement parks, and stores where the families could be filmed and get written approvals for our cameras and use of footage. Still, over the course of four months, we spent at least two to four additional days beyond the interviews with each of the families. If mom and daughter were sewing costumes for a dance recital, we filmed them for the sewing day and the performance day; if the family budgeted for the prom, we filmed the planning, the shopping, and prom night. Once we filmed, our research team would pour over the tapes seeking out the math-relevant moments. There were plenty to choose from and they covered all kinds of mathematical work from calculation to logic to measurement to optimization.

Operating in mathematical ways may be ubiquitous in daily life, although it is characteristically different than formal school mathematics. Daily life mathematics is so based in activity and routine that it is often out of the awareness of its participants. Daily math operations are shared across people or supported by physical props and artifacts, and people can solve problems in their daily lives quite functionally without using highly conventionalized algorithms, jargon, symbols, or formulas. Daily life activities are truly at the informal end of the informal-formal math continuum. These characteristics of mathematics as they appear in the daily life of the families are best seen as they are accomplished—in the context of family life.

The Honey Family Prepares for the Prom

We first met Pat Honey when one of our staff members befriended her while doing business with a photocopy center where she was a manager. She is an energetic woman who works two part-time jobs in order to keep her family afloat. She's the manager at a large copy center, and she also runs a business selling hair extensions from her home. She balances the family income around these two part-time jobs so she can spend more time with her children, who range in age from middle school through high school. Previously, she owned a hair salon, but owning a shop required long hours away from the kids. With some hours at the copy store and some at home, Pat felt she had reached a good balance. Money was tight, but there was enough to keep the family going and to have enough money to spend on the kids for special occasions.

The prom was one of those special occasions. Star, Pat's niece, wanted to attend the school prom. Pat had saved some money and sat down with Star and her daughter Milla to discuss the prom and set the budget. Their conversation starts with the prom dress but quickly moves to money and budgets.

Pat: Are you ready, Star? For the prom, you sure you want to go, now?
Star: Yeah.

Pat: Have you decided on what kind of outfit you want?
Star: Yes, I want a two-piece skirt, I want a long skirt—I don't want it to be short—with two splits on the side.
Pat: Splits? Are you old enough for splits?
Star: And I want the top part to fit me, not like a shirt, but fit like a cute little girly shirt.
Pat: Cute little girly shirt, okay. To the waist! No belly button showing.
Star: No.
Pat: Star, I'm working with a tight budget, but I want you to go to the prom. I'm working with about two hundred dollars. It's not much money, but I had to pay house taxes, had to pay house insurance and my regular bills. So, I did put aside some money and I do have at least two hundred dollars.

Once the total amount that could be spent on the prom is established, the family starts to figure out a budget. Pat has a pencil and paper and a calculator at the table and inputs amounts and records a list on the paper. The conversation goes from item to item and their costs, and there are negotiations about ways to spend money, and what is reasonable considering the tightness of the prom budget.

Pat: So, what do we need to buy?
Star: A dress, some shoes, some stockings, my nails, . . .
Pat: Okay. A ticket, right?
Star: A ticket, and probably put in a limo.
Pat: A limo!!?! Okay Star, about the limo, I think we're going to have to wait for a little bit. We're going to put that on hold and we're just going to worry about your dress, your shoes, your stockings, your nails, tickets, and everything, okay? If we can't afford the limo, I'll drop you guys off and pick you up, is that okay? Do we know the price of the ticket?
Star: The couple ticket, I think, is forty-five dollars.
Pat: What? For one person or for two people?
Star: For two people.
Pat: Okay. Then we have your nails, which is twenty-five and your pedicure which is eighteen—okay, that's eighty-eight dollars right there.
Pat: So, that leaves us with 112 dollars, that's for your dress, your shoes, and your stockings. That's why I chose the outlet cause I think it's affordable. I think we can find you a dress—maybe sixty, seventy dollars and that will leave us with about forty-two dollars for some shoes.
Star: The pedicure won't be mandatory because I'm not gonna get no open-toed shoes.
Pat: Okay, that gives us eighteen dollars extra, which means that your dress can now be up to eighty-eight. I can find probably find an extra two dollars so we can make your outfit up to ninety dollars, okay?

The budget is not just between Star and Pat. It's a family matter, and suddenly Pat informs her daughter Milla that she is going to sacrifice some of her usual spending money in order for Star to attend the prom.

> **Pat:** I'm taking all these extra dollars from your "momma can I have a dollar, can I have two dollars?" Is that okay?
> **Milla:** Well, why do you have to get it from my money?
> **Pat:** Well, Milla, because we need it for her to go to the prom. Is that okay?

There is a long pause while Pat waits for Milla's response. Finally Milla mutters, "Okay," and Pat tells her she is such a wonderful and generous daughter. Budget set, the three head off for the store.

A first look at the mathematical work the family members did while setting the budget shows that it involved fairly straightforward arithmetic. They listed out the costs associated with the prom and basically added them until they met the $200 budget limit. In fact, they actually used a calculator to tally the potential expenses, basically eliminating the burden of mental math or pencil-and-paper calculation. A closer examination of what they did shows a bit more complexity and mathematical work. When Pat asked Star to tell her about the expenses, Star immediately starts listing off expenses for clothing and grooming such as dress, shoes, stockings, and nails. Pat interrupts and asks about whether she needs a ticket. Pat reorganizes the categories of expenses to those that are mandatory and those that are discretionary depending on how much money there is once Star is ticketed. Pat and Star began calculating.

When the three begin shopping, Pat is determined to stay within budget and is requiring Star to stay on budget as they flip through rack after rack of dresses. As they look, Pat not only accounts for the price of the dresses, she also figures in discounts and taxes to make sure the dresses chosen to try on are in the right price range. She shares these calculations out loud with the girls and asks for their occasional participation.

> **Pat:** What's the tax in this area, Star?
> **Star:** 8.25 percent.
> **Pat:** Okay, this is 109, and thirty-three percent off. Like this one?
> **Star:** No.
> **Pat:** Okay, because that's not too bad, it's thirty percent off, 109, it's about seventy-eight, seventy-nine dollars with tax, about eighty-four, eighty-five dollars. You don't like this one? Okay, let's keep looking. This one's 142, it's a little too expensive.

At first Pat calculates the price of dresses even if Star is not interested in them. They learn from these calculations that a dress marked $109 is in the range, but one marked $142 is out of range. They continue looking.

> **Pat:** Okay, let's see. Green? What's the price of this one, 109 dollars; that's the same price, it's about eighty-four, eighty-five dollars with the tax, with the thirty percent off. You like that one?
> **Star:** Yeah, but let's keep looking.

Being a businesswoman, Pat is used to doing quick calculations to estimate price—taking off the 33% discount, then adding back the sales tax all in her head. She employs this skill as they look for an acceptable dress that is within budget.

> **Milla:** Star, how 'bout this one?
> **Star:** Oh yeah, Pat, look at this one. (She holds it up in front of her.)
> **Pat:** Oh, and look at the price. Okay, that's affordable Star, it's on sale. How much is it, eighty-nine dollars? With thirty percent off and the tax, it's about sixty-seven dollars for the dress, Star. It's affordable, and we'll have a little extra left; we can put it on your pedicure or your manicure.
> **Star:** Or the limo.
> **Pat:** Do you want to try it on and see if it fits?
> **Star:** Yes.
> **Pat:** Thank you Star, I'll continue looking . . . (Pat takes a dress from the rack.) That's a nice little summer dress. That's cute, it's cute as a button. With some gold shoes, that is sooo cute.
> **Pat:** (To Star as she returns). Do you like it, does it fit, it looks good?
> **Star:** Yes.
> **Pat:** It's not too short?
> **Star:** Noooo.
> **Pat:** Do we need to buy a jacket for it?
> **Star:** No, because I can use one of your coats.
> **Pat:** Okay, let's buy it then. And thank you, Star, 'cause that's very affordable, we will have extra money.

Pat's mental calculations turned out to be fairly accurate. By the time they finish the conversation, Star and Pat are both running budgets in their heads. Star is figuring on saving for a limo, while Pat is figuring on pedicures and manicures. The point here is that the family members talk as they shop and the mathematics work that Pat does fits right into the flow of their activity. Pat was quick with the mental calculations. She figured the price of the dress, complete with discounts and sales tax, right on the spot, so Star never tried on a dress that was out of their price range.

Let's take a look at how Pat could have figured the price range that would fit within their budget. First, Pat checked the price marked on several dresses, knowing that the actual cost could be known after figuring both discounts and taxes. She knew all the dresses were one-third off, and after checking with the girls, that 8.25% sales tax would need to be added. There are several ways she could have done this calculation, and each method involves multiple steps. One way to take a third off is to divide the entire price by three and subtract one of the thirds. So if the dress was marked $120, dividing it by three would give you $40. Subtracting 40 from 120 would get to the $80 discounted price for the dress. With the first two steps completed, the transaction looked like this:

$120/3=$40

$120–$40=$80

$80 would be the sale price of the dress.

Next, Pat would have to figure the sales tax. To make the calculations easier, Pat could round the 8.5% to 10% so she could figure in whole numbers and work with tens, which are easy to work with. To find 10% of $80, she divides by 10, which gives her $8. This calculation on paper looks like this:

$80/10=$8

Now, she would move to the final step for figuring out the cost of the dress. Pat would add the $8 sales tax to the cost of the $80 dress to get a total price of $88.

It turns out that the mental estimate is within a dollar of the answer that you'd get using exact figures and a calculator. Pat was doing mental math while shopping, and rounding and estimating with whole numbers and easily calculated numbers were easier to handle and basically adequate for solving the problem at hand. The rounding and estimating made the problems easier to handle, even though they resulted in an imprecise cost figure. The strategies were adaptive ones and were possible to manage in conjunction with talking with the girls and looking through racks and racks of dresses. After a few of these calculations with differently priced dresses, Pat established a range of prices that would bring their dress purchase in under the $100 figure in their budget.

Prom Night

When the prom night arrives, Pat, Star, Star's mom, and some friends and their children gather as Star gets ready. As Star's mom puts makeup on her, Pat talks about how the night will go. She gets little information on this front.

Pat: It's her first makeup! Tell us everything you're gonna do this evening, 'cause I don't even know.
Star: I don't know either, I've never been to a prom.
Pat: Well I mean as far as dinner, you guys gonna go to dinner?
Star: Yeah, afterwards.
Pat: But it doesn't start 'til nine, and the limo is going to pick you up at seven, so . . .
Star: Well I don't want to eat first.
Pat: Okay, but what you guys gonna do for two hours?
Star: Probably ride around a little bit.

Star is noncommittal about the prom night plans. The conversation makes more headway when they begin to figure up the success of their budgeting mission. The prom preparations were accomplished within budget and without sacrifice to style. Star had a dress, shoes, a manicure, a unique hairdo—and a limousine! This conversation was mutually engaged and both Pat and Star had much to report as they tallied up their costs as they discussed how they managed the budget:

> **Pat**: The dress, it didn't end up being ninety dollars, the dress was sixty-five. The shoes was thirty-five, the stockings went over—they was ten bucks, the nails instead of twenty were fifteen. So that's how we made it, we made it though, so now we're waiting on the limo and it all worked itself out.
> **Star:** I think I did pretty good for my first time, 'cause I picked out my dress like this, my mom picked out my shoes, my auntie bought me ten-dollar stockings, and let me use her expensive pearls. I got my nails done, my cousin did my toes, and my auntie arranged for my hair to get done. I knew how much to spend and how much I couldn't spend, I knew my range. So, if we went over it wasn't my fault, it was her fault 'cause she kept wanting me to get more and more.
> **Friend:** The limo's here!!

What about that limo? They did some creative budgeting to fit that limo into Star's plan. The conversation about the budget reveals the ways in which it was significant. First, in discussing how the dress came in under budget and how the stockings, shoes, and nails went over budget, Star reveals that she remembered the budget categories and amounts to which she had agreed, and that she understood how to make tradeoffs in costs in order to maintain the bottom line. Second, she recognizes that she has accomplished something important in setting and meeting a budget for the first time. If going to the prom is considered a right of passage, then managing the budget is another. This was a family accomplishment, from setting a reasonable working budget for the prom, to hiring the limousine. The family members discussed the budget and talked as they prepared. Pat was quick on her feet with the mental calculations, figuring the discounted prices of the dresses, and Star tried to stay within range, keeping a running total and manipulating the costs in the situation so she could afford her share of the limousine rental.

Preparing and budgeting for the prom took more than just simple paper-and-pencil calculations. Mental math and estimation came to the forefront of the family budget practices. Once Star and Pat knew the amount of the dress and the cost of the prom ticket, they arrived at the discretionary dollar amount they had to play with as they juggled all other expenses. Since Star wanted the limousine more than she cared about her nails or accessories, she borrowed jewelry, got her hair done at a discount by a hairdresser friend of Pat's, and got makeup help from her mom in order to have the limo and still make budget. With all of this negotiation and activity across family members and friends, the budget-related work turned out to be important skills that Star learned so she could get to the prom on her own terms while keeping family relations copasetic. Star recognizes the importance of the budget accomplishments when she says, "I think I did pretty good for my first time." That it is her first time to learn how to set a budget and to stay within it is not lost on her. What better a way to begin to learn skills than to have them motivated by your social and familial desires and rights of passage? The mathematics skills involving calculation, estimation, and mental mathematics are elementary when they are embedded and accomplished in the excitement of the prom and across the family members and their activities.

How did all of this familial math work correspond with school mathematics? The mathematics work we saw transpire—categorization, figuring percentages, making calculations using division, multiplication, addition, mental calculation, and rounding estimation—are all skills and practices called for in the national mathematics standards (NCTM, 2000). At the most general level,

> For example, in number and operations, these Standards propose that students develop a deep understanding of rational-number concepts, become proficient in rational-number computation and estimation, and learn to think flexibly about relationships among fractions, decimals, and percents. (NCTM, 2000, p. 211)

Several standards specifically correspond with the number work Pat, Star, and Milla performed during the prom preparations. The following are examples:

- work flexibly with fractions, decimals, and percents to solve problems;
- understand the meaning and effects of arithmetic operations with fractions, decimals, and integers;
- compute fluently and make reasonable estimates;
- select appropriate methods and tools for computing with fractions and decimals from among mental computation, estimation, calculators or computers, and paper and pencil, depending on the situation, and apply the selected methods;
- develop and analyze algorithms for computing with fractions, decimals, and integers and develop fluency in their use;
- develop and use strategies to estimate the results of rational-number computations and judge the reasonableness of the results.

The standards recommend that the study of rational numbers "should build on students' prior knowledge of whole-number concepts and skills and their encounters with fractions, decimals, and percents in lower grades and in everyday life." It is also emphasized that students are expected to develop computational fluency, which is defined as "the ability to compute efficiently and accurately—with fractions, decimals, and integers." In this light, the problem encountered on pricing the prom dresses while shopping was a perfect example of a problem arising from a real context. Figuring the percentage discounted and the tax on a couple of dresses could be considered a quintessential middle school problem involving mental mathematics with percents and decimals. In fact, it is a problem that could easily appear in math texts as word problems that apply students' computational facilities, fluencies, and understandings.

The mathematics of rationale number and calculation with whole numbers, decimals, and fractions comprise a major strand in school mathematics in both the elementary and middle school grades. The understanding of numbers and the skill of calculating and calculating in the context of problem-solving are common elements of the school curriculum and are considered essential prerequisites for algebra and other higher order mathematics learning in school. Some of these skills are thought to be difficult to master, especially operations with fractions (Saxe et al., 2001). The fact that we can see Pat move easily between whole numbers and fractions, understand their operations, and use them as needed indicates that she has some knowledge that might have traction in the more formal school math arena. Pat's case is not necessarily extraordinary, and many adults may have similar skills. Other people may have to calculate using paper and pencil or even go to the calculator (as Pat chose to do when she was at home), but they still have the knowledge and resources at their fingertips to do the figuring and determine purchases and make tradeoffs based on their calculations.

The mathematics in the Honey family did not confine itself to the budget and shopping examples examined. There were far more instances than could be included here. They are of interest because they show the breadth of mathematical work the family does. In our time with the Honey family, we went to work with Pat at the copy center and learned about Pat's home hair business. The hair business is of special interest to this discussion because it was completely integrated with family life. Pat previously owned and operated a hair salon, but decided she wanted to spend more time with her children. She replaced that business with the two jobs—one as a manager of a photocopy center and the other as the owner of a business selling hair extensions (real and synthetic hair that is used to supplement real hair and make many styles possible). Pat is involved in mathematics related to the management, operations, and record keeping for both businesses. For the hair business, she set up spreadsheets on the home computer to track inventory, orders, and customer purchases. She balanced many variables in the business such as keeping an inventory based on her customers' preferences and life activities. For example, she kept a running inventory based on her analyses of past and current trends, supply and demand issues, and expenditure management. She knew which times of year were most demanding and adjusted her stock accordingly. She also determined inventory based on the quality, costs, and weights of different hair extensions. Customers choose from different grades of hair, different colors, textures, lengths, and quantities by weight. With different prices for different types of hair, Pat constantly balanced inventory with sales and customer needs. She knows her clientele, their hair preferences, and inventory purchases are based on customers as well as outside factors such as the state of the economy and style changes.

The children help Pat with sales and delivery of hair on an as-needed basis, logging sales and marking inventory in the spreadsheet. If Pat is out when a customer call comes in, the children take the order and make the sale and complete the transaction. Home life is ripe with mathematics. Everyone in the household works in the hair business and participates in record keeping. They all use price charts, sales tax tables, spreadsheets, and sales receipts. Pat and the kids are busy with each other and their activities and rarely think of themselves as transacting mathematically.

At one level, it is not surprising that the Honey family members failed to recognize that they were involved in mathematical practices, but at another level, it is extraordinary. Their lack of recognition of mathematics in their lives mirrored that of other families we studied. Our team saw mathematical practices and transactions in every family we studied, and, consistently, the families recognized only basic elementary school arithmetic as mathematics. They had no frameworks or experiences for connecting, relating, or translating what they did in their lives, with the exception of calculation, to the more formal mathematics their children did in school. Our team saw this pattern of nonconnection to school mathematics in every family we studied. Consistently, three things were true of families.

1. They recognized that they often did arithmetic and that they defined arithmetic as mathematics.
2. They rarely recognized any other mathematical practices outside of arithmetic in their daily activities. They certainly did not apply the label of math to the procedures, representations, or abstractions they applied to the business of getting through the day or everyday life and problem-solving. They consistently identified what their children did at school as mathematics and thought they rarely did those same things. The family as an informal mathematics learning setting was latent.
3. They rarely equated what they did in the course of their lives outside of homework as being at all related, relevant, or helpful to what their children did in school mathematics. The parents knew that the mathematics their children were being asked to do in school went far beyond calculation, and they automatically, and reasonably in light of little information and current institutional practices, assumed no

relation between their knowledge and skills and the mathematics their children were being asked to learn in school. School, with its topics, courses, credits, and requirements was the only mathematics.

These findings are consistent with the findings of researchers who have looked at cognition in action (Lave, 1988; Saxe, 1990). In those studies, people could solve problems in the course of everyday activities in the kitchen and for running a candy-selling business out on the streets, yet were unable to solve typical school problems that involved similar mathematics. No wonder parents saw no connections between their math and life skills; the ways people work mathematically in the course of daily life do not require the particular symbol structures, jargon, and formalisms that school mathematics requires. Their abilities to act mathematically in life activities is similar to their abilities to speak their first languages as native speakers instead of as grammarians. The fact that parents identify and legitimate school mathematics as the "real" mathematics makes a great deal of sense. As far as parents were concerned, they were rightly loeft out of the loop when it came to their children's school mathematics. Also for the parents, mathematics has always been in and about school.

The implications of these disconnects in the ways people think of mathematics in life and school result in a significant loss of math learning potential in both settings. It basically puts parents out of the loop and cuts off opportunities for using the riches of out-of-school learning to bootstrap school learning and vice versa. Both sides lose. Parents and teachers are missing a huge opportunity to better educate children in mathematics as a result of all of this disconnect. It legitimizes school knowledge and puts schools in the position of having to do a difficult job without crucial supports. It puts informal mathematics and parents in a marginalized status and in a position of acquiescence, alienation, and subordination. This is unfortunate, because families actually have a wealth of experiences, connections, and resources on which to draw. PRIMES aimed to make progress on balancing this situation. Ultimately, we devised strategies and materials to help parents, students, and their teachers recognize and legitimize the mathematics they do in their lives; increase their familiarity with school mathematics topics, ideas, and practices; and encourage the connections between the two without privileging one over the other. These were beginning steps.

Getting parents to recognize their life skills as mathematical is a first and necessary step for building more connections for students with mathematics. Parents, with their out-in-the-open yet out-of-consciousness mathematics practice, are diamonds in the rough whose special qualities and brilliance need to be mined for improving math teaching and learning processes. Still, the equation is unbalanced if we work only with parents, and this is where previous efforts may have been insufficient. The responsibility for balancing the equation belongs in the schools, where mathematics learning for children has its formal and compulsory home.

Where do the schools stand on creating more connections between the informal and the formal? The national and state standards documents and available resource materials mention little about parents or family life situations and problem-solving as contexts for school math learning. On a more optimistic note, in a recent newsletter, the president of NCTM emphasized how parents, family life, and nonschool contexts, such as workplaces, offer incredibly rich situations for mathematical work and problem-solving. He called for mathematics teachers to incorporate students' nonschool mathematics practices as building blocks of experience and jumping off points for math learning (Lott, 2003). The NCTM and other organizations have developed a rich set of advocacy materials that help parents approach the school, get information, build communication between the school and the home, arrange services, and have developed math activities for use at home. These amount to the tip of the iceberg. There is much work to be accomplished on building strong bridges that allow the informal and formal to connect and interact productively and reciprocally in both settings. Lott's message to math teachers recognizes that mathematics in life contexts requires few of the formalizations and little of the mathematics language employed in school math contexts. His message is that it is imperative that we work harder to build bridges between school and nonschool contexts.

One consequence of these disconnects between informal and formal maths is that we have gotten the directionality and responsibility wrong. Educators have always recognized that parents are the first and most influential educators of children, but they have always required parents to come to the process on the school's terms. The thinking and activity has been organized around a proposition something like: If parents are to be helpful with school math, then we should create math activities to do at home that set the stage for, practice, or reinforce school math topics. The proposition should become: If parents, families, and communities provide rich and varied contexts for mathematical work, then the schools should come to recognize those mathematics practices as legitimate, come to understand them, and use their expertise to build from them to the special hybrid that is formal school mathematics. The goal would be to have everyone competent at school and at home. Historically, the responsibility has been on parents to learn the formal mathematics of school in order to help their children succeed. This should change. The responsibility and impetus for bridging work should rest with the school, since it has the formal responsibility to serve its institutional and learning goals.

Math educators and parents need to come together and "follow" Pat, Star, and Milla as they shop and conduct a business from the home and learn how the family members were figuring the budget and costs as they moved along. It would enable the parents to know that what they do is mathematical and to feel confident in their continued roles as informal educators. It would enable the teachers to see parents in more central roles and define for them what they must do to create and make use of better connections. It could reduce the exclusivity of the school as the only legitimate mathematics learning setting, decrease alienation of schools and families, increase partnerships, and result in much more mathematical productivity in both school and life. In addition to creating conditions for accomplishing a great deal of math learning based in experience, this could result in an intervention for reorganizing the generally dysfunctional relations that schools have with parents. It could result in parents coming to see themselves as competent to help their children in math. It could increase everyone's access to quality math materials, practices, and learning environments. It could facilitate the schools' evolution from a deprivation model of families to a model that eventually legitimizes and actually values family life and activity. It would give parents an honored place at the table of stakeholders and require a reciprocity of ideas that could open up new opportunities. The Honey family and others we worked with seem unendingly resourceful and amazing in their competences. Every family is within reach. Connecting to the lives of parents and families is the needed step in improving math learning.

ACKNOWLEDGMENTS

I am deeply grateful to the parents, teachers, community members, and PRIMES project staff for their hard work, generosity, and partnership. Without them, the project would not have been possible. Thanks to Ray McDermott for his comments upon reading this article and for the many discussions of the relation between informal and formal learning. The work reported on here was supported by a grant from the National Science Foundation. The findings represent the opinions of the author and do not represent those of the NSF.

REFERENCES

American Association of University Women. (1996). *Girls in the Middle: Working to Succeed in School.* Washington, DC.

American Association of University Women. (1996). *Growing Smart: What's Working for Girls in School.* Washington, DC.Ball, D. L. (1993). With an eye on the mathematical horizon: Dilemmas of teaching elementary school mathematics. *The Elementary School Journal,* 93(4).

Bransford, J., Brown, A. L., & Cocking, R. R. (1999). *How people learn: Brain, mind, experience, and school.* Washington, DC: National Academy Press.

Brown, A., & Campione, J. (1994). Guided discovery in a community of learners. In K. McGilly (Ed.), *Classroom lessons: Integrating cognitive theory and classroom practice* (pp. 229–70). Cambridge, MA: MIT Press.

California Department of Education. (1999). *Mathematics Framework for California Public Schools: Kindergarten Through Grade Twelve.* Sacramento, CA: California Department of Education.

Chaiklin, S., & Lave, J. (Eds.). (1993). *Understanding practice: Perspectives on activity and context.* Cambridge, UK: Cambridge University Press.

Civil, M. (1999). *Parents as learners and teachers of mathematics.* Paper presented at ALM-6, Sheffield, UK.

Cobb, P., Yackel, E., & McClain, K. (Eds.). (2000). *Symbolizing and communicating in mathematics classrooms: Perspectives on discourse, tools, and instructional design.* Mahwah, NJ: Lawrence Erlbaum Associates.

Coleman, J. S. (1996). Equality of Educational Opportunity. Washington: U.S. Department of Health, Education, and Welfare, Office of Education.

Confrey, J., & Smith, E. (1995). Splitting, covariation, and their role in the development of exponential functions. *Journal for Research in Mathematics Education* 26.

de Kanter, A., Ginsburg, A., & Milne, A. (1986). *Parent Involvement Strategies: A New Emphasis on Traditional Parent Roles.* ED 293 919.

Epstein, J. L. (1995, May). School/family/community partnerships. Caring for the children we share. *Phi Delta Kappan,* 76(9), 701–712.

Epstein, J. L. (1986, January). Parents' reactions to teacher practices of parent involvement. *The Elementary School Journal* 86(3).

Erickson, F., & Shultz, J. (1982). *Counselor as gatekeeper.* New York: Academic Press.

Goldman, S. (1996). Mediating micro-worlds: Collaboration on high school science activities. In T. Koschmann (Ed.), *CSCL: Theory and Practice of an Emerging Paradigm* (pp. 45–81). Hillsdale, NJ: Lawrence Erlbaum Associates.

Goldman, S., Knudsen, J., & Latvala, M. (1998). Engaging middle schoolers in and through real-world mathematics. In L. Leutzinger (Ed.), *Mathematics in the Middle* (pp. 129–40). Reston, VA: National Council of Teachers of Mathematics.

Gonzalez, N., Moll, L., Tenery, M., Rivera, A., Rendon, P., Gonzales, R., & Amanti, C. (1995). Funds of knowledge for teaching in Latino households. *Urban Education* 29(4).

Greeno, J. G., & Goldman, S. (Eds.). (1998). *Thinking practices in mathematics and science learning.* Mahwah, NJ: Lawrence Erlbaum Associates.

Greeno, J. G., & The Middle-school Mathematics through Applications Project Group. (1997). Theories and practices of thinking and learning to think. *American Journal of Education* 106: 85–126.

Greeno, J. G., & The Middle-school Mathematics through Applications Group. (1997). Participation as fundamental in mathematics education. In J. A. Dossey, J. O Swafford, M. Parmantie, & A. E. Dossey (Eds.), *Proceedings of the Nineteenth Annual Meeting, North American Chapter of the International Group for the Psychology of Mathematics Education* (pp. 1–15). Columbus, OH: ERIC Clearinghouse for Science, Mathematics, and Environmental Education.

Gutiérrez, K. D., Baquedano-Lopéz, P., & Tejada, C. (1999). Rethinking diversity: Hybridity and hybrid language practices in the third space. *Mind, Culture, and Activity* 6: 286–303.

Hall, R. (1995). Exploring design-oriented mathematical practices in school and work settings. *Communications of the ACM,* September, 62.

Hall, R., & Stevens, R. (1995). Making space: a comparison of mathematical work in school and professional design practices. In S. L. Star (Ed.), *The cultures of computing* (pp. 118–45). London: Basil Blackwell.

Henderson, A. T., & Berla, N. (Eds.). (1994). *A new generation of evidence: The family is critical to student achievement*. Washington, DC: Center for Law and Education.

Hutchins, E. (1995). *Cognition in the wild*. Cambridge, MA: Harvard University Press.

Jencks, C. et al. (1972). *Inequality: A reassessment of the effect of family and schooling in America*. New York: Harper & Row.

Keith, T. Z., Keith, P. B., Troutman, G. C., Bickley, P. G., Trivette, P. S., & Singh, K. (1993). Does parental involvement affect eighth-grade student achievement? Structural analysis of national data. *School Psychology Review*, 22(3), 474–496.

Lampert, M., & Blunk, M. L. (Eds.). (1998). *Talking mathematics in school: Studies of teaching and learning*. Cambridge, UK: Cambridge University Press.

Lave, J. (1988). *Cognition in practice*. Cambridge, UK: Cambridge University Press.

Lichtenstein, G., Weisglass, J., & Erickan-Alper, K. (1998). *Final evaluation report: Middle-school mathematics through applications project*. Denver, CO: Quality Evaluation Design.

Liontos, L. B. (1992). *At-risk families & schools: Becoming partners*. Eugene, OR: ERIC Clearinghouse on Educational Management. ED 342 055.

Lott, Johnny. (2003). Students, Families, Communities and Mathematics Teachers. NCTM President's Message. April 2003. <http://www.nctm.org/news/president/2003–04president.htm>.

McDermott, R., Gospodinoff, K., & Aron, J. (1978). Criteria for an ethnographically adequate description of concerted activities and their contexts. *Semiotica* 24(3/4).

McDermott, R., Goldman, S., & Varenne, H. (1984). When school goes home: Some problems in the organization of homework. *Teachers College Record* 85: 391–409.

McLaughlin, M., & Shields, P. (1986). *Involving parents in the schools: Lessons for policy*. ED 293 920.

Medrich, E. et al. (1982). *The serious business of growing up*. Berkeley, CA: University of California Press.

Mehan, H. (1979). *Learning Lessons*. Cambridge, MA: Harvard University Press.

Middle-school Mathematics through Applications Project. (1998). *MMAP II Final Report to the NSF*. Palo Alto: Institute for Research on Learning.

Moles, O. C. (1996, August). *Reaching all families: Creating family-friendly schools* [Online]. Available: http://www.ed.gov/pubs/ReachFam/index.html

Moll, L. (1992). Bilingual classroom studies and community analysis. *Educational Researcher* 21(2): 20–24.

Moll, L., Amanti, C., Neff, D., & Gonzalez, N. (1992). Funds of knowledge for teaching: Using a qualitative approach to connect homes and classrooms. *Theory and Practice* 31(2).

Moses, R. P., & Cobb, C. E., Jr. (2002). *Radical equations: Math literacy and civil rights*. Boston: Beacon Press.

National Council of Teachers of Mathematics. (2000). *Principles and Standards for School Mathematics*. Reston, VA: The National Council of Teachers of Mathematics, Inc.

National Research Council. (1989). *Everybody counts: A report to the nation on the future of mathematics education*. Washington, DC: National Academy Press.

Nunes, T., Schliemann, A. D., & Carraher, D.W. (1993). *Street mathematics and school mathematics*. Cambridge, England & New York, NY: Cambridge University Press.

Pea, R. (1991). Augmenting the Discourse of Learning with Computer-based Learning Environments. *Proceedings of the NATO ARW Computer-based Learning Environments and Problem-Solving*. Leuven, Belgium, September 1990.

Romberg, Thomas A. (1988). *Changes in School Mathematics: Curricular Changes, Instructional Changes, and Indicators of Changes.* New Brunswick, NJ: Center for Policy Research in Education.

Riley, R. W. (October 7, 1994). Testimony to US Senate Subcommittee, Department of Education Archives. http://www.ed.gov/Speeches/10-1994/promise.html

Saxe, G. (1990). *Culture and cognitive development: Studies in mathematical understanding.* Hillsdale, NJ: Lawrence Erlbaum Associates.

Saxe, G. B., Gearhart, M., et al. (2001). Enhancing students' understanding of mathematics: A study of three contrasting approaches to professional support. *Journal of Mathematics Teacher Education* 4(1): 55–79.

Shields, P. M. (1994, September). *Bringing schools and communities together in preparation for the 21st century: Implications of the current educational reform movement for family and community policies* [Online]. Available: http://www.ed.gov/pubs/EdReformStudies/SysReforms/shields1.html

Silver, E. (1993). *Quantitative understanding: Amplifying student achievement and reasoning.* Pittsburgh, PA: Learning Research and Development Center, University of Pittsburg.

IDENTITY AND AGENCY IN NONSCHOOL AND SCHOOL WORLDS

GLYNDA A. HULL AND JAMES G. GREENO

As authors and readers of this volume are well aware, learning occurs in every kind of situation in which a person participates. At home, at play with friends, at work with colleagues, or in being entertained, people learn ways of participating in the practices of their communities—ways of influencing others and being influenced, giving and taking direction, supporting or challenging or resisting proposals made by others, taking on and fulfilling commitments, or not, and so on. They also learn the information, concepts, patterns of reasoning, and other aspects of the contents of activity that are significant for participating successfully.

In this chapter, we consider an aspect of the relationship between teaching and learning that occurs in school and out-of-school. The centerpiece of our view is a construct of identity. We review different ways of theorizing identity and agency, principally the idea of identity and agency as positional (in respect to interaction and to subject matter), and a notion of identity and agency as connected to entering a discourse. Along the way we challenge two common conceptions related to formal learning (usually associated with the institution of school) and informal learning (usually associated with nonschool worlds), especially learning in after-school or out-of-school programs, the latter an educational phenomenon that is popular and growing in the United States (Hull & Schultz, 2001). One assumption is that how people learn and develop is of necessity different, depending on whether the context for learning is formal or informal, within school settings or outside them. The second assumption that we challenge is the hierarchy that is almost always assumed between school and nonschool: that learning out-of-school—through participation in after-school programs, for example—should be supplemental to learning in school. We will argue for a reversal, that school should be understood as being supplementary to students' out-of-school worlds. Our cases will be drawn from mathematics and literacy and from classrooms, after-school programs, and workplaces.

In some instances, powerful learning takes place at school, where children and youth develop identities full of agency, and in such cases the best relationship to an after-school program is one of seamless continuation. But in other instances, and we would think these are in the majority, school is organized in less than optimal ways, and children and youth have less than optimal chances to develop relationships with teachers and with subject matters that support their learning. In these instances, after-schools and other community-based opportunities can lead rather than follow. Most after-school programs are poorly funded, staffed by volunteers, and in constant need of resources. Yet, because after-school programs are usually voluntary, and thus there are of necessity different relationships of authority in place between children and adults, because fun accompanies work, and precisely because the programs don't often view themselves as supplementary to schools, but as alternative sites for different kinds of learning—because of all of these features, after-school programs can represent important and unique spaces for identity formation.[1]

The concepts of identity and agency are emerging as a central focus of research on activity and learning outside of classes or apart from formal schooling. These concepts also need to be brought into focus in our thinking about in-class learning. In this paper, we draw on ideas that were developed by Dorothy Holland and her colleagues (Holland et al., 1998). One of these is *positional identity,* by which Holland et al. and we refer to the variety of ways in which individuals are entitled, expected, and obligated (by themselves and others) to participate in the practices of a community. Another idea is *voice,* by which Holland et al. and we refer to ways in which individuals present and represent themselves to others and to themselves, thereby authoring and coauthoring their identities in the social worlds in which they participate. They also have access to discursive resources, which they can appropriate into their respective dialogic spaces of authoring boundaries and relations with other people and the subject matter both in the class and elsewhere in their lives.

AN EXAMPLE: WORKPLACE LEARNING INVOLVING GROWTH OF IDENTITY

We begin with an example of learning that we interpret in terms of growth of identity. Hull (2000; 2001) studied activity in a workplace where entry-level employees were asked to carry out increasingly complex and numerous literate and mathematical tasks, in line with the new forms of work organization often referred to as the "new capitalism" or the "new work order" (cf. Gee, Hull, & Lankshear, 1996). These employees were mostly recent immigrants, many had had minimal schooling, and a goodly number were not confident speakers of English. Yet, collectively they rose to the expectation that they become a new kind of worker: self-directed problem solvers, symbol analysts, public speakers, contributors to teams and work groups. Many people would characterize these workers' changes in terms of learning new skills, and they certainly did become skillful in ways that had not been required of them previously. We would argue, however, that they were also successful because in their newly organized workplace (a circuit board assembly plant), new forms of participation became possible that allowed them to internalize a new discourse and begin to refashion their working identities. These new forms of participation allowed workers to position themselves differently in relation to members of management and to develop a different sense of entitlement around the symbolic systems (mathematical, alphabetic, schematic) that had currency in their factory.

None of this, of course, is meant to romanticize difficult working conditions in a nonunion company that hired every entry-level employee initially as a temporary, or to suggest that working in the electronics industry as an assembler is a job to which our youth should aspire. We use this example, rather, because it foregrounds especially well how a shift in contexts of identity can afford different opportunities and motivations for learning and participation.

Circuit board assembly has changed during the past 15 years from an industry dominated by handwork to one that relies on robotics; from shop floors organized in assembly-line fashion to the arrangement of workers into teams and work groups; and from a frontline workforce of whom few intellective activities were required to a workforce increasingly expected to understand and engage in work and the assessment of work through practices mediated by a variety of semiotic systems. In particular, the literate requirements of work in this industry have multiplied (as they have in many others), and some corporations have chosen in the wake of this increase to shift frontline workers' interactions, responsibilities, and entitlements in areas such as record-keeping, goal-setting, problem-solving, and teamwork—activities that have at their center the understanding and use of semiotic systems.

Almost overnight, then, workers who previously had been directed merely to load components on circuit boards by hand were now expected to interact with a range of textual matter through print materials and computer technologies, and thereby to organize work goals; monitor and document work progress, efficiency, and quality; think hypothetically in order to solve production problems; and communicate with each other and management. Literate and mathematical practices had come to mediate work practices in significant ways.

There were shifts as well in how workers interacted with each other and with supervisors, managers, and engineers. The "new work order" has promised an interruption of sorts in the traditional stratification of authority in workplaces, as new forms of and spaces for participation allow new patterns of authority and different senses of entitlement to emerge, sometimes unanticipated ones. In the circuit board assembly example, frontline workers were observed to negotiate new roles with each other through the space created by team meetings, with some workers positioned as team leaders and others positioning themselves as self or team advocate. Quite dramatically, in larger forums that included frontline workers, team leaders, instructors, and supervisors, some workers were able to enact new patterns of relationships that altered responsibilities and work practices. In one instance, a lead worker used the public forum of a cross-area meeting to reveal that his work team had chosen not to set team goals until their rates of work had been recalculated and more realistically realigned. Thus, some frontline employees, long denied access to certain authoritative voices, spaces, activities, and symbolic systems in their factory, were able to claim identities that positioned them as entitled.

We propose that these shifts involved changes in workers' identities, the standard ways people developed of interacting with subject-matter activities, and the set of values, entitlements, and expectations around those activities. Simply put, new forms of participation with systems of knowledge and forms of representation positioned workers to develop what we have come to call literate and mathematical identities. Successful participation in literate and mathematical practices in the workplace co-occurred with the development of a sense of self as a different kind of worker: as someone able to initiate and participate in key activities, to increase in expertise, and be recognized for that expertise by one's co-workers and the company. Literacy and mathematical practices and others involving different semiotic systems lived within, drew their life from, larger activity systems that offered new and desirable roles and positions, different patterns of participating and interacting with others, different responsibilities and entitlements—in short, different identities with more authoritative agency. Let us ask then, if we think in similar ways about contexts of identity in classrooms during as well as after school, what features of programs and participant structures support students' learning?

LEARNING AND KNOWING IN PRACTICES OUT-OF-SCHOOL

To anchor our discussion of learning as a process of developing identity and agency, we focus on two intellective domains: literacy and mathematics. These domains are usually associated with learning in school. But both young people as well as adults become expert in practices that are derived from learning outside of school—at times with more success than characterizes much learning in school. In this section, we review evidence that demonstrates these capabilities and illustrates some of their characteristics.

Language and Literacy Practices

Knowing and thinking that involve literacy occur abundantly in the course of people's everyday lives. Literacy practices are ubiquitous out-of-school—reading and writing and language-based activities diverse in function, form, and purpose. Activities involving literacy range from the functional reading and writing that adults do as part of everyday life (Barton & Hamilton, 1998; Barton & Ivanic, 1991), to the extensive expressive writing engaged in by youth and older adolescents—diaries and plays and raps (e.g., Camitta, 1993; Finders, 1997), to the literacies that accompany engagement in sports and hobbies (e.g., Mahiri, 1998), to Internet-related surfing and chat (e.g., Lankshear, 1997; Knobel, 1999), to the literacy and language practices that anchor a variety of community-based activities (e.g., Cushman, 1998; Heath & McLaughlin, 1993), to the considerable and growing requirements of literacy in many worlds of work (Hart-Landsberg & Reder, 1997; Hull, Jury, & Katz, in preparation). While some literacy activities are born of practical and circumscribed need—making a list of groceries, for example, or reading a subway map—others represent considerable intellectual and emotional investment. Hull and Zacher (2002) and Hull and Katz (2002), for example, describe youth and young adults who choose to spend substantial time at a community center creating written narratives that form the basis of multimedia compositions. These high levels of literate effort and accomplishment prompt us to ask: Why do such literacy practices so often flourish out-of-school, and how is it possible that children and adults thereby reveal themselves as capable learners and doers in the world, in contrast to their poor school-based performance? Similarly, when such engagement with literacy flourishes in formal classrooms, what are its affordances? And what have both of these contexts to say about the literate activities that children and youth might engage in as part of in what we might think of as a hybrid context—after-school programs?

Practices of Mathematical Knowing and Learning

It is widely believed that the ability to learn and use mathematics is a rare talent. Many people—probably a majority—consider themselves as not being "good at math." An example of the view that mathematical talent is rare was stated authoritatively by Poincaré (1956). According to this view, the mathematical capability that can be achieved by all but a tiny proportion of people is limited to learning to perform mechanical procedures that they must work hard to memorize. Poincaré characterized mathematics education as a process in which students who are willing to apply themselves can learn to perform mathematical procedures, which are increasingly complicated as they advance. Students differ in their abilities and motivation to master the increasingly challenging mathematical tasks, so the proportion of students still worthy of mathematics teaching decreases as the cohort advances. The prospect of engaging in significant mathematical thinking—which for Poincaré meant advancing mathematical knowledge creatively—is limited to a handful of people who combine extraordinary intellectual talent in the domain with equally extraordinary interest and commitment.

A vastly different view of mathematical learning and knowing comes from research on everyday reasoning in a variety of practical activities. People with little or no study of mathematics in school, nonetheless reason successfully about the quantities and prices of goods that they sell or purchase (Lave, 1988; Nunes, Schliemann, & Carraher, 1993; Saxe, 1991), and they solve problems involving numbers of items optimally (Scribner, 1984). In games, such as basketball or dominoes, young people perform calculations that figure in their play and understand statistics that represent their levels of success (Nasir, 2002). People whose work requires the use of formal mathematics also need to recognize the applicability of mathematical methods, and to adapt the methods they use to fit them to the problems that emerge in their practices (Hall & Stevens, 1995; Ueno, 1998). Again, we are prompted to consider the characteristics and affordances of those contexts and situations in which mathematical learning and knowing flourish out-of-school.

Identities in Participation

The question of how literacy and mathematical capabilities occur naturally in out-of-school settings can be approached in several ways. One approach considers *contexts of information,* emphasizing the value of informational settings that are familiar and interesting to learners. A somewhat more comprehensive approach uses a concept of *contexts of activity,* emphasizing the importance of meaningful, significant activity in which literacy or mathematical activity can inherit at least some of that meaning and significance.

While properties of information and activity are important, we propose that considering *contexts of identity* is also valuable. This concept calls for an understanding of the relationships of participation between an individual and other people in communities of practice and with the concepts, methods, and information of subject-matter domains. Communities of practice and other "figured worlds" provide examples of the types of people that it is possible for participants in those communities and worlds to become—street vendor, rap artist, lover of books, chess master, public speaker, basketball player, technology whiz, team leader. And they provide opportunities for participants to begin to enact new identities, to take on and to adapt sanctioned ways of behaving, interacting, valuing, and believing.

We conceptualize a person's identity as including interpersonal, epistemic, and discursive aspects. Interpersonally, a person's identity includes her or his interactions with other people, including commitments and the ways in which the person is entitled, expected, and obligated to treat other people in interaction. Epistemically, a person's identity includes her or his interactions with the subject-matter contents of activities, including ways the person is committed, entitled, expected, and obligated to have and seek knowledge, understanding, and use of the contents of a subject-matter domain. Discursively, contexts of identity afford models of self and opportunities to enact selves, a process we will call "discoursal identity."[2]

Interpersonal Identities

These ideas help us organize our understanding of learning away from classes or formal instruction. Individuals in a community of practice have *trajectories of participation,* to use Lave and Wenger's (1991) term, which involves changes over time in relationships of participation with other individuals that we call "interpersonal identity." In the after-school multimedia programs established and studied by Hull and Katz (2002), young people graduated to positions of greater responsibility and authority within the program—becoming tutors for novices, for example, participating in the design of new activities, recruiting other individuals to attend the program—positions that entailed certain valued ways of interacting and communicating as well as investment in particular kinds of creative work. Heath's (e.g., 1998) study of young people working to stage dramatic productions and Long, Peck, and Baskins's (2002) work in an inner-city community literacy center and settlement house also provide examples of learning that included versions of self as valued social participants and change agents.

Epistemic Identities

The process of learning and development also includes what we have called "epistemic identity," or a person's increasing expertise and understanding related to the subject-matter contents of activities, such as a person's belief that he or she is entitled or unentitled to engage in literate or mathematical activity. Examples include Mahiri's (1998) study of adolescent African American males in youth basketball leagues, who engaged in substantial reading in order to learn to operate certain sports-inspired video games. These young people acquired patterns of use and beliefs about literate entitlement, along with technical practice in decoding and comprehending, to use the language of reading research. In addition, these literate activities were bound tightly with a valued sense of self as participant in a "figured world," to use Holland et al.'s (1998) term. Examples involving mathematics include Nasir's (2002) study of adolescent African American males playing dominoes or basketball at the local community center, which can be a significant part of a young person's identity, and also includes patterns of participation that depend on the person's level of experience, skill, and understanding of the enterprise.

Discoursal Identities

We focus here on two ways that language plays an important role in the process of enacting a self. First, we focus on the narrative aspect of discoursal identity—the stories we learn to tell ourselves about the selves we were, are, want to become, and imagine it possible to be. Second, we examine the process of acquiring a new discourse, especially of learning to talk the talk of new figured worlds.

There is abundant research on narrative, or verbal, visual, or embodied representations of past or future events, and the linkage between narrative and the construction of self. Scholars of narrative explain that we construct notions of ourselves by telling stories about who we have been in the past and who we want to become in the future. Narratives of self—telling ourselves and others stories about the people we have been or want to become—can constitute especially significant moments of identity construction. The linguistic anthropologist Urciuoli (1995) calls such moments "performative" and notes that they can result in the "intense creation or realization of self" (p. 202). But as Urciuoli also notes, we are constantly creating our identities from moment to moment through language and other forms of signification. This process is often referred to as acquiring a "new discourse."

Within literacy studies, Gee (1996) has been influential in popularizing the term "discourse" to indicate the "ways of behaving, interacting, valuing, thinking, believing, speaking, and often reading and writing that are accepted as instantiations of particular roles (or 'types of people') by specific *groups of people*" (Gee, 1996, p. viii). Acquiring a new discourse thus means becoming a different person, taking on a new identity. This process, according to Gee and others, is likelier than not to be steeped in tension and conflict, since new discourses can represent conflicting frames of reference and sets of values.

Bakhtin's (1981) writings acknowledge the reproductive powers of discourse while simultaneously allowing a space for self-determination. Especially helpful is his metaphor of voice, by which he means the speaking consciousness, and which he represents as multiple and dialogic in nature, as suggested by these companion terms: "multivoiced," "other-voiced," "double-voiced," and "revoiced." For Bakhtin, voices are continually reaccentuated, interanimated, even ventrioloquated, as individuals encounter and engage in multiple discourses. The process of constructing an identity, then, can be viewed as a linguistic, ideological struggle to make others' words at least somewhat one's own—to create what Bakhtin called an "internally persuasive discourse," perhaps through an orchestration of voices from multiple discourses.

The power of narrative models and opportunities to enact a self can be seen in what Bruner (1994) has referred to as "turning points," or moments when people report sharp changes in their lives and accompanying dramatic changes in representations of self, which can serve as emblems or tropes for how one thinks of one's life as a whole. In recent work on community-based vocational programs, Hull and Paull (2001) have noted that adult students, many of whom have faired poorly in previous schooling and jobs, learn to tell "once I was, now I am" narratives, which serve to guide their search for new careers or job paths. In the case that they reported, the opportunity to tell these narratives through multimedia seemed especially powerful. Likewise, in their work with inner-city youth, Long, Peck, and Baskins (2002) orchestrate literacy-rich, community-based activities in which teenagers are encouraged to "identify their own acts of agency in places where choices make a real difference: staying in school, holding a family together, sustaining day-to-day relationships, building a plan for after graduation" (p. 165).

LANGUAGE LITERACY AND MATHEMATICAL PRACTICES IN SCHOOL

People learn to participate successfully in social practices out-of-school that require significant literacy and mathematical capabilities. We have proposed a hypothesis that this natural learning occurs because these practices support the development of identities, and we have suggested three aspects of identity—interpersonal, epistemic, and discoursal—as being important in supporting development and maintenance of identities in practice.

Why is it that many students who learn practices of literacy and mathematics successfully in practices out-of-school are unsuccessful at learning these capabilities in-school? Of course, there are differences in the contents and technical requirements of successful practice in the school curriculum and the practices in which students succeed out of school. But our hypotheses that the affordances of out-of-school practices for developing identity are important in the support of learning suggests that it is at least worth considering another possibility: If school learning practices could afford the development of students' identities in similar ways, the success of many more students could be fostered. In this section, we review research that has studied school practices that afford successful learning by students who are often unsuccessful in the prevalent school practices. We argue that the success of these practices may be due to their support of students' identities.

Literacy in Students' Intellective Identities in School

For many years, a pendulum of debate has moved teachers back and forth between a focus on the subskills of reading and writing (such as phonics, decoding, grammar, and sentence generation) and more holistic, meaning-centered approaches (such as whole language and "authentic" reading and writing activities or writing process approaches) (cf. Gee, 1999). Although the debates continue to attract participants, especially of late, there is much agreement that subskills need to be taught in the context of meaning-making approaches (cf. Shoenbach, Greenleaf, Cziko, & Hurwitz, 1999). In the same way that an exclusionary emphasis on procedures and memorization of routines can stunt students' epistemic relations to mathematics—resulting in identities that have little authority or agency—we would argue that a misplaced emphasis, on, for example, the correct enunciation of word endings during reading lessons, can result in identities as reluctant readers or even nonreaders.

One rich strand of work on school-based literacy, one that we suggest may encourage students to develop a sense of entitlement as a reader and writer, seeks to recognize and incorporate the personal and community resources of children, youth, and adults, and to use those resources to build bridges to school-based ways of using language and interacting with written texts. There is a long and revered tradition of research on language and literacy that highlights the ways in which many children's patterns of language use differ from the patterns privileged and expected in schools, which are based largely on a white, middle-class norm (e.g., Cazden, John, & Hymes, 1972; Heath, 1983). One goal of this research has been to emphasize that these ways of using language are different, not deficient, a point crucially important for teachers and their expectations about students' abilities and educational trajectories. Another goal has been to figure out how students' existing understandings and patterns of language and literacy practice can be incorporated in the classroom. This work, we would argue, has the effect of enabling the development of agentive literate identities, senses of self as a reader and writer enabled to create and interact with texts in ways that further one's own communicative agenda.

An example is Moll's work with Latino communities in the Southwest and the term "funds of knowledge," which he used to describe the networked expertise woven through community practices (Moll, 1992; Moll & Diaz, 1987; Moll & Greenberg, 1990; see also Vásquez, 1993). Moll's projects provide a demonstration of how funds of knowledge can be used to bridge communities to classrooms when the expertise of parents and community members are acknowledged. Moll also offers examples of lessons in which teachers have brought community members into the schoolroom to share their knowledge and know-how, and he documents the positive effects of such activities on children's interest and investment in the curriculum.

Developing a culturally relevant pedagogy for teaching literary interpretation to African American youth, Lee (1993) also illustrates cultural funds of knowledge, particularly language forms and discourse structures. In more recent work, Lee and her colleagues (Lee, 2000; Majors, 2000; Rivers, Hutchinson, & Dixon, 2000) examine language practices across contexts, identifying community participation structures, in, for example, African American hair salons, and using those structures to inform ways of conducting classroom discussions about texts. This research shows the potential for engaging students in high levels of reasoning about literary texts by drawing on their tacit knowledge of cultural forms found outside school.

Dyson's long-term studies of early writing development acknowledge especially well the resources that young children bring to their writing from their social worlds, including linguistic and symbolic tools appropriated from popular culture (Dyson, 1997; 1999; 2003). Dyson has argued for the permeability of the curriculum, where teachers imagine their classrooms in such a way as to continually welcome the diverse resources that children of necessity bring to their writing. Dyson's research is situated physically within classroom walls, but her conceptual framework embraces children's out-of-school lives and suggests the ways in which children themselves bring their outside worlds into the school through their writing and the oral performances that encircle literacy events.

School Mathematics in Students' Intellective Identities

In many ways, the conversation about what kind of mathematics instruction best supports students' learning has been similar to that in literacy. We hypothesize that successful learning and knowing mathematics out of school results from mathematics being embedded in activities that students invest with their identities. We propose to use this concept of identity to consider school learning of mathematics, emphasizing characteristics of school programs that support students' learning of mathematics that can be integrated with their identities as learners and knowers.

Our consideration of mathematics learning in school has two points. First, we consider alternative practices in mathematics classrooms that follow versions of the standard curriculum of mathematics. The alternative practices involve differences in the ways students are positioned in their participation in mathematical activity, primarily in discourse. We argue that these alternative participation structures, involving authority and accountability in participation, differ significantly in their affordances for students' investments of identity in their mathematical knowing and learning. The second point of our discussion involves examples in which nonstandard curricula have been developed, aimed toward supporting mathematics learning that is substantively more coherent with identities of students than is easily achieved with the standard curriculum.

Identities Afforded by Classroom Practices

We consider how different classroom practices afford different kinds of mathematical identities for students in their participation. Of course, different students in the same class do not all develop the same kinds of identity. Even so, the practices that a teacher and students co-construct in a classroom are much more encouraging for some kinds of identity than for others.

The tasks that teachers define for students to work on influence students' identities in relation to the subject domain of mathematics, which we are calling the "epistemic aspect" of their mathematical identities. Students learn more successfully when their activities include more tasks with significant cognitive demands involving engagement with conceptual meanings of mathematical concepts and representations than when their tasks are limited to remembering routing information and executing procedures without attending to their meanings (Stein et al., 2000). Students who are engaged in extensive project-oriented activity learn to solve open-ended problems more successfully than students whose learning activity is limited to practicing well-defined procedures (Boaler, 1997). We hypothesize that these effects are only partly due to differences in the contents of learning activity. In addition, we hypothesize that activities that make meaningful contact with mathematical concepts and principles afford development of students' interpersonal, epistemic, and discursal identities with authority and accountability in the conceptual domain of mathematics. Boaler and Greeno (2000) reported interviews with students in Advanced Placement Calculus classes that were conducted differently. Students in classes that emphasized individual learning of procedures understood the mathematics they learned as a subject with right and wrong answers. Students in classes that emphasized discussion of concepts and principles involved in procedures understood the mathematics they learned as a subject in which people contribute to each others' understanding and collaborate in the enterprise of learning. They and we interpret this finding as indicating a difference in students' positional identities. When mathematical activities are limited to executing procedures without attending to their meanings, students are not encouraged to adopt use of mathematical terms and procedures in their personal voices; instead, expression of mathematics remains in the voice of others, or of an unpersonalized agency of mathematics, and students (and teachers) are limited in their discourse to animating mathematics, rather than authoring (cf. Goffman, 1981). By contrast, classroom activities that include significant amounts of discussion in which meanings and uses of mathematical concepts and principles constructed by students encourage their development of identities with epistemic entitlements, expectations, and obligations to interpret and adapt mathematical concepts in their thinking and reasoning. These identities involve incorporating mathematical linguistic actions, including questions, assertions, inferences, explanations, and arguments as being authored by "me, for myself" (Holland & Skinner, 2001), in the voice of mathematical conceptual agency (Pickering, 1995).

Contextualizing School Mathematics Content

The examples we have discussed of mathematical identities in classroom practice have involved different ways of teaching and learning mathematical topics that are quite standard in the mathematics curriculum. There also are programs in which the contents of the curriculum have been designed so that mathematical concepts and methods are embedded in activities that make them meaningful in a broader context. These programs locate mathematics in other activities, as it is in everyday activities where people, including children, are known to be successful.

These examples include a curriculum developed at the Institute for Research on Learning, called the Middle-school Mathematics through Applications Project (Goldman & Moschkovich, 1995), in which the students' main activities involve design projects that involve reasoning about and representing quantitative properties and relations that are important for their designs. Another example is a project in Alaska (Lipka, Mohatt, & The Ciulistet Group, 1998) in which mathematics educators have collaborated with Yup'ik Eskimo elders in developing curricula in which mathematics is embedded in situations and problems that are important in Yup'ik culture. A third example is the Algebra Project (Moses & Cobb, 2001), which uses a five-step curriculum process that begins with an activity that students participate in, such as a trip using public transportation. This experience is the basis for students' constructing representations that initially are informal and move progressively to more formal mathematical notations and reasoning.

AFTER SCHOOL IN RELATION TO SCHOOL

The Algebra Project includes an activity, the Young People's Project (YPP), which exemplifies some potentially significant features of out-of-school learning resources that can be constructed in relation to school learning. The YPP is led by young workers who are affiliated with the Algebra Project, including a daughter and two sons of Robert Moses and several high school and college students who were formerly members of Algebra Project mathematics classes. The young people, called Mathematical Literacy Workers, meet after school to become proficient in mathematical activities that Algebra Project teachers use in their classes, and they organize after-school activities for students who are currently studying mathematics in Algebra Project classes. These after-school sessions, which can be held in a school or a nonschool site such as a Boys and Girls Club, include participation in experiential activities that are used in the students' mathematics classes, for which additional time adds to the depth of the students' familiarity and understanding of those activities, and thereby can strengthen their usefulness as a basis for the development of their discourse in mathematics.

The organization and staffing of YPP by young African American people is a particular strength of the program. It provides these students with a setting to contribute to the education of their younger counterparts and involves them with mathematics as teachers, as well as learners, with productive agency in the construction of their and others' mathematical knowledge. And it provides after-school activities for students currently taking mathematics classes that are led by young people, with whom they have a strong basis for identification.

In other after-school programs, the intent is less to provide after-school activities that reinforce or add depth to students' school-based understandings than to provide alternative or different experiences or understandings. Examples include the network of after-school programs begun by Cole and colleagues called The Fifth Dimension, which links community-based after-school programs to universities and undergraduates as mentors, and offers theoretically motivated "activity systems" usually centered around computer games and educational programs (1996). The intent of this after-school network is to improve children's school-based performance, but to do so by alternative participant structures, activities, and roles for children and adults.

Other after-school programs seek to engage children and youth in literacy practices that could be described as "hybrid," as including traditional school-valued versions of reading and writing, but joining those with opportunities to create multimedia compositions that also include music, video, and pictures from popular culture. Such "new literacies" are infrequent in many schools but leverage an engagement by youth that is equally rare. In West Oakland, California, the DUSTY Project (Digital Underground Storytelling for Youth) is one such effort. At this community technology center, youth and adult participants are able to tell personal and community stories through print-based narratives and multimedia and to present and distribute these accounts of their communities, lives, and futures through public viewings at a local theater and the Internet. This project intends to position all learners, but especially those who have not been successful in school, to develop identities as capable, intelligent, and creative users of communication technologies. Another aim of the project is to push the boundaries between school and after-school, exploring how the literate and social development of after-school learning and play can be carried into students' and teachers' classroom worlds. Through the participation of college students as mentors, the program also intends to help urban youth develop college-going identities. Through the participation of community members as instructors and staff, the DUSTY project remains locally grounded and maintains social and cultural ties with participants' primary discourse communities. Analyses of students' participation in DUSTY show that both children and undergraduates develop a rich array of textual and technological skills, while at the same time broadening their repertoires of strategies for working and playing together collaboratively in a literacy- and technology-rich digital storytelling environment (Hull, 2002). Analyses also demonstrate that for some participants, this after-school program provides an especially powerful alternative learning site where children who haven't been successful in school can nonetheless develop agentive identities in relation to new literacies. That is, adolescents who were viewed as lackadaisical students in school nonetheless developed considerable expertise and graduated to positions of authority in the after-school program.

CONCLUSION

In this paper, we have sketched a view of learning and development that privileges the construction of powerful identities for learners across contexts. We have argued the importance of focusing, not on the boundaries that separate school and nonschool worlds but on the kinds of participation that best support learning, and these kinds of participation can be organized in many educational contexts. Differences between learning after-school and learning in school can be very significant, but so can differences in learning between different kinds of after-school programs and between different arrangements for learning in school. The differences we emphasize are not inherent in whether they occur in school. Instead, we emphasize differences in ways that students are positioned in their learning.

We have argued that an understanding of the importance of developing interpersonal, epistemic, and discoursal identities in school and out-of-school. If after-school programs were to take this charge seriously, we might ask what their key features might be. First, we think that after-school programs are good places to make available different roles and positions for children and youth, through opportunities, for example, in which older students work with younger, or students with particular expertise serve as mentors or guides for others, no matter their age. Such redistribution of authority can serve to foster reorientations of self, as children who struggle in schools achieve success and recognition in after-school settings. A second opportunity that after-school programs have is the use of community knowledge and community connections in making such programs comfortable spaces for children and youth to learn and develop. While it's often a stretch for many teachers in public schools to become sufficiently knowledgeable about their students' cultures to make use of that knowledge in the classrooms, after-school programs are typically community-based and staffed. Third, after-school programs don't have to be tied to state tests and other forms of accountability, and thereby they achieve a certain flexibility in terms of the activities they can foster. Hybrid text forms, new uses of technology, explorations of popular culture—all of these can flourish after-school, recruiting participants' motivation and involvement. Such innovations can also be transported to school settings. Fourth, after-school programs can serve as bridges to school and to teachers' understandings of their students, their communities, and the potential of both. After-school programs can be spaces where teachers see different sides of their children and their potential to develop different epistemic, interactional, and discoursal identities.

The view that learning programs can and should focus on students' development of positive and agentive identities can shape the design of after-school programs. The desirability and feasibility of such programs are supported by the research we have cited in this paper, and a commitment to such an effort is required if it is believed that all of the children in our societies are entitled to have access to opportunities for learning of the most significant kinds. We believe that the development of programs for learning after-school can lead, rather than only supplement, the programs of academic learning in school. We hope and believe that such programs can be developed in close concert with school learning programs in which students are increasingly supported in the development of positive identities as learners, knowers, and participants in our society.

We hope that the research we have reported is persuasive in supporting the possibility of designing after-school programs that enable students to learn and develop positively. At the same time, we acknowledge that there is much about this agenda that is not understood as well as it should and can be. We therefore close by noting that initiatives to develop stronger after-school programs should include efforts to analyze and further understand the processes of learning and development that occur as young people participate in them. This is an area in which a combination of design, development, and research can be fruitful and is essential, if we are to strengthen the resources available to all young people in every society to learn and develop.

ACKNOWLEDGMENTS

The authors' research on learning and identity was supported by grants from the US Department of Education's Community Technology Centers program (GH) and by a grant from the Spencer Foundation (JG).

NOTES

1. The alternative nature of after-school and out-of-school programs is currently being challenged in the United States, as federal and state legislation seeks to extend the school day and to establish after-school programs that are a continuation of school.
2. Cf. Ivanic (1998), who uses the term "discoursal self" to mean the impressions that writers convey of themselves, consciously or unconsciously, in their written texts.

REFERENCES

Bakhtin, M. M. (1981). *The dialogic imagination: Four essays by M. M. Bakhtin.* M. E. Holquist (Ed.), Caryl Emerson & M. Holquist (Trans). Austin: University of Texas Press.

Barton, D., & Hamilton, M. (1998). *Local literacies: Reading and writing in one community.* London: Routledge.

Barton, D., & Ivanic, R. (Eds.). (1991). *Writing in the community.* Newbury Park, CA: Sage Publications.

Belenky, M. F., Clinchy, B. M., Goldberger, N. R., & Tarule, J. M. (1986). *Women's ways of knowing: The development of self, voice, and mind.* New York: Basic Books.

Boaler, J. (1997). *Experiencing school mathematics: Teaching styles, sex and setting.* Buckingham, UK: Open University Press.

Boaler, J., & Greeno, J. G. (2000). Identity, agency, and knowing in mathematics worlds. In J. Boaler (Ed.), *Multiple perspectives on mathematics teaching and learning* (pp. 171–200). Westport, CT: Ablex.

Brown, A. L., & Campione, J. C. (1994). Guided discovery in a community of learners. In K. McGilly (Ed.), *Classroom lessons: Integrating cognitive theory and classroom practice* (pp. 229–70). Cambridge, MA: MIT Press/Bradford.

Bruner, J. (1994). The "remembered" self. In U. Neisser & R. Fivush (Eds.), *The remembering self: Construction and accuracy in the self-narrative* (pp. 41–54). Cambridge: Cambridge University Press.

Camitta, M. (1993). Vernacular writing: Varieties of literacy among Philadelphia high school students. In B. V. Street (Ed.), *Cross-cultural approaches to literacy* (pp. 228–46). Cambridge, UK: Cambridge University Press.

Cazden, C. B., John, V. P., & Hymes, D. (Eds.). (1972). *Functions of language in the classroom.* New York: Teachers College Press.

Cole, M. (1996). *Cultural psychology: A once and future discipline.* Cambridge, MA: Harvard University Press.

Cushman, E. (1998). *The struggle and the tools: Oral and literate strategies in an inner city community.* Albany: SUNY Press.

Dyson, A. H. (1997). *Writing superheroes: Contemporary childhood, popular culture, and classroom literacy.* New York: Teachers College Press.

Dyson, A. H. (1999). Coach Bombay's kids learn to write: Children's appropriation of media material for school literacy. *Research in the Teaching of English, 33*(4), 367--402.

Dyson, A. H. (2003). The stolen lipstick of overhead song: Composing voices in child song, verse, and written text. In M. Nystrand & J. Duffy (Eds.), *Towards a rhetoric of everyday life.* Madison: University of Wisconsin Press.

Engle, R. A., & Conant, F. R. (2002). Guiding principles for fostering productive disciplinary engagement: Explaining an emergent argument in a community of learners classroom. *Cognition and Instruction, 20,* 399–483.

Finders, M. J. (1997). *Just girls: Hidden literacies and life in junior high.* New York: Teachers College Press.

Finnegan, R. H. (1998). *Tales of the city: A study of narrative and urban life.* Cambridge: Cambridge University Press.

Gee, J. P. (1996). Social linguistics and literacies: Ideology in discourses (2nd ed.). London: The Falmer Press.

Gee, J. P. (1999). Reading and the new literacy studies: Reframing the National Academy of Sciences' report on reading. *The Journal of Literacy Research, 31*(3), 355–74.

Gee, J. P., Hull, G., & Lankshear, C. (1996). *The new work order: Behind the language of the new capitalism.* Boulder, CO: Westview.

Goffman, E. (1981). *Forms of talk.* Philadelphia: University of Pennsylvania Press.

Goldman, S., Moschkovich, J., & The Middle-school Mathematics through Applications Project Team. (Oct., 1995). Paper presented at CSCL95, Computer Supported Collaborative Learning, Bloomington, IN.

Hall, R., & Stevens, R. (1995). Making space: A comparison of mathematical work in school and professional design practices. In S. L. Star (Ed.), *The cultures of computing* (pp. 118–45). Oxford: Blackwell Publishers/The Sociological Review.

Hart-Landsberg, S., & Reder, S. (1997). Teamwork and literacy: Teaching and learning at Hardy Industries. In G. Hull (Ed.), *Changing work, changing workers: Critical perspectives on language, literacy, and skills* (pp. 359–82). Albany: State University of New York Press.

Heath, S. B. (1983). *Ways with words.* New York: Cambridge University Press.

Heath, S. B. (1998). Living the arts through language plus learning: A report on community-based youth organizations. *Americans for the Arts Monographs, 2*(7), 1--19.

Heath, S. B., & McLaughlin, M. W. (1993). *Identity and inner-city youth: Beyond ethnicity and gender.* New York: Teachers College Press.

Holland, D., Lachicotte, W., Jr., Skinner, D., & Cain, C. (1998). *Identity and agency in cultural worlds.* Cambridge, MA: Harvard University Press.

Holland, D., & Skinner, D. (2001). From women's suffering to women's politics: Reimagining women after Nepal's 1990 pro-democracy movement. In D. Holland & J. Lave (Eds.), *History in person: Enduring struggles, contentious practice, intimate identities* (pp. 93–133). Santa Fe: School of American Research Press.

Hull, G. (2000). Critical literacy at work. *Journal of Adolescent and Adult Literacy, 43*(1), 648–52.

Hull, G. (2001). Constructing working selves: Silicon Valley assemblers meet the new work order. *Anthropology of Work Review, 22*(1), 17–22.

Hull, G. (Oct., 2002). Crossing the digital divide through multi-media and literacy: A proposal to establish and evaluate a model technology program. Final Report to the US Department of Education. Berkeley, CA: University of California, Berkeley.

Hull, G., Jury, M., & Katz, M. (in preparation). *Working the frontlines of economic change: Learning, doing, and becoming in the Silicon Valley.* New York. Peter Lang Publishing.

Hull, G., & Katz, M.-L. (Nov., 2002). Learning to tell a digital story: New literate spaces for crafting a self. Paper presented at the Annual Meeting of the American Anthropological Association, New Orleans.

Hull, G., & Paull, C. (Feb., 2001). Fashioning selves through multiple media: An exploration of digital literacies and digital divides. Invited Paper presented at the National Council of Teachers of English Assembly for Research Midwinter Conference, Berkeley, CA.

Hull, G., & Schultz, K. (2001). Literacy and learning out of school: A review of theory and research. *Review of Educational Research, 71*(4), 575–611.

Hull, G., & Zacher, J. (April, 2002). New literacies, new selves, and second chances: Exploring possibilities for self-representation through writing and multi-media in a community technology center. Paper presented at the annual meeting of the American Educational Research Association, New Orleans.

Ivanic, R. (1998). *Writing and identity: The discoursal construction of identity in academic writing.* Philadelphia: John Benjamins.

Kazemi, E., & Stipek, D. (2001). Promoting conceptual thinking in four upper-elementary mathematics classrooms. *The Elementary School Journal, 102,* 59–80.

Knobel, M. (1999). *Everyday literacies: Students, discourse, and social practice.* New York: Peter Lang.

Lankshear, C. (1997). *Changing literacies.* Buckingham: Open University Press.

Lave, J. (1988). *Cognition in practice.* Cambridge, UK: Cambridge University Press.

Lave, J., & Wenger, E. (1991). *Situated learning: Legitimate peripheral participation.* Cambridge, UK: Cambridge University Press.

Lee, C. D. (1993). *Signifying as a scaffold for literary interpretation: The pedagogical implications of an African American discourse genre.* Urbana, IL: National Council of Teachers of English.

Lee, C. D. (April, 2000). The cultural modeling project's multimedia records of practice: Analyzing guided participation across time. Paper presented at the annual meeting of the American Educational Research Association, New Orleans.

Lipka, J., with Mohatt, G. V. & The Ciulistet Group (1998). *Transforming the culture of schools: Yup'ik Eskimo examples.* Mahwah, NJ: Lawrence Erlbaum Associates.

Long, E., Peck, W. C., & Baskins, J. (2002). STRUGGLE: A literate practice supporting life-project planning. In G. Hull & K. Schultz (Eds.), *School's out! Bridging out-of-school literacies with classroom practice* (pp. 131–61). New York: Teachers College Press.

Mahiri, J. (1998). *Shooting for excellence: African American and youth culture in new century schools.* Urbana, IL: National Council of Teachers of English.

Majors, Y. (Apr., 2000). "Talk that talk": Discourse norms transversing school and community. Paper presented at the annual meeting of the American Educational Research Association, New Orleans.

Martin, D. B. (2000). Mathematics success and failure among African American youth: The roles of sociohistorical context, community forces, school influence, and individual agency. Mahwah, NJ: Lawrence Erlbaum Associates.

Moll, L. C. (1992). Bilingual classroom studies and community analysis: Some recent trends. *Educational Researcher, 21*(3), 20–24.

Moll, L. C., & Diaz, S. (1987). Change as the goal of educational research. *Anthropology & Education Quarterly, 18,* 300–311.

Moll, L. C., & Greenberg, J. B. (1990). Creating zones of possibilities: Combining social context for instruction. In L. C. Moll (Ed.), *Vygotsky and education: Instructional implications and applications of sociohistorical psychology.* Cambridge, UK: Cambridge University Press.

Moses, R. P., & Cobb, C. E., Jr. (2001). *Radical equations: Math literacy and civil rights.* Boston: Beacon Press.

Nasir, N. S. (2002). Identity, goals, and learning: Mathematics in cultural practice. *Mathematical Thinking and Learning, 4,* 213–47.

Nunes, T., Schliemann, A. D., & Carraher, D. W. (1993). *Street mathematics and school mathematics.* Cambridge, UK: Cambridge University Press.

Ochs, E., & Capps, L. (1996). Narrating the self. *Annual Review of Anthropology, 25,* 19–43.

Ochs, Elinor, and Capps, Lisa. (2001). *Living narrative: creating lives in everyday storytelling.* Cambridge, MA: Harvard University Press.

Pickering, A. (1995). *The mangle of practice: Time, agency, and science.* Chicago: University of Chicago Press.

Poincaré, H. (1956). Mathematical creation. In J. R. Newman (Ed.), *The world of mathematics* (vol. 4, pp. 2041–50). New York: Simon and Schuster.

Polkinghorne, D. E. (1991). Narrative and self-concept. *Journal of Narrative and Life History, 1,* 135–53.

Rivers, A., Hutchinson, K., & Dixon, K. (Apr., 2000). Participatory appropriation in a cultural modeling classroom. Paper presented at the annual meeting of the American Educational Research Association, New Orleans.

Saxe, G. B. (1991). *Culture and cognitive development: Studies in mathematical understanding.* Mahwah, NJ: Lawrence Erlbaum Associates.

Schoenbach, R., Greenleaf, C., Cziko, C., & Hurwitz, L. (1999). *Reading for understanding.* San Francisco: Jossey-Bass.

Schwartz, D. L. (1999). The productive agency that drives collaborative learning. In P. Dillenbourg (Ed.), *Collaborative learning: Cognitive and computational approaches* (pp. 197–241). Amsterdam: Elsevier Science/Pergamon.

Scribner, S. (1984). Studying working intelligence. In B. Rogoff & J. Lave (Eds.), *Everyday cognition: Its development in social context* (pp. 9–40). Cambridge, MA: Harvard University Press.

Stein, M. K., Smith, M. S., Henningsen, M. A., & Silver, E. A. (2000). *Implementing standards-based mathematics instruction: A casebook for professional development.* New York: Teachers College Press.

Ueno, N. (1998). Doing mathematics as situated practice. In C. Donlan (Ed.), *The development of mathematical skills* (pp. 111–28). Palo Alto, CA: Psychology Press.

Urciuoli, B. (1995). The indexical structure of visibility. In B. Farnell (Ed.), *Human action signs in cultural context.* Metuchen, NJ: Scarecrow Press.

Vásquez, O. A. (1993). A look at language as resource: Lessons from La Clase Mágica. In B. Arias & U. Casanova (Eds.), *Bilingual education: Politics, research, and practice* (pp. 119–224). Chicago: National Society for the Study of Education.

SCHOOL'S INVASION OF "AFTER-SCHOOL"

COLONIZATION, RATIONALIZATION, OR EXPANSION OF ACCESS?

HONORINE NOCON AND MICHAEL COLE

> After-school programs certainly contribute to adult encroachment on low-income children's already limited ownership of their lives. Yet, at their best, they are relatively sensitive adult institutions in which the adult agenda is relatively modest. As the historical account suggests, after-school programs have struggled, although not always successfully, to respect the importance of the peer group to school-age children and to take children's point of view seriously. They have been cognizant of differences in children's patterns of abilities and interests. After-school programs have striven to make learning and talent development fun through a broad range of experiences to children and have tired to create space for play among their activities. (Halpern, 2002, p. 205)

CHILDREN'S LIVES

Schooling, natural as it appears to modern residents of industrialized nations, owes its rather recent expansion beyond elites to the processes of urbanization and industrialization. As literacy and numeracy became central to the functioning of a broader society and basic skills and a common socialization became requirements for workers in industrialized societies, compulsory schooling expanded rapidly in Western society (Goody, 1977). The first compulsory schools were established in Prussia in 1717, becoming the model for German and, later, American schools (Gatto, 2000). The shared goal was national unification and national consensus, a common social and political ideology (Goodlad, 1990; Richman, 1994; Spring, 2000).

The first US state to adopt compulsory schooling was Massachusetts in 1852. By 1900, 33 states had passed legislation requiring mandatory elementary schooling. Through the first half of the twentieth century, in an inverse relation with child labor, the hours, days per year, and required years of compulsory education expanded. Children were restricted from working until age 16 and, for the most part, were required to be in school for several hours per day through that age.

The advance of common or universal schooling was promoted as both access to economic opportunity and induction into the ideas that govern the nation and the community. These two goals, economic opportunity and participation in the democratic community, continue to drive both state-sponsored education and educational reform as well as debate. While one camp describes schools and school reform as tools for access to participation in a democratic society for future citizens and future workers (Dewey, 1899/1964, 1936; Fenstermacher, 1999; Goodlad, 2001; Olsen, 1999; Soder, 2001), the anticompulsory, or at least more skeptical, education camp (Gatto, 2000; MacLeod, 1995; Richman, 1994; Spring, 2000) describes universal schooling as the colonization of immigrants and the poor by the state and industry in a process of rationalized distribution of access to wealth and power (see also Bourdieu, 1998). Both the former, hopeful reformers, and the latter, harsh critics, share concerns about the advance of sorting practices under the guise of standards. While at best, standards are designed to assure universal access to minimal levels of academic content and basic academic skills, in reality, they act as sorting mechanisms and barriers to those whose access is already threatened by lack of commonality with the mainstream, that is, the poor, minorities, divergent learners, and so on (see Bailey, 1999; Halpern, 2002; Oakes & Lipton, 1990; Sirotnik, 1990; Spring, 2000).

What is clear is that the expansion of compulsory schooling, which magnified with the reform efforts of the Progressive Era,[1] for good or for bad, colonized the lives of children and their families during what had previously been hours devoted to work, play, or other activities. This was done in the interest of standardizing and rationalizing their activity through formal schooling.

Heath, whose ethnography of education has moved from study of formal schooling (1982, 1983, 1986) to informal after-school youth organizations (1994, 2000a, 2000b), notes that:

> One common worry among both theorists and practitioners is that dependence on formal schooling, even in light of all the current reform efforts, will leave students short of the experience needed to establish the expertise, critical skills, and confidence which are critical to the future world of work and to the altered family and citizenship demands of the world. Schools cannot offer the extensive time

> for practice and participation and build-up of moral commitment and group discourse needed for students to develop all that employers, policy makers, and philosophers say will mark the future. (2000a, p. 34)

Moreover, schools in many postindustrial nations increasingly require standardization of product and outcome, determined by quantifiable measures of performance on standardized tests. Thus the agency of individuals in undertaking learning outside of expected roles and structures must be submerged (Ibid., p. 39).

Formal education's sorting, marking, and submergence of individual agency, diversity, and critical thinking has caused theorists and practitioners to both explore and support the value of informal education (Griffin & Cole, 1984, 1987; Lave & Wenger, 1991; Rogoff, 1990; Rogoff & Lave, 1984; Scribner & Cole, 1973, 1981). Recently, the value placed on informal education has been most obvious in the United States in initiatives of the National Science Foundation (NSF), which have emphasized the beneficial complementary role that flexible and more individualized informal education can play in enhancing the necessarily homogenized effects of formal and common schooling (Melber & Abraham, 1999; NSF, 1997, 2003).

Informal education's complementary role in relation to formal schooling has also emerged in the "semi-formal" realm of organized after-school programming. Halpern (2002, p. 186) locates the emergence of adult-organized after-school activities in both the decline of child labor and the passage of compulsory education laws during the last quarter of the nineteenth century. He suggests that one goal of after-school programs was the care and protection of low-income and immigrant children whose out-of-school time sent them from crowded tenements to the streets. As law enforcement and urban development reduced space for these children, a second goal of after-school programs became creating opportunities for play.

In tracing the history of adult-organized youth activities from their expansion in the Progressive Era, James (1993) argues that while some Progressives directed their efforts toward egalitarian aims, the goal of reform was to preserve order in society. He suggests that the youth organization movement, like the expansion of compulsory schooling, led to bureaucratization and professionalization of social services that amounted to the expansion of legally sanctioned intervention in private lives, particularly those of the poor and immigrants. Like Zelizer (1985), James associates the rationalization of children's lives with a redefinition of childhood that characterized the child as sacred and "priceless." Zelizer relates this redefinition to changes in the labor market and the growth of markets in child insurance, services, and products. James points out that the concepts of "adolescence" and "juvenile" emerged in this process along with an enhanced "legitimation of disparities" in social opportunity linked to occupational destinies (1993, p. 181). The legitimate disparities were reflected in playgrounds (for middle-class children) and settlement houses (for low-income and immigrant children).

In their analysis of after-school programs at the end of the twentieth century, Fine and Mechling (1993) describe a process of "child-saving" through ideologically driven homogenization that colonizes children's cultures—their home cultures and their small group, or idiocultures (p. 134), in much the same way that child-saving movements in the Progressive Era sought to assimilate the children of immigrants and the poor into their proper (laboring) position in mainstream US culture. Fine and Mechling (also Adler & Adler, 1994; Ball & Heath, 1993; Zelizer, 1985) argue that this colonization of child culture comes at the cost of expression, negotiation, and discovery.

The colonization of children's leisure is not being accomplished by schools alone, but also by parents who are concerned with safety and optimizing their children's opportunities, by industries such as insurance and educational services (and television, according to Gatto, 1992), by social movements and social elites, and by governmental agencies, as will be addressed later. These groups and entities are engaged in a process of bureaucratization and rationalization that led first to the expansion of schools, and then, simultaneous with the reduction of child labor, to the rationalization of children's lives after school. Halpern (2002) and Heath (2000a, 2000b), who remain optimistic about after-school programming's opportunities for informal education, development of creativity, and exposure to multiple perspectives, express concern about the encroachment of school's rationalizing and sorting practices on after-school's access to informal education.

Rationalization versus Expansion of Access

Changes in the labor force since the 1970s, including the entry of mothers, both married and single, into the workplace and longer hours for all workers, have correlated with an increase in the visibility of, and need for, after-school care for children. According to the US Departments of Education and Justice (1998), "Overwhelmingly, Americans favor providing school-based after-school programs in their own community" (93%). The rationale for this support is that over 28 million school-age children in the United States have both or their only parent in the workforce and between 5 and 15 million of these are left alone at home each week. This is particularly true for low-income children.

Belle (1999) found that the children's after-school arrangements were variable. She conducted a longitudinal study of 53 families (16 African American, 1 Hispanic, 1 Asian American, 35 non-Hispanic White; 33% with annual income below $20,000, 33% with annual income between $20,000 and

$30,000; 33% with annual income over $30,000; 21 two-parent households, 27 single-parent households, 5 joint-custody families), focusing on one child per family who was attending elementary school. She found that often children attended different programs or attended no programs on different days of the week. Additionally, arrangements changed regularly over time. Cost, conflicting work schedules, transportation, and lack of consistent adult attention were issues. Supervised and "semisupervised" after-school arrangements were inconsistent in satisfying parents' desires for structured activities and safety. They were far more consistent in not satisfying children's desires for freedom to "veg out" and play with friends. Children in the study tended to move to self-care as they grew older, with or without their parents' knowledge. Perhaps Belle's most interesting finding was great variability in the children's responses to various kinds of care. Lack of supervision fostered responsibility in some, while it was felt as liberating freedom or constraining restriction by others. For some, adult supervision provided a sense of comfort and happiness, for others a negative experience.

While it was not her focus, Belle's study documents sorting practices in after-school programs. Choice in programs, particularly enrichment programs, is a function of income level. This is consistent with Adler and Adler's (1994) findings that after-school programs act as sorting mechanisms. Adler and Adler point out that during the last generation, children's leisure activities have become less spontaneous and more rationalized. They characterize the change as being from child-directed activities that foster negotiation, planning, and problem-solving to adult-directed activities that are more focused and professionalized. They argue, consistent with Bourdieu, that this rationalization allows adults a means to reproduce the existing social structure and to socialize young people to the corporate values of American culture. Additionally, they describe a prescribed developmental trajectory in which participation moves from recreational, to competitive, to elite activities as children become older and more skilled. Adler and Adler are particularly concerned that like school activities, after-school activities are promoting and sustaining class inequality. This contradicts increasingly prevalent rhetoric that describes after-school programs as a source of access to economic opportunity by way of access to improved academic performance.[2]

The US Departments of Education and Justice's (1998) report "Safe and Smart: Making After-School Hours Work for Kids" advocates connecting the curricula of after-school programs with school curricula as well as linkages between school-day and after-school personnel. Citing several studies, the report suggests that school-based and other school-affiliated after-school programs produce better grades and higher academic achievement. In addition, these programs improve school attendance and reduce drop-out rate, help children turn in more and better quality homework, and provide more time on task for children who, for whatever reason, need more time than others to learn the same material.

The US Department of Education's Office of Educational Research and Improvement's (1999) report "Bringing Education to After-School Programs" provides examples of how to bring enhancement of "critical skills" to after-school programs. These skills include: reading and mathematics, technology and telecommunications, art and music. The examples are taken from among 1,601 school-based after-school programs in 49 states, the District of Columbia, and the Virgin Islands that received federal funding (The 21st-Century Community Learning Centers). This funding and the number of programs have increased steadily and dramatically since 1999.

A study commissioned to evaluate the Wallace-Reader's Digest Funds' Extended-Service Schools Adaptation Initiative (Walker, Grossman, & Raley, 2000) evaluated four school-based after-school programs serving 6,000 primary and secondary-age children and youth in 18 cities. Based on the premise that school buildings are valuable and underused resources that can serve as after-school sites for low-income children and youth, the initiative focused on improving the quality of educational and developmental services for children living in poor communities. A survey of 800 parents found that 76% had enrolled their children because the children wanted to be involved and 53% did so because they felt it would help their children do better in school. The study also found that there were challenges to locating after-school programming in schools. One was conflict between the goals of institutional partners, most often concerning the narrow focus of some principals and teachers on students' test scores. By contrast, when representatives of the partnering institutions, for example, community organizations, nonprofits, and universities, worked together and discovered the low levels of some students' academic skills, the focus on basic skills was more readily engaged.

Related to conflicting partner goals, the report notes challenges to demonstrating academic impacts, including: low intensity of service to individuals in favor of providing service to greater numbers; high mobility among the client children; and low probability of affecting the school's test scores due to the relatively low numbers of children involved. The authors point out that while the possibility of improvement exists for individuals who come frequently, that will not help the principal "whose job depends on the school's aggregate performance." Still, in spite of this and other challenges, the evaluation supports the initiative's goals and practice of extending the school day into what has traditionally been after-school.

This movement into after-school hours, what we might call school's invasion of after-school, appears to be speeding up. Arnold Schwarzenegger, actor and conservative politician, for example, sponsored a proposition (Prop. 49: After School Education and Safety Program Act of 2002) placed on the November 2002 ballot in California that appropriates $465 million, in the first year alone, for grants to California schools for school-based after-school programs. As with the Extended-Service Schools Adaptation Initiative and other school-based after-school programs, Prop. 49 programs are challenged to coordinate with President Bush's No Child Left Behind Act of 2001 (Pub. L. 107–110, 2002), which focuses on increased accountability for schools, proficiency testing, and corrective actions to meet state standards.

Preparation and Contradiction

Because the rationalized sorting practices of formal schooling appear to be actively invading after-school, it is, at this point, useful to stop and consider the contradiction inherent in common schooling as it has evolved since the Progressive Era. As noted above, public schooling was and continues to be supported for two purposes: preparation for participation in civil democratic life and preparation for participation in economic life, that is, the workforce. The contradiction is that the preparation for economic life afforded by the common schools has historically been directed at rationalized, measured productivity, while preparation for participation in democracy requires critical thinking and development of public, and potentially contrary, voice. While extreme, there is truth in Gatto's statement that "Schools are intended to produce, through application of formulas, formulaic human beings whose behavior can be predicted and controlled" (1992, p. 26). There is also truth in Bateson's assessment that "Participation in a democracy, however, requires not only an ability to acknowledge the beliefs and preferences of others but also the capacity to recognize that divergence is essential to the health of the larger system that includes the self and the other" (2001, p. 117). The danger in school's invasion of after-school is that in providing access to preparation for standardized and other testing, opportunities for the development and expression of divergent or free thought and behavior through play, social interaction, and negotiation will be diminished.

In order to illustrate the contradictions that characterize the movement of school, homework, and measurement into the realm of after-school activities, we draw on the case of an informal after-school educational program that uses computers to link diverse children and college students in play and problem-solving.

CALIFORNIA CASE STUDY

The Fifth Dimension Model, developed by Griffin, Cole, and others at the University of California, San Diego's Laboratory of Comparative Human Cognition, LCHC, is a design for the development of after-school programs aimed at improving the academic performance of children who are by language, culture or ethnicity, socioeconomic status, or labeling as learning disabled not likely to be successful in school (see Cole, 1996). This model is used to create systems of mixed activities: children come to play (and learn); adult students come to learn (and play); and researchers and community members come to work (and play and learn). The individual programs provide a range of opportunities for informal, collaborative teaching/learning that link children ages 6–12 and adult learners in joint exploration of computer games and other activities. Because the Fifth Dimension allows for self-paced, voluntary engagement in problem-solving, strategizing, and reflection, it serves as an auxiliary or "enrichment" learning environment located outside school. There are currently more than 40 programs based on the Fifth Dimension Model associated with 20 universities in the United States, the Americas, and Europe (see <http://www.uclinks.org>, <http://5D.org>).

Designed to provide multiple, diverse, and evolving opportunities for informal education, programs based on the Fifth Dimension Model intentionally eschew school-like measurement of academic competence. Rather, informed by Vygotsky's theory of the Zone of Proximal Development (1978, p. 86),[3] they focus on children's learning potential, avoiding quantitative measures and their propensity for sorting and ranking children according to standards of academic success and failure. Progress in the Fifth Dimension programs traditionally has been measured using longitudinal qualitative data to track changes over time. As is typical of informal education, there is no failure in the Fifth Dimension.

In addition to being a model for after-school learning programs, the Fifth Dimension is a model for university-school-community partnerships that co-design, jointly run, and regularly evaluate the programs. The model incorporates an appreciation of the local creativity of each program's participants, placing high value on contributions by people of diverse ages, genders, educational backgrounds, languages and cultures, and socioeconomic status, as well as the contributions of the different institutional partners.

The Magical Dimension: A Case of Colonization

One of the original Fifth Dimension programs opened in 1987 in a Boys and Girls Club. This program, designed and implemented by Cole, and hereafter referred to as "the Fifth Dimension," continues to operate (see Cole, 1995, 1996; Nicolopoulou & Cole 1993). The Fifth Dimension has always been open to all children who are members of the club and has historically, reflective of local demographics, served a mostly Anglo and middle-class population of children who come voluntarily to play with college students and computers. Since 1999, there has been a steady increase in the numbers of Latino and low-income participants. This will be addressed later.

Specific activities in the Fifth Dimension have been variable over time, but have always included a mixture of computer and board games that provide practice with literacy, social science, mathematics, and natural science content. Because the development of the Fifth Dimension has incorporated the loosely organized culture of the club, children who come to play these games are free to wander in and out as they move from one to another of the club's activities.

In 1990, Vásquez opened La Clase Mágica, a bilingual, bicultural adaptation of the Fifth Dimension designed to serve the needs of the same community's Latino children. Since opening, La Clase Mágica has successfully engaged low-income and immigrant children in games directed at Spanish language maintenance, Spanish and English literacy, and heritage culture appreciation. In 1995, however, La Clase Mágica was in serious danger of losing its space and the then tenuous support of its community host institutions (Vásquez, 2003). In 1995, Nocon, with support from Cole and Vásquez, developed the Magical Dimension, a new program based on the Fifth Dimension Model and located at a school that children from the original Fifth Dimension and La Clase Mágica attended (Nocon, 2000). The Magical Dimension was designed as a bilingual program that could serve children from both the Latino and the non-Latino populations. Both Spanish and English were used, as well as a smattering of Russian.

The Magical Dimension was the first local Fifth Dimension program located in a public school. Due to a quick start-up and the availability of computing resources already there, the school's computers were used as well as a significant amount of the school's software. Much of this software was art based and content open, for example, Storybook Weaver©. Eventually, the school's computer teacher became the site coordinator and there was evidence of the Magical Dimension's influence on the school, for example, new computing activities and the child participants being perceived during the school day as computer experts. There was also evidence of the school's influence on the site. The new site coordinator was the only person referred to by title and surname. A bell was rung to gain collective attention. Lights were flashed when it was time to clean up.

The Magical Dimension was successful in attracting diverse children, including a large percentage of Latinos (and their parents) and other children from non-English-speaking homes. Additionally, the program provided a safe place where children from the school's Gifted and Talented Program played and learned along with children with special needs who were regularly referred by the school's resource teacher. The following excerpt from the Magical Dimension's Annual Report 1998–1999 provides a synopsis of the Magical Dimension's history:

> In summer 1997, the prospects for sustaining the Magical Dimension looked good. The school district together with the [Boys and Girls] Club had assumed financial responsibility for site operations. An employee of the district became site coordinator. In the ensuing two years attendance first rose significantly, and then declined. The rise in attendance coincided with the presence of a dedicated LCHC veteran who was paid to be assistant site coordinator by the Club. This individual spoke fluent Spanish and was very engaged in the theory driving the Fifth Dimension. He took on significant responsibility for coordinating the site, and acted as a close link to the university. As more responsibility was assumed by the non-university site coordinator who was paid by the school district, free play rather than engagement in the Fifth Dimension model was privileged at the site. This coincided with a decline in attendance. In addition, whereas in previous years the school resource teacher's help in advertising the program was offered and accepted for collaborative promotion, the district paid site coordinator expressed discomfort with large numbers of children and chose not to promote the program until the spring quarter, during which she made announcements in her school day computer classes. This did not increase attendance.

Based on these experiences and the low attendance figures, Nocon and Cole entered into negotiation with the elementary school (as opposed to the district, which supported the Magical Dimension) to determine how the collaborative effort could continue productively. The principal and the resource teacher along with one or two other teachers agreed to develop together with Nocon and Cole an after-school program that would better meet the school's evolving goals. As a result, the Magical Dimension did not continue, but "morphed" into a homework program that specifically targeted low-achieving children, most of whom were Latino. This metamorphosis was precipitated, in great part, by new pressures on the principal and school to focus on standardized tests and basic needs.

In 1998, California voters overwhelmingly passed Proposition 227, which eliminated bilingual education from state K-12 curricula (California Education Code, 1998). Also in 1998, the California Legislature passed a bill (AB 1626, Chap. 742, 1998) requiring that school districts adopt policies directed at ending social promotion. For grade level promotion, the legislation required the State Board of Education and all public schools in California to adopt minimum levels of pupil performance based on universal use of standardized tests in reading, mathematics, and English language arts. In 1999, the California Senate passed the Public Schools Act (SB 1552, Chap. 695, 2000), which provided for ranking California's public schools according to pupils' performance on the standardized tests (Stanford Achievement Test, 9th ed., or SAT 9) as well as other measures included in an Academic Performance Index.

The passage of this legislation changed the educational, political, and social contexts in which the Magical Dimension (and the Fifth Dimension and La Clase Mágica) were operating. The change in the educational context represented by the move to standardization and quantification had immediate impact on the university-community informal education programs in terms of generating funding. Potential funding agents, local, state, and national, began to seek quantitative measures of program outcomes, basing awards on such measures. This political pressure has been felt by the local and national Boys and Girls Clubs, as well as by other adult organized youth activities, like those described in Heath and McLaughlin (1993), Heath (2000a, 2000b), Halpern (2002), and UC Links (addressed later), which have attempted to engage children and youth disaffected by formal schooling.

Making matters more complex, the change in the social context of schooling is associated with the new needs for schools (and principals) to be competitive in state rankings at the same time that after-school programs' client children face more stringent academic ranking and, in the case of low-income and minority children, very real increases in the probability of retention in grade. A program that seeks to improve children's social and cognitive skills by providing them with confidence-building experiences of productive learning and success with academic content addressed informally can not ignore the children's need to pass the SAT 9 at their grade levels. The potential of retention in grade and its associated stigma is very real for the children. Acknowledging this double bind, Cole and Nocon agreed to work with the school in developing a homework program that would be run in partnership by the Boys and Girls Club, the university, and the school.

Basic Skills versus the Magical Dimension

In March 1999, the principal had indicated a desire to implement a new design in the after-school computer program emphasizing basic skills. The desire to change the use of the space continued to gather momentum in the spring. By late May, the computer teacher had decided, for personal reasons, she could not continue with the Magical Dimension or its derivative the following year:

> I don't want MD to continue as it is now next year for a few reasons. I think it is time for the school to make a program it wants and needs, hence, the basic skills focus. I think me stepping down will bring in a [school-based] teacher which will help with this focus. (Staff field note, sr 5.24.99)

The university and Boys and Girls Club representatives met again with the principal. It was decided not to continue the Magical Dimension the following year. Meetings between the university, club representatives, and the principal did continue through the summer and fall of 1999. Frequently, the resource teacher who had actively supported the Magical Dimension was present. In addition, LCHC sent two researchers to be participant observers at a basic skills summer school program at the school in the interest of using that information to inform collaborative design of the new after-school club.

Basic Skills Summer School

In the summer after the Magical Dimension shut down, the school hosted a K–6 remedial summer school for students in the district who fell below the 40th percentile on the statewide grade level achievement tests. Of the three hundred students invited, 180 attended. The large majority of these students were drawn from the community's Latino population. A study of this group conducted by Nocon, Cole, and others (Solana Beach Coalition, 2000) verified that, in addition to being overwhelmingly Latino, the summer school attendees were predominantly from the community's two poorest neighborhoods.

The four-week, half-day program included remedial work in literacy skills and computer-based practice with reading and oral language recognition. Children were placed in grade-level groups of 20. Each group had a teacher and at least one assistant, most often a high school "Study Buddy." The two researchers from the university participated as participant observers. Based on their observations, they concluded that challenges confronting children with special needs and/or limited English proficiency included the need for special attention to different skill levels, including language and keyboarding skills. The short periods in the summer school days precluded working individually and adequately with the children with the greatest needs.

Another interesting finding concerned the computer program used as both a diagnostic tool and a basic skills practice tool. The program included assessment features, some accessible to teachers and some accessible to the children. During the course of the program, children quickly came to compare scores. Some children, who did not score well, chose to demonstrate how badly they could do, purposely choosing wrong answers, and effectively sabotaging the assessment. This, along with other findings, caused the researchers to note that the program as a whole, and the computer component, in particular, suffered from the lack of a larger support structure, that is, individualized learning aids and social interaction. They recommended that the team designing the new after-school program focus on two goals: (1) literacy in English, with assistance in Spanish; and (2) helping students to become competent self-learners by reinforcing both study skills and self-esteem through social interaction.

Basic Skills After-School (3)

In January 2000, the school implemented a basic skills program in the computer lab that had housed the Magical Dimension from January 1996 through June 1999. The basic skills program was based on a districtwide model. Cole and Nocon determined that the interest of the university undergraduate students would not be best served by assisting in the new program. Their concern was that the college students would be placed in traditional hierarchical roles as teacher-aides, working on basic skills only and thereby participating in school-based sorting practices that had been kindly, but unabashedly, practiced in the summer basic skills program. However, in the interest of continuing the partnership and providing expanded access to the community's children, the principal, with support from the school district, the Boys and Girls Club, and the university jointly designed and opened a new homework club at the Boys and Girls Club. For the school, the Homework Club was justified as part of the school's state-mandated intervention program targeting those children scoring in the lowest quartile on statewide grade-level achievement tests. The school's teachers began to refer children in need of extra help to the Homework Club. Boys and Girls Club employees and teachers began helping the children cross the thoroughfare separating the two institutions. The school district supported the program financially by paying the scholarship fees for the referred children. University undergraduates worked with the children in the Homework Club and also played with them in the Fifth Dimension. The Fifth Dimension integrated new educational software that addressed (if more playfully) the same skills that the school's basic skills computer program addressed.

Homework Club

A total of 27 children were referred to the Homework Club by the school. Between January 3 and June 1, 2000, the average daily attendance was 11.5 children. The average amount of time spent in the homework club was a total of 29 hours, varying between 2 and 77 hours. Based on field note data collected by undergraduates and researchers who participated in the Homework Club, some general trends emerged. The most salient trend was the development of a culture of resistance. Many children were disruptive, talking loudly, moving about the room, etc., and creative in finding ways to avoid doing homework. For example, they often engaged undergraduates in discussion of personal lives, nonschool artwork, popular culture, or even schoolwork not associated with the task at hand. Another trend was that children referred to the Homework Club did not go to the Fifth Dimension after completing their homework, as had been hoped. They chose instead to join the physical play in the gym.

Another trend was the undergraduates' tendency to focus, not on skills or learning activity in their field notes, but on the children's behaviors. In spite of the culture of resistance, the undergraduates noted 75 instances of positive personal and interpersonal behavior, for example, "able to finish assignments," or "asks for help," versus 22 instances of negative behavior, for example, "rude/disrespectful," or "tries to get answers from undergrads."

When interviewed in May 2000, the teachers, in the presence of the school's principal, concurred that they had referred children who were not getting their homework done and would benefit from additional individualized support. Only one of several teachers reported seeing change in one child's academic performance. Three teachers reported better use of homework planners and more consistency in turning in homework. One teacher also reported that the children appeared to feel better about themselves as they turned in their work.

The Homework Club continued to be run by the partnership through the 2000–2001 academic year. Attendance by referred children declined, though some of those originally referred persisted in coming to the Boys and Girls Club and began participating in the Fifth Dimension. This process, as well as collaboration among the club, school, and University in developing an after-school program for kindergarteners, effectively integrated the Fifth Dimension, which, as noted above, served a predominantly Anglo population in 1996, and currently serves a more diverse population, about 35% of which is Latino.

The "official" partnership-run Homework Club was no longer running in the fall of 2001. A Boys and Girls Club homework program took its place, and the school reverted to a more structured silent homework period on school grounds. The issue was not pursued by the university or club for two reasons. First, one reason for declining participation was lack of transportation home, especially during the winter months when darkness fell early. The second was recognition that the referred children were getting extra help at the expense of being publicly marked as "slow," both as they gathered to walk to the Boys and Girls Club and by some less-experienced club staff who kept separate lists of regular Boys and Girls Club members in the homework room and "referred kids." This distinction was at times reinforced publicly as staff allowed the regular kids to come and go at will but required the referred children to stay. Senior club staff quickly intervened and stopped these sorting behaviors, but the differences in the status of participants in the Homework Club and the Boys and Girls Club remained clear.

Colonizing the Fifth Dimension

As noted briefly above, in developing the Homework Club with the local school, the researchers running the Fifth Dimension incorporated corresponding changes in that program's content. Games that were both educational and fun were brought in to provide practice with basic skills (two favorites were Word Munchers© and Troggle Trouble Math©). Other games that provided practice with keyboarding, grammar, and ratios were also incorporated. These games were surprisingly popular and attracted many children.

Concurrent with the opening of the Homework Club, the Fifth Dimension team was experimenting with the incorporation of measurement, using the games mentioned above. Several math and language game tournaments were held, with the children's voluntary and enthusiastic participation. While the fun aspects of these experiments with measurement were impressive, their usefulness as measurement techniques was not. Voluntary participation includes the right not to engage in activities that seem boring and it proved very difficult to get reliable and consistent pre- and post-test measures. Still, the development of the Homework Club and the integration of games targeting basic skills in the Fifth Dimension did influence later development of the Fifth Dimension. In addition to the change in the demographics of the children served, the topic and actual work on homework entered the Fifth Dimension.

During the 1998–1999 academic year, 74 of 454 field notes (16%) written by undergraduates based on their sessions at the Fifth Dimension mentioned homework. In the 1999–2000 academic year, when the Homework Club opened, 34% of the field notes mentioned homework. In 2001–2002, when the homework club was no longer running at the Boys and Girls Club, 16% still mentioned doing homework. What changed was the way in which homework was referenced. In 1999–2000, the year the school-affiliated Homework Club opened, there were numerous allusions to homework behavior. For example, as the Homework Club opened and the partners deferred to school culture, "The teacher directed the kids where to sit as they walked in, presumably to separate friends in order to get them to concentrate on homework. The teacher discouraged talking, even if the kids were asking each other for help" (fn: a199f.44.3). There were numerous references to being quiet, staying in the room for the prescribed time, not eating, not talking, and so on. Later in the year, there were references to help and ongoing relationships, as well as self-selection of homework activity.

In the 2001–2002 field notes, references to homework were both fewer and more incidental. However, there was an emergent pattern of self-selection and homework activity that began to appear outside of the officially designated homework room in different areas of the club, particularly in the Fifth Dimension, where there was a computer with Internet capability.

What interests us is that while the collaborative Homework Club died, in part from lack of attendance, some of the children first referred have continued to come to the club regularly, interacting with staff members, doing homework in different spaces, as well as participating in the informal learning activities in the Fifth Dimension. Similarly, interactions with the school have changed, but persisted, and the partners are again working to coordinate programming that addresses standards and basic skills as well as critical thinking, problem-solving, and participation in social learning situations. Unfortunately, the colonization of the defunct Magical Dimension and the ongoing

Fifth Dimension is not rare, although the sustainability of the school-university-community partnership may be. After-school programs based on university-community partnerships in California and beyond are struggling with the impact of the standards and basic skills movement and its emphasis on homework.

The Case of UC Links: Statewide Expansion

On July 20, 1995, the Regents of the University of California passed a Policy Ensuring Equal Treatment in Admissions (SP-1), which stated that "Effective January 1, 1997, the University of California shall not use race, religion, sex, color, ethnicity, or national origin as criteria for admission to the University or to any program of study." This policy effectively eliminated affirmative action as a tool to be used in ensuring that admissions to the university system reflected the demographics of the state's population. No group, even those that were traditionally underrepresented at the university, could receive preferential treatment. Anticipating that diversity in the student population would be adversely affected, the Regents' policy also provided for the establishment of a task force "to develop and support programs which will have the effect of increasing the eligibility rate of groups which are 'underrepresented' in the University's pool of applicants as compared to their percentages in California's graduating high school classes."

In response to the Regents' policy, in 1995–1996, Cole and Vásquez, together with representatives from the University of California Office of the President and faculty at the nine UC campuses, developed a proposal for a university systemwide initiative based on the Fifth Dimension and La Clase Mágica models. They called the initiative UC Links. The following is from a draft proposal:

> UC Links is a statewide after-school initiative designed to advance the University's role in K–12 education through a University-community-school consortium of model educational systems. The initiative links 9 UC campuses and 2 CSU campuses in computer-based after-school programs at 17 school and other community-based sites throughout California. The purpose is to develop a pipeline of qualified students from elementary school through postdoctoral levels in communities throughout California. The model links after-school K–12 activities with intensive undergraduate coursework combining classroom theoretical study with practice in community settings. This system of coursework and after-school activity serves K–12 students, their families, community organizations, and schools while integrating the University's three-fold mission of teaching, research, and community service.

The UC Links 2001 Annual Report states that the number of California sites has grown to 31, serving 2,125 K–12 students and approximately 1,000 undergraduates (see <http://www.uclinks.org>). Recently, tensions between the UC Links approach and the testing movement has resulted in university-community partnerships leaving schools owing to intransigence regarding standards and training in basic skills, a problem very similar to that reported in the Extended-Service Schools Adaptation Initiative.

In one urban UC Links partnership, the principal, with whom the university partners had enjoyed a long and productive relationship, was dismissed when his school missed its state-based achievement goals by a couple of points. The principal had secured Safe School grants and created a literacy program for adults, in addition to organizing collaborations with both the university and the Boys and Girls Club in order to provide his students with enrichment and access after school. The administration that replaced him determined that the only after-school activity permitted at the school was to be tutoring to raise test scores. The university and the Boys and Girls Club reluctantly severed their partnerships with the school and its children.

In another UC Links partnership, a newly developed system is currently in jeopardy because the principal does not believe that the after-school partnership with the university will have direct impact on students' standardized test scores. Space, supplies, and labor originally designated for the new system have been withdrawn. Similarly, in a long-term partnership between a school and a teaching college, alumni who became teachers at the school have been reprimanded and isolated for devoting volunteer time after-school to a Fifth Dimension–like partnership program dedicated to social justice and access for Latino and bilingual children. In this case, parents are adamant about continuing the partnership in spite of the school administration's stance in opposition.

On the other hand, a UC Links partnership in another city serving a predominantly Spanish-speaking population has adapted to the new emphasis on homework. In this case, the impetus was parents' requests for help. As Spanish speakers, they found themselves unable to provide the necessary homework assistance to their children, and so sought an expansion of access from the university-community partnership. As this case points out, the line between colonization of after-school and expansion of access is not so clear. This ambiguity was also true with the Homework Club and the Fifth Dimension. While some children (and researchers) actively resisted the social controls and worksheets of the homework room, children had real needs for help with those worksheets and found safe and sensitive environments at the Boys and Girls Club and in the Fifth Dimension.

We have chosen to focus on California because of the state's early foray into standardized testing and standardized, homogenized, and rationalized education. Because statewide standards-based reforms have been adapted in 49 states, we consider the California case to be indicative of the pressures experienced by schools and their partners around the United States. For example, a colleague and teacher in Minnesota reports that "district policy has become so rigid we are considered dissenters if we take the 'tests don't really matter' line." He reports, reminiscent of the California case, that summer school has been reserved for the sole purpose of preparing less successful students for passing the basic standards test.

CONTRADICTIONS OF SCHOOL IN AFTER-SCHOOL

The case of the Magical Dimension and the related cases of the Fifth Dimension and UC Links illustrate the basic contradiction in common or public schooling; that is, the contradiction between preparation for critical participation in a diverse democratic society and training in standardized and rationalized cognitive and social behaviors. The Magical Dimension mixed ages, genders, home languages, cultures, and learning styles in an informal learning environment that blended academic content and skills with artistic expression and play. There was room and attention for diverse and divergent voices. This remains true of the Fifth Dimension and the UC Links programs, not only for the children who participate but also for the diverse institutional partners who cooperate in running these programs. Within these informal learning environments, many of the children who self-select to participate (even for those referred, participation is voluntary) choose to do homework, seeking and gaining assistance from staff, college students, researchers, and other children. Along with homework, all the children play games and engage in joint problem-solving, reflection, and writing with collaborating undergraduates and children of different ages, genders, and backgrounds.

The basic skills programs (summer school, after-school, the homework club) sorted children by design (the lowest quartile based on standardized achievement tests) and reinforced social inequities (Latinos and low-income) in doing so. The children in these programs did struggle with basic skills and did face the very real probability of retention in grade or grades. The school, the teachers, and the principal, regardless of personal politics, were forced into the dilemmatic position of trying to help these children by marking and sorting them. We do not believe that the educators involved were intentionally engaged in promoting legitimate disparities in occupational destinies. However, using this approach, the goal of preparing children to participate fully in economic life and democratic society was to be achieved by standardizing and homogenizing the behavior of the poor and immigrant through external controls, while treating them differently from their more advantaged peers. In the face of demeaning external controls that denied interaction with the three upper quartiles and disregarded their strengths, the children resisted. They sabotaged assessments, undermined authority, and stopped coming. When the Homework Club ceased to function as a coercive environment, and the Boys and Girls Club's and Fifth Dimension's traditional focus on children's potentials created safe places for diverse and divergent children, many of the children still elected to do homework in spaces of their choosing and came voluntarily to participate in other informal learning activities with caring adults. This has been particularly beneficial for children who are not successful in school and who find in informal education access to learning and identity formation as successful learners.

In thinking about the cases presented here, the very real issue of inequitable access must be coupled with the question: Access to what? Is access to remedial programming for the poor, the newly arrived, and the divergent equal access? Or, is it access to training in compliance for those who don't make the grade, but can hopefully be made to tow the line? Is access expanded by carrying the sorting practices that defined those who don't "make the grade" into after-school time that could otherwise be dedicated to exploring strengths, developing social skills and confidence, finding and developing modes of expression? How much of a child's identity should be constructed around being in the lowest quartile? How much should be defined by school?

We join Heath and Halpern in arguing that adult organized after-school activities, while they may be characterized as "semicolonizing," should remain different kinds of child and youth development institutions that provide access to informal education without rationalization, sorting, and failure. As Heath points out, "Unlike schools that tend to focus on the need for students to acquire skills and knowledge that may help them obtain jobs, youth organizations focus on building relationships with colleagues, and in so doing, finding ways to work resourcefully with others" (2000b, p. 70). As Halpern argues

> The tasks of middle childhood—acquiring literacy, gaining knowledge of the world, solidifying a sense of competence and agency, exploring interests and discovering talents, becoming more autonomous—do require adult support. Low- and moderate-income children deserve the same access to enriching organized activities as their more advantaged peers. Yet low-income children, as all children, need space—social as much as physical space—to develop their own thoughts, to daydream and reflect; to dabble and dawdle; to pretend, try on, and rehearse different roles and identities; to learn friendship and to learn how to handle interpersonal conflict; to rest and be quiet; and not least to have fun and take risks of their own design and choosing. (2002, p. 206)

We believe that the value of after-school programs is located in their traditionally open, informal, and tenuously institutionalized nature. As flexible sites of informal education, after-school programs have allowed low-income and immigrant children access to safe places and flexible, responsive programming as well as contact with diverse perspectives. The choice and "looseness" that characterize these programs provide opportunities for participation in problem-solving, self-regulation, and learning that goes beyond rigid standards and limited basic content. Informal and potentially limitless education in adult-organized after-school programs is a necessary complement to the formal and limited education provided by schools.

NOTES

1. The Progressive Era refers roughly to the last quarter of the nineteenth century and the first quarter of the twentieth century, a period in US history marked by urbanization, immigration, economic and global expansion, and social movements, including the expansion of common schooling and social welfare programs.
2. See Glass & Walsh, 2001; Heckman & Sanger, 2001; Hock, Pulvers, Deshler, & Schumaker, 2001, and Miller, 2001, for reports on the academic and social benefits of after-school programs.
3. "[The Zone of Proximal Development] is the distance between the actual developmental level as determined by independent problem solving and the level of potential development as determined through problem solving under adult guidance or in collaboration with more capable peers" (Vygotsky, 1978, p. 86).

REFERENCES

AB 1626, Chap. 742. (1998). Pupil Promotion and Retention Act. California State Assembly.

Adler, P. A., & Adler, P. (1994). Social reproduction and the corporate other: The institutionalization of afterschool activities. *Sociological Quarterly,* 35(2): 309–28.

Bailey, M. H. (1999). Access to knowledge. In W. F. Smith & G. D. Fenstermacher (Eds.), *Leadership for educational renewal* (pp. 105–26). San Francisco: Jossey-Bass.

Ball, A., & Heath, S. B. (1993). Dances of identity: Finding an ethnic self in the arts. In S. B. Heath & M. W. McLaughlin (Eds.), *Identity and inner-city youth: Beyond ethnicity and gender* (pp. 69–93). New York: Teachers College Press.

Bateson, M. C. (2001). Learning in layers. In R. Soder, J. I. Goodlad, & T. J. McMannon (Eds.), *Developing democratic character in the young* (pp. 114–25). San Francisco: Jossey-Bass.

Belle, D. (1999). *The after-school lives of children: Alone and with others while parents work.* Mahweh, NJ: Lawrence Erlbaum Associates.

Bourdieu, P. (1998). *Practical reason.* Stanford, CA: Stanford University Press.

California Education Code. (1998). Chap. 1, Article 3, Sections 30–30.5. Language of Instruction.

Cole, M. (1995). Cultural-historical psychology: A meso-genetic approach. In L. Martin, K. Nelson, & E. Tobach (Eds.), *Sociocultural psychology* (pp. 168–204). Cambridge: Cambridge University Press.

Cole, M. (1996). *Cultural psychology: A once and future discipline.* Cambridge, MA: Belknap-Harvard University Press.

Dewey, J. (1899/1964). The school and society. In R. D. Archabault (Ed.), *John Dewey on education* (pp. 295–310). New York: Modern Library.

Dewey, J. (1936). *Democracy and education: An introduction to the philosophy of education.* New York: Macmillan.

Fenstermacher, G. D. (1999). Agenda for education in a democracy. In W. F. Smith & G. D. Fenstermacher (Eds.), *Leadership for educational renewal* (pp. 3–28). San Francisco: Jossey-Bass.

Fine, G. A., & Mechling, J. M. (1993). Child saving and children's cultures at century's end. In S. B. Heath and M. W. McLaughlin (Eds.), *Identity and inner-city youth: Beyond ethnicity and gender* (pp. 120–46). New York: Teachers College Press.

Gatto, J. T. (1992). *Dumbing us down: The hidden curriculum of compulsory schooling.* Philadelphia: New Society Publishers.

Gatto, J. T. (2000). *A different kind of teacher: Solving the crisis of American schooling.* Berkeley, CA: Berkeley Hills Books.

Glass, R., & Walsh, K. (2001). A safe haven. April 2001 Feature Story. *American Teacher, 84*(7). Retrieved October 24, 2004, from< http://www.aft.org /pubsreports/american_teacher/apr01/safehaven.html>.

Goodlad, J. I. (1990). Common schools for the common weal: Reconciling self-interest with common good. In J. I. Goodlad & P. Keating (Eds.), *Access to knowledge: An agenda for our nation's schools* (pp. 1–22). New York: College Entrance Examination Board.

Goodlad, J. I. (2001). Convergence. In R. Soder, J. I. Goodlad, & T. J. McMannon (Eds.), *Developing democratic character in the young* (pp. 1–25). San Francisco: Jossey-Bass.

Goody, J. (1977). *Domestication of the savage mind.* Cambridge: Cambridge University Press.

Griffin, P., & Cole, M. (1984). Current activity for the future: The Zo-ped. In B. Rogoff & J. Wertsch (Eds.), *Children's learning in the "Zone of Proximal Development,"* New Directions in Child Development series, 23 (pp 45–63). San Francisco: Jossey-Bass.

Griffin, P., & Cole, M. (1987). New technologies, basic skills and the underside of education. What's to be done? In J. A. Langer (Ed.), *Language, literacy, and culture: Issue of society and schooling* (pp. 110–31). Norwood, NJ: Ablex.

Halpern, R. (2002). A different kind of child development institution: The history of after-school programs for low-income children. *Teachers College Record,* 104(2): 178–211.

Heath, S. B. (1982). Questioning at home and at school: A comparative study. In G. Spindler (Ed.), *Doing the ethnography of schooling* (pp. 103–27). Prospect Heights, IL: Waveland Press.

Heath, S. B. (1983). *Ways with words.* Cambridge: Cambridge University Press.

Heath, S. B. (1986). What no bedtime story means: Narrative skills at home and school. In B. Schieffelin & E. Ochs (Eds.), *Language socialization across cultures* (pp. 97–115). Cambridge: Cambridge University Press.

Heath, S. B. (1994). The project of learning from the inner-city youth perspective. In F. A. Villaruel & R. M. Lerner (Eds.), *Promoting community-based programs for socialization and learning.* New Directions for Child Development series, 63 (pp. 25–34). Cambridge, MA: Jossey-Bass.

Heath, S. B. (2000a). Making learning work. *Afterschool Matters,* 1(1): 33–45.

Heath, S. B. (2000b). Risks, rules, and roles. *Zeitschrift für Erziehungswissenschaft,* 3: 61--80.

Heath, S. B., & McLaughlin, M. W. (Eds.). (1993). *Identity and inner-city youth: Beyond ethnicity and gender.* New York: Teachers College Press.

Heckman, P. E., & Sanger, C. (2001). LA's Best—Beyond school as usual. *Educational Leadership,* 58(7): 46–49.

Hock, M. F., Pulvers, K. A., Deshler, D. D., & Schumaker, J. B. (2001). The effects of an after-school tutoring program on the academic performance of at-risk students and students with LD. *Remedial and Special Eduation,* 22(3): 172–86.

James, T. (1993). The winnowing of organizations. In S. B. Heath and M. W. McLaughlin (Eds.), *Identity and inner-city youth: Beyond ethnicity and gender* (pp. 176–95). New York: Teachers College Press.

Lave, J., & Wenger, E. (1991). *Situated learning.* Cambridge: Cambridge University Press.

MacLeod, J. (1995). *Ain't no makin' it: Aspirations and attainment in a low-income neighborhood.* Boulder, CO: Westview Press.

Melber, L. M., & Abraham, L. M. (1999). Beyond the classroom: Linking with informal education. *Science Activities,* 36(4): 3–4.

Miller, B. M. (2001). The promise of after-school programs. *Educational Leadership,* 58(7): 6–12.

National Science Foundation. (1997). Informal Science Education: Supplement to Active Research Awards, NSF 9770. <http://www.nsf.gov/pubs/1997/nsf9770/isesupl.htm>.

National Science Foundation. (2003). Informal Science Education (ISE) Program Solicitation, NSF 03–511. <http://www.nsf.gov.pubs/2003/nsf03511/nsf03511.htm>.

Nicolopoulou, A., & Cole, M. (1993). The Fifth Dimension, its play world, and its instructional contexts: The generation and transmission of shared knowledge in the culture of collaborative learning. In N. Minnick and E. Forman (Eds.), *The institutional and social context of mind: New directions in Vygotskian theory and research* (pp. 283–314). New York: Oxford University Press.

Nocon, H. D. (2000). Developing hybridized social capital: Communication, coalition, and volunteering in non-traditional communities. Ph.D. Dissertation, University of California, San Diego.

Oakes, J., & Lipton, M. (1990). Tracking and ability grouping: A structural barrier to access and achievement. In J. I. Goodlad & P. Keating (Eds.), *Access to knowledge: An agenda for our nation's schools* (pp. 187–204). New York: College Entrance Examination Board.

Olsen, L. (1999). The common good. *Education Week on the Web,* January 27.

Proposition 49. (2002). After School Education and Safety Program Act. Ballot for California State Election, November 5.

Pub. L. 107–110, Stat. 1425. (2002). No Child Left Behind Act of 2001. US Congress.

Regents of the University of California. (1995) SP 1. Policy Ensuring Equal Treatment in Admissions.

Richman, S. (1994) *Separating school and state.* Fairfax, VA: Future of Freedom Foundation.

Rogoff, B. (1990). *Apprenticeship in thinking.* New York: Oxford University Press.

Rogoff, B., & Lave, J. (Eds.). (1984). *Everyday cognition.* Cambridge, MA: Harvard University Press.

SB 1552, Chap. 695. (2000). Public Schools Accountability Act of 1999. California State Senate.

Scribner, S., & Cole, M. (1973). Cognitive consequences of formal and informal education. *Science,* 182: 553–59.

Scribner, S., & Cole, M. (1981). *The psychology of literacy.* Cambridge, MA: Harvard University Press.

Sirotnik, K. A. (1990). Equal access to quality in public schooling: Issues in the assessment of equity and excellence. In J. I. Goodlad & P. Keating (Eds.), *Access to knowledge: An agenda for our nation's schools* (pp. 159–86). New York: College Entrance Examination Board.

Soder, R. (2001). Education for democracy: The foundation for democratic character. In R. Soder, J. I. Goodlad, & T. J. McMannon (Eds.), *Developing democratic character in the young* (pp. 182–205). San Francisco: Jossey-Bass.

Solana Beach Coalition. (2000). Extending K-12 Education: Issues facing informal learning programs. Report to the University of California Office of the President. LCHC, University of California, San Diego. <http://lchc.ucsd.edu>.

Spring, J. (2000). *American education.* 9th ed. Boston: McGraw Hill.

Stanford Achievement Test Series, 9th ed., SAT 9. (1995/2000). Harcourt Educational Measurement, Inc.

US Department of Education, Office of Educational Research and Improvement. (1999). Bringing education to after-school programs. Report. Washington, DC: US Department of Education.

US Department of Education and US Department of Justice. (1998). Safe and smart: Making after-school hours work for kids. Report. Washington, DC: US Department of Education.

Vásquez, O. A. (2003). *La Clase Mágica.* Mahweh, NJ: Lawrence Erlbaum Associates.

Vygotsky, L. S. (1978). *Mind in society.* Cambridge, MA: Harvard University Press.

Walker, K. E., Grossman, J. B., & Raley, R. (2000). *Extended service schools: Putting programming in place.* Report. Retrieved October 24, 2004, from the Public/Private Ventures Web site: <http://www.ppv.org/ppv/publications/assets/ 147_publication.pdf>.

Zelizer, V. A. (1985). *Pricing the priceless child.* Princeton, NJ: Princeton University Press.

PARENT-CHILD CONVERSATIONS ABOUT SCIENCE AND LITERACY

LINKS BETWEEN FORMAL AND INFORMAL LEARNING

MAUREEN A. CALLANAN AND GREGORY BRASWELL

Two key aspects of children's informal learning are that it occurs in the *context of meaningful social interactions with family members,* and that it is *interdisciplinary in nature.* In our research, we focus on family conversations as activity settings in which children learn about a variety of school-related topics. We combine constructivist and sociocultural perpectives, exploring children's learning within everyday social interactions. In this chapter, we present findings from an observational study of a thematic exhibit about Alice in Wonderland, which has been designed by the staff of the Children's Discovery Museum of San Jose (San Jose, California). We focus, in particular, on conversations relevant to science education and literacy. In several interactive exhibits, science content is introduced in ways that connect with the theme of Alice's story. In another exhibit, Do Cats Eat Bats?, families explore rhyme and meaning while making up new sentences inspired by the questions Alice asked during her adventure. We discuss ways that parents and children co-construct understanding of literacy and science content while engaging with these exhibits, and we consider the implications of such findings for general discussions regarding informal and formal learning.

Characterizing children's learning in formal and informal settings has been a focus of research for many years (Brown, 1997; Brown & Cole, 2002; Rogoff, Turkanis, & Bartlett, 2001; Vasquez, 2003). The accumulation of findings from various research projects makes it possible for educational researchers to begin to ask how our understanding of informal learning can inform classroom practices, as well as how our understanding of formal learning can inform the development of museums, afterschool clubs, and other nonschool environments. There are many ways that children's learning in informal environments differs from classroom learning. In this chapter, we explore two features of informal learning that are particularly salient. First, children in informal settings typically are learning about the world *in the context of interactions with important people* in their lives, particularly parents. And, second, children in informal settings learn about the world *in an interdisciplinary way,* where topics emerge in the context of activity, and topics are neither neatly divided along disciplinary lines nor presented one at a time or in isolation. We have been involved in an investigation of family interactions in children's museum settings, with a focus on understanding these two crucial features of children's learning in such informal environments.

In this research, our focus on the feature of family interactions is grounded in an attempt to integrate the constructivist theoretical approach of Piaget (1974) with the sociocultural approach inspired by Vygotsky (1978). This integrated approach views children's active construction of knowledge as inextricably linked to the context of everyday activities where they learn about the world around them (Rogoff, 2003). Children's early literacy begins in family activities (Bryant, Bradley, Maclean, & Crossland, 1989; Snow & Goldfield, 1983). Similarly, children's informal learning about science begins in everyday conversations with family members (Ash, 2003; Callanan & Jipson, 2001; Ellenbogen, 2002; Leinhardt & Crowley, 2002). In museums and other informal settings, then, parents' interactions with their children often frame children's experiences of the environment and activities (Crowley, Callanan, Jipson, Galco, Topping, & Shrager, 2001).

The second feature, the interdisciplinary nature of informal learning, is also consistent with a sociocultural approach to human development. As Rogoff (2003) argues, children develop as they participate in the activities of everyday life. Embedded as they are in meaningful activity settings, then, informal learning episodes are likely to engage children in many types of content simultaneously. For example, in a visit to one museum exhibit on earthquakes, children may learn something about the way the earth moves in an earthquake, something about a particular quake that occurred in Mexico City, and a few new vocabulary words (e.g., "seismic," "magnitude"). As educational researchers, we can view the child as learning about several different academic subjects (science, history, literacy), even though the child may see it as just things they know about earthquakes. Linking domains such as literacy and science has been shown to be effective in the "fostering communities of learners" approach of Ann Brown and her colleagues (e.g., Brown, 1997). In that work with urban students, Brown found remarkable achievement gains following classroom activities that integrated literacy skills with subject-matter investigation, for example, in biology.

Well-designed children's museums take into account both the family interaction aspect and the interdisciplinary aspect of informal learning. In this chapter we discuss research that we have conducted on family conversations about science and literacy in the Children's Discovery Museum of San Jose, CA. Our data are videotaped interactions of families as they visited a new thematic exhibition: Alice's Wonderland. Our research, conducted throughout the design phases of the exhibition as part of this NSF-funded project, illustrates some of the ways that parent-child conversations may serve as important settings where children's early science and literacy understanding develop together in an integrated way. In the next sections, we will first describe this innovative exhibition, as well as the role of research and evaluation in the project. Second, we will discuss an analysis of parent-child conversations relevant to science concepts, where we will suggest that conversations with their parents greatly improve the chances that children will link their museum experiences to abstract science concepts. Next, our investigation of parents' conversations with children about reading-related concepts will be described. Parents' guidance for children of different ages will be discussed, and parents will be argued to engage children who are in the beginning stages of reading in potentially valuable experiences. Finally, we will close with a discussion of the role of parents in theoretical discussions of the links between formal and informal learning. Throughout our discussion we will highlight the two features of family interaction and interdisciplinary learning.

METHODS FOR ANALYZING FAMILY CONVERSATIONS IN THE ALICE'S WONDERLAND EXHIBITION

Alice's Wonderland, an exhibit development project, was conducted at the Children's Discovery Museum of San Jose between 1999 and 2002. The project included exhibit design and development for a traveling exhibition that embeds science, mathematics, and logic into a set of hands-on experiences revolving around the theme of Lewis Carroll's *Alice's Adventures in Wonderland*. The exhibit development component of the project is integrated with an education component as well as a research-evaluation component.

The thematic focus of the exhibit is Alice, a curious child who continually tries to figure out what is happening in a puzzling world. In the book, Alice plays with language and logic, and she also becomes more and more curious and tries to understand unusual events that are happening around her. In other words, the inspiration for the exhibition was the notion of linking Alice as a character absorbed with language and words with Alice as a scientist, who can be a role model for visitors as they engage in a variety of hands-on activities that uncover some of the mysteries of our everyday world.

The research reported in this chapter represents the development of a unique partnership between university researchers and museum exhibit design staff. Over the past six years, researchers in developmental psychology at the University of California, Santa Cruz, have collaborated on several funded projects with the exhibit design and education staff at San Jose Children's Discovery Museum. Our research team for the Alice's Wonderland project included faculty, postdoctoral researchers, graduate students, and staff researchers, as well as undergraduate students who assisted with this research as part of earning independent study credit in developmental psychology. Importantly, at least one member of our team regularly attended the exhibit design team's meetings throughout the course of the project.

The research and evaluation component of the Alice's Wonderland exhibition focused on how children learn with parents in museum settings, with a particular interest in science learning and explanatory conversations, as well as equity in science participation across gender and cultural boundaries. Part of the inspiration for the exhibition came from our previous collaborative research conducted at the Children's Discovery Museum, where the findings indicated a substantial difference in the likelihood that parents would explain scientific phenomena to daughters versus sons (Crowley, Callanan, Tenenbaum, & Allen, 2001). In particular, boys were approximately three times as likely as girls to hear an explanation while interacting with an exhibit with their parent. Because these sorts of variations in science talk may impact children's early scientific thinking and their attitudes toward science, Alice's Wonderland was proposed as a thematic exhibit that might help to close the gender gap in family conversation. We asked whether parents might expect the Alice theme to be appealing to girls and hence might explain exhibits to their daughters as often as to their sons. Thus, one focus of the research was to assess the success of this strategy. For the purposes of this chapter, however, we focus on explanation data more generally.

Our methods for data collection and analysis were developed in our earlier work. Video cameras were set up near several exhibits, with wireless microphones attached to the exhibits to provide high-resolution audio recording. Researchers greeted families as they entered the museum, told them about the research, and asked if they would like to participate. Our overall rate of participation has been very high (above 90%). Children whose families agreed to participate were given large stickers to wear to identify them as participants. Whenever a child with a sticker approached one of the target exhibits, the researcher would begin to record the interaction.

Videotapes were segmented into separate family interactions, and then coded, using coding schemes developed to answer particular research questions. For example, parents' explanations were coded into three categories: *Explanations of scientific principles*, *Explanations of how the exhibit works*, and *Analogies*. The results regarding gender differences indicate strong evidence that the exhibition was extremely successful in closing the gender gap. Overall, we have found in this research that parents were equally likely to explain scientific concepts to girls and boys in the Alice's Wonderland exhibition (Callanan, Esterly, Martin, Frazier, & Gorchoff, 2002). Analogies are particularly frequent explanations in these data, partly because of the links that parents make to the story of Alice in Wonderland (e.g., "This looks bigger than it really is, just like Alice got big!"). In general, then, this research has revealed evidence of important gains in determining effective approaches for exhibition design to address concerns about gender equity.

In addition to the overall gender questions, analysis of family conversations around individual exhibits has allowed us to address other questions about informal learning in areas of science and literacy. In the remaining sections of this chapter, we discuss these findings in turn.

FAMILY CONVERSATIONS ABOUT SCIENCE: MAGNIFICATION AND SCALE

In keeping with the theme of *Alice's Adventures in Wonderland*, one of the key scientific concepts explored throughout the exhibition involved relative size, scale, and magnification. Building on the story line, visitors were reminded of the events where Alice changes in size. In several different types of exhibits, families were exposed to experiences that could be understood in terms of scientific content and process related to magnification and scale.

One instantiation of the notion of changing size was embodied in various illusions to help visitors experience the sense that they themselves were changing size. For example, the Hall of Doors presented a room-sized depth illusion such that the angles of the floor and ceiling make you feel larger and larger as you move down the hall. A clever Alice zoetrope shows Alice growing and shrinking as she spins. Fun house mirrors in the legs of an immense table give visitors the chance to experience the feeling of changing their own body's shape and size. In our observations, children and their families were very active in exploring these exhibits and playing with size. Children laughed as they viewed images in the mirror that made them look wider, thinner, taller, or shorter than usual. Others were delighted to notice that they looked "bigger" than their parents if they stood at opposite ends of the Hall of Doors.

In some areas of the exhibition, these experiential notions of changing size were more directly connected to scientific process with exhibits that use technology to change the perceptual experience of size. In particular, a videomicroscope allowed visitors to looks at objects at ten times their normal size. The sign accompanying this exhibit informed visitors that the images on the screen were presented at ten times their normal size, and that this makes the objects look like they would to a mouse. In this exhibit, objects are held over a lens that is embedded in a tabletop, and the objects are immediately magnified on a screen. Unlike most microscopes, this exhibit is very flexible in terms of what objects can be magnified. In addition to items that are provided, visitors often magnified their fingers, strands of hair, and even their eyeballs. Two preteenaged girls entertained themselves for well over 30 minutes by exploring in gory detail a cut on one girl's finger.

Another exhibit, called Microsonics, played with magnification in the realm of sound. This exhibit's appearance as a Victorian-era vanity table soon gives way to the reality that its drawers contain a myriad of sight and sound puzzles. An oscilloscope screen displayed an image that changes shape and size in synch with each noise. This is an exhibit where children spend unusually long periods of time playing and exploring.

One research question in our analysis of family conversations asked about how parents and children discussed the idea of magnification, and how children's visits to exhibits with parents differed from visits with children on their own. Our analysis includes 169 interactions in the Microsonics exhibit and 136 interactions with the Videomicroscope. In both of these exhibits, discussions about relative size and magnification were much more common when parents were present.

In the case of the Videomicroscope, there were no discussions of magnification or size when children interacted with the exhibit without parents. For children who visited the exhibit with parents, although not everyone discussed size, 17% of the dyads discussed the notion of size and 26% talked about explanations for how the exhibit worked. For example, one parent commented that, "Your thumb looks pretty big to a mouse." One parent said, "This is not as solid as it looks," referring to the magnified image of a piece of cloth. A five-year-old boy commented: "It's a close-up of my skin." Another parent looked at a magnified newspaper picture and said, "You can see ink dots. That's how you make a picture, with a bunch of dots." Parents sometimes used technical words such as "magnified" or "magnification." Even if children do not understand the meaning of these words, hearing them may begin to acquaint children with scientific vocabulary that they will hear (and perhaps recognize) later in school settings. Children were not passive observers in these conversations; parents often seemed to take their cue from children's engagement with the exhibit. Often a child's fascination with a particular aspect of an exhibit seemed to be the motivation for parents to connect the exhibit to scientific content.

With the Microsonics exhibit, explanations about sound and amplification occurred mainly when children visited with parents. Explanations occurred in 4% of the cases where parents were not present, but in 24% of the cases where parents were present. Parents and children talked about sound waves: "When you make a sound, it puts waves in the air." They also talked about the amplification of sound that was inherent in the exhibit: "This is how loud these noises would be if you were very small." Some families articulated questions about the exhibit that then guided their exploration of the exhibit, for example: "What do you think the wave is measuring? How high or how loud?" One child made the creative comment: "You can see the sound!"

Our observations also reveal that parents sometimes introduced aspects of the scientific process into their everyday conversations in the museum setting. For example, discussions of the processes of observing, predicting, and testing hypotheses are sometimes mentioned in our data. Parents also make use of the tools provided in the museum setting to discuss abstract representations that have relevance for later science discussions in school settings. For example, the notion of waves is subtly present in several of the Alice exhibits. Representations of sound in the Microsonics exhibit is one example. Another is in an exhibit called Pool of Tears, where droplets of water are released into a pool of water and the resulting waves are visible as shadows cast on a wall. Some parents take the opportunity to link these experiences with terms such as "sound waves." Our sociocultural approach to cognitive development leads us to postulate that such brief mentions of these concepts accumulate over time, leading children to enter science classrooms with some intuitive understandings of the concepts that they will study later in more depth. Exploration of these early conversations in informal settings can perhaps inform classroom practices and science education policy.

In line with our claims about the interdisciplinary nature of informal learning, it is noteworthy that these science discussions were so often linked to the literary theme of Alice. Another area of focus in our work more directly emphasized children's learning regarding literacy.

FAMILY LITERACY CONVERSATIONS: LINKING PHYSICAL SYMBOLS WITH SPOKEN WORDS

Adults and children are constantly immersed in a world of symbols in the form of spoken words, pictures, signs, numbers, gestures, and writing. In order to become a fully functioning member of any culture, a child needs to learn how to both produce and understand a wide of variety of symbol systems. For example, the ability to comprehend and create written symbols is required for becoming a productive contributor to any literate society. Mastering even the basics of written language is no easy feat. In order to read and understand even the simplest of texts, children must master a wide range of skills (e.g., understanding spoken language, the connections between spoken sounds and letters, and the directionality of print on a page). Many of these abilities begin to take shape well before children enter school and begin formal reading instruction. Again, much of this learning occurs in informal settings where parents are engaged with their children, and reading is not completely separated out from other activities.

Many studies have examined children's emergent literacy during social interactions with others, but most of this research has focused on top-down skills (Davidson & Snow, 1995; Gee, 2002; Snow & Goldfield, 1983). Breaking down words into smaller sound components and connecting these sounds to letters is another piece of the puzzle that beginning readers are faced with (Mason & Kerr, 1992; Whitehurst & Lonigan, 1998). Researchers often seem to assume that children's understanding of bottom-up skills such as phonological awareness (i.e., awareness that spoken words can be broken down into component sounds) develop through children's solitary experience with early reading attempts (Ehri, 1998; Goswami, 1998). Understanding rhyme has been linked to phonological awareness, which in turn is linked to early reading performance. There is some evidence that knowledge of nursery rhymes may contribute to an awareness of rhyming patterns that may in turn facilitate phonological awareness (Bryant, Bradley, Maclean, & Crossland, 1989). Further, Goswami (1998) suggests that children can make analogies between words that rhyme—at least in English—in order to help them read before they possess a full awareness of phonemes. For example, knowing what the word "beak" sounds like can help a child figure out what "speak" or "peak" should sound like. Little is known about what role social interactions (e.g., parent-child reading) play in assisting children in using rhyme-based analogies.

The design of the Alice's Wonderland exhibition took advantage of the strong language play inherent in this famous piece of literature. We examined adult-child interactions involving a literacy-based exhibit that was part of the Alice's Wonderland exhibition. The exhibit was inspired by Alice's conversation with herself as she fell through the rabbit hole. Missing her pet cat Dinah, Alice ruminated about what Dinah would eat if she were falling through the air with her: "Dinah, my dear! I wish you were down here with me! There are no mice in the air I'm afraid, but you might catch a bat, and that's very like a mouse, you know. But do cats eat bats, I wonder?" And here Alice began to get rather sleepy, and went on saying to herself, in a dreamy sort of way, "Do cats eat bats? Do cats eat bats?" and sometimes "Do bats eat cats?" for, you see, "as she couldn't answer either question, it didn't much matter which way she put it" (p. 20).

Building on Alice's word play, the exhibit consisted of five drums that were arranged in a row. Each drum contained several words and could be rotated in order to create novel, nonsense sentences (e.g., "True bats meet gnats!"; "Do cats eat bats?"). All of the words on each drum rhymed with one another (e.g., cats, bats, hats, mats) and some words were accompanied by or replaced by illustrations. The rightmost drum contained punctuation instead of words, so that one could form a question, a statement, or an exclamation. Our interest in this exhibit centered on the nature of adults' and children's print-related conversations that occurred while interacting with the exhibit. Such an exhibit should provide many opportunities for adults and children to focus on word-decoding skills. Presumably children and adults may be more likely to talk about print-related concepts when reading text that is not part of a story. Also, the exhibit capitalizes on rhyme as a crucial component of early decoding skills. This exhibit provides little opportunity to discuss higher-level aspects of meaning and increases the potential for print-related talk because of the nonsensical nature of the sentences that could be created.

Our investigation was based on transcripts created from 81 distinct adult-child interactions. This involved almost equal numbers of male and female target children (43 girls and 39 boys), although a majority of the adults involved were female (one female was present in 43 interactions, one male was present in 10 interactions, and multiple adults were present in 29 interactions). In order to examine age-related patterns, target children were classified under four age groups (based on quartiles). Seventeen of these children were 1–2 years old, 20 were 3–4 years old, 21 were 5–6 years old, and 23 were 7–11 years old. Thus a wide age range of children was represented in this sample.

Researchers transcribed family conversations while interacting with the exhibit. Of particular interest for this discussion, we examined instances where parents and children read the sentences off the drums (e.g., "Cats eat bats") as well as instances where they commented on aspects of the written language represented. This print-related speech included five subcategories: letter identification, word identification, word definition, spelling, and rhyming. Not surprisingly, print-related utterances by adults were far more prevalent than such utterances made by children. Forty-one interactions involved print-related speech by adults (50%), and 13 interactions involved print-related speech by children (16%).

We expected that parents of children just beginning to read would discuss print-related concepts more often than parents of either very young children or older, more experienced readers. We also expected parents of older children to simply read the words in the exhibit without adding any print-related commentary. Also, it was expected that young children just beginning to read would ask more print-related questions than older children.

A series of Pearson Chi-squared analyses supported some of these hypotheses. There was a marginally significant difference across age groups in how many interactions entailed adults reading without commentary, $X^2(df = 3, n = 81) = 7.49, p < .06$ This type of speech was more common with older children (76% of interactions with 5–6-year-olds and 69% of interactions with 7–11-year-olds) than younger (41% and 45% of interactions with 1–2- and 3–4-year-olds, respectively). Not surprisingly, the frequency of interactions in which children read without commentary increased across age groups, $X^2(df = 3, n = 81) = 19.6, p < .001$.

There was also a significant difference across age groups in the extent to which adults asked print-related questions, $X^2(df = 3, n = 81) = 8.72, p < .05$. These utterances were most common when 3–4- (45% of interactions) and 5–6-year-olds (57% of interactions) were involved. In contrast, these types of questions occurred in 12% of interactions with 1–2-year-olds and 35% of interactions with 7–11-year-olds. Most of these questions pertained to word identification (28 interactions). Very few questions involved letter identification (five interactions), word definitions (two interactions), or spelling (one interaction). Only two adults made statements regarding rhyming, which was surprising, given the nature of the exhibit.

Conversations about print-related concepts extended beyond individual utterances. Three excerpts from transcripts are included in order to provide a more complete picture of how adults and children talked about print. The first example involves an interaction between a three-year-old girl (whose name has been changed here) and two women:

> [child spins drums]
> **Adult:** Find an M.
> [child continues to spin drums]
> **Adult:** M for Melissa. Where's M? Is there . . . [unintelligible]
> [Another adult female points to "mats" and says, "There's an M."]
> **Adult:** Good! Did you find it? Where's the M for Melissa? M for Melissa!
> [child points to "mats"]
> **Adult:** There it is!

This exchange illustrates how adults and a young child talked about letter identification. The following passage also involved letter identification but with a woman and a slightly older child (a five-year-old girl):

> **Child:** Now let's see.
> **Adult:** What's next?
> **Child:** Gats.
> **Adult** (pointing to "gnats"): It's actually gnats (covering the G) The G is silent.

Child: Gnats. (spins another drum) Cats.
Adult: OK.

In one additional example, a four-year-old boy collaborates with his mother to spell a word on one of the drums.

Adult: What does this word say? (pointing to "cats") What is that?
Child: I don't know.
Adult: Spell it out. See if you can.
Child: C–A–
Adult: T
Child: T–S.
Adult: Spell it—I mean sound it out.
Child: Cats.

These examples of the ways in which adults and young children conversed about the text in the exhibit suggest that museum exhibits such as this one could serve as bridges between formal and at-home literacy practices. The exhibit described above included simple, rhyming words, pictures, and repetitive structures, as do many books used by teachers in early reading activities. Also, adults discussed print-related concepts in ways similar to parents in book-reading activities at home. Given these commonalities, museum settings may provide contexts for learning about reading in the zone of proximal development, much as in home (Sulzby & Teale, 1991) and school (Hiebert & Raphael, 1998) environments.

CONCLUSIONS AND FUTURE DIRECTIONS

How do children learn differently in museums versus in school classrooms? There are many ways of addressing this question, as suggested by the variety of approaches taken by the authors of the chapters in this volume. One approach is to compare the differences in children's performance and motivation in school settings with that in the typically less formal settings of museums, after-school clubs, and other nonschool environments (Schauble, Beane, Coates, Martin, & Sterling 1996). Another approach is to recognize that both formal and informal learning occurs in both types of settings, and to explore the nature of learning across activities that vary along dimensions such as structure, goals, and participants (Rogoff & Angelillo, 2002). A common thread throughout all of this research is the implicit goal of discovering effective ways to support children's learning in all settings.

Parents' interactions with children in the Alice's Wonderland exhibit demonstrated ways that everyday family conversations may give children experiences that are relevant to their emerging skills in literacy and scientific understanding. While the findings reported here do not directly address questions regarding what children have learned from these interactions, they do set the stage for further research by describing some aspects of the discourse and activity that children participate in with their parents. These data also illustrate the ways that school-like content can emerge in informal learning settings. And, in the Alice's Wonderland exhibition in particular, it is clear that informal learning often involves learning that cuts across or integrates diverse topics that represent separate academic disciplines.

The link between literacy and science in the Alice's Wonderland exhibit was facilitated by the narrative theme and the character of Alice. Museum researchers are exploring the notion of narrative in other exhibitions (Allen, 2002; Martin, 2002). Further, this link is very interesting in light of recent discussions regarding the role of narrative in cognitive development (Bruner, 2002) and the role of language and argumentation in science (Osborne, 2002). In particular, Osborne (2002) argues that science education needs to pay more attention to the crucial role of language in scientific work, and to teach children to use and understand scientific language. This research on science conversation in everyday family interaction suggests that children may enter school already familiar with some aspects of the language of science. Perhaps science education can build more effectively on these emerging skills.

By choosing to optimize the spontaneity of the actions we observed in this work, we gave up the possibility of collecting data regarding family demographics, educational background, and attitudes. As previous data suggests, it is likely that these dimensions are related to parents' tendency to discuss science and literacy topics with their children (Tenenbaum, Callanan, Alba-Speyer, & Sandoval, 2002; Grover & Snow, 1998; Snow & Goldfield, 1983). For the purposes of this chapter, however, our point has been to document some aspects of literacy-based and science-based talk in family museum conversations. In these conversations, parents interpret and guide children to interpret the museum experience in ways that potentially connect with their school experiences. As suggested in the beginning of this chapter, then, parents are a crucial link in the quest to more effectively connect informal and formal learning.

In related work, we have attempted to more directly investigate the link between formal and informal learning by exploring interactions during Family Science Nights, where parents and teachers come together to engage with children in inquiry-based learning (Callanan, Alba-Speyer, & Tenenbaum, 2000). One goal in this preliminary work has been to facilitate communication between parents and teachers regarding children's home conversations about science topics covered in school. Extending the "funds of knowledge" approach of Moll and Gonzalez (1994), we investigated ways that parents may serve as experts and resources for teachers. It seems likely that children could benefit from having their teacher know more about their own interest in and understanding of topics covered in school. Preschoolers' spontaneous questions seem very much like the type of inquiry that we hope to encourage in later science classrooms (Simon, 2001). It would be desirable to preserve that natural curiosity throughout the science curriculum so that it doesn't have to be retaught in later years. If we can build on the knowledge that parents have of their own children's interests and beliefs we may be in a much better position to do just that.

In a new project, we plan to further explore cultural variation in the links between formal and informal learning, working again with the Children's Discovery Museum on an exhibition entitled Round and Round. The exhibition will explore circles as mathematical representations, as instantiated in real-world objects such as wheels and as cultural symbols. A major focus of this project will be the study of cultural variation in family conversations about science and symbols. Mexican-descent and Vietnamese-descent families will participate in the project, and the links between informal and formal learning settings will be explored by expanding our work on Family Science Nights, developing a partnership with a local school district, and continuing our studies of family conversations in the museum setting.

Overall, we believe that our findings present compelling evidence that family conversations in museums are settings with potential for children's learning about school-related topics. By integrating constructivist and sociocultural theories we hope to learn more about how children actively explore the world as part of social interactions during everyday activities. Further exploration of the links between informal and formal learning will no doubt uncover important insights that will be of interest to cognitive development and education.

REFERENCES

Allen, S. (2002). *Studying visitor meaning-making at exhibits.* Paper presented at annual meeting of Association of Science-Technology Centers, Charlotte, NC.

Ash, D. (2003). Dialogic inquiry in life science conversations of family groups in a museum. *Journal of Research in Science Teaching, 40:* 138–62.

Brown, A. L. (1997). Transforming schools into communities of thinking and learning about serious matters. *American Psychologist, 52:* 399–413.

Brown, K., & Cole, M. (2002). Cultural Historical Activity Theory and the explanation of opportunities for learning after school. In G. Wells (Ed.), *Learning for life in the 21st century: Sociocultural perspectives on the future of education* (pp. 225–38). Malden, MA: Blackwell.

Bruner, J. (2002). *Making stories: Law, literature, life.* New York: Farrar, Straus and Giroux.

Bryant, P. E., Bradley, L., Maclean, M., & Crossland, J. (1989). Nursery rhymes, phonological skills and reading. *Journal of Child Language, 16:* 407–28.

Callanan, M., Alba-Speyer, C., & Tenenbaum, H. (2000). *Linking home and school through children's questions that followed family science workshops.* Research Brief #8, Center for Education, Diversity, and Excellence (CREDE).

Callanan, M., Esterly, J., Martin, J., Frazier, B., & Gorchoff, S. (2002). Family conversations about science in an Alice's Wonderland exhibit. Paper presented at annual meetings of American Educational Research Association, New Orleans, LA.

Callanan, M., & Jipson, J. (2001). Explanatory conversations and young children's developing scientific literacy. In K. Crowley, C. Schunn, & T. Okada (Eds.), *Designing for science: Implications from everyday, classroom, and professional settings* (pp. 21–49). Mahwah, NJ: Erlbaum.

Crowley, K., Callanan, M., Jipson, J., Galco, J., Topping, K., & Shrager, J. (2001). Shared scientific thinking in everyday parent-child activity. *Science Education, 85:* 712–32.

Crowley, K., Callanan, M., Tenenbaum, H., & Allen, E. (2001). Parents explain more often to boys than to girls during shared scientific thinking. *Psychological Science, 12:* 258–61.

Davidson, R. G., & Snow, C. E. (1995). The linguistic environment of early readers. *Journal of Research in Childhood Education, 10:* 5–21.

Ehri, L. C. (1998). Grapheme-phoneme knowledge is essential for learning to read words in English. In J. L. Metsala & L. C. Ehri (Eds.), *Word recognition in beginning literacy* (pp. 3–40). Mahwah, NJ: Erlbaum.

Ellenbogen, K. M. (2002). Museums in family life: An ethnographic case study. In G. Leinhardt & K. Crowley (Eds.), *Learning conversations in museums* (pp. 81–101). Mahwah, NJ: Erlbaum.

Gee, J. P. (2002). A sociocultural perspective on early literacy development. In S. B. Neuman & D. K. Dickinson (Eds.), *Handbook of early literacy research* (pp. 30–42). New York: Guilford.

Goswami, U. (1998). The role of analogies in the development of word recognition. In J. L. Metsala & L. C. Ehri (Eds.), *Word recognition in beginning literacy* (pp. 41–63). Mahwah, NJ: Erlbaum.

Grover, A. V., & Snow, C. E. (1998). Narratives and explanations during mealtime conversations in Norway and the US. *Language in Society, 27:* 221–46.

Hiebert, E. H., & Raphael, T. E. (1998). *Early literacy instruction.* New York: Harcourt Brace.

Leinhardt, G., & Crowley, K. (2002). Objects of learning, objects of talk: Changing minds in museums. In S. G. Paris (Ed.), *Perspectives on object-centered learning in museums* (pp. 301–24). Mahwah, NJ: Erlbaum.

Martin, L. (2002). Floating the science center on the *Titanic.* Paper presented at annual meeting of Association of Science and Technology Centers, Charlotte, NC.

Mason, J. M., & Kerr, B. M. (1992). Literacy transfer from parents to children in the preschool years. In T. G. Sticht, M. J. Beeler, & B. A. McDonald (Eds.), *The intergenerational transfer of cognitive skills.* Norwood, NJ: Ablex.

Moll, L., & Gonzalez, N. (1994). Lessons from research with language minority children. *Journal of Reading Behavior, 26:* 439–56.

Osborne, J. (2002). Science without literacy: A ship without a sail? *Cambridge Journal of Education, 32:* 203–18.

Piaget, J. (1974). *The language and thought of the child.* New York: Meridian.

Rogoff, B. (2003). *The cultural nature of human development.* London: Oxford University Press.

Rogoff, B., & Angelillo, C. (2002). Investigating the coordinated functioning of multifaceted cultural practices in human development. *Human Development, 45:* 211–25.

Rogoff, B., Turkanis, C. G., & Bartlett, L. (2001). *Learning together: Children and adults in a school community.* London: Oxford University Press.

Schauble, L., Beane, D. A., Coates, G. D., Martin, L. M., & Sterling, P. V. (1996). Outside the classroom walls: Learning in informal environments. In L. Schauble & R. Glaser (Eds.), *Innovations in learning: New environments for education* (pp. 5–24). Mahwah, NJ: Erlbaum.

Simon, H. (2001). "Seek and ye shall find" How curiosity engenders discovery. In K. Crowley, C. Schunn, & T. Okada (Eds.), *Designing for Science: Implications from Everyday, Classroom, and Professional Settings* (pp. 5–20). Mahwah, NJ: Erlbaum.

Snow, C. E., & Goldfield, B. A. (1983). Turn the page please: Situation-specific language acquisition. *Journal of Child Language, 10:* 551–69.

Sulzby, E., & Teale, W. (1991). Emergent literacy. In R. Barr, M. Kamil, P. Mosenthal, & P. D. Pearson (Eds.), *Handbook of reading research.* Vol. 2 (pp. 727–57). New York: Longman.

Tenenbaum, H., Callanan, M., Alba-Speyer, C., & Sandoval, L. (2002). Parent-child science conversations in Mexican-descent families: Educational background, activity, and past experiences as moderators. *Hispanic Journal of the Behavioral Sciences, 24:* 225–56.

Vasquez, O. A. (2003). *La clase magica: Imagining optimal possibilities in a bilingual community of learners.* Mahwah, NJ: Lawrence Erlbaum Associates.

Vygotsky, L. S. (1978). *Mind in society: The development of higher psychological processes.* Cambridge, MA: Harvard University Press.

Whitehurst, G. J., & Lonigan, C. J. (1998). Child development and emergent literacy. *Child Development, 68:* 848–72.

CULTURAL TEACHING AND LEARNING

PROCESSES, EFFECTS, AND DEVELOPMENT OF APPRENTICESHIP SKILLS

ASHLEY E. MAYNARD AND PATRICIA M. GREENFIELD

Cultural teaching can be thought of as the system of socialization that exists to support learners in acquiring cultural knowledge of various kinds (Maynard, 2002). The concept of cultural teaching is meant to complement its counterpart, cultural learning (Tomasello, Kruger, & Ratner, 1993), which emphasizes the processes by which learners acquire culture and the affordances of learners. Cultural teaching focuses on the rituals, routines, cultural practices, and socializing agents that support cultural learning. We see cultural teaching as a central component of informal education. In this chapter we focus on the nature of cultural teaching, its effects on cognitive development, and the development of the ability to teach. We present several studies of cultural teaching and learning that we have conducted over the past three decades.

OVERVIEW OF THE COMMUNITY AND THE STUDIES

Our research on cultural teaching has focused on one community, Nabenchauk, a Zinacantec Mayan hamlet in the highlands of Chiapas, Mexico.

Families living in this community are involved primarily in either farming or commercial activity. Our studies in the community cover the period of time from 1969 to 2003. In this paper, we focus on this entire time span.

The focus of the studies, both naturalistic and experimental, has been on weaving, a complex technical skill acquired by virtually all girls in the community through processes of informal education (Childs & Greenfield, 1980; Greenfield, 1984; Greenfield, Maynard, & Childs, 2000, 2003). Weaving is seen as an alternative to schooling; it is the central skill-learning context for girls in the indigenous culture. Girls begin learning to weave on toy looms, as early as age three. They typically move to adult looms between eight and ten years of age.

An important dimension of these studies has been historical. We have studied two successive generations of girls learning to weave two decades apart; the motivation for the historical study was the economic changes that had taken place during the intervening period, as the community moved from greater economic reliance on agricultural subsistence in 1969 and 1970 toward greater economic reliance on commerce in subsequent decades.

Our notion was that styles of cultural learning and teaching would be adapted to the surrounding milieu, and our research was designed to test this hypothesis under conditions of social change. In other words, the notion of informal education was seen as historically contingent. While we found some important constants, we also found changes that were specifically linked to participation in commercial activities, as well as other changes that were linked to the introduction of television and formal schooling for girls. Our studies of learning to weave established the adult styles of teaching and their adaptation to different economic environments. A logical next step was a study to establish the developmental steps by which these styles, with their commonalities and differences, evolved in the course of individual lives.

A second stimulus to study the development of teaching was Maynard's ethnographic account of how Zinacantecs taught her a number of different everyday activities, including weaving. Her ethnography led to the notion of a general Zinacantec model of teaching and learning that permeates all domains and conditions of informal education (Maynard, 1996; Maynard & Greenfield, in press). This model provided an important endpoint whose development could then be studied.

While many developmental studies have focused on learning, few studies had focused on the development of teaching. Yet teaching is an important adaptation of the human way of life; its ontogeny is very much a part of human phylogeny. In order to study the development of teaching, Maynard (1996, 2002, 2004a) focused on ways that young children, in the course of sibling caregiving, develop the ability to teach their younger siblings everyday activities. In Zinacantán, children are given sibling caregiving responsibilities, starting at age four or five. Maynard found that these responsibilities provide a natural opportunity to learn to teach.

These naturalistic explorations of cultural teaching were complemented by a series of experimental studies of cultural learning. Using one experimental task, we found that weaving apprenticeship had cognitive effects and that changing modes of apprenticeship led to corresponding changes in cognitive representation. In a second study, we found that weaving apprenticeship led to the development of spatial transformation skills in the specific domain of weaving. We also found that the influence of weaving experience, as well as tasks and tools provided to the learner, were constrained by stage of cognitive development.

A MODEL OF INFORMAL EDUCATION: THE ZINACANTEC MODEL OF TEACHING AND LEARNING

The Zinacantec model of teaching and learning is a model of informal education used in our study site. The model comes into play in more structured activities, such as weaving apprenticeship, and in less structured activities, such as making tortillas or other types of cooking. The model was derived based on Maynard's fieldwork in Nabenchauk during which she was taught to do things that Zinacantec women do, such as weaving, making tortillas, and chopping and carrying firewood. The model also comes from Greenfield's earlier studies of weaving apprenticeship in Nabenchauk (Childs & Greenfield, 1980; Greenfield, 1984).

There are five basic features of this model. The features of the model are observation, contextualized talk, scaffolding, guiding the body, and having multiple teachers. All of these are characterized by a lack of direct praise or criticism toward the learner.

Observation means that a learner should observe a task before trying it herself. Zinacantec girls, for example, observe weaving for many hours before they are able to sit in the loom and weave on their own. By the time they are allowed to sit at the loom, they are expected to be able to weave (Greenfield & Childs, 1991). This is in contrast to a more American trial-and-error style of learning. Observation starts as early as infancy. In Figure 1, baby Xunka' Pavlu observes her older sister Paxku' embroidering.

Contextualized talk means that talk about a task happens while the task is going on and not in the absence of the task as an abstract discussion. People talk about the activity of weaving while weaving is occurring, and not while just relaxing or doing another activity.

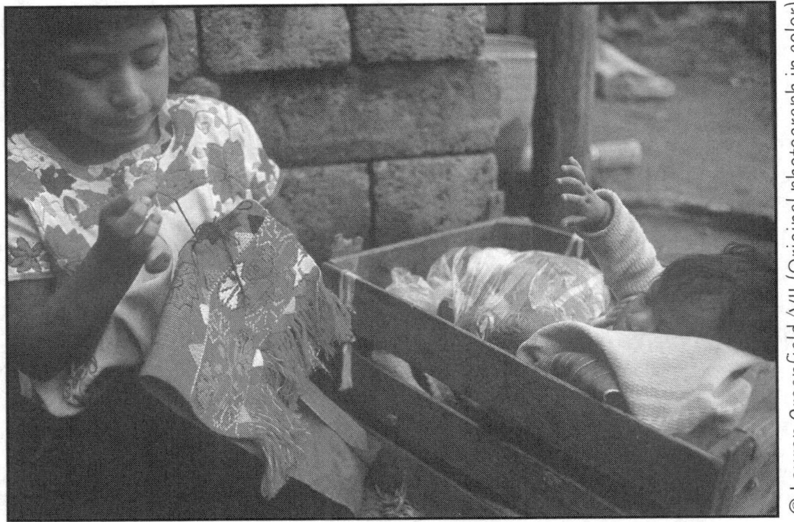

Figure 1: Baby Xunka', daughter of Maruch Chentik and Telex Pavlu, observes her older sister Paxku' embroidering (P. M. Greenfield, 2004).

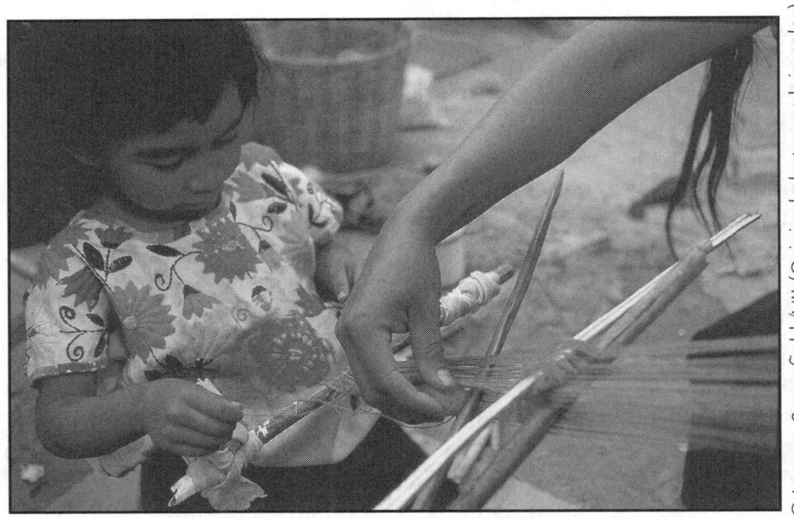

Figure 2: Rosy Xulubte's mother, Katal, inserts thread as Rosy leans back in the loom, maintaining the necessary tension of the warp threads. Nabenchauk, 1991.
(P. M. Greenfield, 2004).

Scaffolding means that tasks are broken down into doable parts for learners to try on their own, such that learners are able to do some parts of tasks with help before they are able to do the tasks by themselves. For example, a child is given some tortilla dough to play with in a press and an older sibling helps by closing the press and pressing down on it. As another example, a very young weaving learner sits at the loom, maintaining the tautness of the warp threads, while her mother creates the heddle (Figure 2).

Guiding the body is when a teacher positions or moves the body of the learner in the position best for the activity. For example, a weaving teacher might push the back of the weaving apprentice forward to achieve the proper angle in weaving.

Multiple teachers. There is often more than one teacher in Zinacantec apprenticeship. This means that anyone who knows more than the learner can provide instruction in the learning process. A frequent scene in the village is a girl learning to weave as others pass by. Some women may stop to talk to the mother of the learner and then make a comment about the weaving, pointing out to the learner how to weave better or to avoid a mistake.

Some of these features, such as scaffolding, are found in other models of informal education (Lancy, 1996), whereas others are not usually mentioned in formulations of models of information education, for example, guiding the body.

CULTURAL TEACHING AND LEARNING: THE CASE OF WEAVING APPRENTICESHIP

We maintain a historical study of weaving apprenticeship in Nabenchauk. We plan to continue it into future generations, as socioeconomic conditions continually change. The study is designed to measure processes of teaching and learning and to examine the ways that those processes are affected by historical changes such as socioeconomic shifts that produce shifts in the daily routines of families. So far we have collected naturalistic video data on weaving apprenticeship from two generations of weaving learners. Girls were observed learning to weave in 1969 and 1970 and the next generation, mostly the daughters and nieces of the girls in the first sample, were observed in 1991 and 1993. We planned to return to the field around 2011 to collect data on the third generation of weaving learners. However, later marriage and childbearing patterns may delay this projected study for a few years.

In 1969 and 1970, Greenfield and Childs (1991; Childs & Greenfield, 1980; Greenfield, 1984) observed a very highly scaffolded process of weaving apprenticeship that maintained a closed stock of about four woven patterns. Each pattern was used for a particular article of clothing: poncho, striped shawl, basketweave shawl, or little girl's blouse. Everyone in the village dressed in one or two of those patterns. All woven garments of a particular type looked basically the same, and everyone dressed the same.

Before returning to the field in 1991, Greenfield and Childs had heard that there were new patterns being woven and they hypothesized that these changes in patterns would be accompanied by a more independent style of learning. They believed that an independent, trial-and-error style of learning was more adapted to the innovative proliferation of patterns they had heard about.

They began our exploration of the developmental implications of social change with a theory of two cultural models of informal education, each adapted to a different ecological environment (Greenfield & Lave, 1982; cf. Edelstein, 1999). The first model is a culturally conservative one: Apprenticeship is highly guided by the master and opportunities for error are therefore limited. This model is strengthened when the cost of error is very high (Greenfield, 1984; Rogoff, 1990) and apprenticeship is product-oriented (Renshaw & Gardner, 1990). Because the master's guidance limits learner experimentation, opportunities to innovate are also limited, and the apprentice therefore acquires an array of skills with little change from the master's set of competencies. This model is well adapted to producing items that express a constant cultural tradition.

The second model emphasizes cultural innovation rather than cultural conservation (Greenfield & Lave, 1982). Instead of guidance by a master, the emphasis is on trial-and-error learning by the novice. The frequency of error of course increases, as does learner independence. Trial-and-error learning intrinsically involves experimentation; innovative processes and products are a natural consequence of experimentation. This model is strengthened when the cost of making an error is relatively low (Greenfield, 1984; Rogoff, 1990), for example, when materials are inexpensive and easily replaced. Under such circumstances one need not be as concerned about preventing error in the final product. Would it be possible to link each of these models to a particular ecological niche? If the ecological niche changed over time, would the model of cultural apprenticeship? These were theoretical questions that drove our historical study of weaving apprenticeship. We believe that there is a relationship between these two models such that ecological conditions may emphasize cultural conservation more than innovation or innovation more than cultural conservation. In our work, we explore the relative emphasis of these models and the ways that the balanced is tipped in relationship to ecological change.

Corresponding to two models of cultural apprenticeship were two possible models of cultural learning and cognitive development. The conservative model stresses learning to reproduce specific known patterns through observation and imitation; the innovative model stresses learning to create novelty and using abstract principles to transfer concepts and strategies to novel situations. Would it be possible to see a shift from one cognitive model to another as a function of ecological change? An experimental study of pattern representation was designed to answer this question.

What kinds of ecological change would be relevant? Theory and evidence link subsistence and agriculture to a conservative cultural model, on the one hand (Collier, 1990; Edelstein, 1983); they link money and commercial entrepreneurship to an innovative cultural model, on the other (Edelstein, 1983; Lerner, 1958; McClelland, 1961). Edelstein, in particular, links movement from the concrete barter of a subsistence-based community to market exchange to abstraction. He contrasts the "concrete exchange of goods" with the "abstract exchange of symbolic equivalents" (Edelstein, 1983, p. 58). As a culture moves from subsistence agriculture toward commerce and entrepreneurship, is there a corresponding change from the conservative to the innovative models of cultural apprenticeship and cognitive development? Is there a concurrent movement from more concrete to more abstract modes of representation? Our experimental study explored this question.

At the same time, ecological change from subsistence to commerce often involves increased schooling (Seymour, 1999). Formal education is, in turn, often associated with abstraction (for example, Greenfield, Reich, & Olver, 1966). To what extent are observed changes from concrete to abstract modes of representation linked to schooling, rather than, or in addition to, commerce? Not only going to school, but also having a school-educated mother were possible factors that could mediate between general ecological change and specific changes in cultural apprenticeship and cognitive representation (e.g., Laosa, 1978; Tapia Uribe, LeVine, & LeVine, 1994; Zukow, 1984). Our studies explored the relevance of these factors as well.

Findings: Changes in Apprenticeship

Indeed, we found some dramatic differences in the way weaving was taught to girls in each generation. There were differences in personnel helping girls learn to weave; there were differences in the ways that girls learned; and there was a shift in the way that errors were handled. In 1970, more weaving teachers or helpers were from an age cohort older than the learner herself; only 7% of the teachers or helpers were in the same age cohort as the learner. By contrast, in the 1990s, more helpers were in the same age cohort as the learner: a full 23%. In the earlier cohort, weaving apprenticeship was highly scaffolded; teachers were next to learners with four hands on the loom. In the 1990s, learners engaged in more independent trial-and-error learning as they practiced weaving. Finally, in 1970 it was teachers who prevented and corrected errors, but by the 1990s, learners were preventing and correcting their own errors. There had been, as predicted, a movement from the conservative to the innovative model of cultural apprenticeship (Greenfield, Maynard, & Childs, 2000, 2003). All of these changes in apprenticeship, including learning to use paper patterns, were concentrated in families in which mothers and daughters engaged in textile commerce. Figure 3 presents a path model indicating that mother-daughter participation in textile commerce mediates the change from a more cooperative style of weaving apprenticeship to a more independent mode of learning.

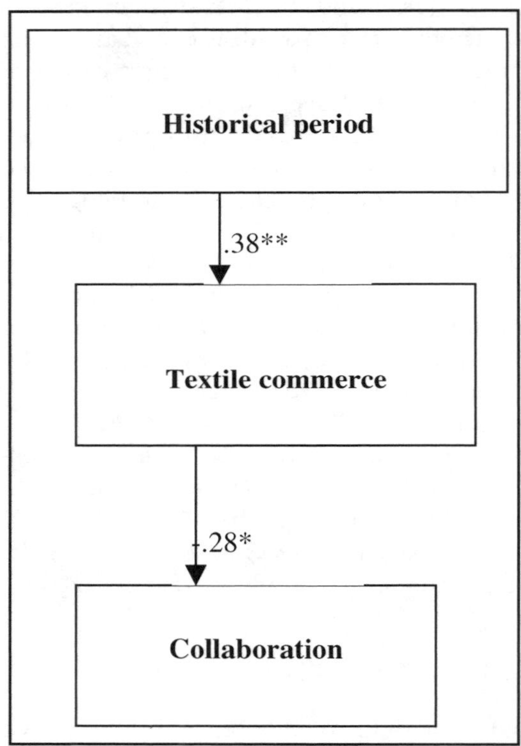

Figure 3. Path diagram of the relationship among the variables of historical period, mother-daughter involvement in textile commerce, and teacher-learner collaboration.

* = Parameter is significant at the .05 level.

** = Parameter is significant at the .01 level. Using EQS (Bentler, 1980, 1995) with maximum likelihood estimation, we found a good fit between model and data. The comparative fit index (CFI) for the tested model was 1.000, and the model chi-square was nonsignificant, C2 = .029, p = .8659. (For the CFI and chi-square test, good fit is indicated by a value greater than .90 and by nonsignificant results, respectively. A CFI of 1 is the maximum possible.) The model includes all weaving participants videotaped attaching the endstick or weaving the first weft thread (N = 69).

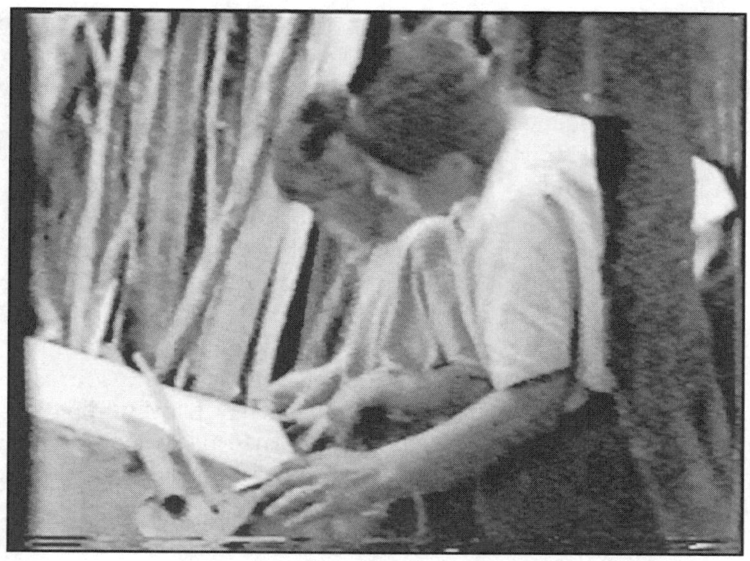

Figure 4a. Mother helping daughter, age nine, learn to weave in 1970 (Greenfield, 2004).

Figure 4b. Daughter's daughter, also age nine, learning to weave in 1991 (Greenfield, 2004). Videos by Patricia Greenfield.

Figure 4 shows a contrast between a young girl learning to weave in 1970 (4a) and her daughter learning to weave in 1991 at about the same age (4b). In these two video frames are visible the difference between a teacher of the older generation (the mother in 1970) and a teacher of the peer generation (an older sister in 1991). We also see a contrast between more guidance and help (1970 frame) and more independent learning (1991 frame).

At the same time, textile patterns themselves had expanded from a few traditional patterns to an infinite range of innovative designs (Greenfield, 2000; Greenfield, Maynard, & Childs, 2000, 2003). This increased range of variability was partially a result of the use of printed paper patterns as design sources. Printed paper patterns had entered the scene as a source for both woven and embroidered textile patterns. In 1991, the printed patterns used for weaving and sewing were cross-stitch patterns arranged in grids of squares and printed in Mexico City. They could be used for either embroidery or brocade weaving (Figure 5).

However, certain processes of visual representation are required to use these patterns, particularly for weaving. The patterns are arranged in a grid of squares, but a loom is not. The loom has threads going at right angles to each other, with warp threads (the white threads in Figure 5) functioning as a frame for the insertion of weft or cross threads. In order to use a cross-stitch pattern for weaving, it was necessary for a weaver to develop a code of correspondences translating a grid of squares into warp and weft threads. One weaver told us that one square would correspond to one thread in the warp dimension (white threads) and to four threads in the weft dimension (the darker, cross-wise threads). This is a fairly complex representational code to create. It is somewhat simpler to use the patterns for embroidery. There we found that by pulling warp and weft threads at even intervals in a piece of store-bought cloth, sewers did create a grid of squares that could be used to correspond to the squares in the pattern book. Paper patterns could also be drawn on paper and transferred to cloth by tracing and other means (see Figure 6).

Textile commerce, either directly or indirectly, provided a form of informal education that favored learning to use paper patterns. In the daughter generation, studied in 1991 and 1993, the use of paper patterns had become highly generalized in the culture. In other words, from mothers to their daughters, there was a significant intergenerational increase in the use of paper patterns to embroider and weave. We found a significant association between a daughter's use of paper patterns and mother-daughter participation in textile commerce. Like other historical changes in informal education in the domain of weaving, learning to use paper patterns was concentrated in girls who, with their mothers, were highly involved in textile commerce.

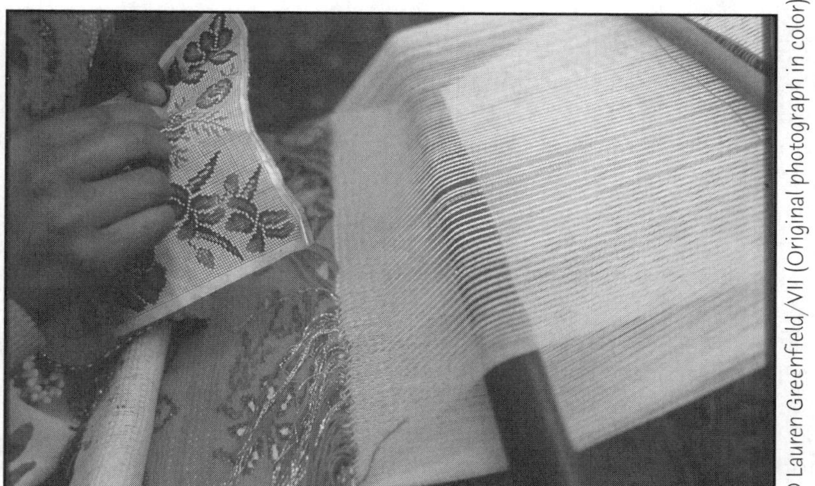

Figure 5. A weaver uses a printed cross-stitch pattern to guide her woven design (P. M. Greenfield, 2004).

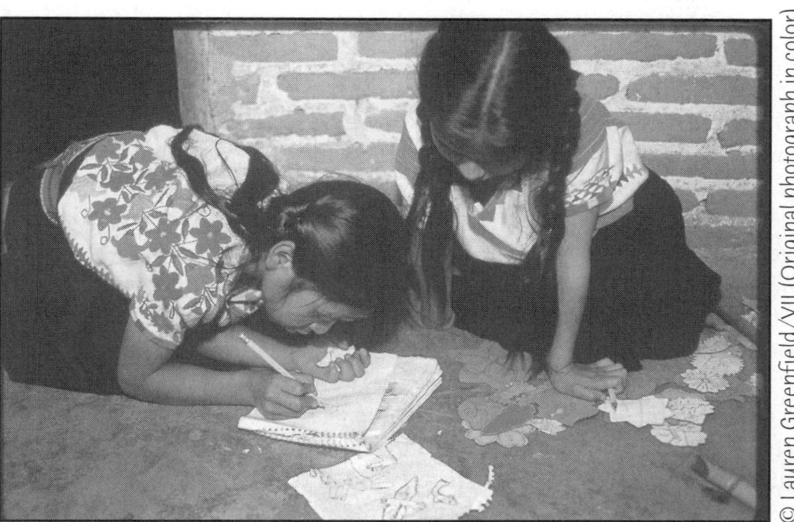

Figure 6. Two girls draw patterns that they will later use for embroidery. Note the cutout patterns on the ground at the right of the picture (P. M. Greenfield, 2004).

The use of paper patterns was also linked to exposure to formal schooling. The introduction of formal schooling for girls was also showing its effects on informal education in the domain of weaving (Greenfield & Maynard, 1997). In 1969 and 1970, no girls over the age of 13 had been to school; in other words, schooling for girls was only a few years. By 1991, the rate of schooling for girls over 13 was about 24%.

The first connection to schooling is that it is said in the community that schoolteachers introduced the first printed patterns. More generally, schooling has introduced modes of external visual representation into a culture that had none, save statues of saints. This has occurred in the form of reading and writing but also pictures and patterns for textile production. Television, present in a significant minority of homes as early as 1991, greatly augmented the introduction of visual representation into homes.

What was the role of formal education in this new cultural learning? One mother told us that it is necessary to go to school to use paper patterns. In Tzotzil, school is called "*chan vun,*" learning paper. Reading is called "*k'el vun,*" looking at paper. The same term "looking at paper" is used to talk about the "reading" of paper patterns. Referring to paper patterns, this mother told us that "to look at paper," that is, read printed patterns, one must "learn paper," that is, go to school. Her statement was confirmed by our quantitative analysis. We found that, for mothers studied in 1991 and 1993, a higher percentage of mothers who had been to school used paper patterns for weaving or embroidery. Unschooled women generally did not use paper; schooled women invariably did.

What was the influence of these mothers' schooling on the informal education of their daughters? We found that mothers who have been to school were more likely to have daughters who did not proceed to the highest level of weaving skill (brocade) and therefore have no need to use paper patterns. In other words, maternal schooling affects the way these mothers socialize their daughters, with less emphasis placed on becoming very expert weavers as a function of maternal schooling. Interestingly, it is the mother's level of schooling that influences girls' level of expertise in weaving, not the girls' own level of schooling. Hence, it is not merely a matter of having less time to weave if you go to school; instead, maternal schooling seems to have changed mothers' socialization priorities, moving them away from the indigenous modality of informal weaving education.

Television has been the major source for bringing visual representations into Zinacantec homes. We looked to see whether it had an influence on the informal education of weaving and embroidery skills. It did: For mothers studied in 1991 and 1993, television in the home was even more strongly related than schooling to the use of paper patterns in weaving or embroidery.

Our two-generation study of weaving apprenticeship and coordinated changes in textile patterns indicates that cultural teaching is not constant.

Cultural teaching is adapted to changes in the ecocultural environment, both economic and educational. When the environment changes, changes in apprenticeship processes change to adapt to new routines and modes of thought (Greenfield, 2000; Greenfield, Maynard, & Childs, 2000, 2003).

Paper patterns can be thought of as a tool of cultural teaching. They also, as we have seen, imply new modes of cognitive representation. In the next section, we move away from ethnography and naturalistic studies to consider the connection between changing modes of cultural teaching and new modes of visual representation through the use of a series of experimental tasks. We then move, by means of a second experiment, to links between modes of informal education and cognitive development in the cultural domain of weaving.

CHANGING MODES OF CULTURAL TEACHING AND COGNITIVE DEVELOPMENT: VISUAL REPRESENTATION

Our research has established that modes of apprenticeship changed over the course of two generations in Nabenchauk, and that those changes are linked to a socioeconomic shift from agriculture to commerce. We hypothesized that there would be coordinated changes in representation such that children exposed to a more independent style of apprenticeship would be better able to represent novel patterns. We report one part of this study here (for further details, please see Greenfield et al., 2003).

In our study of visual representation, we presented participants with patterns of small wooden sticks inserted into wooden frames. Participants were 203 Zinacantec children, adolescents, and young adults, ranging in age from 3.5 to 22 with a mean age of 11.57 years. Participants from the first generation were tested in 1969 and 1970. The next generation, mainly their children, nephews, and nieces, were tested in 1991. We were interested in the ways that subjects would represent woven patterns using the sticks (not reported here), as well as the ways in which they would represent novel patterns (our current focus). Examples of novel patterns included patterns of colored, narrow sticks such as "green, green, yellow, green, green, yellow" and "red, red, green, red, red, yellow." Subjects were asked to continue the patterns using sticks from a large selection of colored sticks of different widths: thin, medium, and broad. We found a significant positive relationship between independent, trial-and-error apprenticeship and cognitive representation of novelty, such that weaving learners in those families with a more independent style of apprenticeship were better able to represent the novel patterns (Greenfield, Maynard, & Childs, 2000). As our model predicted, entrepreneurial commerce, with its intrinsic value of innovation, was associated with a shift toward an innovative model of cognitive development. Central to this model, it stresses learning to create novelty.

CULTURAL TEACHING AND COGNITIVE DEVELOPMENT

We investigated the link between modes of apprenticeship and the development of spatial skills by examining mental transformations involved in creating the warp of a loom (Maynard & Greenfield, 2003). We had observed in prior fieldwork that Zinacantec weaving tools appeared to be adapted to the developmental status of learners (Greenfield, 2000). There is a winding tool, called the toy loom (Figure 7a), adapted to younger girls who are first learning to wind a warp and a winding tool, called a warping frame (Figure 7b), adapted to older girls who have some experience in weaving. The winding tool that is adapted to older girls reflects an advanced stage of cognitive development, one that requires mental transformation. For example, one needs to understand that the left side of the threads in Figure 7b will end up at one end of a loom, for example the top of the loom shown in Figure 8a, while the right side of the threads in Figure 7b will end up at the other end of the loom, for example, the bottom of the loom shown in Figure 8a. Once this transformation is carried out, either mentally or in practice, one implication is that the resulting piece of cloth will be almost twice as long as its length on the warping frame, where it is in essence folded in half, with one half on the right side of the frame, the other half on the left side of the frame.

The winding tool that is adapted to younger girls reflects a less-advanced stage of cognitive development. This tool does not require mental transformations; the weaver simply winds the warp from top (longest stick in Figure 7a) to bottom of the loom (stick closest to weaver in Figure 7a). What you see is what you get: The length of the warp on the loom reflects the length of the resulting piece of woven cloth. We noted that parents and other weaving teachers typically assigned the less complex tool to younger learners, starting about age three, and the more complex tool to older learners, starting about age seven or eight. Note that the latter age is right squarely in the typical range for Piaget's stage of concrete operations.

We made predictions based on children's ages and experience in weaving. We predicted that children would not be able to perform mental transformations before the age of five or six years. Further, we predicted that children who did not have experience in weaving would also not be able to perform the tasks requiring mental transformations. To test this particular prediction we included subjects from Nabenchauk who had exposure to weaving, but no

Figure 7a. A toy loom. The weaver has wound her warp directly on the loom between the two end sticks. Nabenchauk, 1991. Photograph by Patricia Greenfield (2004).

Figure 7b. Warping frame, or komen, which requires mental transformation to visualize how the woven material will appear. A warp is in the process of being wound on a komen at the bottom right of the photograph. Note the rod at the left side of the komen. The threads on one side of the rod will go to one end of the loom, say the top, while the threads on the other side will go to the other, the bottom (P. M. Greenfield, 2004).

experience, namely boys, and we tested children who had neither exposure nor experience, namely American children.

We tested 160 children in Nabenchauk and Los Angeles who ranged in age from 4 to 13 years. The sample represents 80 children in each location and 80 children of each gender, balanced by location. We presented the children with multiple-choice tasks in which they were asked to examine a wound pattern and then choose its match from among an array of woven choices. We designed the answers to represent different levels of cognitive development; some answers reflected an ability to do mental transformation and others did not. There were occasionally some random answers among the choices.

We presented the subjects with two types of tasks: what we call our winding tasks and what we call our "knots" tasks. Both types of tasks included both a testing procedure followed by a "learning" procedure in which we explained to children the problems they had missed. Children were tested again immediately following the "learning" procedure. The winding tasks consisted of six looms with thread wound directly on them (an example is shown in Figure 8a). This is a direct perceptual-matching task; no mental transformation is required. The piece of cloth woven on the warp shown in Figure 8a matches the second choice to the right of the loom. There were also seven winding boards with thread wound on them (an example is shown in Figure 8b). This set included one control test and six requiring mental transformation. There were four woven cloths to choose from in matching each warp stimulus. The correct answer to the item shown in Figure 8b requires a length transformation as well as a pattern transformation; the participant must realize that when the warp is unwound and placed on a loom and woven, its length will almost double from its folded state on the warping frame as well as realizing that the stripes will be in a different configuration when they are unwound from the winding board.

The "knots" tasks were based on work by Piaget (Piaget & Inhelder, 1956). The knots were loops of string with spools of different-colored thread on them. We turned the loops into knots, or figure-eights, thus creating a situation that requires mental transformation to predict what the color configuration will be once the knot or figure-eight is unlooped. Following the pattern of the winding tasks, we presented subjects with one pattern-matching task requiring no mental transformation, and four "knots" with choices for matching, all of which required mental transformation.

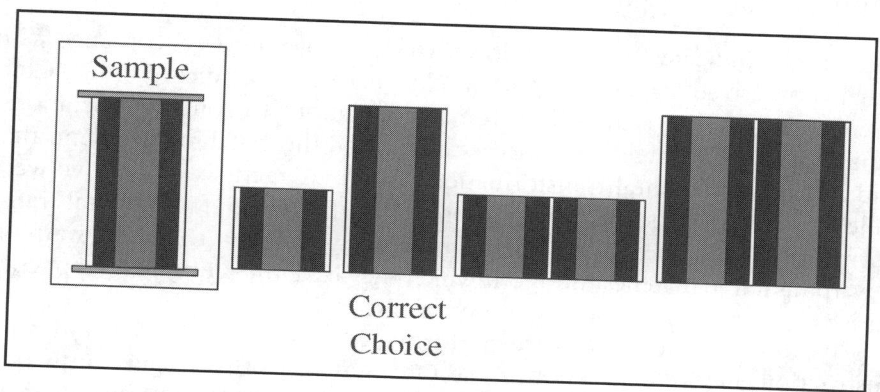

Figure 8a. An example of a loom with four choices. This is a direct perceptual-matching task. The second choice to the right of the loom is what the warp will look like when woven. (Maynard & Greenfield, 2003). Reproduced by permission of Elsevier.

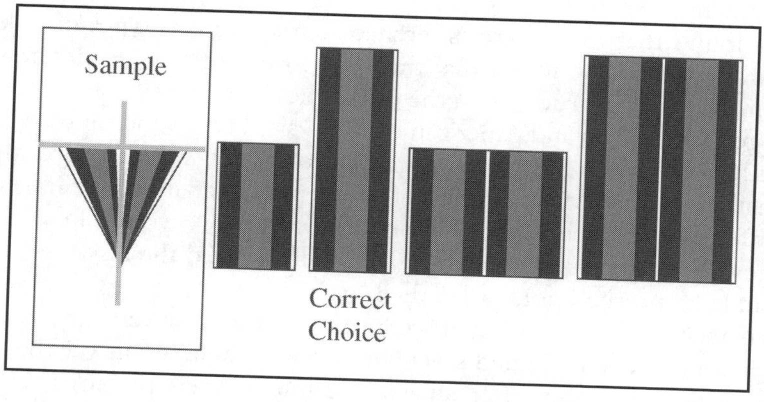

Figure 8b. An example of a komen with four choices. This is a task requiring mental transformation. The correct answer is the second choice to the right of the komen (Maynard & Greenfield, 2003). Reproduced by permission of Elsevier.

Findings: Effects of Cultural Teaching and Experience on Mental Transformation

Our results indicate that the children were performing in accordance with our hypothesized stages of cognition (Maynard & Greenfield, 2003). Children's errors reflect a transition from preoperations to concrete operations. Children under the age of six successfully solved the matching problems that did not require mental transformation. Children aged six and above were able to successfully solve matching problems that did require mental transformation. Thus, the age at which Zinacantec girls begin to wind a warp on a warping frame matches the age at which they have the requisite level of cognitive development, according to our results.

We found that there were performance differences before and after instruction. Before instruction, Zinacantec girls performed significantly better on the winding board tasks than did the Zinacantec boys or American children of either sex. This shows that only participatory experience in weaving had an impact, not the passive familiarity experienced by Zinacantec boys. Before instruction, American children performed significantly better on the knots tasks, the task less familiar to the Zinacantecs. Thus we find that each group is acquiring the ability to mentally transform spatial stimuli in the domain where they have had the most cultural experience. Cultural experience in informal education can lead to domain specificity in cognitive development.

We found that there were differences across the two types of tasks. On the winding board, we found that there were no group or sex differences in performance after instruction on the use of the cultural tool. Zinacantec children aged five and up and American children aged seven and up were able to correctly answer the "learning" question on the winding board after an explanation of the device and their previous, incorrect answers. However, an age difference remained, with US children being two years older than the youngest Zinacantec children who successfully learned the task.

Similarly, on the knots tasks, there were no group or sex differences in performance after the learning procedure. American children aged six and up and Zinacantec children aged seven and up were able to answer the "learning" question correctly after an explanation of their previous, incorrect answers. However, a similar age difference remained; children less familiar with the domain (Zinacantecs in this case) needed to be older to achieve success after the learning experience.

In this study we have found that there is an interaction between cultural teaching and maturational level; the notion of maturational readiness for cultural teaching aptly describes our results. Most interesting of all, this constraint has been built into cultural practices concerning the age at which each winding tool is appropriate for cultural teaching and learning.

THE DEVELOPMENT OF CULTURAL TEACHING

We have explored the nature of cultural teaching, its cultural development, and the effects it has on cognition and cognitive development. We now turn to the ontogenetic development of teaching skills used in informal education in Zinacantán. How do Zinacantec children become mature teachers who can successfully serve as teachers in transmitting cultural activities such as weaving?

Maynard (2002) has explored the social organization and development of teaching in childhood. She used ethnographic video and interview data to examine the development of teaching in the context of sibling caretaking interactions. Older siblings ages three to eleven years of age were observed as they engaged their younger, two-year-old siblings in everyday activities. Children were observed playing out a number of everyday scenarios, such as making tortillas or cooking other types of food, caring for baby dolls, or playing soccer. The older siblings provided verbal and nonverbal guidance to incorporate the two-year-olds into the sibling group activity. The children's verbal and nonverbal behaviors were analyzed by discourse analysis using a coding system designed to examine the development of teaching. The verbal discourse variables were: commands; commands issued from a distance; explanations/justifications for activities; and feedback on the child's performance. The nonverbal discourse variables were: simplifying the task for the learner; and guiding the learner's body in the desired task. One variable that involves the coordination of both verbal and nonverbal information is talk with demonstration; that is, when a sibling describes his/her action while performing the task.

The oldest sibling caretakers, ages 8 to 11, were able to structure tasks, provide necessary materials, simplify tasks into doable parts, guide the bodies of learners, and provide both verbal and nonverbal feedback to help their youngest siblings do a task. The six- and seven-year-olds also could set up materials, but their teaching involved many directives without much task simplification, explanations, or feedback. The three- to five-year-old children mainly served as observational models, engaging in side-by-side activities with learners. It is clear that elements of the adult Zinacantec model of teaching do not develop all at once. Instead, the elements develop sequentially as children get older.

Consistent with the Zinacantec model of teaching and learning, the siblings in the study often organized themselves into groups, rather than dyads (Maynard, 2004b). This afforded the analysis of the ways that children of different ages organized themselves to support the learning of the two-year-old focal children. While the oldest child present took a managerial role, each of the other children contributed to the teaching of the toddler according to his or her own developmental level.

The learners made use of all the information coming from each teacher present. In one typical multiage learning situation, the learner often referenced the behavior of a four-year-old to see how to do a task, used the materials delivered by a six-year-old, and followed the didactic instructions of the eight-year-old present, who was in charge of all the children. Overall, learners often acquired cultural knowledge from more than one teacher, each of whom taught according to his or her own skill level and social status.

Within the social organization, younger children showed an acute sensitivity to the social status of older children. The hierarchical relationships exhibited in children's play are the foundation for the later, Zinacantec adult relationships described by Vogt (1969). Children observed the modes of behavior of their older siblings and then adopted the appropriate behaviors themselves.

The study of the development of children's teaching informs our knowledge of the social and cognitive skills children acquire and use in informal education. Ethnographic inquiry and discourse analysis of moment-by-moment processes led to the finding that children teach each other everyday cultural skills, with the most significant gains in the 8–11-year-old group. Minimal schooling had effects on children's strategies in that schooled children used more discourse in their teaching and taught more often from a distance than did unschooled children (Maynard, 2004a).

The combination of naturalistic methods also led to another important finding: that children can learn from more than one teacher in their joint activities. Teaching and learning do not necessarily imply a didactic, one-teacher model of cultural transmission. Most important, this study shows that teaching, and not just learning, develops.

The ways that the children in this study taught their younger siblings reflect the Zinacantec adult way of teaching more advanced skills, such as weaving (Maynard, 1996; Maynard & Greenfield, in press). First, there is often more than one teacher to help a learner. Second, just as there was no criticism or praise in Zinacantec parent-child apprenticeship processes, there is also none in these children's teaching. The elements of the adult model do not come in all at the same time; the model develops. Thus scaffolding, which requires an understanding of the other's lesser competency in the situation, is relatively late to develop; it is the norm by age eight, when older siblings are very good at helping two-year-olds achieve success at various tasks. Moving the body also occurs as a teaching technique when needed in the two older age groups (six to seven and eight to eleven). Talk about how to do a task is always contextualized (when the task is being performed), but talk about the task at hand increases greatly at age eight. Further research in other cultures is warranted to explore the development of different modes of cultural teaching.

Children's participation in activities with their siblings and peers leads to their acquisition of culturally important skills. Siblings pass on the shared culture of the family and their family's daily routine. Peer teaching and its consequent socialization are probably ways that all children internalize information and culture. The cross-cultural study of cultural teaching in children's sibling and peer interactions is an important step in our discovery of the development of the core processes of cultural transmission in the context of informal education (Maynard, 2004a).

CONCLUSIONS

In this chapter, we have explored the nature, effects, and development of cultural teaching and learning. Cultural teaching adapts to changing ecocultural circumstances; parents and siblings socialize children in adaptation to a changing world. Cultures develop fairly general models of cultural teaching that are the foundation for further adaptation to environmental change. There is a connection between the adaptive modes of cultural teaching and particular emphases in cognitive development. From an evolutionary perspective, adaptation of informal education to a changing environment is connected to cognitive ontogeny. Active participation in learning in a particular domain leads to cognitive development in that domain. Further experience with a given cognitive skill in a new domain can lead to cross-domain generalizations of the skill in question. At the same time, cultural teaching also respects the constraints of cognitive maturation. Cultural teaching is not merely a fixed feature of the child's environment. It is provided by human beings who have developed the ability to teach according to a particular cultural model with techniques and tools adapted to the developmental level of the learner.

ACKNOWLEDGMENTS

This research was supported by the Harvard Center for Cognitive Studies (Jerome Bruner, Co-Director); the Harvard Chiapas Project (directed by Evon Z. Vogt); the Bunting Institute of Radcliffe College; the Milton Fund of Harvard University; the Spencer Foundation; the National Geographic Society; the UCLA Latin American Center; the UCLA Center for Culture and Health; National Institutes of Health Fogarty International Center's Minority International Research Training Program; El Colegio de la Frontera Sur, San Cristobal de las Casas, Chiapas, Mexico; and the UCLA Academic

Senate. Ashley Maynard was supported during data collection by graduate research fellowships from the National Science Foundation (1995–1998) and the Center for the Study of Evolution and the Origin of Life (CSEOL) at UCLA (1995–1997), a dissertation-year fellowship (1998–1999), and a postdoctoral fellowship (1999–2001) from the University of California Office of the President. We would like to express appreciation to Leslie Devereaux, who helped in many different aspects of the fieldwork. Thanks also to field research assistants Matthew Greenfield, Lauren Greenfield, and Hannah Carlson. We thank our friends and study participants in Nabenchauk and our assistants, the late Xun Pavlu and Maruc Chentik.

REFERENCES

Bentler, P. M. (1980). Multivariate analysis with latent variables: Causal modeling. *Annual Review of Psychology,* 31: 419–56.

Bentler, P. M. (1995). *EQS: Structural equation program manual.* Encino, CA: Multivariate Software Inc.

Childs, C. P., & Greenfield, P. M. (1980). Informal modes of learning and teaching: The case of Zinacanteco weaving. In N. Warren (Ed.), *Studies in cross-cultural psychology* (Vol. 2, pp. 269–316). London: Academic Press.

Collier, G. A. (1990). *Seeking food and seeking money: Changing productive relations in a Highland Mexican community.* Discussion Paper 11, United Nations Research Institute for Social Development.

Edelstein, W. (1983). *Cultural constraints on development and the vicissitudes of progress.* Housten Symposium: The child and other cultural conventions, Max Planck Institute of Human Development and Education, Berlin. Praeger Publishers, pp. 48–81.

Edelstein, W. (1999). The cognitive context of historical change: Assimilation, accommodation, and the segmentation of competence. In E. Turiel (Ed.), *Development and cultural change: Reciprocal processes: New Directions in Child and Adolescent Development.* San Francisco: Jossey-Bass.

Greenfield, P. M. (1984). A theory of the teacher in the learning activities of everyday life. In B. Rogoff & J. Lave (Eds.), *Everyday cognition: Its development in social context* (pp. 117–38). Cambridge, MA: Harvard University Press.

Greenfield, P. M. (2000). Children, material culture, and weaving: Historical change and developmental change. In J. S. Derevenski (Ed.), *Children and material culture* (pp. 72–86). London: Routledge.

Greenfield, P. M., & Childs, C. P. (1991). Developmental continuity in biocultural context. In R. Cohen & A. W. Siegel (Eds.), *Context and development* (pp. 135–59). Hillsdale, NJ: Erlbaum.

Greenfield, P. M., & Lave, J. (1982). Cognitive aspects of informal education. In D. Wagner & H. Stevenson (Eds.), *Cultural perspectives on child development.* (pp. 181–207). San Francisco: Freeman.

Greenfield, P. M., & Maynard, A. E. (November, 1997). Women, girls, apprenticeship, and schooling: A longitudinal study of historical change among the Zinacantecan Maya. In I. Zambrano (Chair), Symposium entitled: Women's Schooling in Maya

Chiapas: Naming the Unnamed. 96th Annual Meeting of the American Anthropological Association. Washington, D.C.

Greenfield, P. M., Maynard, A. E., & Childs, C. P. (2000). History, culture, learning, and development. *Cross-Cultural Research: The Journal of Comparative Social Science. Special Issue in Honor of Ruth Munroe,* 34(4): 351–74.

Greenfield, P. M., Maynard, A. E., & Childs, C. P. (2003). Historical change, cultural apprenticeship, and cognitive representation in Zinacantec Maya children. *Cognitive Development, 18:* 455–87.

Greenfield, P. M., Reich, L. C., & Olver, R. R. (1966). On culture and equivalence—II. In J. S. Bruner, R. R. Olver, P. M. Greenfield, et al., *Studies in cognitive growth* (pp. 270–318). New York: Wiley.

Lancy, D. (1996). Playing on the mother ground: Cultural routines for children's development. New York: Guilford Press.

Laosa, L. M. (1978). Maternal teaching strategies in Chicano families of varied educational and socioeconomic levels. *Child Development,* 49: 1129–35.

Lerner, D. (1958). *The passing of traditional society: Modernizing the Middle East.* Glencoe, IL: Free Press.

Maynard, A. E. (1996). An ethnomodel of teaching and learning: Apprenticeship of Zinacantec Maya women's tasks. Unpublished masters thesis. University of California, Los Angeles.

Maynard, A. E. (2002). Cultural teaching: The development of teaching skills in Maya sibling interactions. *Child Development,* 73(3): 969–82.

Maynard, A. E. (2004a). Cultures of teaching in childhood: Formal schooling and Maya sibling teaching at home. *Cognitive Development,* 19 (3).

Maynard, A. E. (2004b). Sibling interactions as preparation for adult life: Social organization and development. University of Hawai'i, Honolulu, Hawai'i.

Maynard, A. E., & Greenfield, P. M. (2003). Implicit cognitive development in cultural tools and children: Lessons from Mayan Mexico. *Cognitive Development,* 18: 489–510.

Maynard, A. E., & Greenfield, P. M. (in press). An ethnomodel of teaching and learning: Apprenticeship of Zinacantec Maya women's tasks. To appear in A. E. Maynard & M. I. Martini (Eds.), *Learning in cultural context: Family, peers, and school* (pp. 75–103). Kluwer Academic/Plenum Publishers.

McClelland, D. C. (1961). *The achieving society.* New York: Free Press.

Piaget, J., & Inhelder, B. (1956). *The child's conception of space.* London: Routledge and Kegan Paul.

Renshaw, P. D., & Gardner, R. (1990). Process versus product task interpretation and parental teaching practice. *International Journal of Behavioral Development,* 13: 489–505.

Rogoff, B. (1990). *Apprenticeship in thinking: Cognitive development in social context.* New York: Oxford University Press.

Seymour, S. C. (1999). *Women, family, and child care in India: A world in transition.* Cambridge: Cambridge University Press.

Tapia Uribe, F. M., LeVine, R. A., & LeVine, S. E. (1994). Maternal behavior in a Mexican community: The changing environments of children. In P. M. Greenfield & R. R. Cocking (Eds.), *Cross-cultural roots of minority child development* (pp. 41–54). Hillsdale, NJ: Erlbaum.

Tomasello, M., Kruger, A. C., & Ratner, H. H. (1993). Cultural learning. *Behavioral and Brian Sciences, 16,* 495–552.

Vogt, E. Z. (1969). *Zinacantán: A Maya community in the highlands of Chiapas.* Cambridge, MA: Harvard University Press.

Zukow, P. G. (1984). Folk theories of comprehension and caregiver practices in a rural-born population in Central Mexico. *Quarterly Newsletter of the Laboratory of Comparative Human Cognition,* 6: 62–67.

"THIS IS OUR SCHOOL OF CITIZENSHIP"

INFORMAL LEARNING IN LOCAL DEMOCRACY

DANIEL SCHUGURENSKY

INTRODUCTION

In educational discourse, informal learning is usually conceptualized as a residual category of a residual category. If formal education refers to the institutional ladder that goes from preschool to graduate studies, and nonformal education refers to any organized educational activity that takes place outside the formal education system (e.g., short courses, workshops, professional development, etc.), then informal learning often becomes a loose category that encompasses "anything else" that is not included in the previous two. Given this characterization, it is not surprising that informal learning is at the margins of the margins of the educational conceptual and research radar. Indeed, most research and policy initiatives still tend to concentrate efforts in formal education, and to a lesser extent in nonformal education. Informal learning is often undervalued and seldom recognized.[1]

Meanwhile, in terms of our understanding of processes and outcomes, informal learning is still largely a black box. This is unfortunate, because much of the relevant (in the sense of personally meaningful and significant) learning acquired throughout our lives occurs in the area of informal learning. This certainly applies to the area of political and civic learning, and particularly to the learning required to act effectively in processes of participatory democracy. This chapter examines the informal civic and political learning that occurs in local processes of deliberation and decision making. It is organized in two main sections. The first advances a conceptual discussion on informal learning. The second, drawing on situated learning theories and participatory democracy theory and practice, analyzes the pedagogical dimensions of the participatory budget of Porto Alegre, Brazil, an experiment in local democracy that has been in place since 1989.

INFORMAL LEARNING: A CONCEPTUAL FRAMEWORK

Taxonomies are always somewhat rigid and incapable of capturing the complexities of real life, or, in this case, the complexities of learning processes. However, since informal learning is typically conceptualized in contrast to formal and nonformal education, a brief description of these two systems can help us to identify what informal learning is not and to begin an exploration of what informal learning is.[2] Formal education refers to a highly institutionalized system that goes from preschool to graduate studies. In most societies, the formal education system includes a period called "basic education" (which varies from country to county but usually ranges from 6 to 12 years of schooling), and is often compulsory. The formal education system is often organized as a top-down system, with ministries of education at the top and students at the bottom. With a few exceptions, schools are supposed to deliver a prescribed curriculum—normally developed or at least approved by the state—with explicit goals and evaluation mechanisms. The state also regulates many of the activities conducted in schools, and is the main provider of funding. The system relies on certified teachers, and after competing successfully each level and grade, students are granted a diploma or certificate that allows them to be accepted into the next grade or level, or into the formal labor market.

Nonformal education refers to all organized educational programs that take place outside the formal school system, and are usually short-term and voluntary. This includes a wide variety of programs that can range from political workshops to tennis courses, second language programs, driving lessons, cooking classes, yoga classes, rehabilitation programs, painting courses, training programs, or professional development. As in formal education, there are teachers (also called instructors or facilitators), and a curriculum with various degrees of rigidity or flexibility. However, nonformal education can also take place without the presence of a teacher. This would be the case, for instance, of study groups that meet regularly with the main purpose of learning something, and whose members plan meetings in advance and rotate responsibilities for preparation and presentation, and so on. Unlike formal education, nonformal education programs do not normally demand prerequisites in terms of previous schooling. Sometimes a diploma certifying attendance or competence is granted, like in the case of a second language, a sport, or driving lessons. Nonformal education is usually directed to adults (and sometimes it is even equated with adult education), but children and adolescents may also participate in this sector through a variety of activities such as evening music lessons, weekend religious classes, scouting programs, heritage language courses, and the like. The term "nonformal education," widely used in educational circles, is not necessarily a good descriptor, not only because it is a negative definition but also because it implicitly suggests that it is second-rate in relation to the formal system. Hopefully a better label will arise in the future to "name" this sector for what it is, and not for what it is not.

After this brief portrayal of formal and nonformal education, we can now examine the remaining category, informal learning. The attentive reader probably has noticed already that in the case of the formal and nonformal sectors I am talking about "education," while in the third category I am using the term "learning." The choice is deliberate, because the first two sectors usually involve some degree of institutional design and organized teaching efforts, while in the third this is not the case. Following Livingstone (1999, 2001), informal learning can be defined as the learning that occurs outside the curricula of educational institutions, or the courses or workshops offered by educational or social agencies. It is pertinent to note that Livingstone does not say "outside educational institutions" but outside the curricula provided by formal and nonformal educational institutions and programs. This is a relevant distinction, because many things that students may learn in school that are not part of the prescribed curriculum (be it in terms of teacher-student dynamics or student-student dynamics) could be considered "informal learning." This encompasses a wide variety of learning, such as patterns of authority or democracy, dynamics of discrimination, and other elements of the hidden curriculum ranging from the architectural design and classroom seating arrangements to rituals and routines. It also includes learning through interaction with classmates, who bring to the school learning acquired somewhere else. This conceptualization implies that informal learning occurs throughout life from cradle to grave, and hence it is not an exclusive domain of adult education. It also implies the need to distinguish between informal learning and informal settings, as these two concepts are often conflated. Such conflation leads to confusion, because it tends to assume that all informal learning is acquired in informal settings. However, as it was noted earlier, while significant learning occurs in informal settings (workplace, media, friends, family, religious groups, neighborhood associations, sport teams, political parties, ethnic associations, etc.), informal learning can also occur in formal and nonformal settings. Hence, informal learning refers to all that learning that is not organized as a pedagogical activity by an educational institution, and it can happen both outside and within educational institutions.[3]

In short, informal learning entails more than the learning that occurs outside the walls of educational institutions, because informal learning can also occur in formal and nonformal educational sites. At the same time, this understanding recognizes that formal and nonformal learning can also occur outside the physical confines of formal and nonformal institutions. An example of this is distance education, be it through correspondence, radio, TV, or computers. In any case, regardless of its location, within informal learning itself, three main forms can be identified: self-directed, incidental, and socialization.

THE FORMS OF INFORMAL LEARNING

Taking the perspective of the learner, and considering simultaneously the categories of intention and consciousness, the following taxonomy of informal learning can be developed.[4]

Self-directed learning refers to "learning projects" undertaken by individuals (alone or as part of a group) without the presence of some form of an instructor, teacher, or facilitator officially recognized as such by an educational institution. However, it can include the presence of a "resource person" who does not regard herself or himself as an educator. Self-directed learning is both intentional and conscious. It is intentional because the individual has the purpose of learning something even before the learning process begins, and it is conscious in the sense that the individual is aware that she or he has learned something. Because of the influential research conducted by Allen Tough (1971) on self-directed projects, for many years there was a tendency to use informal learning and self-directed learning as equivalent. While this is probably one of the most typical expressions of informal learning (and the easiest to capture through research, because it is intentional and conscious), it is not necessarily the only one. Indeed, informal learning can also take at least two other forms: incidental learning and socialization.

	Intentionality	Awareness (at the time of learning experience)
Self-directed	yes	yes
Incidental	no	yes
Socialization	no	no

Table 1: The Forms of Informal Learning

Incidental learning refers to those learning experiences that occur when the learner did not have any previous intention of learning something out of that experience, but after the experience she or he becomes aware that some learning has taken place. As Table 1 suggests, incidental learning is unintentional but conscious.

Socialization refers to the internalization of values, attitudes, behaviors, skills, etc., that occur unconsciously during everyday life. This learning process, often unplanned and unconscious, is often conceptualized as tacit learning. In a pioneering book entitled precisely *The Tacit Dimension*, Polanyi (1966) characterizes tacit knowledge as "that which we know but cannot tell." In an earlier text, Polanyi (1958) notes that tacit knowledge is difficult to identify and to express, and remains inarticulate. Learning a language as a child, for instance, implies a vibrant, rich, and complex tacit system of symbols and rules. This tacit dimension underpins and shapes many subsequent learning processes. It is assumed yet unidentified by the subject. For instance, when we talk, we pay attention to the idea that we want to express, and are only tacitly aware of the rules of grammar and syntax that we are using. A similar process occurs when we play piano, as we are very much aware of the music, but only tacitly aware of the fingers on the keys. Likewise, when we ride a bicycle, we concentrate on our speed and on the traffic, and are only tacitly aware of the basic rules of equilibrium that allow us not to lose balance. In Polanyi's words (1958, p. 50), "rules of art can be useful, but they do not determine the practice of an art." Another interesting example of tacit knowledge posed by Polanyi is when a medical doctor makes a diagnosis of a patient. In order to assess the health of this particular person, the doctor pulls together a vast amount of previous experience and knowledge, but is rarely consciously aware of that knowledge and would find it difficult to articulate it in words.

In the process of learning through socialization, not only do we have not have an "a priori" intention of acquiring them but we also are not aware that we have learned something at the time of the learning experience. This process, then, is unintentional and unconscious. It is pertinent to note that although learning through socialization is usually an unconscious process, we can become aware of that learning later on through a process of retrospective recognition, which could be internal and/or external. For instance, by being exposed to a different social environment, a person can be prompted to recognize that she or he has certain prejudices and biases that were the products of primary socialization. Likewise, some people may not be aware that they have learned something in a particular experience until they have a conversation with a person who asks questions about their learning, eliciting retrospective recognition. This is often the case in the area of informal civic and political learning (Schugurensky & Myers, 2003). One insightful perspective to examine this process is situated learning.

SITUATED LEARNING AND COMMUNITIES OF PRACTICE

Following the contributions of authors such as Vygotsky, Dewey, Bandura, and others to social learning theories, situated learning theories, and experiential learning, we can suggest that learning cannot be isolated from the activity, the culture, and the context in which it takes place. We also can suggest that knowledge is socially constructed and that learning often occurs in social interaction. As Berger and Luckman (1966) pointed out in their classic work, our understanding of reality is a social construct intimately connected to human intersubjectivity and everyday life, and shaped by complex processes of externalization, objectivation, and internalization.

From a situated learning perspective, learners are involved in "communities of practice" that embody a set of values, behaviors, and skills to be acquired by members. This involvement is seldom homogeneous, because people do not usually enter these communities of practice at the same time, and thus an informal system of apprenticeship is often established. As "apprentices" (or beginners, newcomers) move progressively from the periphery of these communities to their center, they become more active and engaged with the culture, and with time they assume the role of "masters" (or experts, old-timers). Furthermore, the literature on this topic reveals that most of this situated learning is unintentional and hence it is incidental rather than deliberate. For instance, in a study conducted by Gear et al. (1994), it was reported that, in spite of using Tough's concept of intentional learning projects to ask about informal learning, 80% of the learning episodes mentioned by their interviewees were not intentionally sought. Similar findings have been reported by Brown, Collins, and Duguid (1989), and by Lave and Wenger (1990). Likewise, Foley (1999, p. 1), in a recent study on informal learning in social action, argues that "the most interesting and significant learning occurs informally and incidentally, in people's everyday lives." Comparable insights are provided by the social movement learning tradition (Adams, 1980; Horton & Freire, 1990).

As Jonassen (1994) points out, situated learning takes place when learners work on authentic and realistic tasks that reflect the real world. The knowledge content and the capacities developed are determined by the demands of the real world and the particular context in which learners are interacting. If knowledge is decontextualized, as happens in many classrooms all over the world, then knowledge becomes inert, and students learn new concepts but may have difficulties applying them in the absence of a real context for its use. This constructivist approach applies also to the learning of citizenship and democracy, the topic of this chapter. Although it may sound like a cliché, it is no less true that one of the best ways to learn democracy is by doing it, and one of the best ways to develop effective civic and political skills is by observing them in the real world and exercising them. In other words, it seems that the old model of apprenticeship, based on observation, modeling, trial and error, and regular social interaction still has something to contribute today to educational theory and practice.

From a Freirean perspective, education is not understood exclusively as a schooling process, but also as an experience-learning process that takes place in daily life and in a variety of community spaces. One of those community spaces is participatory democracy, understood not as pseudoconsultation mechanisms and tokenistic arrangements (see Arnstein, 1969), but to genuine processes of deliberation that are bound to real and substantive decisions.

LEARNING BY DOING: CITIZENSHIP LEARNING AND PARTICIPATORY DEMOCRACY

The idea that the very act of participating in deliberation and decision making has a high pedagogical potential can be traced back at least to Aristotle, and was clearly formulated by Rousseau. As Carole Pateman (1970) noted in her classic book on participatory democracy, the central function of participation in Rousseau's theory is an educative one, using the term "education" in the same wide sense that permeates Freirean thought. Rousseau's ideal system, says Pateman, is designed to develop responsible, individual social, and political action through the effect of the participatory process itself. Along the same lines as Rousseau, J. S. Mill also identified the educative function of participation in local governance.

For Mill, who wrote during the mid-1800s in England, it was at the local level where the real educative effect of participation occurs. This is because the issues dealt with at this level directly affect the individuals and their everyday life, and also because it is at this level where ordinary citizens stand a better chance of being elected by their peers to serve on a local body or committee. It is by participating at the local level, claims Mills, that the individual really "learns democracy." In his own words,

> We do not learn to read or write, to ride or swim, by merely being told how to do it, but by doing it, so it is only by practising popular government on a limited scale that the people will ever learn how to exercise it on a larger one. (Mill, 1963, p. 186, quoted in Pateman, 1988 [1970], p. 31)

Like Mill, G. D. H. Cole argued that it is through participation at the local level and in local associations that people could learn democracy more effectively: "Over the vast mechanism of modern politics the individual has no control, not because the state is too big, but because he [*sic*] is given no chance of learning the rudiments of self-government within a smaller unit" (1919, p. 157) (quoted in Pateman 1988 [1970], p. 38). For Cole, the most appropriate space for the educative effect of participation was industry, because individuals are involved in relationships of superiority and subordination, and because they spend a great deal of their time there.

Following Rousseau, Mill, and Cole, Pateman contends that the existence of representative institutions at national levels is not sufficient for democracy. She argues that other spheres nurturing political socialization (what she calls "social training") for the development of the individual attitudes and psychological qualities that are necessary for good quality participation need to be created and invigorated. Since 1989, one of these new spheres, known in Brazil as a public, nonstate sphere ("esfera publica, no estatal"), is the participatory budget of Porto Alegre, referred to later on in this chapter.

For now, let us remember that in Pateman's framework, the justification for a democratic system in the participatory theory of democracy rests not so much in its effectiveness for governance but primarily on the human results (particularly political learning) that are accrued from the participatory process. She characterizes the participatory model as one where maximum input (participation) is required, and where output includes not just policies (decisions) but also the development of the social and political capacities of each individual. This means that political capacity is both a result and a precondition for good participation, and that there is constant "feedback" from output to input (Pateman, 1988 [1970], p. 43). For Pateman, a central point in her theory is that once the participatory system is established, it becomes self-sustaining because the very qualities that are required of individual citizens if the system is to work successfully are precisely those that the process of participation develops and fosters. Hence, in a virtuous circle, the more the individual citizen participates, the better able she or he is able to participate (Pateman, 1988 [1970], p. 25). The development of political capacities, then, takes place through the process of participation itself, and this is certainly a process of informal learning:

> The major function of participation in the theory of participatory democracy is therefore an educative one, and educative in the very widest sense, including both the psychological aspect and the gaining of practice in democratic skills and procedures. Thus there is no special problem about the stability of a participatory system; it is self-sustaining through the educative impact of the participatory process. Participation develops and fosters the very qualities necessary for it; the more individuals participate the better able they become to do so. Subsidiary

> hypotheses about participation are that it has an integrative effect and that it aids the acceptance of collective decisions. (Pateman 1988 [1970], pp. 42–43)

THE NATURE OF INFORMAL CITIZENSHIP LEARNING IN LOCAL DEMOCRACY

The last quote by Pateman suggests that one important learning dimension has to do with the development of certain psychological attitudes that nurture more participation. These psychological attitudes are closely connected to increases in political efficacy, that is, the confidence in one's capacity to influence political decisions. One of the earliest definitions on political efficacy was the one advanced by Campbell, Gurin, and Miller (1954). For them, political efficacy refers to the feeling that individual political action does have, or can have, an impact upon the political process. In other words, it is the feeling that engaging in civic action is worthwhile. Regardless of the scope of the political system, which seems to be crucial in terms of psychological effects, is the ability and power of a group to influence a decision.

Given the spread of the so-called democratic deficit expressed in high levels of electoral absenteeism and low confidence in political institutions, there is an urgent need for ordinary citizens to learn political efficacy by participating in politics. As Pierre Bourdieu (1991) pointed out, the fact that the political field is monopolized by professional politicians is not a natural phenomenon and can be challenged through social action. This is particularly important for lower income groups, since studies of political efficacy usually find a correlation among socioeconomic status, political efficacy, and political participation: lower income groups tend to have a lower sense of political efficacy, and tend to participate less. Hence, the educative effect of participation for the development of political efficacy is especially relevant for those groups who are underrepresented in participatory democracy and have less experience with these processes.

However, the change in psychological attitudes is not the only educative effect. For instance, Rousseau, Mill, and Pateman also emphasized the broadening of outlook and interests and the appreciation of the connection between private and public interests. They also noted the gaining of familiarity with democratic procedures and the learning of democratic skills, the relationship between local decisions and the wider social and political environment, and the influence of the broader social and political environment on the local reality. Moreover, beyond individual learning, it could be argued that the group as a collective learns too, as it becomes to be more integrated, more fair in its procedures and criteria, and more willing to reach and accept consensus.

The learning that is acquired through participation (be it related to attitudes, knowledge, or skills) often has an expansive effect. This means that, as people become more familiar with, and more effective in, local democracy, they also become more interested (and even more engaged) in broader issues of regional, national, or international scope. Early research on this topic, undertaken by Kojala (1965) with the Yugoslavian Workers' Councils as a case study, has shown that over time participants move from discussing ways to manage their most immediate environment to dealing with policy issues and decisions that transcend their immediate environment.

Indeed, participation in local governance nurtures a wider educative effect because it broadens interests and outlooks and develops more practical capacities for political participation. Such participation, and the consequent learning that derives from it, fosters the development of more informed, critical, and engaged citizens who are eager to learn more and to take on larger challenges. As citizens become more enlightened, empowered, and confident, they become ready to go beyond their circle and become more active in other spheres. Important in this regard is the shift from passivity to the feeling of agency. Drawing on Cole, Pateman argues that industrial working relations nurture obedience and passivity, and that through self-governance and workplace democracy people can acquire the democratic skills and virtues that are necessary to participate in the larger system:

> Only if the individual could become self-governing in the workplace, only if industry was organised on a participatory basis, could this training for servility be turned into training for democracy and the individual could gain the familiarity with democratic procedures and develop the necessary "democratic character" for an effective system of large-scale democracy. (Pateman 1988 [1970], pp. 38–39)

Although many participants may still be more interested in local affairs, their new learning assists them to be better able to assess the performance of national representatives, to weigh the impact of decisions taken by national representatives on their own lives and their immediate surroundings, and to take decisions of national scope when the opportunity arises.

Another aspect of this expansive effect is the transition from narrow self-interest to the common good, and from looking only at one's street as the center of the universe to a more comprehensive understanding of the community as a whole. In this regard, it can be argued that there is a connection between agency and the development of civic skills and virtues. For instance, Rousseau claimed that through the participatory process citizens learn to take into account wider matters than their own immediate private interests because of the need to gain cooperation from others, and learn that the public and private interests are linked. For Rousseau, the logic of the participatory system is such that citizens are forced to deliberate according to their own sense of justice, and they have to reach a common ground in order to make the deliberation possible. Along the same lines, Mill noted that when individuals are solely concerned with their own private affairs and do not participate in public affairs, then the "self-regarding" virtues suffer, and the capacities for responsible public action remain undeveloped. Conversely, when citizens participate in public affairs, they are forced to widen their horizons and to take the public interest into account. Then, as a result of participating in decision making, individuals learn to identify their own impulses and desires, and learn to be public as well as private citizens (Pateman 1988 [1970], p. 25). A case in point is the participatory budget of Porto Alegre, Brazil.

INFORMAL LEARNING THROUGH THE PARTICIPATORY BUDGET

The participatory budget (PB) of Porto Alegre has been in continuous development since its inception in 1989. Its institutional features have been discussed extensively in the literature (see, for instance, Abers, 2000; Genro, 2001; Baierle, 1998; Schugurensky, 2001a, 2001b). In a nutshell, the PB is an open and democratic process of participation that allows ordinary citizens to make decisions together on municipal budget allocations. This includes neighborhood discussions and decisions about priorities regarding investments in local infrastructure, such as pavement, sewage, storm drains, schools, healthcare, childcare, housing, and so on. It also includes thematic forums on citywide issues such as transit and public transportation, health and social assistance, economic development and taxation, urban development, education, culture, and leisure. While the model is far from perfect, the PB has promoted a more efficient, transparent, and accountable administration of public resources, an outstanding achievement in itself in the context of Latin America. By using equity criteria in budget allocations and bottom-up processes, it has also improved the living conditions of poor communities by reversing previous priorities that used to favor higher income areas.

These are important accomplishments that have inspired participatory budget models in many progressive municipalities in Brazil and abroad. However, there is another accomplishment that is particularly fascinating, especially from an educator's viewpoint. This accomplishment relates to the informal learning that is acquired throughout the participatory process, a dimension that is often hidden, seldom recognized, and largely unexplored

(Schugurensky, 2002). This informal learning has nurtured the empowerment of neighborhood associations and popular organizations and the development of a new democratic culture that eliminated political clientelism (the typical exchange of favors for votes). This learning has also promoted the ownership of projects by the community, the preservation of public property, the revitalization of civic life, and an increase in citizen participation, community organizing, and political activism. Moreover, this learning is largely acquired by those who need it the most. Unlike many other experiments of participatory democracy, whose members tend to be predominantly middle class and male, in the PB of Porto Alegre the majority of participants are female and from low-income groups.

In order to explore this learning, I interviewed 30 delegates of the PB and identified 28 indicators of civic and political informal learning acquired through their participation. These were grouped in three areas: knowledge (9 indicators), skills (9 indicators), and attitudes (10 indicators):[5]

Civic and Political Knowledge

K1. city government (e.g., "how things get done")
K2. needs of your community or group
K3. direct knowledge of city councilors
K4. municipal politics, local affairs
K5. jurisdictional differences (municipal, provincial, and federal jurisdictions)
K6. criteria and processes for allocation of public resources
K7. people of other neighborhoods and organizations
K8. needs of other communities and groups
K9. your citizen rights and duties

Civic and Political Skills

S1. public speaking
S2. listening carefully to others
S3. negotiating, bargaining, building alliances
S4. persuading, arguing, building an argument
S5. team work, cooperation
S6. contacting government agencies
S7. understanding and interpreting official documents
S8. ranking priorities, developing local projects
S9. conflict resolution

Civic and Political Attitudes

A1. self-confidence
A2. tolerance and respect
A3. trust in politicians
A4. trust in municipal government

A5. willingness to help others (solidarity)
A6. confidence in your capacity to influence political decisions (political efficacy)
A7. concern for the problems of the city (caring)
A8. potencial to participate in municipal government
A9. interest in community participation
A10. responsibility for preservation of city

Using a 5-point Likert scale, interviewees were asked to rate their knowledge, skills, and attitudes before participating in the participatory budget process, and at the moment of the interview. For each indicator, whenever a change was indicated, they were asked to elaborate on their learning experience and to provide concrete examples. Figure 1 summarizes the learning acquired in the process. The bottom part of the bars indicates the self-perceived starting point at the time of joining the process, and the top part depicts the actual learning that, according to participants, occurred through the process.

As can be noted, in some areas the changes reported by the participants were minimal (e.g., A3 "trust in politicians" remained low), but for the most part the changes were significant. Since this table presents an average, it does not reflect the variation of change among participants. Depending on their previous experience and the context in which they interact, people learned different things; in some cases the learning or the change was relatively modest, in others there was no change at all, and in others it was really impressive. For some participants the perceived change was so large (particularly in relation to certain knowledge and skills), that they remarked during the interview that they went from 0 (zero) to seven or eight, something that a 1–5 point scale was obviously unable to capture. In general terms, though, changes were larger in terms of knowledge and skills than in attitudes. In some cases, the relatively low change in civic attitudes was due to the fact that participants perceived themselves as already highly rated in these areas before joining this process. For instance, most of them had already an inclination to help others (A5), and to tolerate and respect those who think differently (A2). In terms of knowledge, there was significant learning in most areas, particularly in reference to criteria and processes for budget allocations (K6), which is at the crux of the model. Changes were also noticeable in relation to knowing city councilors (K3), and knowing people from other groups and neighborhoods as well as their needs (K7 and K8). In the area of skills, most self-perceived learning occurred in relation to public speaking (S1), to the ability to make alliances and negotiate solutions with other groups (S3), the capacity to contact government agencies when needed (S6), and the ranking of priorities and developing local projects accordingly (S8).

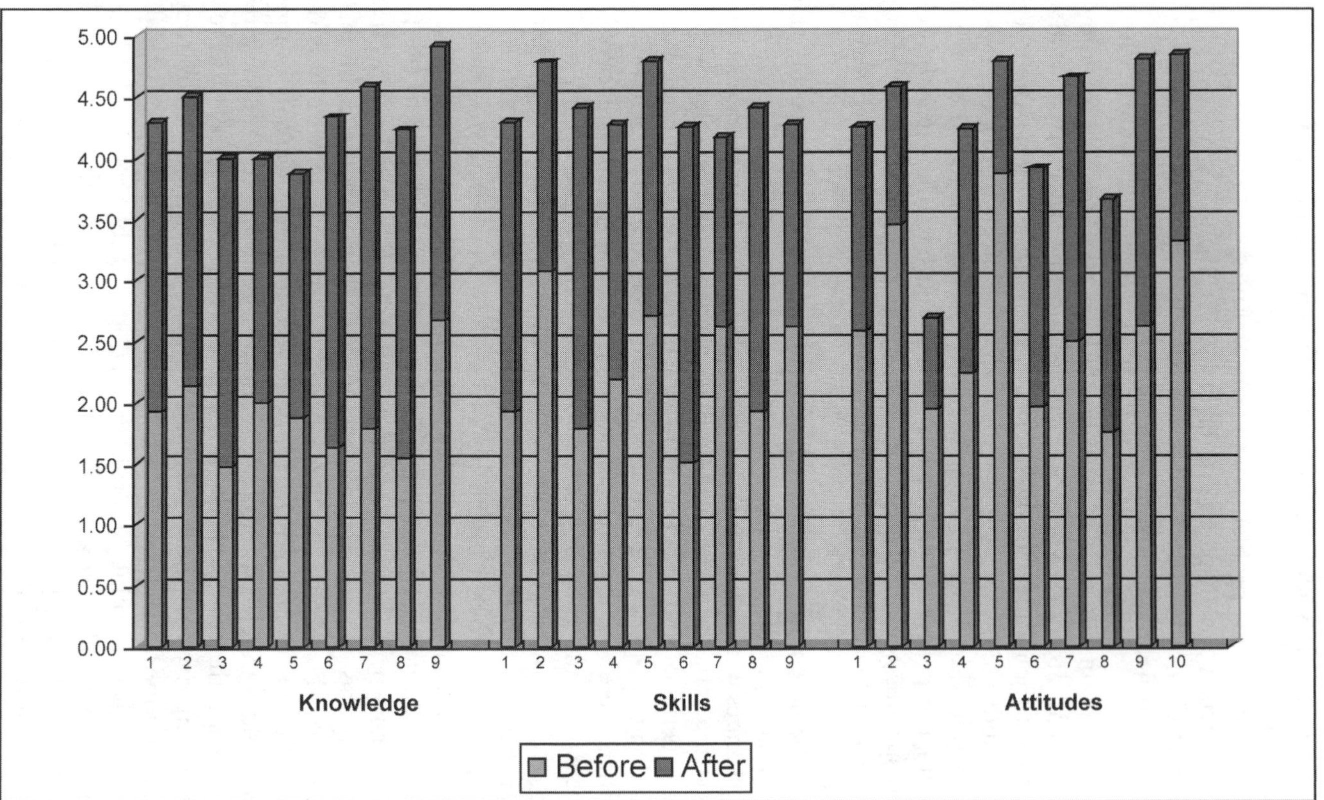

Figure 1: Informal Learning in the Participatory Budget of Porto Alegre

An interesting finding of this study was that most of the informal learning acquired through the participatory budget was incidental or as part of socialization, in the sense that such learning was not intentionally sought and was seldom a conscious process at the time it happened.[6] As Eraut (1999) points out, one of the methodological challenges for research on informal learning is to provide the right questions and opportunities for respondents to elicit and describe their tacit knowledge, skills, and values, and eventually the time, place, and forms of their acquisition. Indeed, when at the beginning of the interviews I asked participants (in an open-ended question) what they have learned as a result of their participation, the typical response was "nothing" or "very little." However, when we went item by item through the different indicators, and they began to provide examples of learning in each area, it was evident for them that a significant amount of learning took place. In many cases they mentioned this at the end of the interview, pointing out that until that moment they had not been aware of all the learning that they had acquired by participating.

Through the interviews and focus groups (particularly with PB participants with low levels of formal schooling), this study found that informal learning acquired through the participatory budget process is significant. After one neighborhood meeting, one woman defined the participatory budget as "our school of citizenship." Indeed, through the very process of participation, neighbors learned a variety of ways to become more active, informed, responsible, tolerant, and democratic citizens. They found a space in which they could develop civic and political capacities that probably could not be learned at the same pace and with the same intensity in many other places. This includes learning about the city as a whole beyond the particular issues of a particular street or neighborhood, and understanding the specifics of democratic deliberation and decision making. It also includes skills and attitudes such as speaking in public, listening respectfully to others who hold different opinions without interrupting them, solving conflicts, and reaching agreements. They also learned about public administration, community organizing, and the working of the formal political system.

Because elected delegates to the participatory budget have to rotate continuously, many ordinary citizens have the opportunity to develop their leadership skills, avoiding the risk of power concentration in a few hands. Perhaps more important, and this brings back the issue of political efficacy, because participants can see almost immediately the results of their decisions in terms of public works: They learn that they can make a difference, and thus develop more confidence in their ability to influence the political system. In short, through experiential learning, people learned democracy by doing it, acquiring a great deal of knowledge, skills, values, and attitudes that are seldom acquired in schools and even nonformal settings. Moreover, this learning is often translated into new behaviors, such as participating in politics and social movements, promoting democratic rules in other institutions and organizations, or taking better care of their city.

To provide an example of the last new behaviors, in one interview a delegate from a poor neighborhood mentioned that when he was a street kid he used to vandalize public property all the time. "Now I know how many public telephones are vandalized per month in my region and in the city," he said, "and I know how much money it costs to repair them. I also know how many extra school lunches we could provide with that money. So, now I tell the youth in my neighborhood that every time they vandalize a telephone we have less food in schools for them and for their siblings." The participatory process allowed this delegate to learn something about the public budget, and to make a mental connection between vandalizing telephones and school lunches that he was not able to make before participating in the process. Now he was aware of this learning, and was able to translate it into taking better care of his community.

The informal citizenship learning, however, does not only apply to low income participants. For example, a middle-class woman from a middle-upper-class neighborhood mentioned that she was invited to attend a budget session by one of her neighbors. Her neighbor wanted more illumination in their public park for safety reasons. She went to the meeting ready to vote for the demand of her group, but things changed when she listened to the issues and demands raised by residents from a poorer neighborhood, a favela (shanty town) located on a hill about a kilometer or two from her house. After listening to their problems, she changed her mind and voted for their demand. The participatory budget gave this woman the chance to meet for the first time with people from the other neighborhood as citizens instead of as employees (e.g., as plumbers, gardeners, carpenters, or maids). Before, all encounters with them were limited to hiring and paying them once the job was done. This time, however, she met with them not in the marketplace but in a public democratic forum. She listened to their issues, witnessed a process of mutual persuasion, and was persuaded that the open sewage and the proliferation of mice in the schoolyard were more urgent than her park lights. This is also informal learning, a learning that probably would have not taken place if there was not a meeting space like this. Along the same lines, several interviewees mentioned that the participatory budget prompted them to change some perceptions and attitudes that were deeply entrenched in their ways of understanding the world and acting on it. The findings of the study also suggest that, given certain conditions, people are willing to move from narrow self-interests to the common good, and from individualism to solidarity.

SUMMARY AND CONCLUSIONS: PARTICIPATORY DEMOCRACY AS AN INFORMAL SCHOOL OF CITIZENSHIP

In this chapter informal learning was conceived of as any learning, purposeful or not, that involves the acquisition of knowledge, skills, attitudes, or values that are not formulated in an externally imposed curriculum. Confirming the arguments of classic theories in the field, it was found that participatory democracy is a particularly effective setting to learn the values, skills, and competencies for the effective exercise of citizenship. Indeed, John Stuart Mill claimed that participatory democracy fosters among participants an "active character." G. D. H. Cole made references to the development of "a nonservile character." For Rousseau, participatory democracy nurtures a cooperative character, which includes an interest for the common good, and a capacity to define collectively the common good and to make democratic decisions to put it into practice. For Pateman, it promotes a democratic character, which consists of a capacity for self-governance, and political efficacy.

As the experiences recounted by interviewees in this study suggest, participatory democracy has the potential to fulfill those expectations if there is a proper space to learn democracy by doing it. Through a good process of participatory democracy, people learn to become more informed, engaged, and critical citizens who can deliberate and make decisions in a democratic fashion, who can think not only about their specific grievances but also about the common good. This means learning a new political culture that is based on active citizenship, solidarity, and equity, that is, a culture in which we are not only spectators but also actors, and in which the common good and the needs of the most marginalized members of society come before our particular demands. It also means learning new ways to relate to each other and to the government, building relationships based on collaboration and respect. Paraphrasing that woman from Porto Alegre, an informal school of citizenship provides opportunities for political and democratic learning that is as broad as possible and enjoyed by as many people as possible. Thus, political capital, understood as the capacity to influence political decisions (Schugurensky, 2000b), is more equitable redistributed, and is no longer an exclusive monopoly of professional politicians and the so-called professional citizens.

The development of political efficacy and political capital, however, is only part of the educative effect of participation. There is also the broadening of perspectives, the awareness of the connections between private and public interests, the gaining of familiarity with democratic procedures, the concern for improving the urban landscape and the quality of life for residents, and the development of political and democratic skills and attitudes. A school of citizenship also means to learn how to practice democracy in-between elections. We are not born democrats, and often we are not raised to be active democratic citizens. Democracy is something that we can learn everyday beyond the occasional act of voting, and the more democratic the enabling structures that nurture the deliberation process, the more significant the democratic learning will be. Most political forums today, be they right, center, or left, are characterized not by dialogue but by monologues and confrontation. Participatory democracy, although it is not a perfect model, at least allows for listening, which is a precondition for learning. It is the creation and functioning of true democratic spaces that allow people to learn democracy by doing it through research, deliberation, and decision making. This implies that we need to find new ways of doing politics, and to create a multiplicity of healthy democratic spaces. These are nonrecognized educational institutions that nonetheless fulfill an important educational purpose.

NOTES

1. Historically, the learning acquired through informal means has not been recognized by formal educational institutions or by the workplace, although the recent emergence of systems of evaluations and accreditation such as PLAR (Prior Learning Assessment and Recognition) is slowly changing this.
2. No hierarchical relationship is implied among formal, nonformal, and informal education. On the contrary, it can be argued that the learning acquired informally and in nonformal educational institutions is as important (and sometimes more important) than that acquired through the curriculum of formal educational institutions.
3. Although it could be argued that all institutions are educational in one way or another, here I am using the term "educational institutions" to allude to institutions that were created and are operated with the main purpose of delivering a particular content in a certain time period.
4. This taxonomy is described and discussed in more detail in Schugurensky (2000a).
5. After having conducted similar studies in Montevideo and in Toronto, this inventory has been expanded to 56 indicators.
6. According to a recent study with 1,039 representatives to the participatory budget, participants join the process for a variety of reasons. The most frequent one (56.5%) is to advocate for a community need such as pavement, sewage, potable water, electricity, healthcare, childcare, and so on. Others (about 24%) join mainly to serve their communities or because they want to participate. Only 8.19% said that they entered the process because they "wanted to know" (CIDADE, 1999). This means that the majority of participants did not focus purposefully on learning at the time of joining the process, and in this sense their acquired knowledge, skills, and attitudes were unintended. It may be argued, however, that although this learning was not intended by participants, it was intended by the designers of the participatory budget. This is an interesting thesis to explore in future research. From my interviews with the designers and coordinators of the participatory budget, my preliminary hypothesis is

that the pedagogical dimension was not on their radar screen during the first phase of the process. Their focus was placed on ensuring a fair and equitable allocation of public resources and on nurturing the mobilization of neighborhood associations.

REFERENCES

Abers, R. (2000). *Inventing local democracy: Grassroots politics in Brazil.* Boulder, CO: Lynne Rienner Publishers.

Adams, F. (1980). Highlander folk school: Social movements and social change in the American South. In Rolland Paulston (Ed.), *Other dreams, other schools: Folk colleges in social and ethnic movements.* Pittsburgh: University Center for International Studies.

Arnstein, S. (1969). A ladder of citizen participation. *Journal of the American Institute of Planners* 35(4): 216–24.

Baierle, S. (1998). The explosion of experience: The emergence of a new ethical-political principle in popular movements in Porto Alegre, Brazil. In S. Alvarez, E. Daguino ,and A. Escobar (Eds.), *Culture of politics, politics of culture* (pp. 118–38). Boulder, CO: Westview Press.

Berger, P., & Luckmann, T. (1966). *The social construction of reality: A treatise in the sociology of knowledge.* New York: Doubleday.

Bourdieu, P. (1991). Political representation: Elements for a theory of the political field, in Pierre Bourdieu: *Language and Symbolic Power.* Cambridge, MA: Harvard University Press.

Brown, J. S., Collins, A., & Duguid, S. (1989). Situated cognition and the culture of learning. *Educational Researcher* 18(1): 32–42.

Campbell, A., Gurin, G., & Miller, W. (1954). *The voter decides.* Illinois: Row & Peterson.

CIDADE. (1999). Quem é o público do orçamento participativo: seu perfil, por que participa e o que pensa do processo. Porto Alegre: CIDADE (Centro de Assessoria e Estudos Urbanos) and Prefeitura de Porto Alegre.

Cole, G. D. H. (1919). *Self-government in industry.* London: G. Bell & Sons.

Eraut, M. (1999). Nonformal learning, implicit learning and tacit knowledge. In F. Coffield (Ed.), *The necessity of informal learning.* Bristol: Policy Press.

Foley, G. (1999). *Learning as social action: A contribution to understanding informal learning.* New York: Zed Books.

Gear, J., McIntosh, A., & Squires, G. (1994). *Informal learning in the professions.* Hull, UK: University of Hull, Department of Adult Education.

Genro, T. (2001, January 25). A better world is already possible here. *Zero Hora,* 3.

Horton, M., & Freire, P. (1990). *We make the road by walking.* Philadelphia: Temple University Press.

Jonassen, D. H. (1994). Thinking technology: Toward a constructivists design model. *Educational Technology* 34(4): 34–37.

Kojala, J. (1965). *Workers' councils: The Yugoslav experience.* London: Tavistock.

Lave, J., & Wenger, E. (1990). *Situated learning: Legitimate periperal participation.* Cambridge, UK: Cambridge University Press.

Livingstone, D. (2001). *Adults' informal learning: Definitions, findings, gaps and future research.* NALL Working Paper # 21. Available online: <http://www.oise.utoronto.ca/depts/sese/csew/nall/res/21adultsifnormallearning.htm>.

Livingstone, D. (1999). Exploring the icebergs of adult learning: Findings of the first Canadian survey of informal learning practices. *Canadian Journal for the Study of Adult Education* 3: 49–72.

Maguire, P. (1993). Challenges, contradictions and celebrations: Attempting participatory research as a doctoral student. In P. Park (Ed.), *Voices of change: Participatory research in the United States and Canada* (pp. 157–76). Toronto: OISE Press.

Mill, J. S. (1963). In G. Himmlefarb (Ed.), *Essays on politics and culture.* New York: Doubleday.

Pateman, C. (1988 [1970]). *Participation and democratic theory.* New York: Cambridge University Press.

Polanyi, M. (1966). *The tacit dimension.* New York: Doubleday.

Polanyi, M. (1958). *Personal knowledge: Towards a post-critical philosophy.* Chicago: University of Chicago Press.

Schugurensky, D. (2002). Transformative learning and transformative politics: The pedagogical dimension of participatory democracy and social action: Essays on theory and praxis. In E. O'Sullivan, A. Morrell, & M. A. O'Connor (Eds.), *Expanding the boundaries of transformative learning* (pp. 59–76). New York: Palgrave.

Schugurensky, D. (2001a). Grassroots democracy: The participatory budget of Porto Alegre. *Canadian Dimension* 35(1): 30–32.

Schugurensky, D. (2001b). The enlightenment-engagement dilemma and the development of the active citizen: Lessons from the Citizens' Forum and the Participatory Budget. Proceedings of the 20th anniversary conference of the Canadian Association for Studies in Adult Education (CASAE), 159–64. Toronto: CASAE.

Schugurensky, D. (2000a). The forms of informal learning: Towards a conceptualization of the field. NALL working paper #19. Available at <http://www.oise.utoronto.ca/depts/sese/csew/nall/res/19formsofinformal.htm>

Schugurensky, D. (2000b). Citizenship learning and democratic engagement: Political capital revisited. Proceedings of the 41st Annual Adult Education Research Conference (AERC) (pp. 417–22). Vancouver: AERC.

Schugurensky, D., & Myers, J. P. (2003). A framework to explore lifelong learning: The case of the civic education of civics teachers. *International Journal of Lifelong Education* 22 (4) 352–79.

Tough, A. (1971). *The adult's learning projects: A fresh approach to theory and practice in adult learning.* Toronto: OISE.

CULTURE MATTERS

INFORMAL SCIENCE CENTERS AND CULTURAL CONTEXTS

SALLY DUENSING

ABSTRACT

Science and technology museums and science centers are cultural creations and cultural institutions. As with formal education institutions, informal education institutions reflect the cultural contexts in which they exist. In their exhibits and educational programs these centers develop and disseminate images and understandings concerning both the content and process of science and of learning. Different museums and centers do this in different ways, but they are all embedded in sociocultural contexts of museum practice, science, and public education as well as national and local cultural milieus that influence the form and content of their presentations. This chapter examines different ways in which exhibits and programs have been designed and adapted by museum staff to fit particular cultural contexts in science centers in a variety of different countries. Discussion will center on ways in which these adaptations perpetuate certain cultural norms, thought, and practice. The overall intention is to further understand and question relationships of cultural contexts and variations in learning environments, both informal and formal.

> Every museum exhibition, whatever its overt subject, inevitably draws on the cultural assumptions and resources of the people who make it. Decisions are made to emphasize one element and to downplay others, to assert some truths and to ignore others. The assumptions underpinning these decisions vary according to culture and over time, place, and type of museum or exhibit.
>
> Ivan Karp, *Culture and Representation*

The underlying premise for this chapter is that science and technology museums and science centers[1] are cultural creations and cultural institutions. Cultural assumptions about learning are reflected in exhibit and program design, as well as methods for explaining exhibits to museums visitors. Informal science museums are embedded in sociocultural contexts of museum practice, science, and public education as well as national and local cultural milieus that influence the form and content of their presentations (Alexander, 2000; Broadfoot et al., 2000; Rosier and Keeves, 1991).

To illustrate ways in which science centers both reflect and generate the cultural contexts in which they exist, I will discuss a variety of ways in which science museum exhibits, programs, and pedagogical practices subtly and not so subtly vary in different cultural contexts. These examples come from observations I have collected in my long-term work with science centers from widely diverse cultural contexts and from an ethnographic study (Duensing, 2000) on staff belief that I conducted to further investigate some of these observations. This chapter is not meant to be an encompassing comparative account, but rather a highlight of differences in cultural museum practice to explore and question relationships of cultural contexts and variations in learning environments, both informal and formal.

BACKGROUND

For the past twenty years there has been an enormous growth in informal science museums and centers. Worldwide it is estimated that there are now more than 1200 science centers or museums that are visited by over 200 million people annually (ASTC, 2001; Persson, 2002). From Bombay, India, to Santiago, Chile; Beijing, China, to Cincinnati, Ohio, these informal science educations environments serve diverse populations and a range of local and national educational objectives and needs. Although these centers are in a wide variety of countries, little research work has been focused on cultural variations in informal science center practice in these different communities (Bandelli, 2001; Bradburne & Janousek, 1993; Cooper, 2001; Duensing, 2000; Mahovsky, 1992). Additionally there are few studies on how museum staff, such as exhibit and program designers and developers, reflect and perpetuate certain cultural norms in their thought and practice that shape the learning environment of a science center—and thus the kinds of visitor experience the museum creates (Anderson & Rennie, 1995; Rowe, 1998; Toon, 2002). There are some publications on access and equity issues regarding staff and visitors (AAAS & ASTC, 1995; Beane & Pope, 2002) that do offer discussion on the role of design of exhibits and programs to enhance or diminish access, but the emphasis in general is on the importance of and methods for diversifying museum staff and board and community involvement.

In contrast, in the art and natural history museum fields there is a growing body of literature on relationships of culture and museum practice (Bradburne & Janousek, 1993; Clifford, 1991; Coombes, 1994; Corrin, 1994; Karp & Lavine, 1991; Vercoe, 1996; Paris, 2002). Much of this work concerns the display of objects with the position that the display itself is a cultural object. Although this literature is primarily on collections in art and natural history museums, and not science centers per se, it is of relevance for any kind of museum in showing some of the different ways a museum reflects cultural points of view.

OBSERVATIONS

Observations discussed in this chapter grow out of my 20 years as coordinator of the Exploratorium's work with the international science museum community and my doctoral research. The Exploratorium, located in San Francisco, California, is a recognized leader and resource in the field of informal science education through its highly interactive exhibits and programs. This form of exhibit, which is also often referred to as hands-on or participatory, is generally defined as an activity that offers a range of possible actions within the individual exhibit for the museum visitor to pursue (Duensing, 2000; Gregory, 1983; Tressel, 1984). For example, rather than having an optics exhibit in which a visitor can only turn a lens a few degrees to see light refract, in an interactive exhibit at the Exploratorium visitors can freely move loosely cabled lenses and prisms to explore a myriad of refraction and other optics phenomena that occur between lenses and beams of light.

A primary focus of my work at the Exploratorium has been to help museums from a variety of different countries who were interested in setting up Exploratorium exhibits and/or programs in their own institutions. As a result of this work, I began noticing adaptations made to ideas by staff to better fit their environments (Duensing, 1999). These changes often built upon perceived cultural differences between the local institutional cultural environment and the Exploratorium's.

For example, a simple design change in Caracas, Venezuela, was to add bright colors to their versions of Exploratorium exhibits that are in more neutral tones in San Francisco. The Venezuelan staff creating this new children's museum in Caracas felt that colorful rather than muted-toned exhibits would more effectively attract children because it would reflect the emphasis of bright colors in the Venezuelan culture.

Sometimes the title of an exhibit would be changed to more directly relate to a particular community. An Exploratorium exhibit, for example, on stereovision and eye rivalry is called Cheshire Cat since part of someone's face seems to disappear much like the cat in *Alice in Wonderland*. Thinking that many visitors in Caracas would not be familiar with this Lewis Carroll story the title was changed to a descriptive Disappearing Face. And interestingly in Paris, France, the home of Marie Antoinette, this exhibit is called Moins le Tête (Minus the head).

In another example, staff at a new children's museum in Mexico City said that they modified ideas from the Exploratorium and other US museums to have more space around each exhibit. They anticipated that family groups visiting their museum would be larger on average than those in San Francisco. They wanted to make sure the design would allow these visiting groups to watch and interact with each other.

At a small neighborhood science center, Espaço Ciencia Viva, in Rio de Janeiro, Brazil, many of the exhibits began as versions of Exploratorium exhibits designed to require little or no assistance from museum staff. However, the exhibits in Brazil were redesigned to be more like activity tables with a variety of loose materials. Museum staff would show visitors some of the effects one could explore with the various things on each table. There was at least one staff member for every three of these exhibits. The staff in Rio said that to effectively reach their public, the highly social culture of Brazil should be reflected in the format of the exhibits.

Science subject areas in a museum can also reflect cultural considerations in terms of what is exhibited. The routine demonstration in many US science centers of a cow's eye dissection is not in most science centers in the UK. Museum staff in the UK said that due to the strong animal rights feelings in the UK, these kinds of demonstrations would initiate a huge negative outcry from the British public. They said that it is very difficult to do any kind of animal dissection at their museums. In turn, UK staff are surprised at the controversy and reluctance of some science museums in the US to address evolution in their exhibit halls.

An Exploratorium exhibit developer noticed a striking difference between what was considered appropriate to have in an exhibit on human sexuality and AIDS in Brazil as compared to one in the US. Here are excerpts from her notes while visiting Brazil:

> AIDS is a major health problem in Brazil and there were many good exhibits done by students. Their frank and straightforward presentation was a revelation to me—that we were so constricted by US cultural taboos from communicating effectively and openly to raise awareness about AIDS and how to protect yourself from being infected. Sexual activity was just an openly acknowledged part of human life, there was no embarrassment or giggling about explaining it as one of the ways you could become infected with AIDS.

Even subjects as apparently neutral as light and optics can reflect cultural considerations in their design. For example, an educator from Kenya became quite angry with the design of a mirror exhibit at the Exploratorium in which there is a coin that appears to be floating in space created by reflections from two parabolic mirrors. You put your hand in to touch the coin where you see it, but your hand seems to go right through the coin. What you're actually seeing is an image in space of the coin created by the mirrors and not the coin itself. The salience of the surprise bothered him. He felt that if this exhibit were set up this way in his country, it would be promoting magic and not helping understanding.

Staff Belief and Science Center Practice

Observations like those mentioned above were the catalysts for me to carry out an ethnographic study on staff belief with the staff of Yapollo, the National Science Center Trinidad and Tobago in the West Indies, a center I have been involved with for over ten years (Duensing, 2000). The approach I used is based on a sociocultural theoretical framework (Rogoff, 1993, 1998, 2003; Vygotsky, 1978; Wertsch, 1991) that emphasizes both the role of the environment in shaping the cognition and behavior of individuals and the role of individuals in shaping the environment in mutual co-creating ways. I employed the sociocultural perspective looking at the dynamic interplay between the people who create the museum and the cultural contexts of the museum within the local communities as well as the international science and education communities. From a sociocultural perspective, museum practice is a culture-shaping enterprise that is itself shaped by culture.

In this study I looked at the multiple cultural perspectives, the beliefs, values, and actions, held by the staff, as a reflection of what is considered and not considered in the choice and design of exhibits and programs. These perspectives are formed from their participation in different local communities such as the formal British-based school system in Trinidad and Tobago, the out-of-school everyday learning activities, as well as the cultural practices of the worldwide science museum community. The synthesis of these perspectives creates its own cultural ways of thinking and practice about exhibits and pedagogy that form the shared common wisdom at Yapollo.

A dominant practice and value repeatedly expressed by Yapollo staff that I will highlight here was the importance of social interaction in the learning of science. This social emphasis was repeatedly reflected in the pedagogy and design of Yapollo's exhibits and programs. The staff stated that they recognized that Trinidadian culture in general has a strong value and emphasis on social interactions and connections, and some staff felt that this social emphasis was stronger in general in Trinidad than in the US. For example, several of the floor staff one day were talking about different places they had visited and mentioned feeling uncomfortable and strange in New York City, saying that on the city's subways people don't look at each other and just look up at the ceiling. They said that they felt bothered by this lack of acknowledgment and seeming invisibility. I remembered feeling uncomfortable when I first visited Trinidad and Tobago for the opposite reason. I felt like everyone was looking at me. After being there a few weeks I was able to begin to see that everyone looks at everyone. On the street, for example, it is common practice to look and nod at people walking by. This form of social contact and acknowledgment is basic in Trinidadian culture.

Social Design

The overall arrangement of the public floor space of Yapollo itself is an expression of Yapollo's social approach. In most US, UK, and European science centers, exhibits that can be used by individuals or small groups of people dominate the public floor. At Yapollo at least half of the entire public floor space is devoted to group activity programs that include the demonstrations, project-making areas, a computer activity area, and a planetarium.

The staff who lead demonstrations, called demonstrators, often said that the demonstrations and other activities in this area were more interesting than the exhibits for visitors. It was felt that social interaction with the activities was where the engagement with ideas happened. One of the demonstrators said that the high level of interaction with the staff at the demonstrations excited children far more than their individual exploration at the exhibits.

The idea of museums and science centers as places for social activity is not a unique, new, or unusual idea. There have been numerous accounts of ways in which science centers and museums provide ideal environments for social interaction (McLean, 1993; McManus, 1987). However, what was unusual for me was the degree in which Yapollo staff explicitly and implicitly applied the use of social interaction throughout the center. I have not encountered a social emphasis to this degree in US or European science centers. It is only with the science center in Brazil that I have experienced a similar approach.

This emphasis can be seen in the number of staff that are on the public floor to interact with visitors. For example, in Trinidad and in Brazil there is one facilitator for every three to five exhibits. US science centers, in contrast ,in general have one staff person for every 15 to 20 exhibits (or less). The floor staff in Trinidad are considered by exhibit and program-planning staff as integral as the exhibits in their informal science learning environment; some science centers in other countries have said that they don't see the need for floor staff at all.

Social Explaining of Exhibits

A focus on social interaction can also influence the ways in which floor staff explain exhibits to the public. Explaining an exhibit was often constructed to be a two-way transaction in Trinidad. Their teaching at exhibits or in the demonstrations frequently involved asking visitors to give an explanation of what was going on. Unlike the more one-way form of explaining that I was used to seeing in many US science centers, in which the staff members tell the visitors an explanation, demonstrators would regularly solicit explanations from the visitors as part of explaining an idea. Observing and listening to the demonstrators, I would regularly see that after explaining aspects of a particular exhibit to visitors, the demonstrators would then say, "Okay, now you tell me," asking the visitor to now explain it back.

One of the demonstrators described the way he uses this technique to help visitors understand a more complicated exhibit. He asks them to say what they do and do not understand in a step-by-step process. Breaking down the concept of the exhibit in smaller components, he would walk them through it, explaining and asking them to tell him what was going on at each step.

Making Mistakes Socially

A salient feature I noticed in this back and forth interaction in working through an explanation with museum visitors was the energy or fun people seemed to have in the interaction itself, not in being correct. Interactions were used to help participants figure something out through the right and wrong guesses put forward. The thing was to try—being right or wrong was part of it but seemed secondary.

Yapollo staff said that a social situation provided encouragement for kids to have to say something. Rather than be intimidated, having to explain something in front of a group was perceived as a positive motivating technique that contributed to a person's understanding. As one staff member said, "It is at the demonstrations more [than exhibits] that you get the children to talk, to try and explain why they think it worked and you can access the science more."

Demonstrators described various ways in which guessing techniques were used in their science demonstrations as well as in explaining the exhibits. They told me that they encourage visitors to figure something out through the process of guessing. The process of guessing was seen as a way to begin to understand something. This form of dialogue is often purposely competitive. Audience members are encouraged to guess out loud—often competing with each other or the demonstrator.

One of the most lively presenters of these demonstrations told me how he encourages the audience to guess and prove him wrong through setting up a situation with a fellow demonstrator in which they each have a different opinion about why or how something works and the audience is encouraged to side with one of them.

He went on to explain that he also has developed the role of a magician, a magician who challenges the students to try to prove wrong him. He described how during one of these demonstrations as the kids were guessing both what and why a particular thing would happen, something went wrong and the effect he was trying to show malfunctioned. He said as a result it became a successful learning opportunity in that he had the whole group competing both with him and each other to try to figure out why the magician was wrong.

> "And the children they laughed, they laughed and I laughed too, we talked, and the discussion went very good. Even though it didn't work they understood."
>
> *You told them why it didn't work?*
>
> "Exactly, I told them why it didn't work, and they understood what was going on. The teacher laughed, she almost cried. She came up and shook my hand and said, 'Very well, very well done, magician.'"

When I was watching David conduct one of his energetic demonstrations, after someone correctly guessed the answer to a question he had asked, he said to the audience, "Everybody heard her, right? What did she say?" And then he called on various people in the audience to tell him and everyone else in the audience what she said to make sure others got the answer as well. There was a social form in which problems were solved.

In a focus group discussion with all of the Yapollo demonstrators, I asked them how they had learned this technique. I expected that they would say something about applyng the social construction of knowledge or a scaffolding (Brown et al., 1993; Edwards and Mercer, 1987) form of teaching as part of their training to work with the public. However, no one remembered how they came by it, nor that it was anything that they were explicitly taught as an effective teaching technique.

Alternatively, in other discussions, demonstrators, when describing the social kinds of learning they were promoting at Yapollo, would refer to some of the other informal learning activities that are common in Trinidad and Tobago. One of those mentioned on a number of occasions was the process for learning how to play in a steel band, an orchestra comprised of the musical instrument invented in Trinidad and Tobago using the steel drum, also called steel pan. Starting in December as part of the lead up to Carnival these orchestras form and start rehearsing songs they will play in events and competitions that are part of the Carnival events. Ranging from 40 to 100 players, in almost every town, however large or small, steel band orchestras can be found rehearsing in places called pan yards. When I was living in Port of Spain, for example, within an eight-block radius there were five different pan yards.

There is a wide range of expertise. Most groups have a flexible informal process for newcomers to become part of the orchestra. Novices often join by showing interest. They are given increasingly difficult parts to see what role they would be best able to undertake. Novices and more experienced members of the orchestra practice together. Yapollo's director of education, a well-known composer and leader of steel orchestras, told me how great it is that once a year anyone from any walk of life can have the experience of playing in a full orchestra. Watching some of the rehearsals in the pan yards, some of these connections mentioned by staff were quite apparent. For example, errors were not something to be avoided but seen as part of learning of the musical composition, and there was noticeable excitement in being part of a group effort.

School Visits to a Museum

The school field trip program, in which museums around the world are visited by school groups, can also reveal cultural variations in formal and informal practice. For example, Yapollo staff said that since they were currently only open on weekdays when school groups would visit, and were not yet open for families on the weekends, their exhibit maintenance problems were relatively low. In their view, kids in general were much rougher and wilder when they visited with their families than with their school class.

I wondered if I had heard them wrong. What they were reporting was the opposite of my experience at the Exploratorium as well as what staff say about field trips in many if not most science centers in the US and Europe. In these other science centers, exhibit maintenance goes way up during school visits. The experience of museum staff in the US and Europe is that in general kids are much wilder when they visit on a school field trip than they are when they come with their families or even on their own.

When I observed some of the classes on school field trips to Yapollo, the students did not appear docile or blindly obedient. Rather, I had the impression that they were respectful as well as playful.

In speculating with Yapollo staff about what might contribute to such a distinct difference between Yapollo and Exploratorium field trip behavior, Yapollo staff said that the teacher has a lot of authority in the classroom. There was an impression by many of the staff that the kids in the US were less respectful of their teachers and that many middle-class parents in the US (as well as in Trinidad) allow their kids to get away with anything. One of the demonstrators thought that San Francisco kids would be rougher than West Indian kids.

> "San Francisco kids' minds work different because it's a different way of life, if West Indian kids sees kids in San Francisco they [will] say 'but we don't get on like this.'"

DISCUSSION

In the images I have presented in this chapter there are important lessons for understanding informal learning practice in science museums and technology centers. The most important point is that science center presentations, exhibit designs, and styles of learning are rooted in the cultural contexts in which the centers are located and the cultural communities and practices in which museum staff participate.

At each turn of the road, center staff are making decisions about individual exhibit design, how exhibits will be used, groups of exhibits, pathways by which visitors will be guided as they make their way through the museum, kinds of teaching and learning that will occur, and what kinds of excitations will be present for visitors in terms of the sights, sounds, experiences, and individual or group activities that are presented. All these decisions are culturally informed and culturally mediated.

Cultural considerations such as those I have presented so far have implications for museum policy, such as design, pedagogy, and evaluation. In diverse cultures, for example, there are diverse patterns of sociability and learning and the question becomes how these patterns of learning are accounted for. In evaluating museum effectiveness, cultural thinking must be employed to discern the learning goals, methods, and expectations of both the various communities the center attempts to serve and museum staff.

Practices of Informal Practice

An interesting set of questions, for example, can be asked about the explanation practices of young demonstrators described above. A reviewer of an earlier draft of this chapter asked why was I surprised at the style of teaching the demonstrator employed, likening it to the well-known scaffolding approach in teaching that is a prevalent approach in current educational practice (Edwards and Mercer, 1987; Palinscar and Brown, 1984) that offers common understanding through structured and sequenced questioning through joint activity and shared conceptions.

What I see is that ideas such as scaffolding must themselves be seen in cultural context. There are two things to be noted here. First is that although it is a well-known pedagogical practice in many US classrooms, I have not experienced it as a common form of exhibit explanation practice in US science centers. Watching the demonstrators in Trinidad, I realized that I rarely, if ever, saw this practice on the museum floor with the general public in San Francisco or other US science centers. Second, it is rooted in particular aspects of the local culture from which it derives, but it is also a created process by the demonstrators involved. There was no idea about scaffolding per se from which the practice was consciously derived by the demonstrators.

Social Mistakes

Further cultural aspects of the social construction of knowledge can be seen in the following two examples involving the use of errors from formal learning. The social problem-solving much like what I observed at Yapollo, has also been described in studies on cultural variations in formal classroom practice as well, providing a possible connection to explore between informal education environments and formal education practices. For example, Catherine Lewis (1995) describes the use of errors as a learning tool in an elementary mathematics lesson in Japan. Children would go to the blackboard to solve a problem, when errors were made, the whole class would be encouraged to think through the problem together. The focus was on the problem-solving/thinking something through as a group, not on the individual not getting it right.

Similarly, Robin Alexander in his book *Culture and Pedagogy* (2000) describes a classroom in Russia in which questions and mistakes involve the whole class thinking through problems, a process that is unlike common practice in many UK and US classrooms.

> The child who comes to the front and works through a problem, aloud and at length, is less an individual being tested and compared with others than their representative. For the moment, that child *is* the class, and all are participating.

Alexander contrasts this form of social problem-solving with the more individualistic approach in US and UK classrooms he observed.

> In England and Michigan we see many pupils answering questions but each pupil answers at most one or two questions over the course of a lesson . . . In Russia we also encountered this pattern of exchange, but alongside it we regularly observed episodes during which the same child answered one question, then another which built on the first, and then another and another. . . . a single child provides nor just one piece but several . . . In Russia in contrast, the process is invariably a public one, so what pupils do not do themselves they hear and see another doing, in terms and at a conceptual level which they have a good chance of comprehending. If it is indeed the case that one has only understood something if one can explain it to a child, then for one child to explain something to another is double guarantee of understanding. (p. 454)

Although Alexander's work focuses on classroom practice, the idea led me to wonder about possible variations in response in science centers in the US to the kind of guessing games as described in Trinidad. Would US students who are not accustomed to this positive use of errors in classroom practice be motivated in the same way? Does this social problem-solving reflect a broader cultural practice of response to challenges in a nonpersonalized way? Japanese teachers have developed a classroom culture in which students are skilled in learning from one another and respect that the use of error is part of learning (Hatano and Inagaki, 1996). While the culture of American classroom, is often very different—many emphasize the importance of being right and contributing by talking. Could offering this kind of social learning activity in the informal environment influence the way students respond in the formal setting and vice versa?

Cultural Contexts of Student Behavior

The impact of an individualistic cultural emphasis can also be seen in relation to the differences noticed in student behavior in families and schools described above. In a discussion on the behavior of Trinidad school groups with a director of a science museum in England, she said that when she was a teacher in the London schools her experience was that the West Indian immigrant kids "go wild" with the lack of strict authority that often occurs when they come from the Caribbean schools to the UK or have a UK teacher instead of one from the West Indies. She said that she took over a class of immigrant children from the West Indies and that they were really out of control because her style of teaching was very self-directed and nonauthoritarian.

Her experience directly relates to a study by Cynthia Ballenger (1992) regarding effective adult authority approaches to dealing with immigrant Haitian children in a Massachusetts classroom. Ballenger describes her own need to learn new ways of thinking about control and authority in working with four-year-old Haitian children. She had to undo her assumptions about the universality of classroom management techniques to learn other techniques that worked with these young students. As if responding to the British science museum director's saying that her "self-directed and nonauthoritarian way of teaching" didn't work, Ballenger describes watching a Haitian teacher controlling the students better than she and says that she is "struck and troubled by the powerful individualism underlying the approach I characterize as typical of me and many North American teachers." She went on to say:

> "[It's] as if something like the child's 'enlightened self-interest' were the ultimate moral guidepost. In comparison to the language used by the Haitian teachers, North American teachers' language seems to place very little emphasis on shared values."

The discussion with the British museum director and the related study by Ballenger as mentioned above raise interesting questions and implications for science center practice. Ballenger's work could be used as a lens to question the experience that most US and European science centers have that school groups in general "go wild" when they visit, as compared to Yapollo where they do not. Would Trinidadian students also "go wild" in San Francisco or other US and European science centers as it was with the Haitian kids in

Massachusetts or West Indian students in London? And are there differences in practice that Yapollo staff use in working with the visiting school groups that contribute to these differences in behavior in Trinidad? Is it possible that, like Ballenger who noticed differences she needed to learn from Haitian teachers about how to effectively work with the Haitian students, there are differences of approach that staff use in Trinidad that might be of benefit to US and European staff with the existing problems that they encounter with some of the visiting school groups?

There is a further implication in that the way families themselves use the science center in Trinidad might be different than in the US or Europe. Are the staff observations that Trinidadian kids are wilder with their families indicating a significant behavior difference due to cultural context? There is a growing body of research on family interactions and learning in museums (Ash, 2002; Bitgood, 1993; Borun, 1999; Crowley and Callanan, 1998; Diamond, 1986; McManus, 1987) that has generated a number of assumptions about differences in families visiting science centers in the US and Europe. The influence of cultural context and cultural background is an important, yet mostly missing, ingredient in this field of visitor research.

Evaluating Informal

Because behavior in museum settings can differ and can also be interpreted in other ways in different cultures, variations of context can influence research and evaluation considerations regarding school groups and family behavior as well as the general area of evaluating exhibit effectiveness. Evaluating what is effective is cultural and the goal is culturally mediated. What gets evaluated as effective informal practice can reflect these social or individualist cultural priorities. The goal of having large groups work together, for example, is different than the goal of individual visitor learning.

Christian Heath and Dirk vom Lehn (2001) have conducted a number of studies of visitor interaction with exhibits and with other visitors and have begun to document ways in which exhibits often discourage attempts by visitors to do things together. In their research in UK museums, Heath and vom Lehn have noticed that often hands-on kinds of exhibits are designed for individual interaction. They have documented some of the problems that occur when these exhibits are approached by multiple visitors at the same time, perhaps reflecting a less social emphasis or value by exhibit designers (Heath and vom Lehn, 2001).

Perhaps also reflecting a more individualistic approach, they also feel that many of the exhibit evaluation studies have only focused on the elements of the exhibit itself and not on the kinds of interaction that the exhibit can encourage or discourage (vom Lehn and Heath, 2001). In their work they find that observing visitor interaction at exhibits is as important as the components of the exhibit in trying to understand factors that contribute to the richness of the experience in museums.

> To a large extent, studies of visitor behavior in museums and galleries have paid little attention to the presence of strangers features in how people navigate and examine exhibits. [von Lehn et al., 2001a, p. 204] . . . Museums provide an opportunity to explore how the "affordances" and experience of objects emerge within and are constituted through interaction that inextricably relies on social organization which informs the very ways things are seen and experienced. (p. 209)

Of course, there are exhibits in most any museum that do encourage interaction, visitors with other visitors or visitors with museum staff, but many US and European exhibit areas are filled with computer screens and other displays that can be used by only one or two visitors at a time. Even if the subject matter is something people might like to jointly observe and discuss, the design may frustrate conversation.

Defining Informal

Interactive Learning

As the evaluation discussion implies, what is considered informal can be seen to vary from situation to situation. On the surface it might appear that the definitions are the same, but just below the surface some important differences can be found. For example, science centers almost anywhere highlight the fact that they offer interactive forms of learning. However, at Yapollo interactivity refers to the social interaction as much as an individual's manipulation of the exhibit. The design emphasis of group activities, much like the table form of exhibits mentioned earlier at the Espaço Ciencia Viva in Brazil and the design for families at Papalote in Mexico City, stands in contrast to exhibit design in most US science centers where socially oriented group activities such as demonstrations and activities are generally thought of as secondary enhancements to the exhibits, not the central components of design. Exhibits are often designed to be what are often called stand-alone experiences. The exhibits considered most effective are those that need the least mediation by museum staff.

Free Choice and the Right to Participate

The group activities and methods of explaining exhibits at Yapollo often contain a high degree of mediation between staff and visitors on the floor, far more than I was used to seeing in US science centers. Yapollo staff said that it was more important for the visitors to *have* the opportunity of experience more than have the *choice* of the experience. This perspective is articulated by

Yapollo's director of education; when she was discussing the value of activities as compared to exhibits. she said:

> "As you said at the Exploratorium it's a visitor's choice to go to an exhibit, (if) they don't go to that exhibit, they've just lost that privilege of knowing that. Whereas at an activity they are directly faced with doing the thing to the end, from beginning to end. And they participate in all its parts. With an exhibit, it may be there for them to use, but they (the visitors) may not."

Providing a visitor with a series of guided activity experiences to offer the "privilege of knowing" that the visitor might or might not have selected to do on their own is considered a high priority in the design of informal learning at Yapollo. In contrast, staff in science centers and museums in the US and Europe frequently use the term "free choice" to describe an essential attribute of informal or interactive science museum environments. Generally this means that the visitor decides where to go, what to explore, and for how long.

> Museums are free-choice environments—not only places where individuals can freely select what to learn but also places where individuals freely choose whether to come in the first place. (Falk and Dierking, 2000, p. 71)

Free choice is not irrelevant at Yapollo, but it would not be seen as the primary way to engage visitors. Since free choice is now considered the essential element of informal learning in many science centers it is important to consider that this seemingly fundamental attribute of informal learning is not necessarily a universal attribute but rather is itself a reflection of specific cultural values. "Free choice" does not represent Yapollo's goal of emphasizing the right or privilege to participate. Additionally this term often has an emphasis on individual exploration as is eluded to in the Falk and Dierking quote above. And thus as with exhibit evaluation and design, considerations of what is informal learning can accentuate the idea of the museum visitor as the "lone scientist" interacting with objects more than people (Bruner, 1995), a common western European image of science learning.

Formally Informal

And a further definition of what is considered to be basic or essential elements of informal learning can be seen to come from how the museum sees itself in relation to the formal school culture. Yapollo's emphasis of social interaction in its teaching and learning approaches was a reflection of Trinidad and Tobago out-of-school everyday learning culture—but not a reflection, the competitive, exam-driven British-based school culture. Yapollo's role was often described by staff as helping to address the deficits caused by this restrictive, exam-driven formal education process.

This dialectic critique of museums in relation to schools is not only occurring in Trinidad and Tobago but is a long-term debate within the international science community. For example, the Association of Science and Technology Center's January/February 1999 News Journal *Dimensions* focused the entire issue on differing points of view regarding how much science centers should embrace or separate from a new national standards program being implemented in US schools. Frank Oppenheimer when founding the Exploratorium in 1969 often expressed a desire to offer a learning environment that was unlike the dominant school culture in being less judgmental or test driven, saying,

> "No one flunks a museum."

And to repeat what was said at the beginning of this chapter, museum staff are not just one part of culture but are embedded in multiple cultures. Yapollo staff reflect both formal and informal cultural perspectives of Trinidad and Tobago. The fact that all of the staff have secondary and in many cases university level education backgrounds makes it interesting to note what parts of the formal education practice staff consciously or unconsciously discard, adopt, and adapt to build the informal learning environment of Yapollo.

Yapollo staff's conscious effort to create a learning environment that intentionally was not a reflection of the school culture raises intriguing ideas to explore further on how a science museum establishes its own culture of learning in relationship to the school culture of a particular community. In what ways does taking an oppositional stance augment and not just stand in opposition? How does the opposition itself alter both the museum and the schools, allowing for the possibility for new things to emerge in both environments?

> [I]individuals and whole generations may question and transform a community's traditions and institutions, especially if the values conflict with those of another community in which the individuals also participate. (Rogoff, 2003, p. 234)

SUMMARY

What I hope these examples indicate are ways in which cultural variations in pedagogical practice in informal settings can provide questions and ideas to consider for both informal as well as formal learning environments. Additionally understanding some of the variations and how staff reflect and perpetuate certain cultural norms in their thought and practice can empower institutions to more consciously and thoughtfully respond to the diverse communities that both museums and schools have stated that they want to serve.

> The process of gaining multicultural understanding in education . . . by forcing me to attempt to empathize with and understand a view of the world that is in many ways very different from my customary one, have put me in a position to reexamine values and principles that had become inaccessible under layers of assumptions. (Ballenger, 1992)

NOTE

1. I will use the terms "science center" and "museum" interchangeably.

REFERENCES

Alexander, R. (2000). *Culture and Pedagogy: International Comparisons in Primary Education,* Blackwell Publishers, Inc., Oxford UK & Malden, Massachusetts, USA.

American Association for the Advancement of Science and Association of Science and Technology Centers. (1995). *Diversity in Science and Technology Centers,* ASTC Publications, Washington DC.

Anderson, D., and Rennie, L. (1995). *Perceptions of Visitors' Learning at an Interactive Science and Technology Centre,* Paper presentation at NARST Annual Meeting, San Francisco, California, April 1995.

Ash, D. (2002). Negotiations of Thematic Conversations about Biology, in *Learning Conversations in Museums,* Leinhardt, Crowley, & Knutson (Eds.), Lawrence Erlbaum and Associates, Inc., Mahwah, New Jersey.

Association of Science and Technology Centers. (1999). News Journal *Dimensions,* January/February, 1999, Vol. 27, Issue 1.

Association of Science and Technology Centers. (2001). *ASTC Sourcebook of Science Center Statistics,* ASTC Publications, Washington DC.

Ballenger, C. (1992). Because You Like Us: The Language of Control, *Harvard Educational Review,* 62, 199–208.

Bandelli, A. (2001). Bicycles and Traffic Jams: Translating a Web Site in *Cultural Reflections: Museum in a Global Society, Journal of Museum Education,* Duensing (Ed.), Vol. 26(2).

Beane, D. B., and Pope, M. S. (2002). Leveling the Playing Field through Object-Based Service Learning in *Perspectives on Object-Centered Learning in Museums,* Paris, S. (Ed.), Lawrence Erlbaum Associates, Inc., Mahwah, New Jersey.

Bitgood, S. (1993). Social influences on the Visitor Museum Experience, *Visitor Behavior,* 8(3), 4–5.

Borun, M. (1999). *Family Learning in Museums: The PISEC Perspective,* Franklin Institute Publications, Philadephia, PA.

Bradburne, J., and Janousek, I., Eds. (1993). *Planning Science Museums for the New Europe,* UNESCO, Paris.

Brah, A., & Coomes, A. E., Eds. (2000). *Hybridity and Its Discontents,* Routledge Press, London and New York.

Broadfoot, P., Osborne, M., Planel, C., Sharpe, K. (2000). *Promoting Quality in Learning: Does England Have the Answer?* Cassell, London and New York.

Brown, A., Ash, D., Rutherford, M., Nakagawa,K., Gordon, A., Campione, J. (1993). Distributed expertise in the classroom, in G. Salomon (Ed.), *Distributed Cognitions:Psychological and Educational Considerations* (pp. 188–228), Cambridge University Press, New York.

Brown, C. (1992). The Museum's Role in a Multicultural Society, *Patterns in Practice, Selections from the Journal of Museum Education,* Museum Education Roundatable, Washington, DC.

Bruner, J. (1995). Vygotsky: A Historical and Conceptual Perspective, in Wertsch, J., (Ed.), *Culture, Communication and Cognition: Vygotskian Perspectives,* Cambridge University Press, Cambridge.

Chisholm, J. (1996). Learning "Respect for Everything": Navajo Images of Development, in Hwang, Lamb, & Siegel (Eds.), *Images of Childhood,* Lawrence Erlbaum, Mahwah, NJ.

Clifford, J. (1991). Four Northwest Coast Museums: Travel Reflections, *Exhibiting Cultures, the Poetics and Politics of Museum Display,* Smithsonian Institution Press, Washington D.C.

Coombes, A. E. (1994). *Reinventing Africa: Museums, Material Culture and Popular Imagination,* Yale University Press, New Haven and London.

Cooper, L. (2001). Whose Scientific Culture Is It Anyway? in *Cultural Reflections: Museum in a Global Society, Journal of Museum Education,* Duensing (Ed.), Vol. 26(2).

Corrin, L. (1994). *Mining the Museum: An Installation by Fred Wilson,* The Contemporary, Baltimore, & The New Press, New York.

Crowley, K., and Callanan, M. (1998). Describing and Supporting Collaborative Scientific Thinking in Parent-Child Interactions, *Journal of Museum Education* (Special issue on Understanding the Museum Experience, Paris, S. Ed. 23, 12–17.

Diamond, J. (1986). The Behavior of Family Groups in Science Museums, *Curator,* Vol. 29, No. 2.

Diamond, J. (1999). *The Practical Evaluation Guide,* Alta Mira Press, Walnut Creek, New York, Oxford.

Duensing, S. (1993). Explainers, Learning and Culture, *ECSITE, European Collaborative for Science, Industry and Technology Exhibitions Newsletter,* Spring Issue.

Duensing, S. (1999). Creating a Culture of Learning, *Dimensions Journal,* Association of Science and Technology Centers Press, Nov/Dec. 1999.

Duensing, S. (2000). *Cultural Influences on Science Museum Practices,* UMI Microform 9949651, Bell & Howell, Ann Arbor, Michigan.

Duensing, S. (2002). Using Galperin's Perspectives to Explore Generative Learning in Informal Science Centers, *Human Development* 43; 107–114.

Edwards, D., and Mercer, N. (1987). *Common Knowledge: The Development of Understanding in the Classroom,* London: Routledge.

Falk, J., and Dierking, L. (2000). *Learning from Museums, Visitor Experiences, and the Making of Meaning,* Alta Mira Press Walnut Creek, New York, Oxford.

Gregory, R. L. (1983). A Feeling for Science, *New Scientist,* November, 484–489.

Hatano, G., & Inagaki, K. (1996). *Cultural Contexts of Schooling Revisited: A Review of the Learning Gap from a Cultural Psychology Perspective*. Paper presentation at conference of Global Perspectives for Education, University of Michigan.

Heath, C., and vom Lehn, D. (under review). "Interaction and Interactives," submitted to *International Journal of Science Education*.

Hein, G. (1998). *Museums: Places of Learning*, Routledge, New York.

Hood, M. (1993). Staying Away: Why People Choose not to Visit Museums, *Museum News*, pp. 50–57.

Hipschman, R. (1980). *Exploratorium Cookbook*, Vol. 2, Exploratorium Publication, San Francisco.

Hipschman, R. (1987). *Exploratorium Cookbook*, Vol. 3, Exploratorium Publication, San Francisco.

Karp, I., and Lavine, S. (1991). *Exhibiting Cultures: The Poetics and Politics of Museum Display*, Smithsonian Institution Press, Washington.

Kennedy, J. (1990). *User Friendly: Hands-On Exhibits That Work*, Association of Science and Technology Centers Press, Washington, DC.

Leinhardt, Crowley, & Knutson (Eds.). (2002). *Learning conversations in Museums*, Mahwah, NJ: Lawrence Erlbaum Associates.

Lewis, C. (1995). Educating Hearts and Minds: Reflections on Japanese Preschool and Elementary Education, Cambridge University Press, Cambridge, England.

Mahovsky, M. (1992). *A Comparison of Visitors in Three Science Museums*, Doctoral Dissertation, University of Vienna, Austria (unpub.).

McLean, K. (1993). *Planning for People in Museum Exhibitions*, Association of Science and Technology Centers Publication, Washington, DC.

McManus, P. (1987). It's the Company You Keep: Social Determination of Learning-related Behavior in a Science Museum, *International Journal of Museum Management and Curatorship*, 6 (33).

Palinscar, A. S., & Brown, A. L. (1984). Reciprocal Teaching of Comprehension-Fostering and Monitoring Activities, *Cognition and Instruction*, I(2), 117–75.

Paris, S. (Ed.). (2002). *Perspectives on Object-Centered Learning in Museums*, Lawrence Erlbaum Associates, Inc. Mahwah, New Jersey.

Persson, E. (2002). Unpublished study of international science center statistics.

Rogoff, B., Chavajay, P., Mistry J., Göncü, A., and Mosier, C. (1993) Guided Participation in Cultural Activity by Toddlers and Caregivers, *Monographs of the Society for Research in Child Development*, Serial No. 236, Vol. 58 (8).

Rogoff, B. (1998). Cognition as a Collaborative Process, Handbook of Child Psychology, Vol. 2, *Cognition, Perception and Language*, Wiley, New York.

Rogoff, B. (2003). *The Cultural Nature of Human Development*, Oxford University Press.

Rosier, M.J., and Keeves, J. P. (1991). *The IEA Study of Science I: Science Education and Curricula in Twenty-three Countries*, Pergamon Press.

Rowe, S. (1998). *Learning Talk: Understanding How People Talk and Think about Learning in the St. Louis Science Center*, St. Louis Science Center, St. Louis, Mo.

Sauber, C. (1994). *Experiment Bench: A Workbook for Building Experimental Physics Exhibits*, Association of Science and Technology Centers Press, Washington, DC.

Saxe, G. (1994). Introduction to Studying Cognitive Development in Sociocultural Context, *Mind, Culture and Activity*, Vol. 1(3).

Serrell, B. (1990). What Research Says about Learning in Science Museums, Association of Science and Technology Centers Press, Washington, DC.

Toon, R. (2002). Science Centres and Legitimacy, Unplublished Doctoral Dissertation, University of Leicester, UK. (unpublished).

Tressel, G. (1984). A Museum Is to Touch, *1984 Yearbook of Science and the Future,* in Calhoun, D. (Ed.), Chicago, Encyclopedia Britannica, pp. 214–31.

Vercoe, C. (1996) Postcards/Signature of Place, *Art Asia Pacific Journal,* Vol 3, No. 1

vom Lehn, D., Heath, C., and Hindsmarsh, J. (2001a). "Exhibiting Interaction: Conduct and Collaboration in Museums and Galleries," *Symbolic Interaction* 24(2): 189–216.

vom Lehn, D., and Heath, C. (2001b). Communicating Science in Your Amazing Brain (Explore@Bristol). King's College London, Work, Interaction & Technology Research Group 33.

Vygotsky, L.S. (1978). *Mind in Society* (Cole, John-Steiner, Scribner & Souberman Eds.) Harvard University Press, Cambridge, Ma.

Wertsch, J. (1991) *Voices of the Mind: A sociocultural approach to mediated action,* Harvard University Press, Cambridge, Ma.

Wertsch, J. (1998). *Mind as Action,* Oxford University Press, New York.

INFORMAL LEARNING

CONCEPTUAL DISTINCTIONS AND PRELIMINARY FINDINGS

D. W. LIVINGSTONE

CONCEPTIONS OF FORMAL EDUCATION AND INFORMAL LEARNING

The continuing acquisition of knowledge and skills is probably the most distinctive feature of the human species. Learning is a continual process and any identification of forms of learning is a somewhat arbitrary exercise. But several basic forms of learning may be roughly distinguished in terms of the primacy of teachers and the type of organization of the body of knowledge to be learned.

While no form of human learning is devoid of the influence of other people, the distinctions that are proposed in this chapter focus on the degree of directive control of learning. These forms of learning range from dominant teacher control, through other forms that involve teachers/trainers/mentors, to dominant learner control. In addition, there are at least two different knowledge traditions: a rational or scientific cognitive knowledge form that emphasizes recordable theories and articulated descriptions as pre-established, cumulative bases for increased understanding, and a practical knowledge tradition that stresses direct experience in various situated spheres (Molander, 1992). Practical knowledge frequently remains tacit, unable to be described symbolically. In reality, both teacher-learner and theory-practice relations are best understood as continua.

The basic forms of learning are formal schooling and further education courses as well as informal education and self-directed learning. **Education**, which derives from the Latin verb (*educere*) meaning "to lead forth," encompasses the first three forms of learning characterized by the presence of a teacher, someone presumed to have greater knowledge, and a learner or learners presumed to have lesser knowledge and expected to be instructed or led by said teacher.

When a teacher has the authority to determine that people designated as requiring knowledge effectively learn a curriculum taken from a preestablished body of knowledge, the form of learning is **formal education**, whether in the form of age-graded and bureaucratic modern school systems or elders initiating youths into traditional bodies of knowledge.

When learners opt to acquire further knowledge or skill by studying voluntarily with a teacher who assists their self-determined interests by using an organized curriculum, as is the case in many adult education courses and workshops, the form of learning is **nonformal education** or **further education**.

When teachers or mentors take responsibility for instructing others without sustained reference to an intentionally organized body of knowledge in more incidental and spontaneous learning situations, such as guiding them in acquiring job skills or in community development activities, the form of learning is **informal education** or **informal training**.

Finally, all other forms of intentional or tacit learning in which we engage either individually or collectively without direct reliance on a teacher or an externally organized curriculum can be termed **self-directed** or **collective informal learning**. In the most expansive conceptions of human learning, self-directed learning may be seen as coterminous with life experience itself. Figure 1 portrays these different forms of learning in terms of primary agency and extent of institutionalization of knowledge.

		Primary Agency	
		Learner(s)	**Teacher(s)**
Knowledge Structure	**Preestablished**	Nonformal education Further education	Formal schooling Elders' teachings
	Situational	Self-directed learning Collective learning	Informal education Informal training

Figure 1: Basic Forms of Learning

This discussion will focus on adult learners because the conflation of formal education with other forms of learning may be somewhat lessoned beyond the age of compulsory schooling. Nevertheless, there has been considerable conceptual confusion among adult learning researchers over types of adult learning. Both earlier typologies and much of the research to date on adult learning have also tended to conflate some of these different types of learning (see Mocker & Spear, 1982; Padberg, 1991). Drawing boundaries between these four forms of learning can be very difficult. Distinguishing teachers from learners is often complicated in educational settings in which extensive interaction or independent inquiry are encouraged. More specifically, the nonformal or further education of adults typically occurs in courses or workshops with a preestablished curriculum and an externally designated instructor; adults also may decide to resume formal schooling in the same settings as compulsory age initial cycle students. But because adult participation is more discretionary, the curriculum of further education processes is likely to become quite learner-centered and situational in response to specific adults' interests, and therefore similar to an informal education process. The informal education of adults that occurs through contact with institutionally authorized guides in situations without a preestablished curriculum may be very comparable to and difficult to distinguish from a self-directed informal learning process if the guide is freely chosen in an ongoing informal relationship. Formal education that occurs outside state-approved educational institutions may be ignored or regarded as informal education by state officials, whereas such preestablished bodies of knowledge as the traditional wisdom shared by elders can remain central to the reproduction of aboriginal culture, for example. Conversely, self-directed informal learners may decide to follow a preestablished curriculum on their own, and therefore engage in a learning process much like formal education. But self-directed informal learning per se is most simply understood as learning that is undertaken on the learner's or learners' own terms without either prescribed curricular requirements or a designated instructor.

Most adults probably engage in multiple forms of learning on an ongoing basis, with varying emphases and tendencies. Only the state-sanctioned forms of schooling and further education are very fully identified or widely documented. Other adult learning activities have tended to be ignored or devalued by dominant authorities and researchers, either because they are more difficult to measure and certify or because they are grounded in experiential knowledge, which is more relevant to subordinate social groups (see Gereluk, Briton, & Spencer, 1999; Burns, 2001). In any case, it is clear that both adults' informal education/training and their self-directed informal learning have been relatively little explored to date and warrant much fuller attention from those interested in comprehending the nature and extent of adult learning.

Some of the most influential contemporary theories of adult learning focus on the learning capacities of adults outside standard teacher-directed classroom settings, such as Malcolm Knowles's (1970) work on individual self-directed learning and Paolo Freire's (1970, 1994) reflections on his initiatives in collective learning through dialogue. Both theorists stress the active practical engagement of adult learners in the pursuit of knowledge or cultural change. Theories of cognitive development that take more intentional account of subordinate groups' actual conditions and their sociohistorical context and that recognize the importance of diverse social relations beyond the realm of established educational institutions to the shaping of adult social consciousness (Vygotsky, 1978; Moll, 1990) have encouraged some researchers to begin to more fully conceptualize and conduct grounded studies of the dimensions of adult self-directed informal learning and informal education practices situated in the everyday lives of ordinary people (see Lave & Wenger, 1991; Engestrom, Miettinen, & Punamaki, 1999; Livingstone & Sawchuk, 2004; and others represented in this book).

Given this context, I can suggest a generic nominal definition of informal learning. ***Informal learning*** *is any activity involving the pursuit of understanding, knowledge, or skill that occurs without the presence of externally imposed curricular criteria.* Informal learning may occur in any context outside the preestablished curricula of educative institutions. The basic terms of informal learning (e.g. objectives, content, means and processes of acquisition, duration, evaluation of outcomes, applications) are determined by the individuals and groups that choose to engage in it. Self-directed or collective informal learning is undertaken on our own. Informal education or training is distinguished from such self-directed informal learning by the presence of some form of institutionally recognized instructor. Unless otherwise specified, the term "informal learning" will refer to both self-directed/collective informal learning and informal education/training in the remainder of this paper.

Conceptions of both self-directed informal learning and informal education to date have been quite insensitive to distinctions between intentional and more diffuse forms of learning. **Intentional self-directed informal learning** and **intentional informal training** can be distinguished from everyday perceptions, general socialization, and more tacit informal learning or training by peoples' own conscious identification of the activity as significant learning or training. The important criteria that distinguish intentional informal learning and training are the retrospective recognition of both (1) a new significant form of knowledge, understanding or skill acquired outside a prescribed curricular setting; and (2) the process of acquisition, either on your own initiative in the case of self-directed informal learning or with aid of a recognized mentor in the case of informal training. This is the guideline for distinguishing between intentional informal learning and training and all of the other tacit forms of learning and other everyday activities that we go through.

For example, there are the basic forms of socialization that we experience as young people, when older family members engage with us in many forms of anticipatory socialization that neither we nor they recognize as informal training because they are so incorporated in other activities, such as the various ad hoc day-to-day interrelationships between parents and children through which youths are inducted into the cultural life of their society. In basic socialization, tacit informal learning and acting constitute a seamless web in which it is impossible for most of us to distinguish many learning activities. Did I actually learn this in some discrete way or was it something that emerged in a much more diffuse experiential way that became part of my consciousness? Can I retrospectively identify deliberate and sustained efforts to gain a new form of understanding, knowledge, or skill, and attribute to these efforts a recognizable amount of time? It is important to stress here that self-reported estimates of informal learning and training very likely substantially underestimate the *total* amount of informal learning that people do because of the embedded and taken-for-granted character of this tacit learning (see Eraut, 1999, pp. 36, 40).

More inclusive approaches to informal learning that attempt to identify tacit knowledge through such means as direct observation in situation or in-depth interviewing may serve to sensitize both learners and researchers to previously taken-for-granted learning processes. Case studies using these methods can identify numerous dimensions of previously obscured but vitally important learning in social contexts that underpins more evident learning practices. These dimensions range from the hidden curriculum in elementary school classrooms to the implicit organizational learning that occurs among marginalized workers (e.g., Anyon, 1980; Church, Fontan, Ng, & Shragge, 2000). But all such approaches to date have only scratched the surface of tacit learning and remain prone to researcher presumptions whenever they go beyond respondents' self-reports.

The actual time that we allocate informally to gain intentional knowledge, skill, or understanding may vary in terms of our circumstances, the amount of concentration we can place on it, our actual learning capacities, and a number of other factors. A large number of case studies have now been done to document the content and time invested in actual self-directed learning activities by various adults (see Adams et al., 1999). The cumulative findings in Canada and internationally in the 1970s were that in the vast majority of social groups—whether distinguished by gender, age, class, race, ableism, or nationality—the vast majority of adults engaged in self-directed learning projects and the basic amount of time that people were spending on such learning projects showed very similar distributions across most groups. The average number of hours devoted to informal learning of this delineated, recognized sort was generally found to be around 10 hours a week or 500 hours a year in most of these case studies (Tough, 1978). But the corpus of case studies, most of which were conducted in the 1970s, were not done with sufficiently large or diverse enough samples to make representative claims about specific populations, at least not in statistical terms.

To study self-directed informal learning using the sample survey techniques normally required for representative readings of human behavior, we have to strike a resolve to focus on those things that people can identify for themselves as intentional learning projects or deliberate learning activities beyond prescribed curricula and without externally authorized instructors. Documenting informal training requires a similar reliance on respondents' self-reports. More sensitive ethnographic case study research should be encouraged. But "thin" versions of adults' intentional informal learning and training generated through survey research can at least provide more complete profiles of their actual array of learning practices. Well-designed surveys of intentional informal learning may thereby contribute to more nuanced appreciation of the multiple dimensions and relationships of the learning continuum. Such measures can at least provide benchmarks for understanding the extent and changing patterns of informal learning activities.

EMPIRICAL RESEARCH ON INFORMAL LEARNING

One of the first empirical studies to attempt to estimate the extent of informal learning activities among adults was the 1961–62 US national survey (N = 2845) of voluntary learning (Johnstone & Rivera, 1965). After a detailed set of questions about further education course participation, the survey then asked whether respondents had ever tried to teach themselves some subject by means of independent study strictly on their own, followed by asking them if they were currently engaged in any studies of this sort. Nearly 40% of US adults indicated that they had engaged in such learning activities at some time and nearly 10% said they were currently involved; respondents were also almost twice as likely to indicate participation in independent studies as in further education courses, and most of those engaged in further education were also involved in independent studies (pp. 33, 38, 129). As Johnstone and Rivera (1965, p. 37) concluded:

> To the authors' knowledge, this type of measure has never before been extracted from a national sample of the population—which in itself suggests that self-instruction is probably the most overlooked avenue of activity in the whole field of adult education. . . . About the only comment that can be made at this point is that the incidence of self-education throughout the adult population is much greater than we had anticipated.

As noted above, the most substantial subsequent body of empirical research dealing with adult learning activities beyond organized schooling and further education courses has been the case studies of adults' self-directed learning projects. This research was inspired by Malcolm Knowles (1970) and pioneered by my colleague Allen Tough (1971, 1979). Tough's early case studies, since replicated by numerous others, found that well over two-thirds of most adults' intentional learning efforts occurred completely outside institutionalized adult education programs or courses, hence the image of the adult learning iceberg (Brookfield, 1981; Brockett & Hiemstra, 1991). The case studies initiated by Tough in the 1960s suggest that virtually all adults are regularly involved in deliberate, self-directed learning projects beyond school and training programs. As Tough (1978, p. 252) summarized the central finding from a wide array of case studies in the 1970s:

> The typical learner conducts five quite distinct learning projects in one year. He or she learns five distinct areas of knowledge and skill. The person spends an average of 100 hours per learning effort—a total of 500 hours per year.

Because the extensive character of informal learning was first indicated by these case studies, there have been very few larger scale surveys to verify and further explore the social relations of informal learning with representative samples. The first large-scale national survey focused on informal learning—inspired by Johnstone and Rivera's incidental findings and guided by Tough's case study interview format—was conducted by Patrick Penland (1977) in the United States in late 1976. The interview began with the general framing questions on informal learning. Just as in Tough's research, the initial questions were followed by some probes to provide further opportunities for respondents to recall their relevant intentional informal learning activities during the past year. Penland found that over three-quarters of US adults were involved in self-planned learning activities and that, as in the prior case studies, they were spending an average of about 500 hours per year in such informal learning.

Most of the other sample surveys conducted in North America and Europe since the early 1970s on the general frequency of informal learning are summarized in Table 1.

After Penland's study, very few further large-scale general surveys of informal learning were conducted until the mid-1990s. But some national surveys have recently begun to ask about aspects of informal learning in the context of inquiries focused on adult education course participation. A 1995 Finnish survey (Blomqvist, Niemi, & Ruuskanen, 1998, pp. 34, 91), using much more restrictive questions than Penland and excluding registered students, found that 22% of Finnish adults between 18 and 64 had been involved in self-directed learning for at least 20 hours in the past year. A UK survey covering the 1994–97 period and focused primarily on taught learning has found that

Survey*	Sample Size	Total Hours Per Year	Informal Learners (%)
Hiemstra (1975) [Nebraskans over 55]	256	325	84
Penland (1976) [US national adult population]	1,501	514	76
Tough (1971-78) [Estimate based on 1970s case studies]	N/A	500	98
Leean & Sisco (1981) [Rural Vermont school dropouts]	93	425	98
Blomqvist, Niemi, & Ruuskanen (1995) [Finnish adult population]	4,107	20+	22
Livingstone, Hart, & Davie (1996) [Ontario adult population]	1,000	600	86
Beinart & Smith (1994-97) [United Kingdom adult population]	5,653	N/A	57
Statistics Canada (1998) [Canadian national adult population]	10,749	230	30
NALL (1998) [Canadian national adult population]	1,562	750	95
Livingstone, Hart, & Davie (1998) [Ontario adult population]	1,007	750	88
Livingstone, Hart, & Davie (2000) [Ontario adult population]	1,002	650	86

*Years cited refer to period of learning surveyed rather than time of publication

Table 1: Estimated Incidence of Informal Learning Activities, Selected Countries, 1975–2000

57% of all adults indicated involvement in some form of nontaught learning during this period (Beinhart & Smith, 1998, pp. 200–17, 309, 315). This included 51% of those who were employed who indicated that they had spent time keeping up to date with developments in the type of work they do without taking part in a taught course (for example, by reading books, manuals, or journals or attending seminars); it also included 29% of all nonstudents who were deliberately trying to improve their knowledge about anything or teaching themselves a skill without taking part in a taught course, and 1% of all adults who were studying for any qualifications without taking part in a taught course.[1] A follow-up survey 18 months later found that the participation rate in nontaught learning over the entire 4.5–year period increased to 65% (LaValle & Finch, 1999, p. 11). No estimates of the duration of informal learning were attempted in these surveys; in the UK case this was because pilot surveys found that respondents were unable to give precise start and end dates for these more informal nontaught types of learning (Beinhart & Smith, 1999, p. 269).

The 1998 General Social Survey (GSS) in Canada (Statistics Canada, 1999) also contained a few questions on undertaking informal learning instead of taking courses. About 30% of respondents gave an initial positive response. After responding to the other two general questions, the remaining respondents then estimated that they were spending an average of about 19 hours per month on these learning activities, which translates into nearly 5 hours per week or about 230 hours per year. Averaged over the entire sample, this would reduce to about 1.5 hours per week.

All of these recent surveys of informal learning (i.e., the Finnish, UK, and 1998 GSS surveys) very likely produce *serious underestimates* of the actual current extent of intentional informal learning. The questions on informal learning are typically posed immediately after a series of questions about initial schooling, adult credit courses and noncredit courses. This initial emphasis may serve to predispose respondents to think of learning in terms of organized education, especially when only cryptic definitions of informal learning are provided, and no opportunity is offered to consider informal learning activities in relation to any other specific learning context besides educational institutions. These survey questions also tend to dichotomize courses and learning on your own, suggesting—explicitly in the case of the GSS survey—that you normally only do one or the other. Virtually all the earlier surveys, informed by Tough's case study research, demonstrated this is clearly false, that most course participants also engage in substantial informal learning activities. It is likely that these recent surveys have merely rediscovered the iceberg of intentional informal learning rather than plumbing its depth.[2]

Surveys conducted in Ontario, Canada, in 1996, 1998, and 2000 on public attitudes to educational policies have included a few questions that used a similar format to the original Tough studies and the Penland survey. These surveys have found that the vast majority of adults indicate involvement in some form of informal learning during the past year. Estimated time commitments have fluctuated between averages of about 12 and 15 hours per week during this four-year period (Livingstone, Hart, & Davie, 1999, 2001).

Finally, in 1998, the research network on New Approaches to Lifelong Learning (NALL) conducted the first national survey in Canada focused on adults' informal learning practices (NALL, 1998; Livingstone, 1999). NALL is centered at the Ontario Institute for Studies in Education at the University of Toronto (OISE/UT). It has been funded by the Social Sciences and Humanities Research Council of Canada (SSHRC) to identify the extent of adult learning, the existence of social barriers to learning, and more effective means of linking learning with work.[3] The NALL survey of adults' current learning was planned to attend to the full array of adults' learning activities, including not only schooling and continuing education courses but also informal learning that occurs outside organized education. We reviewed and borrowed from virtually all prior studies of informal learning that have previously been conducted (see Adams et al., 1999). We did extensive pilot testing with dozens of individuals and groups. The final interview schedule addresses schooling, further education courses and workshops, as well as informal education and various aspects of self-directed informal learning, but the primary focus is on the diverse aspects of intentional informal learning; a variety of social background factors are also addressed. (Those interested in reviewing the full interview schedule can find it at the NALL Web site: <http://www.nall.ca>.) A representative telephone survey of 1562 Canadian adults was conducted for NALL between June 6 and November 8, 1998, by the Institute for Social Research at York University. This survey asked respondents to talk about informal learning from their own standpoints. The NALL survey sample includes adults 18 and over, who speak English or French, reside in a private home (not old age/group homes/penal or *educational* institutions) with a telephone. All provinces and households and individuals within households were given an equal chance of selection using random digit dialing. The average telephone interview time was 32 minutes, which is about half of the administration time of the earlier US national survey (Penland, 1977, p. 23). An in-depth follow-up interview was also conducted with a subsample of the original respondents in the summer of 2000 (see Livingstone, Hart, & Stowe, 2003).

The NALL survey respondents were first given a definition of informal learning as including anything people do to gain knowledge, skill, or understanding from learning about their health or hobbies, unpaid or paid work, or anything else that interests them outside of organized courses. They were then asked to indicate their participation in four aspects of informal learning: employment-related; community volunteer work-related; household work-related; and other general interest-related. In each aspect, respondents were asked about informal learning activities on several specific themes. The most relevant NALL findings are summarized briefly in the remainder of this section.

Those Canadian adults in the active labor force (including over 60% employed and about 8% designated as unemployed) were first asked to identify any informal learning they had done during the past year related to their employment. These employment-related learning activities included such matters as new job tasks, employment-related computer learning, and occupational health and safety. The proportion of respondents who indicated participating in each of these topical areas of learning ranged from over 70% (keeping up with new general knowledge in job/career) to around 10% (job-related second language skills). Respondents were then asked to estimate the time they spent on employment-related informal learning. On average, currently employed respondents estimated that they spent about six hours per week in all of these informal learning activities related to their current or future employment during the past year. Around 10% estimated that they spent less than an hour per week in employment-related informal learning activities. Very few employed people stated that they did no job-related informal learning but some found it too difficult to provide a specific estimate; all of them were treated as "less than an hour" responses and were coded as zeros, thereby contributing to a conservative estimate of average hours. The remainder were about equally divided into those who spent one to two hours, three to five hours, and six or more hours per week in job-related informal learning. Less than 10% estimated that they spent more than 20 hours per week, which suggests that even when respondents are given fairly extensive opportunities to identify job-related informal learning they are very unlikely to regard informal learning as a seamless web occupying most of their paid work time.

Similar questions were asked in each of the other three spheres of informal learning. Those involved in household work over the past year (over 80%) averaged about five hours per week in informal learning related to their household work. The household work-related learning activities included such matters as home cooking, home maintenance, shopping, child or elder care. Participation ranged from 66% in home renovations and gardening to about 40% in cleaning activities. Again there are small numbers at the extremes, with around 10% indicating they devote less than an hour per week to housework-related informal learning and about 5% saying they spend more than 20 hours per week in such learning. Given the greater proportion of adults involved in housework than in paid employment and the only slightly higher average hours devoted to informal learning related to employment, it appears that Canadians are now devoting about as much aggregate time to informal learning related to housework as to paid employment.

Those who have been involved in organized community work over the past year (over 40%) devote about four hours a week on average to community-related informal learning. The community-related informal learning activities include such matters as communication skills, social issues, organizational/managerial skills, and fundraising. Participation rates ranged from over 60% in interpersonal skills to around 25% in other technical skills. The majority of community work participants indicate that they devote no more than two hours per week to related informal learning activities, while less than 10% devote more than 10 hours per week. The relatively low levels of participation in community volunteer work and related informal learning are consistent with the fact that this is the most discretionary type of work in advanced industrial societies and many people simply choose to opt out.

Finally, most people engage in some other types of informal learning related to their general interests and not directly connected with any of the three forms of work. Those who do so (around 90%) spend on average about six hours a week on these learning activities. The basic sorts of general interest learning range widely from hobbies to religion. Participation rates varied from about 75% in health and well-being to 35% in science and technology topics. Around a third of respondents spend an hour or less per week in informal learning related to all of these general interests. The majority spend no more than three hours, while less than 10% devote more than 10 hours a week to such general interest learning. While there is evidently very wide participation in informal learning related to many diverse interests, the incidence of work-related informal learning is considerably greater if we include both paid and unpaid work.

Overall, according to the NALL survey, nearly all Canadian adults (over 95%) are involved in some form of informal learning activities that they can identify as significant. This survey provides estimates of the amount of time that all Canadians, including those who say they do no informal learning at all, are spending in all four areas (employment, community, household, and general interest). The estimated average number of hours devoted to all forms of informal learning activities by all Canadian adults during 1998 was around 15 hours per week. The average figure masks considerable variation in the total amount of informal learning that Canadian adults say they are now doing. Less than 5% insist that they are either doing no informal learning, doing less than an hour per week, or are unable to offer a specific estimate, while 25% say they are doing over 20 hours per week of total informal learning activity. About three-quarters of Canadian adults are now spending six hours or more each week in some kind of informal learning activities, most of this related to paid or unpaid work.

The NALL survey estimate for the amount of time that Canadian adults are spending in organized courses (including time in class and doing homework and class assignments) is about three hours per week averaged over the entire adult population, or about 12 hours per week among those who actually participated in courses. The most recent national survey of adult education, which focused in more detail on different types of nonformal course participation but only asked about hours participants took the course rather than explicitly asking them to consider homework time, generated an average of about one hour a week for the entire adult population or four hours a week per participant (Arrowsmith & Oikawa, 2001, p. 35). Even if the focus is restricted to those who participated in courses, they appear to devote more time to intentional informal learning activities than to course-based learning. If we consider the entire adult population, *Canadian adults are clearly spending vastly more time in informal learning activities than in nonformal education courses, a ratio of about five to one.* The use of the metaphor of the submerged part of an iceberg to describe the informal portion of adult learning may not be exact, but it is fairly close.

It is important to recognize here that the NALL time estimates have been generated through a survey that was *primarily* devoted to identifying the multiple possible sites and topics of informal learning. Virtually all prior empirical studies of informal learning have found considerable initial reluctance among respondents to identify their learning outside educational institutions as legitimate learning (see Tough, 1979). It is only when people are given an opportunity to reflect on actual learning practices in relation to their daily lives that much informal learning is recognized as such by the learners. In addition, informal learning activities often occur in combination with other social activities. While this makes time estimates more difficult and less exact, it is not a sufficient basis to either devalue or ignore informal learning processes. In any event, when adults are given even brief opportunity to reflect on their informal learning practices along the topical lines summarized above, the average estimated time devoted to informal learning is now around 15 hours per week, which is both much more time than they devote to organized educational activities and a significant portion of their waking time. Of course, future surveys will need to both confirm and track trends in the NALL benchmark estimate.

A major *non*finding suggested by earlier case studies on adults' informal learning is also confirmed by this national survey. While school attainment and adult education participation are strongly associated, neither is a good predictor of the incidence of informal learning activities. Second, while participation in adult education declines as we age, older people generally sustain their involvement in informal learning activities. Similar rates of participation in informal learning are found between nearly all other sociodemographic groupings as well (e.g., sex, class, and income and ethnicity, region, nation), with greater variations within particular subgroups than between them. There appear to be no discernible demographic prerequisites to general involvement in informal learning nor are there major institutional barriers, as virtually everyone can participate on their own terms if they are interested.

In summary, the few inclusive and directly comparable surveys on adult informal learning suggest that North Americans were spending around 10 hours per week in intentional informal learning activities in the 1970s, and that the incidence may have increased by the 1990s (see also Candy, 1993). Clearly, the overwhelming majority of Canadian adults are now spending a substantial amount of time regularly in these pursuits and are able to recognize this intentional informal learning as a significant aspect of their daily lives. The recent proliferation of information technologies and exponential increases in the production of information have created greater opportunities for informal learning beyond their own direct experience for people in all walks of life. Whatever the actual extent and trends over time are found to be through further, more refined studies, virtually all empirical studies to date that have estimated the extent of adults' intentional informal learning have confirmed that it is a very substantial activity.

CRITICAL ASSESSMENT OF RESEARCH TO DATE ON INFORMAL LEARNING

The early body of empirical research on self-directed informal learning was subjected to numerous serious criticisms that any further studies of informal learning should remain sensitive to, including tendencies to individualistic, dominant class, and leading question biases, as well as the profound difficulty in validly identifying intentional informal learning that may be initiated incidentally, occur irregularly, and have diffuse outcomes (see Brookfield, 1981; Livingstone, 1999).

The *individualistic bias* is the implicit assumption that you learn most of what you learn individually rather than in collective or relational context. Early empirical research focused on individual respondents and documenting their self-directed learning projects. But the collective aspects of our informal learning, the social engagements with others, are an integral part of any actual knowledge acquisition process, as some leading general theories of learning now clearly acknowledge (see Engstrom, Miettinen, & Punamaki, 1999; Livingstone & Sawchuk, 2004). Collectively conducted learning processes continue to constitute the least well-documented part of adults' informal learning. But the individualistic bias can be partially overcome by research methods that either engage with people in the social contexts of their lives (such as participant observation) or by questioning them collectively (as in discussion groups of various kinds). Even the individual interview methods required for a large-scale survey can more explicitly address the social relational aspects of respondents' specific learning activities.

The *dominant class bias* charge emerged because the vast majority of the early case study research was conduced with white, middle-aged, professional-managerial people and university students. But further case study research done with less affluent classes, visible minority groups, and seniors do support the general conclusions that Tough (1978) made about self-directed learning being fairly common in its incidence across most social groups (see Adams et al., 1999). The dominant group bias surely can be more fully addressed with greater sensitivity and respect for other standpoints by further in-depth studies that document the informal learning of working-class and underclass people, women and people of various sexual orientations, visible minorities, disabled people, and older and younger generations. This requires extensive pilot testing of instruments with representatives of subordinate social groups to try to ensure their general accessibility (e.g., Livingstone & Sawchuk, 2004).

In the enthusiasm of the early empirical research in the self-directed learning tradition, there was often a tendency toward *leading questions,* in the sense of "of course you do informal learning, don't you?" and "what is it?" as opposed to asking people whether or not they do it, and taking what they tell you as valid. The basic procedure in early studies was for the interviewer to react skeptically to responses that denied any significant informal learning, and then proceed to a series of probes to ferret out actual informal learning projects (Tough, 1979). The genuine difficulty here is that researchers do have to engage in an initial orienting process precisely because most people do not register much of the informal learning they do until they have a chance to reflect on it. Later research studies have been less leading, including a growing tradition of situated learning case studies that have confirmed the extensiveness of intentional informal learning activities through direct observation (e.g., Lave & Wenger, 1991). Future surveys and other studies should give respondents numerous thematic cues based on prior empirical studies but accept all responses as given without insistent probing that could encourage respondents to overestimate their informal learning activities.

If we recognize the general importance of informal learning for the reproduction and development of social life, and if we agree that it is feasible to get past the early critiques to engage in empirical research that may validly identify people's intentional informal learning, there are still other major challenges. These include recognizing *incidentally initiated learning, irregularly timed intentional learning, and the distinction between learning processes and learning outcomes.* The predominance of planned learning may be clear enough when we are talking about schooling decisions. But you can do informal learning any time, anywhere, with anyone. It can be planned in a very deliberate way or it can be stimulated with no prior intent. Many informal learning activities that result in the accomplishment of new knowledge, understanding or skill begin in an ad hoc, incidental manner and are only consciously recognized after the fact (see Eraut, 1999). Retrospective views of the amount of time spent in *incidentally initiated informal learning processes* are likely to remain very approximate underestimates. But approximations of the significance of important phenomena should be preferred to either continuing to ignore them or to imposing false precision in measurement efforts.

Informal learning never ends. But much of it occurs in *irregular time and space patterns.* You can learn life-course shaping or influencing knowledge at any place and within a very short period of time, in a moment of "perspective transformation" (Mezirow, 1991) or an "organizing circumstance" (Spear, 1988). Much of the most important learning that we do occurs in these moments of transition, whether it happens to be a birth, a death, a marriage, divorce, a transition between careers or locations, or some other major influential event that provokes us into a concentrated period of informal learning. Survey respondents' estimates of the amount of time they devote to informal learning activities are helpful to compare the perceived amounts of time available for such activities in different social groups. But such estimates of learning patterns should not obscure the fact that the most significant informal learning continues to occur in these irregular, intense moments of our lives (see Merriam & Clark, 1991).

It is also important to observe that the amount of time that people spend in *learning processes* is not necessarily positively correlated with successful *learning outcomes*. A less capable learner may have to spend considerably more time to achieve a successful outcome. Much of the research to date on adult learning focuses on documenting the types of learning processes that people are involved in, the amount of time that they engage in these processes, and their particular substantive areas of learning. Very little of this research addresses the question of the actual competencies that people have gained from their informal learning activities. This is at least partially because many of the criteria of successful informal learning are themselves informally determined. No external authority can pose an inclusive set of criteria about either the curriculum that should be learned or satisfactory levels of achievement, let alone ensure intersubjectively meaningful comparisons between informal learning outcomes. So, the initial recourse here again is to self-recognition: What have learners accomplished through informal learning activities that they perceive as significant?

In light of general conceptual confusion, varied measures, and the very limited amount of comparative data, researchers' knowledge of the extent, processes, content, outcomes and trends of adults' informal learning and training remains very crude. The extensive case study research on self-directed learning in the 1970s has led to **very little cumulative development** of understanding of the phenomenon of informal learning to date. Researchers keep rediscovering portions of informal learning anew with little effort to date to replicate earlier discoveries. For example, while early self-directed learning researchers developed protocols to probe the topical foci and duration of informal learning projects, the recent UK and Finnish survey researchers were apparently unaware of this research and abandoned any attempt to either identify topical foci or estimate actual duration of adults' informal learning activities. The Statistics Canada (1999) questions in the General Social Survey of 1998 generate estimates of duration and topical foci but mainly for those who have learned informally "instead of taking a course," ignoring the well-established fact that most adults who take courses also engage in other informal learning. All of these surveys also present the notion of informal, independent, or nontaught learning cryptically after extensive questioning on participation in organized education, ignoring the earlier finding that most people may tend to deny that they do any significant learning outside educational settings until they are given an opportunity to reflect at least briefly on their experiential learning. Our replications of the 1976 US survey in Canada in the late 1990s (i.e., the NALL and OISE/UT surveys) represent a beginning in this regard, but further survey research is needed to reach much confidence in these estimates of the extent, topical foci, and trends in adults' informal learning.

None of the empirical research to date on informal learning has distinguished very clearly between **informal self-directed learning** and **informal education or training**, as defined in the first part of this paper. For example, it may be the case that a great deal of job training occurs in the form of informal education of newer entrants by more experienced workers, but the relative importance of informal learning without such teachers by workers individually and collectively learning on their own has not been well documented. A single item in the 1998 NALL survey indicates that the most important general sources of employment-related knowledge from the standpoints of those in the current Canadian labor force are workers' own independent learning efforts (44%), followed by informal education by their co-workers (28%). Nonformal education in the form of employers' training programs is regarded as most important by a small minority (15%). Whether particular informal learning activities are done with the aid of a teacher/mentor and therefore qualify as informal education and training or whether they are done by individuals or groups on their own and constitute self-directed informal learning should be addressed more carefully in subsequent research.

The **boundary between intentional and tacit informal learning** has only begun to be explored and most studies of intentional informal learning continue to ignore or underestimate the depths and complexity of tacit learning. However, the now well-established tradition of conceptual and empirical research on implicit learning is beginning to provide clearer insights into the interplay of implicit and intentional learning and memory generally (see Reber, 1993; Stadler & Frensch, 1998). Further progress in probing the depth of intentional informal learning will probably require similar intensive interviewing and experimental research designs.

Another reason for highly variable results in surveys of informal learning and training has been a failure to contextuate such learning in the **activity structure** of respondents' daily lives. If people are merely asked to identify and estimate informal learning activities without reference to the other activities and time commitments that they are involved in, both the time constraints and the learning incentives associated with everyday life are more likely to be ignored. The mid-2000 follow-up with a subsample (N = 328) from the 1998 NALL survey incorporated a series of related questions on general time use prior to items on informal learning time (Livingstone, Hart, & Stowe, 2003). The average estimated total informal learning time was reduced by about 20%. We hypothesize that this reduction may be related to the introduction of general activity structure time constraints into the second interview schedule, as well as to other contextual changes between 1998 and 2000. Future surveys will need to include similar items on other contextuating activities in order to generate reliable estimates of informal learning.

A closely related problem that has hardly been hinted at to date in empirical research estimating the extent of informal self-directed learning and training is the matter of **simultaneity**. We learn while we act continuously. To distinguish learning components from other aspects of our everyday practices can be extraordinarily difficult. Time use research has attempted to deal with the general problem of simultaneous activities by asking respondents to record primary and secondary activities in a given time period. Further research on informal learning and training will probably have to resort to some similar strategy of identifying informal learning as either a primary or secondary activity within a more clearly identified time and space structure of activities.

Only with more reliable estimates of informal learning over time and in different jurisdictions will it be possible to evaluate the relationships between organized schooling and nonformal education, on the one hand, and informal learning and training, on the other. The possibility of recent **substitution effects** in Canada, and Ontario in particular, is supported by survey evidence that suggests that the levels of participation in adult education courses declined during the mid-1990s (Arrowsmith & Oikawa, 2001; Livingstone, Hart, & Davie, 1999), while perceived material barriers to participation and the incidence of informal learning both increased (Livingstone, Raykov & Stowe, 2001; Livingstone, Hart, & Davie, 1999). The most recent Ontario evidence for 2000 suggests that adult course participation may have again increased and that the incidence of informal learning may have declined somewhat (Livingstone, Hart, & Davie, 2001, 2003). The possibility of such an inverse relationship, with increased incidence of informal learning substituting for diminished access to further education courses and vice versa, should be examined by additional longitudinal surveys. But any examination of such an inverse relationship should not lose sight of the following facts: (1) there has been a dominant trend of increasing formal/nonformal course participation in the post–World War II era; (2) informal self-directed learning and informal training remain far more pervasive than course participation; and (3) that all four types of learning practically complement each other throughout the life course.

There is also virtually no prior systematic research beyond scattered ethnographic studies on the **relations between informal learning and training and different types of work**. Correlation analysis of the association between the time devoted to different types of work (employment, housework, and community volunteer work) and informal learning specifically related to these three types of work in the 1998 NALL survey finds that correlations are highest between community volunteer work and community-based informal learning and lowest between paid employment and job-related informal learning (Livingstone, 2002). This suggests that the greater discretion one has to engage in the work, the stronger the association between the hours of such work and the related incidence of informal learning. Prior research on relations between degrees of autonomy in paid employment and personality characteristics is of some relevance (e.g., Kohn & Schooler, 1983), but no other empirical studies have to date addressed these relations between types of learning and work inclusively.. Further studies on these relations, which include discretionary forms of (informal) learning and (unpaid) work, may be very useful guides for the redesign of paid work (see Livingstone, 2003).

With regard to the lack of social group differences in informal learning, the most provocative findings involve aging. Prior research on aging and learning has focused on declining speed and efficiency of skill acquisition. No comparable decline has been found to date in the incidence of informal learning. Case studies and experimental research examining the actual informal learning practices, topical foci, and skill outcomes of older adults are much needed to overcome stereotypes of decline and to understand the interaction of cumulative experience and new skill acquisition. Similarly, more attention needs to be paid to the distinctively high incidence of both organized education activities and informal learning among those making the transition to adulthood. The general finding of no significant differences in incidence of informal learning activity between most other sociodemographic groups also needs to be tested much more thoroughly against more reliable measures of informal learning over time. Furthermore, sensitive case studies also may discover significant content differences in the informal learning practices of socially disadvantaged groups.

Much further grounded research is needed to document actual processes of informal learning and training, prevalent thematic foci, and quality of outcomes in order to generate clearer profiles of intentional informal learning. Only then will we be able to begin to carefully assess the impact of informal learning and training on specific skill development as well as the aggregate effects of informal learning and training on such central social policy areas as workplace productivity, community development, and effective citizenship.

CONCLUDING REMARKS

It is should now be clear that informal self-directed learning and informal training constitute the most elusive and shifting domains of adult learning but also the most extensive. **Given the centrality of informal learning, it is imperative to establish benchmarks of its general incidence, basic contents and modes, and any differential patterns of intentional informal learning and training, and to continue to track trends in relation to other dimensions of learning**. Further large-scale sample survey research on informal learning and training is necessary to obtain reliable, representative estimates of the extent and content of informal learning in the adult population in different countries. We should be under no illusion that a survey questionnaire is capable of uncovering the deeper tacit levels of either individual or collective knowledge gained in informal learning and training practices. But by building on prior research and critiques, we should now be able to generate useful profiles of the basic patterns of the incidence of intentional informal learning and training and examine their association with organized forms of education more fully than most prior studies.

In sum, survey research on adults' informal learning should adhere to the following basic guidelines:

- focus on intentional informal learning that respondents can identify as significant for themselves;
- distinguish informal learning occurring outside established curricula from nonformal education occurring in organized courses and workshops;
- distinguish between self-directed informal learning that most people do on their own individually and collectively, and informal education and training that involves a mentor;
- assess informal learning activities in relation to other activities of everyday life including different types of paid and unpaid work, and allow for simultaneity with some of these other activities;
- provide sufficient contextual and thematic referents in any empirical study for respondents to effectively identify their major intentional informal learning activities, without leading them into gratuitous overestimates;
- insist on directly examining the informal learning practices of all adults without any presumption that specific sociodemographic groups (e.g., older people, marginalized groups) have greater or lesser learning predispositions.

In the longer term, the more comprehensive documentation of organized and informal learning activities in relation to the existing job structure and patterns of unpaid work should provide a more adequate basis for developing employment policies that are more responsive to the actual employability of the current and prospective labor force. For example, the issues of whether there are skill surpluses or shortages in specific sectors and whether training or economic policy initiatives are most appropriate really requires such intelligence to aid effective, sustained government decision making. There is mounting evidence, based on organized education and training measures, that there is now no general skill shortage in many advanced industrial societies (see Lavoie & Roy, 1998). There is also a large body of empirical evidence indicating that aggregate educational attainments have increased much quicker than aggregate educational requirements to perform existing jobs, particularly in Canada and the United States (see Livingstone, 2003). Taking systematic account of the informal self-learning and training relevant to actual job performance and to unpaid work activities would provide a fuller understanding of the complex relations between learning and employment. Aside from the small but important proportion of adults with low literacy and increasing marginalization from the credential-based labor market, the most basic problem now may not be skill supply shortages but underemployment of people's available skills and knowledge in our current job structure. In any event, neither researchers nor public policymakers can afford to ignore the growing problem of training-employment gaps, and more comprehensive ongoing surveys of adult learning are clearly needed to inform employment and training policies. As the OECD *Manual for Better Training Statistics* (1997) suggests, the temptation to focus narrowly on the most easily identifiable and immediately applicable aspects of informal vocational learning in such research should be resisted.

Efforts to measure returns to informal learning and training should proceed very cautiously given their elusive character, and the differential interests of employers and employees and other citizens in controlling access to working knowledge. Further case studies and comparative sectoral studies should address the relative and complementary effectiveness of informal learning and training and organized education programs/courses in relation to a wide range of indicators of social benefit, including productivity and sustainable employment. But future rate of return estimates should beware of the "most immediately tangible measures bias." A pragmatic fixation on monetary rates of return for the employed excludes consideration of benefits of education and training for the unemployed and nonemployed (about 40% of adult population); other nonmonetary benefits for all people, including the employed (consumption effectiveness, informed citizenship, familial health); and macrosocietal benefits (besides GDP these include Quality of Life measures). While both the extent and rates of return to informal learning and training are much less well documented than either schooling or nonformal training, informal learning and training could well turn out to be the most productive investments in terms of a more inclusive cost-benefit analysis of lifelong learning.

While there are conceptual difficulties in distinguishing informal self-directed learning, informal training, nonformal education, and formal education, as well as methodological challenges in generating reliable readings of informal learning and training, the empirical research to date has at least established that adults' intentional informal learning activities are both very extensive and warrant continuing documentation and assessment in relation to other economic and social activities. The insights generated by the early adult education research on self-directed learning should be taken into fuller account in future large-scale surveys of informal learning activities. The consistent finding of virtually all prior studies that the basic incidence of adult informal learning is not closely related to either prior formal educational participation or most sociodemographic differences suggests that the more effective recognition of prior informal learning in both work settings and educational institutions—through further research on and fuller use of prior learning recognition mechanisms—could stimulate both greater educational accessibility and enhanced workplace utilization of knowledge. All of those committed to the principles of lifelong learning and the democratic development of the emergent information age (see OECD, 1998) should be interested in further exploration of the still largely hidden informal dimensions of the iceberg of adult learning.

ACKNOWLEDGMENTS

Portions of this chapter are revised from a position paper (Livingstone, 2001) for Human Resources Development Canada (HRDC). The views expressed in this paper are those of the author and do not necessarily reflect the position of HRDC. The NALL national survey on informal learning was funded by Social Sciences and Humanities Research Council of Canada research grant #818–1996–1033.

NOTES

1. The summary figure of 57% in this UK survey also includes some who declared that they received supervised training outside of taught courses while actually doing a job, when a manager or experienced colleague has spent time helping them learn or develop skills as they do specific tasks at work. About 30% of employed workers indicated this form of learning (Beinhart & Smith, 1998, pp. 208, 315), which we have classified as informal education or training rather than self-directed informal learning. Eliminating those who only indicated involvement in supervised training on the job would probably reduce the summary figure somewhat. However, none of the other surveys reported in this table have distinguished clearly between self-directed informal learning and informal education or training.
2. This conclusion is confirmed by a mid-2000 follow-up to the 1998 NALL survey, which replicated the first GSS 1998 item on informal learning, but substituted "outside of" for "instead of" in the stem. The NALL follow-up survey was otherwise similar to the GSS in asking this question prior to any other items on informal learning. This survey drew a positive answer from over 70% of respondents, compared to only 30% of GSS respondents.
3. In addition to the first national survey of informal learning practices, NALL has also conducted a parallel national survey of teachers' informal learning practices, and has completed follow-up surveys, as well as over 30 related case studies. Most of these studies examine the relations among informal learning, schooling, and nonformal education, as well as their relations with paid and unpaid work and other sociodemo-

graphic characteristics. For further information, see the NALL Web site: <http://www.nall.ca>.

REFERENCES

Adams, M., et al. (1999). *Preliminary bibliography of the research network for New Approaches to Lifelong Learning (NALL)*. Toronto: Centre for the Study of Education and Work, OISE/UT. Retrieved April 14, 2003 from <http://www.nall.ca>.

Anyon, J. (1980). Social class and the hidden curriculum of work. *Journal of Education, 162:* 67–92.

Arrowsmith, S., & Oikawa, C. (2001). Trends in Canadian adult learning. In *Statistics Canada: A report on adult education and training in Canada: Learning a Living.* Ottawa: Statistics Canada and Human Resources Development Canada.

Beinhart, S., & Smith, P. (1998). *National Adult Learning Survey 1997.* Sudbury, Suffolk: Department for Education and Employment. Research Report No. 49.

Blomqvist, I., Niemi, H., & Ruuskanen, T. (1998). *Participation in adult education and training in Finland 1995.* Helsinki: Statistics Finland.

Brockett, R., & Hiemstra, R. (1991). *Self-direction in adult education: Perspectives on theory, research and practice.* New York: Routledge.

Brookfield, S. (1981). The adult education learning iceberg. *Adult Education (UK), 54*(2): 110–18.

Burns, G. (2001). Dichotomization of formal and informal education, the marginalization of elders, and problems of aboriginal education and native studies in the public educational system. In P. Gamlin and M. Luther (Eds.), *Exploring human potential: New directions in facilitating growth in the new millennium.* Concord, ON: Captus Press [see also <http://www.nall.ca>].

Candy, P. (1993). *Self-direction for lifelong learning: A comprehensive guide to theory and practice.* San Francisco: Jossey-Bass.

Church, K., Fontan, J-M., Ng, R., & Shragge, E. (2000). *Social learning among people who are excluded from the labour market. Part one: Context and studies.* NALL Working Paper Series, Paper No. 14. Retrieved April 14, 2003, from <http://www.nall.ca>.

Engestrom, Y., Miettinen, R., & Punamaki, R-L. (Eds.). (1999). *Perspectives on activity theory.* Cambridge: Cambridge University Press.

Eraut, M. (1999). *Nonformal learning in the workplace—the hidden dimension of lifelong learning: a framework for analysis and the problems it poses for the researcher.* Plenary paper presented at the First International Conference on Researching Work and Learning, Leeds University, September 10–12.

Freire, P. (1970). *The pedagogy of the oppressed.* New York: Herder and Herder.

Freire, P. (1994). *The pedagogy of hope.* New York: Herder and Herder.

Gereluk, W., Briton, D., & Spencer, B. (1999). *Learning about labour in Canada.* NALL Working Paper Series, Paper No. 8. Retrieved April 14, 2003 from <http://www.nall.ca>.

Hiemstra, R. (1976). *Lifelong learning.* Lincoln: Professional Educators Publications.

Johnstone, J., & Rivera, R. (1965). *Volunteers for learning: A study of the educational pursuits of American adults.* Chicago: Aldine.

Knowles, M. (1970). *The modern practice of adult education: Andragogy versus pedagogy.* Chicago: Follett.

Kohn, M., & Schooler, C. (1983). *Work and personality: An inquiry into the impact of social stratification.* Norwood, NJ: Ablex.

LaValle, I., & Finch, S. (1999). *Pathways in adult learning.* Sherwood Park, Nottingham: Department for Education and Employment. Research Report No. 137.

Lave, J., & Wenger, M. (1991). *Situated learning: Legitimate peripheral participation.* Cambridge: Cambridge University Press.

Lavoie, M., & Roy, R. (1998). *Employment in the knowledge-based economy: A growth accounting exercise for Canada.* Ottawa: Applied Research Branch, Strategic Policy, HRDC.

Leean, C., & Sisco, B. (1981). *Learning projects and self-planned learning efforts among undereducated adults in rural Vermont.* Washington, DC: National Institute of Education.

Livingstone, D. W. (1999). Exploring the icebergs of adult learning: Findings of the first Canadian Survey of Informal Learning Practices. *Canadian Journal for the Study of Adult Education, 13*(2): 49–72.

Livingstone, D. W. (2001). *Adults' informal learning: Definitions, findings, gaps and future research.* Position paper for the Advisory Panel of Experts on Adult Learning, Applied Research Branch, Human Resources Development Canada.

Livingstone, D. W. (2002). *Working and learning in the information age: A profile of Canadians.* Ottawa: Canadian Policy Research Networks. [free download from <http://www.cprn.org>].

Livingstone, D. W. (2003). *The education-jobs gap: Underemployment or economic democracy.* Toronto: Garamond Press. (2nd ed.).

Livingstone, D. W., Hart, D., & Davie, L. E. (1997). *Public attitudes toward education in Ontario 1996: Eleventh OISE/UT Survey.* Toronto: University of Toronto Press.

Livingstone, D. W., Hart, D., & Davie, L. E. (1999). *Public attitudes toward education in Ontario 1998: Twelfth OISE/UT Survey.* Toronto: University of Toronto Press.

Livingstone, D. W., Hart, D., & Davie, L. E. (2001). *Public attitudes toward education in Ontario 2000: Thirteenth OISE/UT Survey.* Toronto: OISE Press.

Livingstone, D. W., Hart, D., & Davie, L. E. (2003). *Public attitudes toward education in Ontario 2002: Fourteenth OISE/UT Survey.* Toronto: OISE Press. Retrieved April 14, 2003, from <http://www.oise.utoronto.ca/OISE-Survey>.

Livingstone, D. W., Hart, D., & Stowe, S. (2003). *Adult informal learning and training in Canada: Findings of the 1998 NALL National Survey and 2000 follow-up survey.* Toronto: Centre for the Study of Education and Work. Retrieved April 14, 2003, from <http://www.nall.ca>.

Livingstone, D. W., Raykov, M., & Stowe, S. (2001). *Interest in and factors related to participation in adult learning and informal learning.* Ottawa: Human Resources Development Canada. Research Paper R-01–9–3E.

Livingstone, D. W., & Sawchuk, P. (2000). Beyond cultural capital theory: Hidden dimensions of working class learning. *Education/Pedagogy/Cultural Studies, 22*(2): 121–46. [see also <http://www.nall.ca>]

Livingstone, D. W., & Sawchuk, P. (2004). *Hidden Knowledge: Organized labour in the information age.* Toronto: Garamond Press and Boulder, CO: Rowman & Littlefield.

Merriam, S., & Clark, M. C. (1991). *Lifelines: Patterns of work, love, and learning in adulthood.* San Francisco: Jossey-Bass.

Mezirow, J. (1991). *Transformative dimensions of adult learning.* San Francisco: Jossey-Bass.

Mocker, D., & Spear, G. (1982). *Lifelong learning: Formal, nonformal, informal, and self-directed.* Information Series, No. 241. Columbus, OH: ERIC Clearinghouse on Adult, Career, and Vocational Education, National Center for research in Vocational Education, Ohio State University.

Molander, B. (1992). Tacit knowledge and silenced knowledge: Fundamental problems and controversies. In B. Goranzon & M. Florin (Eds.), *Skill and education: Reflection and experience.* London: Springer-Verlag.

Moll, L. (Ed.). (1990). *Vygotsky and education: Instructional implications of sociohistorical psychology.* Cambridge: Cambridge University Press.

NALL. (1998). *Lifelong learning profiles: General summary of findings from the First Canadian Survey of Informal Learning.* [<http://www.nall.ca>].

OECD Documents. (1997). *Manual for Better Training Statistics: Conceptual, measurement and survey issues.* Paris: OCED.

OECD. (1998). Lifelong learning: A monitoring framework and trends in participation in the Centre for Educational Research and Innovation. *Education Policy Analysis 1998.* Paris: OECD, pp. 7–24.

Padberg, L. (1991). A study of the organization of learning projects of adults of low formal educational attainment. Ph.D. Dissertation, University of Missouri.

Penland, P. (1977). *Self-planned learning in America.* Pittsburgh: University of Pittsburgh.

Reber, A. (1993). *Implicit learning and tacit knowledge.* New York: Oxford University Press.

Spear, G. E. (1988). Beyond the Organizing Circumstance: A Search for Methodology for the Study of Self-Directed Learning. In H. Long et al. (Eds.), *Self-directed learning: Application and theory.* Athens: University of Georgia Adult Education Department.

Stadler, M., & Frensch, P. (Eds.). (1998). *Handbook of implicit learning.* Thousand Oaks, CA.: Sage.

Statistics Canada. (1997). *Adult education and training in Canada: Report of the 1994 Adult Education and Training Survey.* Ottawa: Statistics Canada.

Statistics Canada. (1999). *Public use tape for the general social survey 1998.* Available from the University of Toronto Data Archive.

Tough, A. (1971). *The adult's learning projects.* Toronto: OISE Press.

Tough, A. (1978). Major learning efforts: Recent research and future directions. *Adult Education Quarterly 28*(4): 250–63.

Tough, A. (1979). *The adult's learning projects: A fresh approach to theory and practice in adult learning.* Toronto: OISE Press.

Vygotsky, L. (1978). *Mind in society.* Cambridge, MA: Harvard University Press.

"DANCING WITH WORDS"

NARRATIVES ON INFORMAL EDUCATION

ZVI BEKERMAN

INTRODUCTION

The pedagogy with which we are concerned in this paper could be identified as equivalent to that which is described by Reid (1981) as "social goals group" work, which is group work geared towards problems related to the social order and values (p. 202). The Hebrew name for this type of activity is *Hanchaia,* which can be variably translated as leading, guiding, moderating. It exists in Israel primarily in the sphere of values education, by which we near educational efforts directed at strengthening, for example, democratic, conciliatory, and/or national/religious values. This pedagogical practice relies heavily on the use of spoken language as the central mediator in educational work and operates principally in informal educational frameworks. Those active in it seem, when at work, to be engaging with words in a dance. The dance that we will describe in this article abounds with "pirouettes"—wanderings and rotations, whose ultimate destinations remain unclear.

Informal educational frameworks have been variously described, by sociologists, as being based on an informal code (Kahane, 1997) characterized by structural components such as voluntarism, multiplicity, symmetry, and moratorium; by anthropologists (Greenfield & Lave, 1982; Lave, 1996) in terms oppositional to formal education as that which is embedded in daily life, carried out in familial spheres, directed by little or no pedagogy or curriculum, and motivated by social contribution; or as moving in a pedagogical continuum tuned into an heteroglossic (Bakhtin, 1981) modality of didactic practices and characterized by the performance of "phenomenological learning," which generates specific ways of processing knowledge; by creating spaces for dialogue while personalizing or directing it toward specific, ideologically loaded issues; and by using varied mediating tools (Bekerman & Keller, 2003; Silberman-Keller, 2000); and they have been heralded as possible strong contributors to reforming the maladies of formal educational strategies.

Informal educational frameworks can and should be exposed to the same critical analysis applied to formal education: that is, an examination of the political-cultural aspects that shape their participants into a specific pattern of sociocultural perspectives (Apple, 1982; Bekerman & Silverman, 1999; Bourdieu, 1998; Giroux & McLaren, 1990; Giroux & McLaren, 1994). Such an examination, which resists the traditional proclivity to sever all educational and learning processes from contexts of power, history, and ideology, assumes that state educational institutions are the places in which the ruling hegemony perpetuates its economic, social, and cultural forms. Accordingly, educators have a central function in all that concerns socialization toward hegemonic worldviews. It is thus critically important to research pedagogical practices and perspectives in order to better understand social and cognitive processes taking place between the teacher and the student (Hariman, 1989; Lather, 1994; Varenne & McDermott, 1998) and the sociohistorical constructs they help shape and perform (Gilmore, 1985; Lather, 1994). In light of the above, this article will examine the extent to which the dance of words performed by informal educators contributes to or challenges the perpetuation of the prevailing hegemonic sociopolitical ideology.

SITE AND METHOD

In brief I will report on and analyze the interviews I conducted with a group of educators (facilitators, leaders, etc.) who work within an Israeli Jewish-Zionist non-profit organization that sponsors informal educational and extracurricular activities. Among these activities are one- and two-day seminars for both religious and nonreligious state schools in Israel, which are overseen by the Ministry of Education and Culture. The students that participate in these seminars do so not on a voluntary basis but, rather, in consequence of their school's commitment to be part of the project. The declared purpose is to "arouse in young Israeli Jews an awareness of their Jewishness and to help them investigate ways in which this Jewishness influences their views concerning themselves, their families and friends, their country (Israel), the Jewish nation and the minorities in the state of Israel

. . . utilizing an educational perspective anchored in humanistic, democratic and pluralistic values" (cited from unpublished document).

All interviews were conducted in accordance with qualitative ethnographic principles (Seidman, 1991; Spradley, 1979); the interviewer remained focused on a number of topics that seemed relevant to the study, but allowed subjects to tell their stories without binding the interview to any fixed agenda of questions. All interviews were audio taped and fully transcribed. The qualitative data were carefully analyzed, looking for patterns and thematic issues of relevance which were then coded so as to allow for further analysis. The interviews were conducted in the workplace and lasted between an hour-and-a-half and two hours. All the interviewees had worked in the institution between one and two years and were selected on the assumption that they would feel skilled in their roles as educational leaders but not yet jaded and worn as many do after numerous years in the field. The average age of the interviewees was 24, although one facilitator was comparatively older at 45. All of the facilitators worked with high school students, for the most part with pupils in the 11th grade (ages 16–17). Eight out of the twelve educators conducted the seminars in non-religious state schools, the remaining four worked in state religious schools. Seven of the facilitators defined themselves as "not-religious," and five defined themselves as "religious," "religiously observant," or the product of "Bnei Akiva" (a religious Zionist Youth movement). Apart from two facilitators who immigrated to Israel at a very young age (two and eight), all were born in Israel. Apart from one who had yet to start her university studies, all held B.A. degrees or were studying for a M.A. All but one studied subjects in fields within the social sciences and the humanities. They all served in the Israeli Defense Force but for one, who, because of her religious outlook, chose to perform national service (a community service option officially offered to religious woman who might choose for religious reasons not to serve in the army). Eight out of twelve of the educators had been involved in youth movement activities since the age of fifteen as youth leaders, and six of these had held teaching or leadership positions while serving in the army. Of the remaining four, only two reported that when they joined the organization they had had no former experience in youth leadership or teaching.

In the course of the interviews, all the interviewees were asked to describe the seminars they conducted, the meaning they found in their work, the pedagogies they used, and the influence they think their work may have. The facilitators were also asked to describe their own personal histories in brief. The open interview method adopted enabled all the interviewees to direct the interviews toward topics that interested them or issues they felt were of relevance to their lives as educators. The interviews were carried out in a relaxed atmosphere and the interviewees spoke very willingly and openly. Throughout the interviews I had the sense that whenever I asked further and probing questions about their work and the meanings they attached to it, they felt they were being allowed to articulate thoughts that they had not articulated before. Many expressed this feeling openly in the interviews, saying that in the conversation they had had the opportunity to analyze certain ideas and concepts that, because of time restraints, they could not deal with in their daily work. Some of them asked to talk to me again after I had analyzed the interviews, and I met with a few of them again to discuss my conclusions and hear their responses.

The interviews were very rich in content. The accounts offered flowed from the interviewees' personal experience unmediated by any theoretical perspectives. The facilitators had a high level of personal involvement in their work. Because of their deep involvement, they tended to stray from the original foci of the interview a number of times. Nonetheless, the analysis of the individual interviews pointed unequivocally to four central areas of interest that constituted the foci of the narrative that the interviewees shaped and reported on. These areas are: What is involved in the pedagogical activity they conduct? What does this activity achieve for the participants? What does the activity achieve for the facilitators? What are the processes and contents that characterize the activity? In the following sections, I report on the pictures that emerge from these four areas of interest, presenting them as a kind of collage that embodies the sum total of each individual representation.

HANCHAIA: STRUGGLE AND DIALOGUE

In the interviews the facilitators related to their educational work primarily in terms of the practices that they carried out within the framework of the seminars; more specifically those practices that took place in discussion groups within a defined geographic location (a hall or classroom) in which students and the facilitator sat in a circle. From the perspective of the facilitators, the term *Hanchaia* defines the activities that occurred within the special arena we have just defined. These activities had unique rules and were designed so as to enable the maximum degree of freedom of expression. The facilitators could not think of anything that was forbidden to say within the boundaries of the discussion group. As opposed to regular school practice where the teacher holds the key to the development of bi-lateral discussion by way of questions and evaluation of acceptable answers (Edwards & Mercer, 1993), in the *Hanchaia* activity the opposite is true. The facilitators did not feel that anything said in this educational situation merited an evaluative response. They saw their role as one that was designed to encourage and support an open discussion in which they also took part. They became involved with directives only when a participant's comments did not elicit a response from other participants, when responses overlapped each other, or when responses were so disorganized that it became impossible to follow the discussion.

The facilitators had no theoretical training in education. Their knowledge was based entirely on their own experiences as students as well as on the few days of practical training they were given before they started work. Thus their observations and reports throughout the interviews where based on this minimal training they had received, the practical experience they garnered, and what they defined as "gut instinct." On the basis of these "instincts," the facilitator clearly understood her role to be primarily a listener. If she continually interfered, the objectives of the discussion would not be achieved. "If I want to accomplish the objectives, I cannot physically bring it about," one of the facilitators emphasized in the interview.

Everything, including understanding the unstated objectives of the sessions, must come from the participants themselves. In essence, the facilitators argued that the objectives already "exist" in the participants. Their somewhat Socratic method was aimed at helping their students to reveal and understand these objectives for themselves. According to the facilitators, an activity was successful if they themselves were surprised at the conclusions reached. They did not direct the group, but helped it reach its own conclusions. Unexpected new articulations and formulations arose that differed from those that they would have used, but that were ultimately relevant to what they conceived as the purpose of the educational activity.

For the facilitators, the central core of this educational activity lies in the process, not in the content. This is the crux of their differentiation of their work from the work of teachers. "With us," they said, "the process is what sets the rules, the process is what counts." "We are not interested in academic achievements," they argued, "but rather in the development of the person and the group." In the eyes of the facilitators, the formation of a fitting formula takes time to develop. A too speedy arrival at the "correct" conclusions can be a sign of less than serious work. "If it happens too fast, I'm not happy, because it isn't 'real'—or maybe it is real, but it's superficial. I want it to stem from the stomach and not from the mouth." Their expectation was that *Hanchaia* would cause behavioral or cognitive changes, something that depended primarily on the group's activity and participation as well as on the facilitator's flexibility toward change. In essence, *Hanchaia* was a partnership between each of the group's individual components as well as between the participants and the facilitator. The chances of success increased, in their opinion, when this interaction was built on personal relations that were themselves based on trust among all the different elements of the group.

The creation of trust, essential for the development of a successful encounter, was achieved through much debate and endless questions raised during the discussion, all of which carried with them no punitive evaluation. The debate and questions were meant to help the participants to "open their eyes," to look at things from "a different perspective," to "encourage them to express different opinions," and "to learn to listen to one another even when one doesn't agree with their opinions." Everyone was asked challenging questions from different standpoints and it made no difference if the facilitator personally agreed with what was being said. "I'm tough with them, I attack them, irrespective of which side they come from." "I check if he really thought about what he is saying. I want to know if he really underwent a [thought] process."

The questions the facilitators repeatedly raised were not expressions of ideological positions or expressions of their own personal approaches. Countless times in the interviews, in one way or another, the facilitators emphasized the importance of not expressing personal opinions. "If I express my opinion, I destroy everything that I have done." That said, the facilitators were also well aware of the problems that arise from advocating such a position. According to the facilitators, withholding their own personal opinions in a debate that focused on the participants' personal opinions most likely gave the facilitator an unintended and undesired authoritative voice. They acknowledged that their position in the group was somewhat different from that of the participants but yet not similar to that often adopted by teachers in regular school activities.

Thus the first parameter that could help us define *Hanchaia* work becomes the perceived differences between the facilitators' positioning vis-à-vis the students and that of the teachers in traditional school situations vis-à-vis students. A second parameter was defined in the interviews when one of the facilitators argued: "I differentiate between what I do here and what I do in my house—there I have to give answers." Thus when considering these two boundaries, *Hanchaia* is positioned in the interviews in an intermediary space formed between the school and home.

The decision not to express their personal opinions was for the most part limited to group debate and discussion. The majority of the interviewees claimed that when they were asked specific questions outside of the debate group, they were ready to let the questioner in on their feelings about one topic or another. Another situation in which stating one's position and/or judgment of a given statement was considered acceptable was when a participant expressed an "extreme" opinion, or one that "could possibly hurt" others' feelings, even when those others were not present at the encounter. An example of this included "racist" statements such as "We have to kill the Arabs" or comments that mock other people's statements. In addition, the "distortion of facts" also drew assertive, "corrective" statements from facilitators.

The impression drawn from the interviews suggested that, apart from a few solitary corrective or "leading" statements, the chief goal of the debate was to sustain, as much as possible, a critical and introspective conversation through provocative and probing questions. "The most important thing is that they should go through the process, that they listen to others." "The point is to take something that seems simple, obvious, and to examine it from every side. Everything that is obvious, apparently comprehensible (without examination) is bad." "It is necessary to take seemingly clear-cut issues and examine them. To be at one with issues that sound clear-cut can sound good, because then you can build on them, but if one part is wrong, everything falls apart." According to the facilitators the only "truth," apart from the "truth" that one shouldn't express personal opinions and positions on issues, was the "truth" that everything that had not been discussed and examined carefully was not expedient and could not stand the tough test of reality.

We should not conclude from this that the facilitators' sole intention was to change what the students said. In fact, the opposite was true. The facilitators repeatedly emphasized situations where participants, as a result of the critical dialogue, sustained and strengthened their beliefs. What was expected was that the participants carefully examine and criticize their beliefs and be willing to listen openly to the opinions of others.

The emphasis on the need for each individual to thoroughly review her positions points to the fact that the *Hanchaia* process is founded on the assumption that people are autonomous creatures. However, this autonomy was considered to be intricate and complex. The interviewees argued that before individuals can make and accept decisions as free and autonomous agents, they must understand, principally through the polemical process developed in the seminar, the freedom into which they were born. Understanding the polemical nature of this freedom enabled people to take proper advantage of it. "Without considerable, real, internal struggle, humans are shallow, superficial and risk the possibility of being spoon fed all of their life." When thus, "their true voice can never be heard, not to themselves and not to others who surround them." According to the facilitators, the process of *Hanchaia* was meant to ensure that individuals reached decisions only after they had heard their own internal voice—a voice that, in the dialogue created at the educational activity, awakened conflict and indecision. These women argued that: "*Hanchaia* does not deal with specific issues or decisions. *Hanchaia* simply guides the student in thinking of things that he has never thought about before. *Hanchaia* throws light on selected issues."

Beyond the mere posing of questions, the facilitators hoped to construct a real dialogue between themselves and the students. The dialogic event does not come about automatically but is in need of careful preparation so that "the group does not panic . . . and you don't panic either." "Chiefly, the idea is to create a feeling amongst the participants that you are truly willing to listen to them and to seriously consider their concerns." Bringing about such an atmosphere requires significant effort. In comparison to the teaching practices used in schools, facilitation is daunting. The facilitator cannot rely on having a defined area of knowledge or a pre-prepared lesson plan. They only have the meeting between themselves and the group—a meeting whose outcome cannot be predicted in advance. When the facilitators raised their concerns and fears about their work, two metaphors were used to define the process of *Hanchaia*. The first metaphor was taken from the world of theater. One facilitator expressed herself in the following way: "I enjoy and I direct. It is a play, and I direct it in the same manner as does a director." The second metaphor compared the facilitator to an architect or a sculptor. Only through slow, patient, and painful work, and in constant dialogue with the resources available, can either create the desired product.

The resources available were the words in which the discussion was conducted. The facilitator sculpted his words in such a way as to move the discussion forward, primarily by opening for analysis the issues that the participants brought with them to the discussion forum: their sense of belonging and identity, their perspectives on social issues, etc. The interviewees suspected these conceptions to be baseless slogans. That said, the facilitators were sensitive to the fact that they sometimes got carried away in their constant challenging of what the group said, as if this persistent clarification game proved that the group was involved in the activity and advancing appropriately. In this spirit, one facilitator made the following comment immediately after her director/theater metaphor; "It took me time to say, 'the drama is over, now listen to them properly' . . . it was as if I had finally realized that what was important was not the drama of the meeting but where the participants actually were." The facilitators felt very positive about their work. As they described it, they struggle with crucial, essential issues and become partners in the process of their revelation. They initiate a process that helps others discover and understand themselves, while simultaneously discovering and revealing things significant to their surrounding world.

The interviewees considered the process of discovery to be creative and challenging as well as exceedingly difficult. The central focus of their work was not the lone individual. Instead, the group dialogue sought to direct all of the participants, including the facilitators, to examine honestly their personal positions in light of the positions of others. The facilitators themselves in each meeting were challenged and strengthened by the groups' remarks.

In contrast to the formal educational frameworks that traditionally aspire toward higher achievements, *Hanchaia* aims toward totally different goals—not forward and upwards, but backward and inward. The *Hanchaia* process strives to go back to an examination of the development of the current ideas and notions of the participants, and inward to the inner depths where the true voice of the participant is heard.

Thus *Hanchaia* can be described as a tangled, complex process within which the rules of personal and interpersonal performance are overturned. Similarly, normative value systems that had seemed firmly established are reopened for debate. The remainder of this article focuses on three components central to *Hanchaia:* the students, the facilitators, and the world of content.

THE STUDENT: IS SOMETHING HAPPENING HERE !?

The student is a figure that merits attention, even though her presence in the interviews I conducted is rather small. This might follow from the fact that, as we will see below, most of their descriptions of the students reflect much of what was said previously about *Hanchaia* as an educational process. The facilitators assumed that, for the student, the *Hanchaia* was a meaningful experience whose influence was unexpected if not shocking: "90% of the students don't know what has hit them." Although the facilitators did not state this explicitly, the descriptions given in the interviews assumed a world wherein the student had no place for introspection. Occasionally, they mentioned school or the MTV generation, as spheres that lacked serious questioning or as media that encouraged no introspection. The *Hanchaia* seminar was perceived as standing in binary opposition to these spheres, and the facilitators believed the participants "leave the seminar with the feeling that, indeed, something happened here." This "something" was not necessarily the transformation of ideas or self. In essence, the interviewees reminded me that whether or not the participants changed their mind was irrelevant to their work. Instead, this "something" was tied primarily to the way the students thought of themselves and their relationships in the future. The interviewees argued that students left the seminars more aware of themselves. This awareness allowed for a different way of "looking at" and "understanding" the world. The facilitators repeatedly stated that the students "sharpen their vision" in the course of the group discussion. Their questions on various subjects brought the participants to see topics from a different angle and ultimately to "know how to recognize and how to choose."

In the eyes of the interviewees, the goals of the discussion process were fourfold: to encourage the student to observe and understand differently what surrounds him; to enable him to understand that, essentially, nothing happens by accident; to demonstrate that he has fundamental responsibilities regarding that which surrounds him; and to show him that "freewill is given." Accordingly, a successful *Hanchaia* activity resulted in a person understanding that he is an autonomous decision maker, and more important, that, "if you are free, you are responsible." In their decision making they should decide responsibly and from a perspective that has taken into account a multiplicity of choices (choices the student has uncovered through the discussion process in which she participated). "In this way democracy will be protected," said one of the interviewees. By "democracy," she seemed to be relating to more than just the political system implied by the word. The word "democracy," in this instance, was meant to include a vision on the types of individuals that can have a part and a place within such a system. The hope was that "what is done in the seminar session somehow seeped through to one's consciousness" and contributes to the larger political picture where democracy needs to be sustained.

The questions the facilitators asked destabilized the positions and opinions of the students, creating an opening for a more critical view on issues that previously seemed transparent. After the process the participant felt that everything she "had or knew before were mere slogans," "and now he is striding forward and understanding more deeply." This "deeper understanding" was twofold: first, an understanding of external influencing factors; second, an understanding of the need to listen to one's internal voice. The process was considered successful when the pupil "goes out agitated with a need to find answers to the questions that he is now asking" on issues that previously seemed crystal-clear or simply meaningless. Similarly, "he leaves with a need to express his own voice and to hear others," so that he does not "remain apathetic and indifferent and doesn't bury his head in the sand."

In order for this process to happen, the first stage in the educational activity must give the student the feeling that, indeed, "here [in the educational event] they will be listened to," whether he speaks or is silent. He needs to understand that "here" he is allowed to take a break from his "daily worries," and that "here we confront each other and each others ideas honestly, and develop personally," and, most important, "here, one doesn't harm others or get harmed." The interviewees described the trust formed between the group and the facilitator as something central that results from the process of personal "wrestling" that turns "a person into a person." The components of the process were varied: they enjoyed, they learned new things, and they entered into a dialogue with themselves and others. Typically, they started to speak "from the place from which everyone speaks" (a common/external place). "If we succeed to move the discussion to their inside, to a meaningful level for the individual, then they start uncovering things that they had never thought about." They suddenly "uncover conflicts. And suddenly what was for long peripheral becomes central/internalized." Then they feel that "something significant happened to them." For the student, "the seminar is truly profound and not just a bunch of slogans, if you first and foremost help him develop backwards—always checking why this, why that" (the 'true' sources of the students beliefs). "The facilitator wants the students to back up their words, to ask questions, to encounter and confront their own positions and the positions of others in the strongest possible way." "At the end of the day the question of choice needs to be up front and center stage. The student needs to take a stand, to make a choice. Maybe he will again adopt the notions he arrived with but even if this is the case he will be, by the end of the process, so much more enriched."

Accordingly, *Hanchaia* "works" for the student because ultimately he is made to grapple with, analyze, and challenge issues relevant to his present reality. Despite all the warnings and reservations voiced by the facilitators about creating a dialogue that is intended to serve the examination of the internal world of the participants in light of and in dialogue with the larger social world outside, it becomes apparent from the interviews that the self and its self-questioning remained at the center of the educational enterprise. Many difficult questions arise from this emphasis on the individual and the "challenging" of him, and whether this is a barren introspective exercise or whether it has relevance beyond the individual are questions to which we will return later in this paper.

THE FACILITATOR: TO REACH THE DESTINATION TOGETHER

Regarding the influences of *Hanchaia* on the facilitators, the descriptions are, for the most part, isomorphic to those described for the pupil. According to the reports, *Hanchaia* triggers strong emotions for those practicing it. The interviewees use numerous superlatives and very emotional terms to describe the influence of *Hanchaia* on themselves as educational agents. "It grabs me." "It isn't rational but I really, really love it." "It causes me to be entirely different, not passive." "I go from stage to stage and do things that I would otherwise have not done" (in regular life situations). "I also go through the process. It gives me satisfaction." "To stand in front of a group boosts my energy and fuels my adrenalin." "It does something for me. I understand myself differently, and uncover a new world each time." The facilitators "love"*Hanchaia*, because *Hanchaia* is a dialogue between human beings. "At the center of this work [are] my interactions with people, which is not meaningless; these shape my personality." "In a normal interaction there is give and take, in *Hanchaia* I am in the position of giving throughout." "The bond that is created offers a sense of complexity and depth. I learned that there isn't such thing as a black and white, there's gray in the middle." "Going into the conversation is as exiting as embarking on a journey whose final destination is unknown."

The group interaction produces changes in the facilitators—change that is similar to that which is their goal to produce in the participants. "Suddenly I am learning how to listen, I already hear them differently . . . If I have succeeded in a workshop it means that I have personally developed. It's good to develop together with someone." "I enjoy learning new opinions, new outlooks, and different forms of grappling with issues. Every person is essentially a world, and it is possible to be acquainted with different levels of this world and with multiple worlds. You see, you relate, you feel, and this gives you a sense of gratification. It's unexpected. Surprising things happen, and it's exciting." "I always ask leading questions so as not to lose the group. I want to arrive there together with them."

Through *Hanchaia* the facilitators themselves developed and learned how to relate in a totally different way to the "other." However, these changes did not happen easily and were accompanied by a number of difficult feelings. "I always want to listen. This produces a feeling of great vitality, but to reach this stage of enjoyment isn't something that comes easily. It is bound up in a technical process, as is to be expected, but also, and primarily, in a spiritual process that is accompanied by great fears." "Before the seminar, I'm stressed; I have to prepare myself. Every individual group can touch on a thousand issues. You have to understand, because you never know where they're going to surprise you . . . In the beginning you don't want to start at all."

The facilitators occasionally described their feelings about *Hanchaia* in terms of fear and power. Despite the symmetry that they talked about earlier, they clearly understood that their position as facilitators was different from that of the students. "It gives me a feeling of power, a feeling that you can bring people towards cogitation. You make things happen." "I do not rule in the sense of domination, but in the sense that I lead them from place to place and help them to recognize their own freedom." "There is an element of power when standing in front of the group. It gives me energy and fuels adrenalin, gives me satisfaction, a good feeling, but this doesn't have to be interpreted in a negative way. Power is the power to influence. This is my contribution to society. To stand in front of a group gives me the feeling of being a better citizen." "It took me some time to understand that I am in a position of power."

The tangled maze of emotions described here seemed worthwhile when, in retrospect, the facilitators could say something happened within the group. "I feel gratified when causing people to think, to cause new ideas and perspectives to drip slowly, to sink in a little. Otherwise I feel bad." "What I mean by this is causing people to open their eyes, to stir up something, something small. Then you are causing this 'drip,' because the new ideas might be small but they penetrate deeply." Together with the need to "penetrate," to "drip," to "turn over," the interviewees carried an awareness that this situation was not always desired or possible. "The work is essentially to go in, not to go out, to go into the deep waters. But you can't go in and stay there for ever." Ultimately, the descriptions portrayed *Hanchaia* as requiring great emotional resources and constant involvement. Without these components, *Hanchaia* could not take place. One interviewee expressed this succinctly when saying, "It requires inexhaustible resources from me. I come out completely wrung out."

Thus far we have given a definition of *Hanchaia* and a perspective on how this work influences the facilitators and their students. We read descriptions that ultimately sketched a world of educational processes positively experienced by those involved, a more symmetrical world that offers recognition and respect to those who partake in it. I will now turn to issues related to the contents of these educational activities.

THE WORLD OF CONTENT: A SPACE FOR THE PROCESS TO TAKE PLACE

Before we address what was said in the interviews about content, we must remember the framework in which the facilitators conducted their work. We have defined this framework as one that functions in extracurricular or informal educational spheres and as dealing with values education centered on Jewish-Zionist concepts. These topics never became a central issue in the interviews I conducted. In the cases in which they were expanded upon, comments were limited and disconnected from the areas centered around educational processes on which we have reported above. Religious women working in the seminars intended for state religious schools raised topics related to Judaism and Zionism more frequently than those facilitators who worked within the secular schools. That said, for both populations content seemed to be secondary to process and, if at all related to, they identified two different types of content. The first was "the process content," which dealt with social issues whose principal concerns were human qualities and relationships, the second, the realm of Jewish Zionist ideological content—which never acted as a focus in and of itself, except for the advancement of the process content.

After analyzing the interviews of the facilitators that work with religious populations, it emerges that they were more aware of these different conceptualizations of content than were their colleagues working in secular schools, and more forceful in their preference for process content than for ideological content. The latter facilitators made an effort to explain this situation by stating that they had linked ideological contents to other points in the course of the interviews.

Jewish Zionist issues indeed arose in multiple contexts in the interviews. The first context related to the facilitators' personal biography. Though only five out of twelve interviewees described themselves as religious, eight of the interviewees felt that the religious world had influenced them significantly. These women recounted a significant, meaningful story about their parents' or grandparents' connection to the religious world. Generally speaking, as evident in the interviews, the facilitators' outlook on Judaism was no different from those of the bulk of Israeli society (Bekerman & Silverman, 1999). The secular amongst them defined their identity, for the most part, around the world of national images, and the religious amongst them around their relationship to faith and the observing of religious laws. As opposed to the accepted "norm" in Israeli society, the facilitators saw these different Jewish perspectives as enriching the Jewish experience, and not as a dividing factor. Both groups pointed out the importance of belonging to the Jewish people and the state of Israel. Ultimately, all the facilitators expressed a sense of partnership and a belief that in working professionally in *Hanchaia* they are committed to a personal process wherein they examine closely their positions on these issues.

As I pointed out earlier, in the eyes of the interviewees one of the principles of *Hanchaia* is openness to any and every opinion, in as much as it does not offend or harm anyone. Because of the very nature of *Hanchaia,* every facilitator I interviewed accepted, from the start, this commitment to openness. However, a certain discrepancy in the definition of openness existed between religious and secular groups, which was expressed in their view on content. Those facilitators working within the secular community were committed to an openness with almost no boundaries. Those working within the religious community pointed out in their interviews that this openness expressed itself within the boundaries that prefigure and take into consideration the religious way of life. These parameters were not always the result of personal conviction or of a formal rule dictating the way things should be. Instead, some of the facilitators expressed a sense of responsibility toward the educational framework in which they worked. In other words, the religious school trusted them not to deviate from its educational parameters and they felt that they had to comply with these expectations.

One other area where the issue of ideological contents becomes central relates to the intersection between the individual and the societal. As we mentioned, a central goal of *Hanchaia* is to create a process of introspection and of deep self-scrutiny. At the same time, through this process the individual was meant to consider that which surrounds him and the society in which he lives and develops. The process was meant to develop sensitivity to the "other," a readiness to listen and to come to grips with different ideas, and to encourage a true dialogue. At the end of the process, the participant ideally reached a better understanding of himself, along with a recognition of the need for dialogue between himself and society. In this space in which the individual and the group engaged in dialogue, Jewish Zionist contents served as a pretext that allowed for this conversation to take place.

For the most part, these subjects, when talked about by the interviewees, reflected the dominant hegemony and were compatible with the official traditionally accepted discourse of the need to sustain the Jewish people as a collective with religious and national characteristics. In other words, the participants expressed their commitment to a degree of religious observance within the framework of public proceedings and in regard to the central events of the calendar year as they relate to the communal Jewish life cycle (i.e., festivals, etc.), and an obligation toward the continuity of the Jewish people and its unity within the framework of a sovereign nation.

DISCUSSION

The interviewees' descriptions of *Hanchaia* emphasized, again and again, the need to examine and reexamine in detail the foundations of all views expressed and positions taken by the participants in the seminars. Every ideological argument, even the simplest amongst them, was unacceptable if presented as "obvious." Lyotard (1984) points out that the postmodern era brings to an end the great narratives meant to govern human life in the modern period. His views are echoed in the interviewees' arguments.

The facilitators suggested, even demanded, that the students free themselves from the traditional scripts—the scripts that had held sway over them and had, until now, helped them interpret and give meaning to their lives in their given historical-political context. According to the facilitators, hegemonic texts had no place in *Hanchaia* activity, or at least there existed a strong demand to examine these texts anew from every possible angle. *Hanchaia* is presented in the interviews as a postmodern call for the fragmentation of the "givens" of their interpretation of human experience, for the erasure of reified signifiers, and for a pluralism that cannot be subjected to reduction (Brooker, 1993; Harvey, 1990).

Together with this thrust, which mainly addresses the individual him/herself, another parallel objective addresses the individual's relationship with the "other." In the framework of *Hanchaia,* every participant is expected to examine himself and his attitudes. However, in addition he had to listen to the other and try, truly try, to hear her voice. This requirement is also compatible with the postmodern conception that challenges the monologic character of Western perspectives—perspectives that dictate that the "other" is beneficial only as means for the self to define what it is not (Sampson, 1993). For the interviewees, *Hanchaia* was an invitation to a dialogue between the individual and himself and between the individual and society. The dialogue sought to change the power relations between the "I" and everyone else, and to shift the weight from the single individual to the relationships between individuals and society. One can hear the voice of Bakhtin's heteroglossia—which brings about a play of multiple voices, not just individual but also social (Bakhtin, 1984; Clark & Holquist, 1984)—echoing in these descriptions.

From the perspective of the facilitators, their work is as almost absolutely different from that of formal educational work. In their descriptions, the facilitators emphasized the need to construct dialogical relations. In contrast, traditional teaching depends routinely on a monologue wherein the overwhelming power of the teacher can easily prevent dialogue and the adoption of critical standpoints of any kind by the students (Edwards & Mercer, 1993). In the discussion groups, in addition to each individual receiving encouragement to build an internal dialogue, a space was created for social dialogue between the members of the group, including the facilitator. To a certain extent, in the *Hanchaia* activity the facilitators succeeded in creating what is described by Gutierrez (Gutierrez, Rymes, & Larson, 1995) as the "third space." In this space, certain structures of culture, dialogue, and knowledge became accessible to the participants. In this space, the teacher and student were able to free themselves from traditional hierarchical scripts. They created a dialogue with the potential for revealing political aspects of knowledge and identity, and in so doing challenged the hegemonic narrative.

Nevertheless, the interviewees were aware of their relatively different place in the group, despite their efforts to create symmetry. They were also aware that the content ideological boundaries they themselves constructed in the debate were in line with the (hegemonic) dominant narrative. This was particularly true for those instances in which they relied on Jewish Zionist ideological contents to delimit the parameters of what was legitimate in the discussion; it was much less so when they dealt with human qualities and relationships. Indeed, as we have pointed out, these acknowledged Jewish national religious aspects that emphasized the need for continuity, *were precisely* what characterized the entire discussion, whether or not the group had a religious background. In conclusion it seems that despite the facilitators' absolute commitment to bring about a process of self-examination and thoughtful reflection, to the point where "nothing will seem obvious and clear-cut," at a certain moment the process stopped and the pedagogy they adopted kept the discussions on the topic of cultural/ethnic affiliation and far from critical sociopolitical perspectives.

I wish to remark on another dimension that caused the interviewees some discomfort when they sided pedagogically with critical approaches in the field of education. The reader may recall that the interviewees felt the need to emphasize their obligation not to express their personal opinions in the group discussions. In contrast, the facilitators also expressed their readiness to reveal their personal positions in one-to-one discussions during breaks or informal encounters. The fact that they avoided expressing their personal opinions within the discussion forum exposes their *Hanchaia* work to criticism from critical pedagogical standpoints (Freire & Macedo, 1995). This criticism warns educators not to fall into the trap of "neutrality" that eventually undermines the emancipatory process (Lusmed, 1986). Since all pedagogy is located and reliant on a given cultural space, neutral arguments, if at all possible, prevent the exposure of the power sources that feed the educational discourse.

We should also consider a collateral question that arises concerning an "emancipatory" pedagogy that actually forces its "redeeming" interpretation on students, and in doing so, defines and directs the "other" who was meant to be freed by dialogue. Thus, despite the explicit liberatory efforts of the facilitators, they actually serve the ruling power and sustain its strength.

Another issue I address concerns the focus on the individual. I discussed this briefly when I talked about the facilitators' views on the influence of the *Hanchaia* activity on the participants. As stated, this focusing took place despite the stated intentions of the facilitators to create an honest dialogue between the participants and themselves, in which all voices were equally heard. The picture drawn by the interviewees emphasized their perception of a decontextualized individual, detached from the social conditions that surround him. Within the educational activity no effort was made toward creating associations between the abstract and philosophical concepts used in the dialogue and the social conditions that produce and sustain them. Despite their good intentions, the facilitators, to a certain extent, prevented linkage between talk concerning the individual "I" and the political, social space. One can say that the facilitators, in acting in this way, supported (perhaps unintentionally) modernist perspectives, in which the solipsistic autonomous individual is in need of no context to be explained and understood. The demand that I repeatedly heard from the facilitators was that participants should be encouraged, through the questions posed throughout the seminar, to understand the essence of freedom in an independent way. The facilitators encouraged participants to recognize their own autonomy, without which humanity cannot be achieved. Their requirement essentially served a modern monologic outlook that seeks to encourage individualism and autonomy in order to dominate and prosper (Sampson, 1993). Moreover, there was an apparent further danger that since the monologic outlook was disguised as dialogue, every redemptory effort that is meant to exist within dialogue was pushed back even further.

When considering the above, the answer to the question of "what is it that is happening here?" seems gloomy and disheartening. The facilitators, who deploy a rhetoric of critical pedagogy, find themselves reconstituting the power relations that they wished to counteract. We ask ourselves how are bright facilitators, critically struggling with their own approaches, brought to a halt at the hegemonic boundaries? If we go back to our initial metaphor of dancing with words, we can conceptualize this situation in terms of a band playing and the facilitators dancing to its tune. It is the band that decides the melody and the specific tempo. This description is true to a certain extent, but, just as we learned from Gramsci (Fontana, 1993; Gramsci, 1929–35

[1971]), hegemony can work only in a constant social dialogue. The band might influence but cannot impose its tempo on the dancer or force the dancer to dance to its tune; any coordination achieved is a joint one always. For this reason, those who are dancing are also partners to the hegemony. Had they so desired or made the effort, they could have danced at a different tempo. Despite this partial "truth," I wish to widen the context, and consider, precisely, the dance floor on which the meeting of band and dancers takes place. What I want to point to is the larger institutional framework.

My focus on this framework stems not from a desire to free the interviewees and the surrounding society from responsibility but, rather, from a (hesitant) belief that institutions can contribute, under certain constraints, to innovative educational experiments, with, perhaps, redeeming qualities. The seminar organizers who hired the interviewees were successful in recruiting positive educational figures and encouraging them in their work. Given present sociopolitical conditions in Israel, the institution, apart from some general principles that aim at enabling the students to become critical and introspective, does not seek to expose the loci of hegemonic influence that support the ruling Jewish Zionist ideology. The institution's existence is dependent on the Ministry of Education and it is careful not to overstep its mandate. In their work, the facilitators reflected symbolically the position of the institution in the political-social sphere. As an organization, the institution is neither public nor private. This matter receives full expression when the facilitators pointed out their reservations in expressing their personal opinions in the course of the seminar. The facilitators avoided expressing personal opinions in the discussion groups (the public sphere), but in private discussions with participants (the private sphere), they would indeed reveal their positions. At the center of their educational approach was the concept of challenging each opinion. This matter was presented as one of the distinguishing factors between school (the public sphere), at which, at first sight, answers are given only to questions that were not asked, and home (the private sphere), where constant challenging is interpreted as something impossible or undesirable.

The constant desire to challenge expressed ideas along with the avoidance of giving expression to personal opinions represent the hidden potential for change. They also, quite possibly, reveal the close connection between the knowledge and culture that nourish the hegemony. Despite this, there isn't enough in their educational work to turn them into an antihegemonic force. Those that struggle against ruling ideologies need more than this.

Teitelbaum (1991) described the Socialist movement's resistance as it was reflected in their Sunday afternoon schools in early twentieth-century America. These schools were similar in structure and in pedagogical approach to the institution with which we are now dealing, with a critical difference. In contrast to the facilitators, who focused their work on discussion that translated into examining questions, these schools constructed appellant questions, but also adopted texts that constituted the bases of this profound questioning. These texts offered competing outlooks to those that were accepted as natural in the given historical context, and enabled the participants to weigh up, argue their arguments, and examine their situation in a new light. Thus, it seems, if the institution were to take up a stronger position, it indeed could create an educational context in which an emancipatory dialogue could actually take place. This could gain expression if they chose alternative cultural texts rather than those that are proposed by the ruling ideological system. The assumption is that a new identity is not built merely by critical approaches or on the rejection of existing ones. Instead, we see the need for a method that proposes alternative symbolic systems to those that are under scrutiny or negated. One can assume that without choosing alternative texts, every "innovative" educational effort will be judged as a failure. The source of the texts that they choose is not important, as long as they stem from a cultural context that is relevant to the participants.

On this point I wish to close by summing up a critical comment stated by one of the interviewees. This woman argued, perhaps more than her friends, that the constant challenging is not necessarily desirable. She also stated that she endeavors to use texts in her work. She related a story of a visit to "Yad V'Shem" (the central Israeli holocaust memorial museum in Jerusalem) with a group of students that was considered "weak" according to school achievement measures. While in front of a picture wherein a number of women stood naked covering their pubic hair, one of the participants asked a question. "Why did these women cover precisely that part of their body and not the rest of their nakedness?". The interviewee related that in the background she heard one of the accompanying teachers in uproar at his question, as if concealed in the question was a disregard, a derision of the holiness that surrounds the sacrifice (so to speak) found in the picture. The interviewee commented that precisely at this point she had a text from which she could begin.

REFERENCES

Apple, M. W. (1982). *Education and Power.* Boston: Routledge and Kegan Paul.

Bakhtin, M. M. (1981). *The dialogic imagination: Four essays by M. M. Bakhtin* (C. Emerson & M. Holquist, Trans.). Austin: University of Texas Press.

Bakhtin, M. M. (1984). *Problems of Dostoevsky's poetics* (C. Emerson, Trans.). Minneapolis: University of Minnesota Press.

Bekerman, Z., & Silverman, M. (1999). Slaves of tradition—Slaves of freedom: Social constructivist perspectives on the "culture" of Israeli traditionalists and liberals. *Israel Studies, 4*(2), 90–120.

Bekerman, Z., & Keller, D. S. (2003). Non formal pedagogy, epistemology, rhetoric, and practice. *Education and Society, 21.*

Bourdieu, P. (1998). *Practical reason.* Stanford, California: Stanford University Press.

Brooker, N. C. (1993). *Dialogue in teaching: Theory and practice.* New York: Teachers College Press.

Clark, K., & Holquist, M. (1984). *Michael Bakhtin.* Cambridge, Mass.: Harvard University Press.

Edwards, D., & Mercer, N. (1993). *Common Knowledge: The development of understanding in the classroom.* New York: Routledge.

Fontana, B. (1993). *Hegemony and Power.* Minneapolis: University of Minnesota Press.

Freire, P., & Macedo, D. P. (1995). A dialogue: Culture, language and race. *Harvard Educational Review, 65,* 377–403.

Gilmore, P. (1985). Silence and sulking: Emotional displays in the classroom. In D. Tannen & M. Saville-Troike (Eds.), *Perspectives on Silence* (pp. 139–62). Norwood, NJ: Ablex Publishing Corporation.

Giroux, H., & McLaren, P. (1990). *Critical pedagogy, the state and cultural struggle.* New York: SUNY Press.

Giroux, H., & McLaren, P. (1994). *Between borders: Pedagogy and the politics of cultural studies.* New York: Routledge Pess.

Gramsci, A. (1929–35 [1971]). *Selections from the Prisions Notebooks* (Q. Hoara & G. N. Smith, Trans.). London: Lawrence & Wishart.

Greenfield, P., & Lave, J. (1982). Cognitive aspects of informal education. In D. A. Wagner & H. W. Stevenson (Eds.), *Cultural perspectives on child development* (pp. 181–207). San Francisco: Freeman.

Gutierrez, K., Rymes, B., & Larson, J. (1995). Script, counterscript, and underlife in the classroom: *James Brown v. Board of Education. Harvard Educational Review, 95*(3), 445–71.

Hariman, R. (1989). The Rhetoric of inquiry and the Professional Scholar. In H. W. Simmons (Ed.), *Rhetoric in the human sciences.* London: Sage.

Harvey, D. (1990). *The condition of postmodernity.* Cambridge: Blackwell.

Kahane, R. (1997). *The origins of postmodern youth: Informal youth movements in a comparative perspective.* New York: Walter de Gruyter.

Lather, P. (1994). Staying dumb? Feminist research and pedagogy within the postmodern. In H. W. Simons & M. Billig (Eds.), *After postmodernism: Reconstructing ideology critique.* London: Sage.

Lave, J. (1996). Teaching as learning in practice. *Mind, Culture, and Activity, 3*(3), 149–64.

Lusmed, D. (1986). Why pedagogy? *Scree, 27*(5), 2–14.

Lyotard, J. F. (1984). *The postmodern condition* (G. Bennington & G. Massumi, Trans.). Minneapolis: University of Minnesota Press.

Reid, K. E. (1981). *From character building to social treatment: The history of groups in social work.* Westport, Conn.: Greenwood Press.

Sampson, E. E. (1993). *Celebrating the other: A dialogic account of human nature.* Hertfordshire: Harvester Wheatsheaf.

Seidman, I. E. (1991). *Interviewing as qualitative research: A guide for researchers in education and social sciences.* New York: Teachers College Press.

Silberman-Keller, D. (2000, June 26–30). *Images of places and time in non-formal education.* Paper presented at the 13th International Congress World Association for Educational Research, University of Sherbrooke, Quebec Canada.

Spradley, J. P. (1979). *The ethnographic interview.* New York: Holt, Rinehart and Winston.

Teitelbaum, K. (1991). Critical lessons from our past: Curricula of socialist Sunday schools in the US. In M. Y. Apple & L. K. Christian-Smith (Eds.), *The politics of the text book.* New York: Routledge.

Varenne, H., & McDermott, R. (1998). *Successful failure: The schools America builds.* Boulder, Colo.: Westview Press.

IMAGES OF TIME AND PLACE IN THE NARRATIVE OF NONFORMAL PEDAGOGY

DIANA SILBERMAN-KELLER

"... Life is a dream and dreams, dreams are ..."

Calderón de la Barca, *Life is a Dream*

INTRODUCTION

The assumption underlying this essay is that a given pedagogy,[1] whether humanistic, conservative, liberal, or critical, creates and reflects a narrative that includes its ideal vision of educators, learners, and teaching and learning processes. Images of time and place are created and shaped within the exclusive narrative framework of each and every type of pedagogy (Keller, 1997).

The concept of nonformal pedagogy does not yet exist in the professional literature. This essay describes the images of time and place in the educational activities and organizational structures of nonformal educational settings and through them attempts to characterize the uniqueness of nonformal pedagogy.[2]

Two conceptual frameworks are integrated into the theoretical approach through which the place and time images in the nonformal pedagogy narrative were detected and analyzed. The first is based upon the work of Michael Bakhtin (1988), who in researching the nature of fiction introduced the term "chronotope," borrowed from Einstein's theory of physics (Bakhtin, 1981). The second derives from the philosophical studies of Deleuze and Guattari (1991), specifically their discussion of the nature of philosophy, in which they coined the term "geophilosophy"—the relationship between a philosophy and the geographical location where it emerged.

Bakhtin's concept of the chronotope marks "the intrinsic connectedness of temporal and spatial relationships that are artistically expressed in literature." Indeed, Bakhtin defines chronotopes based upon their expression in a variety of literary forms, for example, idylls, folktales, or picaresque novels.

In their book *What is Philosophy?* Deleuze and Guattari (1991) refer to the term "geography" as, among other things, a variable that participates in the creation of a mental state in which physical surroundings have an impact upon philosophy. According to them, the location and milieu of Greece played a significant role in the philosophy of ancient Greece.

Pedagogy, no less than philosophy, is affected by the formative impact of its actual or seeming position in space and time. That is, the surroundings of a particular pedagogy play a part in creating a metaphysical landscape that impinges upon its essence. When we discuss pedagogy, the term "geophilosophy" is transformed into "geoideology" based upon the assumption that pedagogy is moderated by ideology rather than by philosophy (Burbules, 1992; Keller, 1994; Lamm, 2002).

Images of time and place, or chronotopes, are structured and reflected in an exclusive narrative and constitute an inseparable element of the geoideology of nonformal pedagogy.

DATA COLLECTION

Data collection for this essay focused on out-of-school educational organizations. Data was collected based on two criteria, organizational attributes and pedagogical attributes, with the assumption that the two criteria are related. Tools used in data collection included interviewing officials and reading and analyzing texts issued by an organization or pertaining to it, such as instructional booklets, programs, promotional flyers, newspaper advertisements, administrative texts, and educational circulars. The collected data was interpreted on two levels. The first level involved clarifying information regarding the common images of time and place in the activities of nonformal educational organizations. The second level was composed of categorizing, comparing and interpreting the images of time and place in each organization, and then pinpointing the consistencies in these images (activities, values, and behaviors that were observed to repeat themselves). The generalization to be presented in this essay was based upon these detected consistencies.

The selected out-of-school organizations were classified into representative prototypes, including youth movements; youth organizations; community centers; "alternative" educational systems; municipal departments for youth, culture, and sport; and art, science, and history museums with educational departments or branches.[3] A review of pedagogical and theoretical texts in the field of narrative criticism and semiotics provided additional theoretical foundations for analyzing and interpreting data.

PEDAGOGY AND LITERATURE: SOME THEORETICAL BACKING

According to Bruner (1986), there are two types of cognitive functioning or two forms of thought offering alternative ways of organizing experience and structuring reality. The first type is paradigmatic or scientific-logical. It seeks to realize the ideal of describing and explaining reality through a formal and/or mathematical system that is subject to validation. The second type of cognitive functioning is narrative. It organizes reality through stories, dramatic structures, and credible (though not necessarily "real") historical reports. This type considers the intentions that motivate human activities based upon events as they unfold as well as upon the results marking the progress of these events.

Expanding upon Bruner, I have made the assumption that all forms of pedagogy structure and reflect a narrative that supplies the pedagogy's basic assumptions as well as all the components that take part in its expression or comprise its activities. This narrative constitutes a unique genre known as "the text of educational ideologies" and is composed of the textual procedures that play a part in its structuring. These procedures engender a high level of verisimilitude in educational texts and contribute to their credibility and hence to their public acceptance. The textual procedures that have generated ideological educational texts characterize these texts as well and are expressed on a variety of levels: the rhetorical level responsible for the degree to which the texts are convincing; the narrative level responsible for designing the characters and plot that take part in the pedagogical program; the communicative level that determines the nature of the text through its relationship between sender and receiver; the inter-textual level that contributes to the text being understood and accepted by the public (Silberman-Keller, 1997, 2000; Keller, 1992, 1994).

Adding images of time and place when formulating and characterizing pedagogy constitutes yet another way of studying the narrative elements that, together with plot and characters, participate in the structuring and reflection of a pedagogical narrative.

As in any other pedagogy, nonformal pedagogy implements its own narrative as part of its way of existing in the world, and this very narrative has supplied the case study for the narrative inquiry of pedagogy.

IMAGES OF PLACE IN NONFORMAL PEDAGOGY

Margins—Within the Space of the Nonformal Educational System

Formal education defines the place of nonformal pedagogy in a given educational system. Compulsory education laws, along with the sociological, cultural, and political functions of formal education in modern nations, place systems of formal education at the center of educational activities related to socialization processes, which are characterized by accumulated achievements in the form of certificates required by the laws of compulsory education (Bentley, 1998; Heimlich, 1993; McGiveney, 1999; Mocker & Spear, 1982; Reed & Loughran, 1984). This central feature of formal education allows it to be seen as a canonical educational activity. In contrast to formal education, nonformal education operates on the basis of the open participation of its clientele. The option of choosing to participate in nonformal educational activities—even if only superficial—is also evident in its content as well as in the way this content is translated into activities. These two factors—the nature of participation in nonformal education along with the way its unique content is incorporated into its activities—place nonformal education at the edges of the canonical center, that is, at the margins of formal education.

This location to a large extent determines the self-image of nonformal pedagogy. Its operators, its clients, and the general public as well believe that it fills roles different from those filled by the formal educational system, including "complementary education" and "alternative education."

Complementary education touches upon processes of cultural, social, religious, and political socialization that complement the socialization processes taking place within formal educational settings. For this reason, and despite its being indicative that what goes on in the schools is not complete, complementary education to a great extent still adapts itself to and is guided by what happens in school. Thus, even if this form of education takes place in out-of-school organizations, it does not stand on its own and constitutes a continuation of what happens in school, thus enhancing school activities and underlining their significance.

Alternative education is related to educational patterns intended to serve as an alternative for formal education. Its role is not to fulfill the primary function of providing basic learning skills or general education, nor to help cope with social, health, or political problems (LaBelle & Sylvester, 1990; Torres, 1990). According to LaBelle and Sylvester—as well as research for this essay—educational organizations that use nonformal pedagogy as an alternative to formal education are autonomous and are usually created upon government or citizen initiative. In either case, this form of pedagogy is openly critical of school by creating an alternative to it. Often, complementary education is also considered alternative, for its organizers and its clients see it as filling some lack according to a "better" model of education than that existing in the schools.

Nonformal education in Israel offers a model that combines complementary education and alternative education. In part it is initiated by the canonical center, while in part groups with special interests or needs instigate it.

The implementation of nonformal pedagogy at the margins of canonical education, be it in the form of complementary or of alternative education, to a large extent shapes its internal discourse and practices, mainly in two central directions. One is the tendency toward leniency and is related to educational achievements considered to be "creative," "unconventional," "politically identified," "innovative," and tied to the avant-garde significance of marginality. The other relates to margins as somewhere that is "unimportant" or "not to be taken into account," that is, on the margins of the essential and canonical system, where the very nature of learning settings is socially defined and legitimized.

This dual interpretation of the marginality of nonformal pedagogy creates tension, which is expressed in, among other things, the structuring of its routine practices that provide ontological weight for the existence of marginality in the world.[4]

Margins, then, signify the placement of nonformal pedagogy within the system. They supply the narrative of this pedagogy with a motif of difference in its practices. Those involved in this pedagogy transmit this message in their work, while planning their activities and carrying them out, and they perceive themselves as educators who are different from or other than schoolteachers. Often, this difference or otherness generates avant-garde self-images among those involved in nonformal pedagogy, and often it is used to critically censure the centrality of the school and its practices. This sense of otherness can also evoke severe criticism and social condemnation regarding the distribution of resources among the institutions of formal education and organizations dealing with nonformal pedagogy. Thus, to a large extent it creates independence in the mobilization of resources for the operation of those organizations using routine practices.

Networks—Mapping Nonformal Educational Systems

Networks are a metaphor for the structure of nonformal education that operates in accordance with nonformal pedagogy as well as helps to formulate this pedagogy. This system is composed of autonomous or semiautonomous organizations that themselves generate a networklike configuration, both in their organizational structure and in the models of communication serving them.

Such organizations emerged largely as a result of the actions of those who initiated the development of critical approaches to what was going on in the formal educational establishment, which was typically represented by government agencies, or as a response to a need or a social interest. Such organizations exist based on ideological advocacy justification for their fields of endeavor and their achievements. Together these organizations reflect a broad spectrum of social and political interests and needs that are pedagogically shaped through practices characterized by a large degree of flexibility.

In contrast to a formal-hierarchical system of education, the nonformal educational system is set within the bond between the center and the periphery in every organization, as well as in the links among the organizations that are part of the system. This relationship among organizations is not conditional upon any requirement whatsoever, and is usually created upon interests and needs that arise by chance, thus moderating the existence of hierarchical structures.

The structure of the nonformal educational network has an impact upon nonformal pedagogy in at least two areas: on intra- and inter-organizational communication and on the feelings of belonging among the members of a particular organization. Intra-organizational communication takes place via negotiation and dialogue between the center and the periphery that contributes to consolidating the organization as a specific ideological community. Inter-organizational dialogue defines the activity environment for each of the organizations. The activity environment sometimes generates competition and sometimes cooperation, depending upon the changing situation in the field. For example, cooperation and/or competition between a community center and a local branch of a youth movement can emerge around a common interest. Another example involves the points of contact between "green organizations" or social advocacy organizations, creating factions or short-term coalitions according to changing circumstances. The network, a representative pattern of organizational structure and communication, reinforces feelings of belonging among the members of the organizations as a consequence of its being an alternative to hierarchical structure. This structure is maintained and recycled through organization-wide meetings as well as through the existence of an organizational system of cooperation and participation in various decision-making processes.

Networks are important on a more general level because they generate channels of communications that permit the transfer of information—directly and overtly as well as indirectly and covertly—within and between organizations, in order to enhance and institutionalize nonformal pedagogical practices. Via such transmission, the specific terminology of nonformal pedagogy is created and established. This terminology shapes the organizational patterns existing around it and because of it, including patterns of pedagogical training, teaching and instructional techniques, and the methods through which it is implemented.

One of the most outstanding instances of the relationship between the network structure and the systemic frameworks of communication within nonformal pedagogy can be seen when tracing the occupational biographies of educators and officials in the organizations that participated in this research study. These biographies indicated that employees tended to "migrate" from organization to organization and that their initial "learning," which constitutes a process of socialization for a social role, creates a specific language that, seemingly invisible, proceeds across the network and is transformed, from "migration" to "migration," into cultural capital that shapes a vocabulary not limited to one organization but rather is the property of the entire system. This diagnosis, which is most typical of the nonformal educational system in Israel, was also tested in a meeting between Israeli educationalists and their counterparts from abroad. Apart from the use of local terminology, here, too, uniformity was apparent in the educational perceptions of those working in nonformal pedagogy.[5] It is therefore quite likely that the educational perceptions and forms of discourse among nonformal educators point to the existence of a linguistic code specially characterized by the marginal self-placement of nonformal educators. This marginal code is apparently transmitted via the network and bases its subject matter on the unique nature of nonformal pedagogy. This phenomenon becomes more significant as its transmissions are used as an alternative for a unified professional idiom while the professional stature of nonformal pedagogy is still in the early stages of its formation.

Networks represent patterns of existence and communication as part of the total environment in which nonformal pedagogy functions. In metaphorical terms, networks are what spin and drive the microspatial environments in which educational activities actually take place: "alternative homes" and "anywhere."

Alternative Homes and Anywhere—The Micro-Space of Nonformal Pedagogy

Youth movements refer to their meeting places as "nests," "tribes," or "branches." Community centers call them "centers," while green organizations term them "field schools." A number of youth education groups have recently opened "pubs," museums hold "workshops," and youth movement counselors often live in "communes." This short list reflects the varied ways in which organizations practicing nonformal pedagogy refer to their meeting places.

Despite this diversity in names, the concept of alternative home has been uniformly perceived among those dealing in nonformal education. This outlook is expressed in the way these meeting places are designed as part of the educational activities that take place in them, including how they are decorated, how their walls and furnishings are fixed up, and what is "allowed" or "forbidden" to take place within them. All of these benefit from a flexibility that creates arrangements, decorations, and activity spaces inspiring a comfortable feeling resembling the common public perception of a family home, thus making it possible to refer to these places as alternative homes. This image is also fed by statements made by those who organize or participate in the activities, referring to the activity center as a place "where you can be at home" or even a place where you can behave differently than what is allowed in more formal settings. The physical setting of nonformal activities creates an atmosphere of belonging and security, of freedom and of warmth, one that determines the very nature of the place. When a place is defined as home, nonformal educational activities can actually take place anywhere. Therefore, alternative homes embody a pedagogical resource generating feelings of belonging that make it possible to move back and forth confidently among various other geographic or social spaces.

Interviews with those active in this field have indicated that the more they succeed in developing a feeling of belonging to their activity center, the more they are also able to involve their clients in decoration and maintenance as an inseparable part of the pedagogical practice ritual.

These three images of place both shape nonformal pedagogy and are shaped by it on a number of levels. On the general level of the total educational system, the clear distinction between the canonical center and the margins determines that the margins represent the overall space for nonformal pedagogy. Networks are an inspirational and practical metaphor that guides the communicative and organizational channels within the nonformal educational system. And the concepts of alternative home and anywhere reinforce the immediate surroundings of nonformal pedagogy. In such places, it is possible to develop more secure patterns of relationships in response to marginality or networking. The images of time in nonformal pedagogy shed light on these places as components of its chronotope.

IMAGES OF TIME IN NONFORMAL PEDAGOGY

In his article "The Constitution of Human Life in Time," Thomas Luckman states (Luckman, 1991, p. 151):

> Time is constitutive of human life in society. Of course it is also constitutive of human life in nature: *all* life is in time. But as a dimension of human life it is only the matrix of growth and decline between birth and death. It is also the condition of human sociality that is achieved again and again in the continuously incarnated contemporaneity of face to face interaction.

Luckman's comments indicate that time is constitutive of pedagogical activities as a flexible resource that takes on and changes its form in accordance with the narrative needs making up part of its very nature.

Leisure Time: The Mantle of Time Surrounding Nonformal Pedagogy

In the modern era, and to some extent in the postmodern era as well, the bureaucratic tendency to allocate and truncate time has also had an impact upon the way in which time serves as a factor in shaping our social and personal lives. This doling out of time determines that parts of the day, week, or year not related to particular functions are termed "leisure time" or "vacation time." This definition is, first and foremost, in terms of time, but in effect it represents a form of social authorization for how time is used. That is, human beings are "allowed" to spend their vacations wherever they want and with whomever they choose, yet even so their vacations and leisure time are officially limited to the time "permitted" for such activities. In general "private time," which includes vacation or leisure time, falls within a category signaling the time people have "left over" after they have allocated time to the general social context (Eviatar, 1990).

The distinction between formal and nonformal education is a specific case of bureaucratic time allocation. This differentiation determines the institutionalized living space and internal timetable of nonformal pedagogy.

The French sociologist Joffre Dumazedier (1974), who investigated the notion of leisure time from the sociological perspective, has defined leisure time as the space in which the individual can fulfill himself. In his view, this is a specific social time in which the individual can "allow" himself to rest after having completed his social, familial, and political obligations. It is a time when he can free himself of worries, physical and mental exhaustion, and anxiety. Thus, leisure time offers the possibility for socially legitimate self-fulfillment and pleasure. In contrast to Dumazedier, who saw leisure time as an opportunity for pleasure and development, Foucault (1980) critically described leisure time from the perspective of modern politics as an expression of control. According to him, work is what regulates time. But as leisure time increases, it also must be regulated in order to achieve control and discipline. According to Foucault, television determines an individual's daily schedule. In places where there is no television, an entire industry has developed utterly devoted to organizing the apparent leisure time of the citizens. A variety of institutions fill up this leisure time with cultural programs and public activities. Continuing Foucault's line of thought, Joseph Ramoneda believed that political movements could be classified according to how they organized time. The most open and free societies can be found in the category of political movements that showed the greatest degree of flexibility in their use of time and the respect they gave to the personal space of their citizens (in which only subjective considerations determine how time is used).

Defining nonformal pedagogy as taking place during leisure time implies that it procures a form of organized and institutionalized time. If it responds to an individual and subjective initiative, or alternatively, to an initiative coming from an institution, it will apparently be determined according to the society in which it exists, but it always is part of a social institution situated within leisure time. This placement can even be assumed to contribute to the formation of normative behavior that, among other things, is intended to prevent what is perceived as social control whether it is shaped differently in different political regimes.

Israel reflects a model that integrates governmental and semi- or nongovernmental organizations. In both types of organizations, nonformal pedagogy serves to generate diverse cultural, social, political, and educational activities.

The definition of nonformal pedagogy in these two types of institutions as taking place after the "compulsory" time spent in school or at work portrays leisure time as contributing to the symbolic and practical creation of "otherness" as an inseparable element of its essence. This is because leisure time, in which educational activities take place in accordance with nonformal pedagogy, breaks the cycle of required social meetings arranged by means of formal definitions, allowing a more or less voluntary meeting of individuals who have chosen to belong to social groups based upon interest or common need.

During this time, individuals, groups, and communities can allow themselves to be "atypical" by filling social roles other than those they fill in formal settings at compulsory times.

These atypical social roles generate alternative narratives to those that take place during compulsory time through the adoption of diverse play rhetorics (Sutton-Smith, 1997) that blur the lines between what is "important" and what is "unimportant," "real" and "not real," "coincidental" and "noncoincidental," "serious" and "not serious." These spatial contrasts expand the significance of social existence beyond the possibility of shattering the routine self-image resulting from formal definitions. Thus, it may be that these alternative narratives enhance the significance of their formal equivalents by intensifying the rift and the distinction between work time and leisure time.

Leisure time serves as an entryway of sorts to "other time" that permits "otherness" on a variety of expressive levels and creates additional unique images of time in the practice of nonformal education. The following images of time refer to definitions of the target audiences of nonformal pedagogy as well as to the timetable of its activities and to time as it is internally perceived and constructed through the intervention of nonformal pedagogy.

Life Cycles: Defining the Target Audiences for Nonformal Pedagogy

As in the organizations of formal education, nonformal educational organizations also divide up their target audiences according to the age of the participants. Thus, nonformal educational settings are composed of distinct educational organizations geared to different age groups, including children, teens, adults, and seniors. Organizations targeted at age-diverse audiences exist as well, for instance, community centers, green organizations, municipal culture departments, and museums.

Despite the above, the issue of participants' age in nonformal educational activities is marked symbolically as well as practically relative to the integration of age and education. For according to the nonformal pedagogy narrative, education is seen as taking place throughout life. Some of the alternative names for nonformal education, such as "continuing education," "adult education," and "community education," demonstrate a breaking of the accepted pattern in modern formal education by defining its existence in relation to life cycles and the ages of its participants.

The time image of "all the cycles of life" is a contradiction in terms. On the one hand, nonformal educational organizations compartmentalize the age boundaries of their participants within their activities. On the other hand, they take leave of such compartmentalization through practices that push the end of the educational process beyond a particular age limit, thus enabling the process to continue throughout life.

The Internal Timetable of Nonformal Pedagogy: Calendar Time

An examination of the internal timetable of nonformal pedagogy as it is manifested in nonformal educational institutions makes it possible to differentiate between two different planes on which time can be divided. One singles out images marking the sequence of the activity year, while the other demarcates the continuity and rhythm of the activities. Both represent distinct images within two categories: "the activity time schedule" and "time spent in nonformal educational activities."

The Activity Time Schedule

Nonformal educational activities take place after regular work and school hours and increase during seasonal vacations and holidays when there are also vacations from work and school, or after retirement.

Lewis and Weigart (1990, pp. 77–104) pointed out that the two time axes, "the seasons of the year" and "the holidays," intertwine and that this intermingling grants a unique significance to both:

> Two significant changes come with the seasonal cycles and add to their distinctive social definitions. First, our life-styles reflect changes in weather and temperature as we adopt the food, the clothing, work and recreational activities, appropriate for the season. Second, each season is characterized by dominant holydays . . . and this aura and mood penetrates our lives from season to season probably far more than we realize consciously, whether we react with joy or depression.

The cross between leisure time and holiday time in nonformal pedagogy is particularly prominent in planning the activity schedules of organizations working in nonformal education. These times determine periods of heightened and diminished activity when planning time schedules, personnel assignments, facilities, and budgets.

The character of the seasons and the holidays determines the content of educational activities as well. Distinct sets of holidays or festivities can be identified. For example, the seasonal field trips taken by youth movements are given distinctive names, such as "From Sea to Sea," "To the Judean Desert," "To the Negev," "To the Galilee," and "The Expedition to Poland." These regularly scheduled trips integrate weather and seasonal variables with specific educational content. For youth movements and nonformal educational organizations, these trips "celebrate" their unique ethos.[6]

Most nonformal educational organizations make special preparations for the period falling between the end of the Passover holiday and *Yom Ha'atsma'ut* (Israeli Independence Day). In most organizations involved in nonformal education, summer vacations as well as winter and spring breaks are also activity-intensive.

Based on the above examples, we can say that time images incorporating holidays and seasons of the year have a close affinity to the pedagogical activity cycles in the schedule of nonformal educational organizations.

The images representing this combination of the seasons of the year, the religious holidays, and the secular calendar include "linear time" and "cyclical time." The image of linear time refers to the passage of time, while that of cyclical time relates to recurring events or festivities. Linear time and cyclical time mark two axes used to represent time graphically and metaphorically in a unique geometrical form marking recurring repetitions along the ongoing stream of time. Moreover, the significance of linear time derives from the concept of progress that is usually related to the advancement of human civilization and the perception of time as irreversible. The significance of cyclical time stems from the concept of perpetual repetition and to a large extent characterizes time as "mythic time" that produces rituals, as defined by Mircea Eliade (1959).

The schedule marking time duration in nonformal pedagogical activities is thus represented along a linear axis whose lines of progress integrate time cycles that seem to hinder the advancement of time. This "delayed" or cyclical time itself produces a separate axis leading to comparisons of one year to another and one season to another, thus reinforcing tradition.

Linear time and cyclical time differentiate between ordinary days and holidays, celebrations, and ceremonies, and they create the borders within which educational activities take place, activities that themselves affect and are shaped by specific images of time.

TIME AND RHYTHM WITHIN NONFORMAL EDUCATIONAL ACTIVITIES

According to the nonformal pedagogy narrative, perceptions of time in nonformal educational activities can be illustrated by three images: "images of duration and rhythm in educational activities," "images of developmentality," and "images of trial, error, and rejuvenation" that provide a bridge between the first two types.

Images of Duration and Rhythm in Educational Activities: Flashes

An examination of the educational activities within the organizations that contributed data to this essay shows that in most organizations the image of time representing the rhythm of nonformal educational activities is the "flash." This image expresses short-term activities composed of a few meetings. Usually the activity begins with a trigger[7] such as a field trip, a movie, a simulation, an assignment, or a text. Such a trigger launches the activity, the nature of which is usually a discussion integrating various types of dialogue.[8] During this discussion, the subjects making up the issue under discussion are pinpointed, and they are used in the learning nourished by a variety of sources, including examining the origins of information, positions, and feelings that arise during the group discussion with regard to the issue under consideration in the activity. The activity ends with a summarizing event that can become a new trigger for continued discussion or development from different viewpoints, or alternatively as a summary marking the transition to a new subject.

The flash as an image representing the rhythm of activities in nonformal pedagogy has a great deal of weight, for it generates the group meeting and organizes the course of development of the educational activity. It also creates interest and motivation for continued participation among the members of the group for a particular activity. The importance of the flash, then, lies in its ability to engage people in an activity, and in this capacity it receives serious consideration from activity planners and executors and constitutes a place that calls for invention, innovation, and variety in planning activities that serve as a gateway to participation in nonformal education. This claim is backed by the methods reviewed in the *Haphalopedia* (Goldberger & Steintsler, 1994), an encyclopedia of nonformal educational methods that demonstrate the variety of activities available for use in flashes. Nonetheless, these activities have a modular structure that alternately integrates many methodological components or parts into different and recurring combinations, thus structuring a wide variety of activities. It may be that this modular repetition of methodological variety marks the essential nature of innovation in all components of the flash as a generator of very adaptable processes of dismantling and assembly as flexible modules intended to create diversity and ongoing innovation or modular construction and reconstruction.

The integration of a trigger (to launch a single activity) and a flash (to regulate the sequence and therefore the rhythm of a number of activities) generates a distinction in the significance of time in the narrative of nonformal pedagogy. First, the trigger creates a type of passageway between compulsory time and leisure time while it also exists under the umbrella of leisure time. In some sense, the trigger is an invisible and initial gong or ring that shapes disorder while at the same time marking a new beginning and order characterized by the liminality generated by a different type of learning. This new order, which is neither here nor there in time, allows for a carnivalesque atmosphere providing the opportunity to don other masks and thus expanding the possibility of realizing social roles.

The typical triggers in nonformal pedagogical activities include, among others, relaxation games, competitive games, simulations, sculpture, drawing, films, and dance. Only after the trigger is employed does the activity begin, involving discussion or group action.

Second, the flash as a series of activities produces learning modules that generate a beginning and an end. On the average, it includes from three to ten activities and forms a nonformal pedagogical learning unit. Ongoing repetition turns this image into the dynamics of teaching and learning while coping with a high stimulation threshold and motivating attention and focus among participants. Its very nature stresses the here and now, transforming them into the focal points for concentrating the cognitive or emotional knowledge gathered during the learning process.

The Image of Developmentality

Development marks a passage in time as well as a change from one condition to another. The passage between two conditions contains an assumption, at least in modern education, of progress. Development also assumes causality and thus creates a chain of links based upon seeing one or more factors as preceding subsequent events or happenings.

The concept of developmentality as an image of time (a motif that includes a variety of concepts regarding development as a product of education) lies at the heart of all pedagogies. Most implement a broad system of rhetorical images to represent this concept that also describe intentionality in the educational act. This is evident, for example, in agricultural and sculptural images marking growth, sunrise, flowering, and design, as well as in more abstract images found in contemporary critical libertine pedagogy based upon positioning educational intervention to generate development of talents, skills, and knowledge, most of which are intended to support the realization of personal freedom among students.[9]

The developmental basis of most modern pedagogies relies on psychological or psychosociological theories that have supplied their theoretical platform. The writings of Freud, Piaget, Fromm, Maslow, Skinner, Rogers, and Colberg have provided the basis, presumably scientific, for the development of the personality, of cognitive skills and moral growth, of realizing personal needs, and of behavioral autonomy according to a variety of pedagogical narratives.

Nonformal pedagogy also relies upon the description of education as a developmental process. Consequently, a variety of organizations specialize in providing educational services to distinct age groups, and even these are divided into groups where the passage from one to another imitates the growth process.

Thus, the developmental image of time amalgamates with the image of time describing the target audience of nonformal education and the perception that it permits development throughout life. The uniqueness of nonformal pedagogy stems from the creation of an interdependent relationship between individual development and group development: the individual develops within the group, and the group develops as a result of the individuals comprising it. Individual development and group development are the declared aims of nonformal pedagogy and are an inseparable part of the intentions behind each and every activity within nonformal education. Over the past three decades, this ideological pattern of activity has gained theoretical support in the field of nonformal education in articles on social psychology and group leadership (Rosenwasser, 1997).

Developmental time in nonformal pedagogy, then, is first and foremost shaped by ideology and thus represents an approach that links the individual to society through the agency of the small group to which the individual belongs. To a certain extent, this image alludes to the familial belonging that ties individuals to their social surroundings at a time of inevitable existential alienation. Therefore, developmental time in nonformal pedagogical terms offers additional forms of "otherness." This otherness exists because there is no gap between the individual and the group, thus negating current alienation and providing the basis for an ideal future picture in which the individual is an inseparable part of society.

The integration of order and rhythm in nonformal pedagogy, by relying upon the concept of flash time and by gearing educational activities and their goals to developmental time, in essence, provides the answer to the following question: how can the desired development be shaped in nonformal pedagogy? The answer to this question is the creation of the time images of trial, error, and rejuvenation.[10]

Trial, Error, and Rejuvenation: Fragmented Time

In nonformal pedagogy, the educational process as well as teaching-learning processes assume development on at least two levels: the orientation level that directs the planning of educational activities and the level of the outcome expected from participating in the educational process, that is, the development of the individual and the group as representing the ideal development direction of the entire society.

The image of trial, error, and rejuvenation or of fragmented time determines the shape of developmental time. This shape is characterized by a variety of metaphorical lines; they can be circular, elliptical, or branched. All of these shapes represent the bond between the present when the educational activity takes place and the pace at which its effects are expected to be recognized by its participants. In nonformal educational and teaching-learning processes, the expected outcomes after educational activities have taken place are imprecise and flexible and can be expressed in a number of different ways. Thus they provide the individual and the group with "processing time."

Fragmented time, then, represents processing time or the subjective time of those who participate in educational activities, expressed, among other things, by traditional Hebrew slogans, such as "educate the boy according to his own way."

Fragmented time is positioned perpendicular to the chronological, linear, irreversible time of the educational activity calendar, and it is built upon the assumption of variation in the developmental rate of individuals within a group.

The developmental maturity of an individual or of a group in the field of nonformal education is tested, for example, within a discussion where individuals in the group come to an agreement or a decision regarding a joint activity, even when this agreement or decision incorporates consensus and/or conflict. Definitive maturity or complete development is not the goal of nonformal pedagogy, which generates opportunities for ongoing learning, for this pedagogy is based upon the notion that for the individual "education, like life itself, goes on as long as it exists." In this regard, groups, communities, and even societies are seen as dynamic developmental entities.

CONCLUSION

The analogy between the novel as the realization of a particular form of narrative and the narrative of nonformal pedagogy as expressed in a number of its images of time and place enables us to use a concept coined by Bakhtin (1988, p. 333)—"ideologeme." The significance of this concept becomes clear in Bakhtin's explanation:

> The speaking person in the novel is always, to one degree or another, an *idiologue,* and his words are *ideologemes.* A particular language in a novel is always a particular way of viewing the world, one that strives for a social significance.

In this essay, the central character representing the narrative of nonformal pedagogy is the chronotope, signifying a combination of time and place images. This character exists within the self-perception of those who design this pedagogy as well as among its clients, and thus it aspires toward social significance among the general public. The chronotope in nonformal pedagogy is part of its ideologeme.

Over the course of history, the subject of time has played a role in the speculations and studies of both philosophers and scientists.[11] Its disclosure within a limited context, along with the subject of space, makes it possible to link it to the concept of geoideology. That is, time marks the setting of a given pedagogy as participating in the creation of a metaphysical landscape that has an impact upon its very essence.

Therefore, the descriptions accompanying nonformal pedagogy, which are usually found in its internal discourse but also in public discourse concerning it, include, among others: "otherness," "marginality," "originality," "nontraditional work hours," "freedom," "permissiveness," "fellowship," "family," "intimacy," "nonconventionality," "entertainment," "debate," "volunteerism," "political-social involvement," "tolerance," "acceptance of others," "play and enjoyment." These descriptions for the most part result from the way in which images of place and time exist as part of the interaction between the self-perception of nonformal pedagogy narrative and its practice.

Even if the positive formulations of these descriptions create an impression of referring to nonformal pedagogy as an ideal, for us they are only a reflection of the way in which this pedagogy perceives of itself.

All of the self-descriptions of nonformal pedagogy are subject to criticism (although not to censure). Questions with regard to such criticism can shed light on the nature of nonformal pedagogy with respect to the following: its role in the context of the ruling hegemony in a given society; political regimes that it supports or that support it; interpretations it grants to the notion of equality in education or cultural pluralism; the possibility of introspective and subjective thought within the activities it generates; and mechanisms of social supervision, renewal, and/or preservation that are developed by and that develop in light of it. The answers to such questions are important, particularly because contemporary educational philosophy, research, and practice promote the subjects of teaching, formal learning—and nonformal learning as a possible alternative to teaching—that for a number of years have been experiencing an unavoidable and ongoing crisis because of the loss of exclusivity of the school as a place of learning, as well as in light of scientific and technological developments and current globalization processes (Boud & Garrick, 1999; Burbules & Callister, 2000; Burbules & Torres, 2000; Coffield, 2000, Dale & Bell, 1999; Marsick & Watkins, 1991).

This essay was intended to study the chronotope of nonformal pedagogy by means of describing several images of time and place common in the discourse of those who use this pedagogy. According to the best traditions of this pedagogy, the reader is invited to examine the possible identity, correspondence, or conflict between these images of time and place and to contemplate their significance.

NOTES

1. Three definition strategies for the concept of pedagogy can be found in the relevant literature. The first is based on the dictionary definition, the second on encyclopedia definitions, and the third is the definition given to the concept as representing a specific form of pedagogy. In this article, "pedagogy" is defined as a theoretical and practical framework according to which and as a result of which educational activities take place. See Houssaye 1993; Bertrand & Houssaye, 1999).
2. A multitude of terms, the products of diverse theoretical approaches, are used to refer to and conceptualize educational practices outside of the school setting. These terms and theoretical approaches exclusively color the various aspects of this educational form. Nevertheless, there is still no overall definition of this perspective that directs and includes both nonformal teaching/learning and the administrative/organizational structuring that generates and reflects this educational approach. This article attempts to include these elements as the dynamic components of an exclusive form of pedagogy. This attempt is the outcome of my ongoing experience as the head of the Department of Non-Formal Education at Beit Berl College as well as the result of dialogue and joint research with Dr. Zvi Bekerman of the Hebrew University in Jerusalem, some of which is reported in this book. I am grateful to him for the opportunity to discuss these issues.
3. I want to thank the Research Committee at Beit Berl College, Israel, for its support in financing this research. I also extend my thanks to my research assistants: Anat Kuzi, Liat Levy, Oshrat Ganei-Gonen, and Lior Yaakovivitz.
4. The term "ontology" has a long tradition in philosophical discourse. Its definition in this article is based on Gadamer's discussion of the ontology of art (Gadamer, 1989, p. 92): "The 'subject' of the experience of art, that which remains and endures, is not the subjectivity of the person who experiences it, but the work itself. For play has its own essence."
5. These meetings took place between students in the Department of Nonformal Education and graduate students from many Latin American countries who have taken part in a continuing education program held over the past five years at the International Institute of the Histadrut Labor Federation on the campus of Beit Berl College.
6. The field trips mentioned in this article are from a youth movement known as *Ha'Noar Ha'Oved Ve Ha'Lomed* (Working and Studying Youth). In all the youth movements and in many strata of the organizations operating in nonformal education, field trips have unique names that mark a significant subject or event.
7. The term "trigger" has been inspired by the terminology developed by Barthes (1974). Like all pedagogy, nonformal pedagogy builds its self-narrative using strategies that mark the desired starting point for all activities no less than the textual modalities. The way in which the jumping-off points for nonformal pedagogical activities are constructed is reminiscent of a similar concept in the terminology of Paulo Freire (1970): "generative subjects." The Israeli experience with nonformal education, however, shows that for the most part an initiated topic does not fulfill the need to liberate the oppressed, as Freire postulated, but rather serves to integrate between the ideological guidance of the nonformal educational organization and contextual educational situations.

8. In his book *Dialogue in Teaching: Theory and Practice,* Nicholas Burbules (1993) categorized the types of dialogue in the educational act. Among them are dialogue as conversation, dialogue as investigation, dialogue as argument, and dialogue as teaching mechanism.
9. The tradition of libertine or critical thinking in education has a long history. One option is to trace its development by placing its first stages within the context of the modern age, in the work of Rousseau. Subsequently, it is also apparent in the work of Pestalozzi, Montessori, Rogers, Illich, Freire, and others as well. Recently, Jeffs and Smith set up an Internet site with an encyclopedia of nonformal education and a bibliography that relates nonformal education to corresponding elements in a variety of pedagogical approaches (see <http://www.infed.org>).
10. The work of Reuben Kahane (1997, pp. 20–25), "Trial and Error," is an integral part of the moratorium, one of the structural components of the nonformal code. Perhaps there is a parallel between the two concepts, but within the discussion of time and place in nonformal pedagogy, the notion of "trial, error, and rejuvenation" represents the internal illustration of the image of fragmented time as requesting a delay in the rhythm of evaluating the educational "products" of nonformal pedagogy.
11. As noted, there is a long tradition of considering the subject of time. Time has been directly considered in the works of Aristotle, Plato, St. Augustine, Kant, Husserl, Heidegger, Bergson, Ricoeur, Deleuze, as well as in some of the writings of Galileo, Newton, Einstein, and others. Certainly, this topic is indirectly part of every philosophical, scientific, historical, and artistic discourse, indeed of any discourse considering life and its significance.

    The subject of time has also been discussed in many literary works, including those of Jules Verne, Umberto Eco, Virginia Woolf, and Jorge Luis Borges, just to mention a few. Cinematic arts and film criticism also consider this issue, perhaps intrinsically, as evident in the works of Deleuze (1983, 1985), Collins, Radner, and Collins (1993), and Zizek (Wright & Wright, 1999), as well as in the catalogue of the exhibition *Le temps vite,* published by the Pompidou Centre in 2000.

REFERENCES

Bakhtin, M. M. (1981). *The dialogic imagination: Four essays by M. M. Bakhtin* (C. Emerson & M. Holquist, Trans.). Austin: University of Texas Press.

Barthes, R. (1974). Introduccion al analisis structural de los relatos. In *Analisis estructural del relato* (pp. 9–44). Buenos Aires: Tiempo Contemporaneo.

Bekerman, Z. & Silberman–Keller, D. (2004). Non-formal pedagogy epistemology rhetoric and practice. *Education and Society, 22* (1), 22-41

Bentley, T. (1998). *Learning beyond the classroom: Education for a changing world.* London: Routledge.

Bertrand, Y., & Houssaye, J. (1999). Pedagogie and didactique: An incestuous relationship. *Instructional Science,* 27: 33–51.

Boud, D., & Garrick, J. (Eds.). (1999). *Understanding learning at work.* London: Routledge.

Bruner, J. (1986). *Actual minds, possible worlds.* Cambridge, MA, and London: Harvard University Press.

Burbules, N. C. (1992). Forms of ideology-critique: A pedagogical perspective. *QSE,* 3(1): 7–17.

Burbules, N. C. (1993). *Dialogue in teaching: Theory and practice.* New York: Teachers College.

Burbules, N. C., & Callister, T. A. (2000). *The risks and promises of information technologies for education.* Boulder, CO: Westview Press.

Burbules, N. C., & Torres, C. A. (Eds.). (2000). *Globalization and education: Critical perspectives.* New York and London: Routledge.

Centre Pompidou. (2000). *Sciences: C'est l'an 2000, il fait vraiment un temps de temps.* Belgique: Snoeck-Ducaju & Zoon.

Coffield, F. (2000). *The necessity of informal learning.* Bristol: The Policy Press.

Collins, J., Radner, H., & Collins, A. P. (1993). *Film theory goes to the movies.* New York and London: Routledge.

Dale, M., & Bell, J. (Eds.). (1999). *Informal learning in the workplace.* London: Department for Education and Employment.

Deleuze, G. (1983). *L'Image-mouvement.* Paris: Les Editions de Minuit.

Deleuze, G. (1985). *L'Image-temps.* Paris: Les Editions de Minuit.

Deleuze, G., & Guattari, F. (1991). *Qu'es-ce que la philosophie?* Paris: Les Editions de Minuit.

Dumazedier, J. (1974). *La sociologie empirique du loisir.* Paris: Seuil.

Eliade, M. (1959). *Cosmos and history.* New York: Harper.

Eviatar, Z. (1990). Private time and public time. In J. Hassard (Ed.)., *The sociology of time* (pp. 168–77). New York: St. Martin's Press.

Foucault, M. (1980). *Power and knowledge: Selected interviews and other writings 1972–1977.* New York: Pantheon Books.

Freire, P. (1970). *Pedagogy of the oppressed.* New York: Seabury.

Gadamer, H. G. (1989). *Truth and method.* New York: Crossroad Press.

Goldberger, D., & Steintsler, D. (Eds.). (1994). *Haphalopedia.* Tel Aviv: Yedioth Aharonoth.

Heimlich, J. E. (1993). Nonformal environmental education: Towards a working definition. *CSMEE Bulletin: Eric:* 3–93.

Houssaye, J. (Ed.). (1993). *La Pedagogie: Une encyclopedie pour aujourd'hui.* Paris: ESF.

Kahane, R. (1997). *The origins of postmodern youth: Informal youth movements in a comparative perspective.* New York: Walter de Gruyter.

Keller, D. (1992) *State religious education: Two ideological frameworks.* Ph.D. Dissertation, Hebrew University, Jerusalem.

Keller, D. (1994). The text of educational ideologies: Toward the characterization of a genre. *Educational Theory,* 44(1): 26–43.

Keller, D. (1997). Plot and characters in ideological educational texts. In A. Gur Zeev (Ed.), *Education in the era of post-modern dialogue* (pp. 221–43). Jerusalem: Magness.

LaBelle, T. J., & Sylvester, J. (1990). Delivery systems—formal, nonformal, informal. In R. Murray-Thomas (Ed.), *International comparative education* (pp. 9–23). Oxford: Pergamon Press.

Lamm, Z. (2002). *In the whirlpool of ideologies: Education in the twentieth century.* Jerusalem: Magness Press.

Leadbeater, C. (2000). *Living on thin air: The new economy.* London: Penguin.

Lewis, J. D., & Weigart, A. J. (1990). The structures and meanings of social-time. In J. Hassard (Ed.), *The sociology of time* (pp. 77–104). New York: St. Martin's Press.

Luckman, T. (1991). The constitution of human life in time. In J. Bender & D. E. Wellbery (Eds.), *Chronotypes: The construction of time* (pp. 151–67). California: Stanford University Press.

Marsick, V. J., & Watkins, K. E. (1991). *Informal and incidental learning in the workplace.* London: Routledge.

McGiveney, V. (1999). *Informal learning in the community: A trigger for change and development.* Leicester: NIACE.

Mocker, D. W., and Spear, G. E. (1982) "*Lifelong Learning: Formal, Nonformal, Informal, and Self-Directed.*" Information Series No. 241. Columbus: ERIC Clearinghouse on Adult, Career, and Vocational Education, The National Center for Research in Vocational Education, The Ohio State University. (ERIC Document Reproduction Service No. ED 220 723).

Ramoneda, J. (2000). Le Temps de la Politique. *Journal de la exposition: Le Temps vite* (pp. 6–7). Belgique: Snoeck—Ducaju & Zoon.

Reed, H. B., & Loughran, E. L. (Eds.). (1984). *Beyond schools: education for economic, social, and personal development.* Amherst: Community Education Resource Center, University of Massachusetts.

Richardson, L. D., & Wolfe, M. (2001) *Principles and practices of informal education, learning through life.* London and New York: RoutledgeFalmer.

Rosenwasser, N. (1997). *Anthology for group training: A reader.* Jerusalem: Zippori Center, Hahevra Le'Matnasim.

Silberman-Keller, D. (1997). A New Reading of Educational Goals in Israel: The Intertextual Arena. *Iyunim Be'Hinuch:* 249–68.

Silberman-Keller, D. (1997). Margenes y Lugar de la educacion no-formal. In Secretaria de Desarrollo Social (Eds.), *Los Jovenes como sujetos de Politicas Sociales* (pp. 203–11). Buenos Aires: Presidencia de la Nacion, Programa de Fortalecimiento del Desarrollo Juvenil.

Silberman-Keller, D. (2000). Education in a multicultural society: The case of state religious education. *Education for culture in a multicultural society, issues at teacher workshops, 4th Compilation:* 139–58.

Sutton-Smith, B. (1997). *The ambiguity of play.* Cambridge, MA: Harvard University Press.

The encyclopedia of informal education, http://www.infed.org/index.htm

Torres, C. A. (1990). *The politics of nonformal education in Latin America.* New York, N.Y: Praeger Publishers.

Wright, E., & Wright, E. (Eds.). (1999). *The Zizek reader.* Oxford & Massachusetts: Blackwell Publishers Inc.

SELF-EDUCATING COMMUNITIES

COLLABORATION AND LEARNING THROUGH THE INTERNET

NICHOLAS C. BURBULES

I

The Internet has become one of the most important resources for formal, nonformal, and informal learning. Here I want to focus on one of its aspects, its capacity to support new kinds of community, usually in the absence of face-to-face contact, and including the capacity to form international networks, around shared interests and concerns—from political movements, to devotees of barbecue recipes, to medical researchers, to cricket fans, to owners of Yorkshire Terriers.[1] Some of these communities have the character of what I will call "self-educating communities," in that one of their most striking features, regardless of the subject matter they share in common (and no matter how trivial or obscure that topic may seem to others), is an overt commitment to sharing information, initiating newcomers, and extending their collective knowledge through such processes as shared problem-solving, experimentation, and independent inquiry—new knowledge that typically gets fed back into the network of collaborative edification for which they share responsibility.[2] The video gaming community was one of the earliest self-educating communities on the Internet, using it to exchange tips and shortcuts about game strategies and problem-solving, and sometimes melding gaming into social interaction through venues such as MUDs and MOOs (multi-user role-playing environments).

Certain capabilities within the Internet have extended and facilitated these self-educating processes. Early on, groups with common interests formed email lists and newsgroups; and these have remained effective and lively forums for discussion, debate, information sharing, and answering questions pertinent to an amazing variety of topics. These electronic forums constitute a public space of sorts, generally open to new participants, and with a variety of well-established norms and strategies for building community: FAQs, for example (Frequently Asked Questions), which summarize basic information about the topic at hand, partly geared toward speeding up the process for newcomers to access a common storehouse of knowledge, and so to become minimally conversant—but also partly designed to define the community in terms of its uncontroversial shared values and beliefs.[3] Not incidentally, FAQs also serve to minimize the amount of discussion space and time devoted to repeating the same questions and answers over and over again: newcomers—newbies—quickly get advised to take their questions there before posing them to the group as a whole. These communities are not *always* entirely welcoming to newcomers however; they can be particularly scornful, for example, when newcomers ignore information readily available through the FAQ; when newcomers introduce topics that are collectively judged irrelevant to the main subject matter; when they belabor the obvious, thinking something is new to the group when it is only new to *them;* or when they violate norms, often tacit ones, about proper modes of address and expression.[4] As with other communities, over time some participants distinguish themselves through frequency of contributions, quality and originality of contributions, and consensually recognized expertise or wisdom—and newcomers who fail to appreciate this and act with appropriate respect are often chastised, until they are judged to have earned the right to challenge the authorities of the group. Given repeated violations of these norms, other members will often "plonk" or "killfile" newcomers, that is, block their incoming messages through filters; this does not prevent the newcomer from posting messages to the group (although in worst-case scenarios it is possible to ban them, if the forum is moderated)—it simply means that the individual filterer can choose never to see that person's messages again.

In all of these dynamics, email lists and newsgroups resemble other sorts of communities that are similarly devoted to shared knowledge, value, and belief. They encourage a certain amount of free exchange and coeducation around their shared interests, but also manifest overt and implicit status relations and norms of interaction about which they can be quite self-protective.[5] The absence of face-to-face contact in Internet-mediated forums (which is changing now with the rise of video chats) can give these interactions a particular intensity, because it can be easier to say blunt and hypercritical things when you cannot see the other participants, do not know them, and will likely never meet them (hence the phenomenon of "flaming").[6] Many participants use email addresses or signatures that shield their name or identity, and this also can create a sense of detachment from personal obligations. Furthermore, other sorts of communities typically include members who interact, or at least can interact, along many dimensions of shared interest. Online communities, by contrast, are much more likely to comprise participants joined together *only* by the topic or occasion at hand—this can give their interactions greater intensity because such interactions are somewhat decontextualized, cut off from other social consequences, and undiluted by ameliorating lines of association along other dimensions. If we disagree strongly about *this* issue, in this domain, it may not matter that we agree (or would agree) about several other areas—they probably will never come up in this context. These capacities for anonymity, virtually consequence-free statements of whatever one wants to say, and intense, even obsessive preoccupation with a specific topic that matters a great deal to the members of the community, even if it matters little to anyone else, all help explain why allegiances to these communities can be very strong—even to the point of people preferring online interactions within these groups to interactions in "the real world."[7] This also helps explain the commitment members often feel to contributing to the overall knowledge of the group, even when they receive no credit for doing so; and why newcomers sometimes must undergo a trial period before being accepted as fully qualified members.

Let me give an example of how powerful these online dynamics can be. I enjoy DVDs, and try to find them at a discount whenever possible. I have been a longtime participant in a Web-based discussion site called DVD Talk.[8] Its main purpose is to share information about DVDs, comparative pricing, discounts or coupons, and so on. It is a prototypical self-educating community: before a new movie even comes up for sale, members have advance information about its quality, about where it can be bought for the lowest price, whether alternative versions are in production, and so on. In 2000, Amazon.com, without making any announcement, instituted an experiment in differential pricing for their DVDs: that is, if person A went to the Web site to purchase a particular DVD, one price came up; if person B went to the same site looking for the same DVD, a different price would come up. Amazon never announced the precise criteria they used for assigning these different prices, but presumably they included factors such as whether a person had purchased through Amazon before, or not; what their overall volume of previous purchases had been; what types of movie they had purchased before, and so on. Amazon clearly never considered the possibility that persons A and B might be in contact with each other, comparing the prices they were finding on the site. This is precisely what DVD Talk is designed to do, of course. Almost immediately after this new pricing policy was put in place, members of DVD Talk realized what Amazon was doing; within a few hours after that, the pros and cons of doing so had been argued out at length (was it discrimination, or just savvy marketing?); and a few hours after that a nationwide boycott had been organized against purchasing DVDs through Amazon until they ended the differential pricing policy. Within a day or two Amazon did so.[9] Now, DVDs are not the most important thing in the world, but this case shows how the capacities of a self-educating community can have wider social, political, and economic effects. In this instance the sharing of information, debate over issues, and strategizing about possible responses fired the collective imagination and interests of the group; but the group also *acted,* probably for the first time, as an organized advocacy group. Consumers normally engage large companies as individuals, and their knowledge and leverage with the firm are correspondingly limited. Joined together in these kinds of networks, knowledge and leverage become more collectivized. (Of course, similar narratives could be constructed around anti-globalization protesters; parents committed to home schooling; or other, more important areas of social commitment and common purpose.)

Probably the best-known example of the power of networked actors is the community that grew up around Napster and other venues for sharing music (MP3) files. While this instance is not exactly a self-educating community, the person-to-person (P2P) technology and ethos that grew up around sharing and distributing music files has much wider relevance: with increasing bandwidth and access to multimedia resources, participants can establish nearly instantaneous, real-time exchanges around, say, video feeds from citizens recording live events with handheld video cameras (war atrocities, or natural disasters); political speeches; classroom lectures; data from remote instruments or scientific experiments; and real-time access to an enormous range of live inquiries. These feeds no longer need to go to a central agency to disseminate it (and giving it the option, therefore, of editing, filtering, or suppressing it). This decentralized network means, simply, that if one person in a networked community has something, everyone can have it. The implications for communication, information sharing, and new forms of publishing are profound here.

Web-rings are a similar kind of networking, organized through the cross-linking of Web pages on a shared subject matter. They typically include a procedure by which new pages can request inclusion into the ring; the existing community can then decide which new participants (pages) are to be included. Thus, Web-rings have many of the features of any other kind of community, whether online or not. They are overtly self-educating communities because their reason for being is to multiply sources of credible information and perspectives within an area of shared concern. Their structure of cross-linking grants authority and credibility to included pages, as well as facilitating access to those pages since, as with other kinds of networks, one can enter the rhizome anywhere and still have more or less direct access to any other point or node in the network.[10] Hence, even while being quite dispersed, Web-ring communities have a definite "inside" and "outside"—sources on the topic that are not part of that network are typically disadvantaged in attracting attention (unless they happen to be part of some other network that gives them visibility), and sometimes this inside/outside demarcation can be a way of marking dominant versus marginalized perspectives in a field. But for those *inside* the community, access to new information and the ability to reach and influence others are greatly facilitated.

Finally, a more recent development with similar effects is Web logging (or "blogging"). Blogs are Web pages that can be easily updated with information, commentary, and Web links, gathered or produced by the blog author and organized in the format of a daily journal or notebook that can be easily updated several times a day. Blogs have become an extremely powerful form of self-publishing, since a blog author can quickly copy and organize a large volume of material from other sources, add analysis or commentary to it, and produce a distinctive "take" on the subject matter (some of the most visible blogs have to do with news and political analysis, for example). There is something deeply democratic about the ability of anyone with Web access to produce their own newsletter or journal and make it available to anyone with shared interests; some of the most influential political blogs, for example, are by previously unknown individuals who simply have the time and energy to scour the news for information and have an interesting, if idiosyncratic, perspective to share. Because blogs often borrow from one another, a new blogger can quickly gain visibility by being cited by others. As digests or archives of a sort, blogs can be extremely useful when the author reviews and collects information from a large number of other sources and publishes it in one place. Instead of reading 20 newspapers (or 100 cookbooks), for example, one comes to depend on those people who filter and select only the most important or worthwhile examples and organize them in one easily updated site. Moreover, as noted, blogs are themselves highly interlinked; so as blog authors themselves review and link to one another's materials a very large volume of material can be distilled into a relatively small number of pages. Here, as with Web-rings, the interlinking process provides a network that grants credibility to one another; and while this certainly can be an imperfect process, over time the implicit community of bloggers on a subject tends to select and highlight the sources that have best proven themselves as worthy of attention. Here again, I would call this a self-educating community, both because a large amount of information is shared, discussed, criticized, and commented upon by participants, but also because it has a developmental structure: It grows precisely through the links of particular claims or views that are picked up, combined, criticized, or added to by others. A novel bit of information or commentary can spread rapidly through a blog community, growing as it propagates through additions and contributions from others. Like a rumor, it can morph into something very different from what it started out to be. But unlike a rumor there is usually a palimpsest of the undistorted original, because this propagation is normally through cutting and pasting of links that can easily return a reader to the first source; thus it is more easily possible to compare the elaborated version with the original.

II

In discussing these examples of online self-educating communities (email lists, news groups, Web-rings, and blogs), I do not mean any sharp distinction or typology between them. Functionally they can work in very similar ways: even in an email list, for example, one can cut and paste material from other sources and then propagate them, along with commentary perhaps, to the others in a group—hence, the effects of blogging don't depend solely on that specific technology. Or one can have many of the effects of a Web-ring within moderated discussion groups that maintain control over who can post to them. New technologies for achieving these kinds of networked information sharing and discussion are arising all the time. But they all share certain features in common *as* self-educating communities. First, they each must balance the respective values of *internal* and *external* expertise. Internal expertise is important because sources who are familiar, closely affiliated, and have a track record over time may have earned a reputation for credibility, honesty, or integrity that a newcomer or stranger by definition cannot have. Moreover, members within a self-educating community share a set of assumptions, a vocabulary and mode of expression, and a shared background knowledge that often makes their contributions more valuable to others within that community. But external expertise is also important because the very virtues of familiarity and shared assumptions that strengthen a self-educating community internally can also reinforce its blind spots and prejudices. Misconceptions can cycle endlessly within the group without ever being challenged. External perspectives can often recognize and point out these foibles, and can interject much-needed new information or new perspectives that enrich the conversation. Finally, of course, new members need to be drawn into a community if it is to grow and thrive numerically over time. The problem here, of course, is that the values of internal and external expertise can be in conflict with each other, and the very things a self-educating community does to strengthen itself in one regard can weaken it from the other point of view. In this paradoxical sense, a self-educating community always needs to have boundaries, but they must be semipermeable.

Another potential issue for self-educating communities is the very ethos of shared information that vitalizes them. It is perhaps the most striking thing about the Internet that—apart from those sources that are commercialized, along with other spaces that may be copyrighted (academic journals, for example)—the dominant sensibility is a "come one, come all" spirit of sharing that views the frictionless propagation of information as a good in itself. From blogs to shareware to self-published literature, countless people devote countless hours of effort to creating and distributing resources that can be of great interest and use value to others, but which may return little or nothing to the original creators in terms of payment, credit, or recognition. A link to their site or "word of mouth" testimonials may grant to them some degree of acknowledgment, notoriety, and appreciation—but this is not what animates them, generally speaking. Self-educating communities cannot exist without such a strong ethos, at least within and among their members, but here, too, tensions can arise. The amount and forms of appropriate acknowledgment and appreciation that can be expected may not be widely agreed upon. Misappropriation, misuse, misquoting, or misinterpretation can generate resentments. Or, at the other extreme, so can being ignored. Seeing someone else get credit for something you feel responsible for—or even when someone else gets credit for something that you believe you arrived at independently first—can strain even the most altruistic, community-oriented spirit. Clearly, there is nothing here that is unique to online self-educating communities; but it may be that the "cut-and-paste" capabilities of digital communication make it more likely that something can be plucked out of an original context and either propagated in a misleading way, or taken without attribution from its original source. In certain cases it might be very difficult, or impossible, ever to identify a single originary source.

A self-educating community is an experiment in collective intelligence; how the wisdom of the whole can be more than the sum of its parts. In a real sense the knowledge of such groups is *distributed*—any specific thought or belief only inheres in individual minds, of course, but to the extent that something is *known* it is often known by the group interacting *as a group*. The epistemology of distributed knowledge depends on the same sorts of processes of evidence, testing, argument, and confirmation that any epistemology does, but in a distributed framework these are not simple Baconian criteria; rather, they are inquiry processes embedded in social networks, and therefore inseparable from the social dynamics of those networks (status, envy, competition, loyalty, flattery, selfishness, and so on). A self-educating community, to the extent that it sees itself as such, approaches these dynamics with a tacit (or openly acknowledged) commitment to enhancing the knowledge and understandings of all its members; and so approaches these epistemological processes with less of a sense of competition, intolerance, or hierarchy (although these certainly might remain present), and more of a sense of inclusion and patience with disagreements *at least among members within that community*.

An epistemology of distributed knowledge highlights the collective processes of circulating and questioning claims; juxtaposing alternative perspectives as an approach to problem-solving; and offering arguments to and sharing evidence with others, as opposed to simply making assertions. Such activities play a role, not only in persuading others to respect, or come to accept, one's views—which may be, again, a typical and understandable motivation for certain individuals—but because of a sense that such things properly *belong to* the group, and that the group as a whole (including one's self) benefits most from the fullest and widest engagement with all the evidence, experiences, and perspectives its members can bring to the topic of common concern. Hence the vitality and success of a self-educating community depends on the exercise of certain "civic" virtues (most notably, perhaps, generosity) toward the interests and concerns of the group as a whole.

My focus here on *online* self-educating communities, and their manifestations of distributed knowledge, is intended to highlight the ways in which the online context encourages and supports a value orientation to these processes that is often different from other institutional contexts, including many educational institutions. It isn't that people acting online are by nature more generous or less self-interested than people acting in other contexts (formal institutions of higher education, for example)—it is more a matter of customs, reward systems, and status markers that tend to motivate certain sorts of behavior in each respective context. For example, it is in many respects the very conditions of distance, anonymity, and lack of face-to-face engagement (which so many use to criticize the "impersonal" and "cold" nature of online interactions) that may actually have the effect of minimizing the status concerns or need for credit that can stand in the way of committing to the interests of an online community as a whole. Such impersonality may make it easier for people to risk being questioned or disagreed with by others, and so more willing to put their positions out to be analyzed and tested by the group as a whole.

But the situation is complicated, and there is no reason to enshrine online self-educating communities as necessarily superior to other alternatives. The very impersonality that some see as liberating, others see as alienating, and so they may be *less* willing to risk putting their views into circulation. The in-group feeling that motivates a high degree of openness and sharing within a self-educating community may also have the unintended effect of suppressing disagreement (even when participants deny this and say they are quite tolerant toward disagreement), because in some instances disagreement might be tacitly regarded as threatening to the collective ethos. Self-educating communities often run into a tension between being self-critical (which is necessary for remaining open to new and challenging points of view) and being self-congratulatory (which can reinforce internal bonds of commitment, but which can also yield a kind of complacency)—indeed, some groups may be very self-congratulatory about how self-critical they are, and their belief that they are relentlessly open to question may itself become a rationale for deflecting certain kinds of questioning.

Finally, no community can be fully inclusive and still maintain the qualities of a community that make it attractive to its members; there will always be exclusion as well. There may be different strategies and criteria for exclusion (and, again, some of them may be largely tacit and unintended in their effects), but however strongly these strategies and criteria may be based on persuasive rationales *within* the group, they will undoubtedly be viewed by some of those outside the group as arbitrary and unjust. In general, these in-group/out-group dynamics are a risk for any community, not only self-educating communities, and not only *online* self-educating communities; but they have a higher stake in self-educating communities that deal with important or valuable knowledge, because the social dynamics of community building and maintenance, as I have sketched them here, may be in deep tension with the values of education and knowledge building that are the community's reason for being. Actions taken to keep the community active and involved may interfere with the activities to which the community is overtly devoted. This irony may simply highlight the general fact that communities cannot always pursue all the different ends they value simultaneously.

III

My comments here about online self-educating communities have numerous implications for formal, informal, and nonformal education. Most obviously, programs in "distance education" can basically be understood as an attempt to foster the characteristics of a self-educating community in formal education; and when these programs are established through online media (I prefer to refer to them simply as "online education" programs because distance is no longer their central defining feature), they partake of all the sorts of possibilities, and difficulties, of other online self-educating communities.

Having taught several online courses through my university, in which participants rarely, or never, meet me or one another face-to-face, I have found that the most important task in my teaching is not that of binding their loyalty, affection, or dedication to me and my expectations as a teacher; but of persuading them of their obligations to themselves and one another as a learning community.[11] Certainly, their commitments to me (or to earning the grades I administer) may be an invaluable motivation—at least initially—in directing their energies toward this common purpose; but because online teaching and learning inevitably require a greater degree of independent motivation on the part of the learners (since they are cut off from the traditional disciplining and motivational practices of the classroom), this independent motivation, in my experience at least, is most productive when it grows out of a desire to participate in, and benefit from, the collective intelligence of the group. Designing course activities and projects that foster this sense of the group as a self-educating community have proven invaluable in deriving very high levels of effort and satisfaction from student work. I would never argue that online courses are therefore superior educational experiences; I still generally favor the atmosphere and interactions of the traditional classroom. But for certain kinds of students, and subject matters, the structure of an online self-educating community—for reasons I have described previously—can elicit more intense and open-ended commitments to independent and shared learning. The trick, then, is how to turn a group of students with a set of traditional assumptions about what a class, a student, and a teacher are into a self-educating community. In this regard, group projects, less "high stakes" grading policies, and decentered communication networks (where the teacher is no longer the hub of all interactions) can all play an invaluable role.

Having highlighted these possibilities in the context of formal education (even when practiced in a twenty-first-century medium like the Internet), it is a short step to see their more general relevance for informal and nonformal education. I see the distinction between informal and nonformal education here as having primarily to do with the degree of *structure* and the degree of *intentionality* in the teaching-learning process. Nonformal education is characterized by some kinds of structure (though different ones from formal educational institutions and processes), and includes some level of conscious intent to achieve learning, whether by overt teaching or other means. Informal education, as I understand it, is more continuous with the activities of everyday life, in which some teaching and learning might occur, but largely in an unintentional and tacit way. (Admittedly, the line between these may be exceedingly difficult to demarcate sharply.)

In this sense, self-educating communities of the sort I have described here (whether online or not) are more appropriately labeled "nonformal" than "informal" in most cases. The examples of self-educating communities I have given are certainly aware of themselves as such, and may have been established explicitly along those lines (in other cases, a community organized initially for some other purpose may come to see its role as *centrally* educational in nature). Certainly in the online venue a good deal of informal teaching and learning also takes place; but the examples I have given involve people *intentionally* using technological capabilities to establish a network with specific purposes in mind. The ongoing dynamic of participation in the group, through processes of discussion, debate, and information sharing, is where education happens. In self-educating communities, the roles of teacher and student may be fluid; most or all participants may regard themselves as students of the ongoing subject matter, and each a potential learner as well as a potential teacher.

Elsewhere I have written about the architecture of online spaces and how these design features shape the kinds of interactions that take place within them.[12] These include:

- movement/stasis
- interaction/isolation
- publicity/privacy
- visibility/hiddenness
- enclosure/exclusion

There are many contexts and activities for which these structures of online space (and in some related instances time) shape the kinds of activities that people engage in. Certain kinds of virtual spaces (chat rooms, "cyber-lounges," or the aforementioned MUDs and MOOs, for example) are designed precisely to facilitate online conversation, social interaction, and information sharing. For online self-educating communities, their ethos of open access to information and their general openness to involving newcomers imply certain kinds of architectures rather than others (whether a site is password-protected or not, for example). Hence, "nonformal" education in this context does not mean a lack of structure, but favoring *certain kinds* of structure.

Finally, such self-educating communities are important for certain kinds of lifelong (and, as they say, "lifewide") education—whether of formal, informal, or nonformal varieties. The kinds of learning essential to these concerns (independently motivated, usually of strong personal or professional concern or interest, and by nature open-ended and perpetually unfinished) are of the sort most amenable to the structure of a self-educating community, whether online or not. The kinds of self-directed study, mentoring, and active collaboration that support such learning are readily supported by community networks. In the context of this essay, I am highlighting the particular usefulness of *online* self-educating communities for these purposes; and in the context of lifelong, lifewide education involving adult learners, the advantages and possibilities of online interactions may be most evident, particularly those that depend upon participants having a strong sense of motivation, affiliation, and responsibility to the group as a whole.

In closing, unfortunately, I think we must remind ourselves of the vast majority of people around the world who have no access to these sorts of online educational interactions and opportunities. While this study highlights the particular advantages of such interactions and opportunities, one cannot argue that online education can or should *replace* other sorts—first, because different media each have distinctive advantages and disadvantages (there can never be just one best way to teach or learn); but, second, because self-educating communities, to the extent that they are educationally beneficial, must exist within the venues most readily available to the learning population. In the vast majority of cases, then, they will have nothing to do with modern information and communication technologies. But if my analysis here has merit, they can still exhibit many of the same common characteristics.

NOTES

1. Nicholas C. Burbules, "Does the Internet Constitute a Global Educational Community?" *Globalization and Education: Critical Perspectives,* Nicholas C. Burbules and Carlos Torres, eds. (New York: Routledge, 2000): 323–55.
2. <http://dkrc.org/>.
3. Patricia Wallace, *The Psychology of the Internet* (New York: Cambridge University Press, 1999), 55–87.
4. It also appears that discussion groups are rather scornful of those accessing the Internet through such avenues as WebTV, and even AOL—since these are seen as the preferred mediums of technology novices; there is probably a social class factor at work here as well.
5. Wallace, *The Psychology of the Internet,* 88–109.
6. Wallace, *The Psychology of the Internet,* 110–32.
7. Sherry Turkle, *Life on the Screen: Identity in the Age of the Internet* (New York: Simon & Schuster, 1995).
8. <http://www.dvdtalk.com/>.
9. <http://www.cnn.com/2000/TECH/computing/09/13/amazon.reaction.idg/>.
10. See Nicholas C. Burbules and Thomas A. Callister, Jr., "Knowledge at the Crossroads: Alternative Futures of Hypertext Environments for Learning." *Educational Theory,* Vol. 46, No. 1 (1996): 23–50; Nicholas C. Burbules, "Rhetorics of the Web: Hyperreading and Critical Literacy," *Page to Screen: Taking Literacy into the Electronic Era,* Ilana Snyder, ed. (New South Wales: Allen and Unwin, 1997), 102–22; and Nicholas C. Burbules, "The Web as a Rhetorical Place," *Silicon Literacies,* Ilana Snyder, ed. (London: Routledge, 2002), 75–84.
11. <http://cter.ed.uiuc.edu/>.
12. Nicholas C. Burbules and Thomas A. Callister, Jr., *Watch IT: The Promises and Risks of Information Technologies for Education* (Boulder, CO: Westview Press, 2000), Ch. 8: "What Kind of Community Can the Internet Be?"

SITUATING GENIUS

RAY MCDERMOTT

A history of the very idea of genius can be used as a display board for wider social and political tensions that shape the environments in which people are asked to learn. At present, we are given genius as:

- first, and relentlessly first, in the head, mysteriously so, the stuff of inspiration and then, in retrospect, attribution;
- second, situated, shared, borrowed, and stolen, the stuff of hard work in an active community;
- third, inscribed, advertised, managed, and manipulated, the stuff of public relations in an unnecessarily competitive community;
- and, as a subset of its inscribed appearance, but under the worst conditions, fought over, fought with, fought against, lorded over, and destroyed, all in all, the stuff of politics in a divided and duplicitous society.

The inside-the-head genius shares with school the claim that smartness and achievement are a natural pairing evident in both the commodification of genius as a kind of intelligence and its use in the explanation of exceptional accomplishment. The situated and collaborative genius has been a corrective to the excesses of brain power versions of learning. Accounts of the institutionally inscribed and managed genius promise relief from the hegemony of the inherent genius that has in the twentieth century become a point of celebration and, in ugly circumstances, a target for invective.

I can offer one historical and one ethnographic reason why genius is a proper focus for theories of knowledge, learning, accomplishment, and adoration in a society that dices most everything up for sale. The first offers genius as a chapter in a natural history of theories of the mind. The English term *genius* joins two Latin words, *genius* and *ingenium,* the first for a guardian spirit, the second for natural disposition and ability (Murray 1989). The term had a stable history as a spirit until the seventeenth century when, as part of a package of terms including *creativity, intelligence, individual, imagination, progress, insanity,* and *race,* it began to refer to an unusually able kind of person. All these words, Owen Barfield says, "began to suffer that process which we have called 'internalization'" (1967: 208). In the early eighteenth century, genius became a focus for theoretical claims and critique. The term is an entry in Diderot's *Encyclopédie, ou dictionaries raisoné des sciences, des arts, et des métiers* of 1758 (tome 7: 581–84). It is not an entry in Samuel Johnson's *Dictionary of the English Language* of 1755, but in his preface he complains that a dictionary is not the work of a genius. The term was in the air.[1] A rough history of the modern genius starts with:

- a renaissance genius as the medium of moment for rare gifts from supernatural sources (Screech 1983);
- an early eighteenth-century genius as poet or scientist, still rare, as a kind of person across contexts. Joseph Addison (1711) announced the importance of individual genius two years after England's first copyright law.[2] Authorship was a new unit of exchange, and plagiarism a new violation. By the 1750s, "a craze of theoretical writings urges that the inspired need not have a genius; instead, the inspired author has genius or is a genius" (Frieden 1985:66);
- a late eighteenth-century genius, less rare, as a social role, for which every generation must have its representatives: after Mozart, then, gulp, Hayden, until, finally, Beethoven (DeNora 1995);
- the nineteenth-century romantic genius, as a role and a goal, sought after, trained for, and dependent on others to realize and celebrate (Carlyle 1841; Bone 1989);
- a barrier to next steps forward: "A people is the detour made by nature to arrive at six or seven great men. Yes, and then to get around them" (Nietzsche 1884; Pletsch 1991);
- a name for what most people are not, a source of unproductive alienation (Nietzsche again; Plekanov 1908).

In the late nineteenth century, even as the critique of the lone and inspired genius by Nietzsche and Plekanov is taking shape, a more invidious form of genius—the inherent genius—comes to the fore. Making ingenious contributions is one thing, being called a genius is another, and being born a genius still a third. The late nineteenth century adds birth to the conditions for attribution. Genius becomes:

- an inheritance and soon thereafter a genotype (Galton 1869);

- a stereotype in invidious racial comparisons, no less inherent, but especially so for populations accused of having too little genius, blacks (Mosely 2000) and women (Battersby 1989) in particular, or too much of it, Jews (Gilman 1996) and homosexuals (Elfenbein 1999) in particular.

In the twentieth century, genius set into decline, not because great achievement went away but because it became all too easy to attribute and all too unrelated to accomplishment. Genius in decline goes the way of much else we treasure, institutionalize, and, as a result, lose access to as a category inviting focus and power. To the present day, inherent genius owns the popular imagination. Genius, like everything else in the nineteenth century, had become a commodity. It became worth money, and conceptions of genius have delivered their object ever since to be measured, quantified, bet on, and bought and sold as a unit of exchange and capital investment.

A recent issue of the *Atlantic Monthly* (December 2002) displays the tensions of the moment. It offers, first, a paper by a historian complaining about current uses of the term, then a description of a student's attempt to sell her eggs to a couple in search of a super baby destined for high SATs and beauty pageants, and, finally, a portrait of a celebrated genius, chess master Bobby Fischer, now living madly and hawking anti-Semitism around the world. It is all there, the whole genius thing: *intelligence, genes, great success, market values, insanity,* and *racism*. For four hundred years, genius has changed shape with nuances serving different conditions. Its current packaging displays our own situation and illustrates the cultural demands we place on theories of intelligence, learning, and achievement.

The second reason for focusing on genius relies on an ethnographic sense of when genius appears in daily conversation. When do claims of genius become important?

- Genius exists most obviously in institutions that celebrate the success of a few over the many: the normal over the disabled, the talented over the normal, and the genius over the talented.
- Genius exists most poignantly in the dreams and whispers of parents before their children are erased by schools (regular schools, art, dance, and music schools no less, sports schools, and so on) that measure them one against the other until only a few are left.
- And genius exists most paradoxically as an apology for the celebrated rewards of higher education and the failed dreams of parents.

All this makes sense in competitive societies focused on failure for many as the context for the success of a few. The invocation of genius makes the system rhetorically fair and legitimate. Sorting children prematurely and by arbitrary standards, by labels that reproduce class and race inequalities across generations, gets justified by people saying, "Not everyone can be Einstein." The genius story is available to counter any claim that a more democratic society—one less organized to document failure—could produce more competent and promising students. Because it is possible to be a genius, it is possible to be a dunce. When measured against genius, failure is ever ready for invocation. Because genius is rare, stupidity is rampant. Visits to math classes for children in the U.S. show most with pictures of Einstein, hanging there, like Newton in centuries prior (Fara 2000), to inspire, but with the opposite message also available: middle-school math, simple scale and proportion in multiple forms, requires genius, and only a few can make the grade. In American schools, only one-tenth of the children make it beyond tenth grade math, and every child is far more likely to murder someone than to take a doctorate in mathematics. Simple math is difficult if the only goal is to learn faster than others. Why should students have genius as their goal or stupidity their fear?

The historical rise of genius as genotype and its present use as an apology for failure makes a terrifying combination. A skewed distribution of wealth is one problem. A skewed distribution of educational pedigree is a second problem. When a skewed distribution of wealth and pedigree attends schools in which everyone must do better than everyone else, and when these conditions are tied to a static biology with degrading theories of disability and race, the situation is dangerous (McDermott 1988, 1993; Varenne and McDermott 1998). The commodification of genius and other measures of learning are a small part of this predicament.

Contrary to received theory and practice, learning is not well modeled as:

the property, of a static subject,
facing well defined tasks with clear and measurable outcomes,
as if time stood still between stimulus and behavior,
as if the world stood still between pretest and posttest,
as if purpose and sensuous engagement were only a passing consideration.

The enemy has been clear. Most new theories and the best new tools for organizing learning have offered process over stasis and critiqued the reified entities—the cognitive *property,* the well-defined *task,* the disembodied *subject,* and the unsituated *outcome*—that restrict a view of learning and an appreciation of those struggling to organize it. The new theories assert that there is more to learning than the assessment of who has acquired how much information and skill and how fast, and that we should develop theories better tuned to everyday demands. In the school-dominated theory, institutional attribution trumps actual learning, and the new theories have emerged to resist academic degrees as the only index of learning.

This chapter emphasizes a more comprehensive culprit, namely, the division of labor that is the primary context for genius being proposed, interpreted, and evaluated under received conditions. The division of labor we must confront unjustly divides those seemingly with from those seemingly without knowledge. The division—all those people on salary—takes many forms in educational institutions: teacher/learner, enabled/disabled, smart/dumb, genius/talented, researcher/practitioner, counselor/client, etc. The problem is not that these divisions do not make sense. **The problem is that they make sense so easily they obscure the arrangements that have fostered their existence and hide their consequences**. The problem is not that there are not people who know much more than others. **The problem is that the distinction makes sense all too easily, as if knowledge were the only thing separating those who know more and those who know less, as if persons knowing more in one setting uniformly know more in other settings**. The distinction between knowing more and knowing less obscures the work that arranges for the distinction to be institutionally useful in a competitive society—to the point that the distinction can appear applicable ***even when it does not and should not apply***. An unfair division of labor makes invidious distinctions appear natural and easy. They must be confronted if there is to be equal access to the rewards of a society.

An account of the historical uses of the term *genius* complicates a focus on learning by asking how exceptional learning is institutionally inscribed and made visible, regardless of how actual learning is organized. **It is a harsh reality that no one has to learn anything for apparent learning to be measured, recorded, and used as a gateway to institutional access**. Assessments do not have to measure actual or relevant learning to supply institutions with a score for gauging access. Students of French or calculus do not have to learn French or calculus to set the curve; they only have to do better than the rest. Upon graduation, students must only sometimes display learning, but must always show credentials. If no one learns anything, but some are declared better learners than others, the system can go forward. Assessment techniques claim to measure learning, but must only balance access to be institutionally viable. That is their job. We should call them "accessments."

Most societies have done well without explicit theories of learning. Others have plied them in a different division of labor. Theories of learning serve the extensive record keeping done by modern states. Alternatives are rampant in prestate societies or in alienated institutions within a wider state apparatus. Current alternatives can make change only in confrontation with state-established inscription practices. For recent examples, we have:

- a sophisticated theory of learning at market and mosque in precolonial Egypt contrasted to the narrow learning inscribed by the school-

based theory of colonial powers; at the mosque, all knowledge is understood as tentative, under construction, and context sensitive (Mitchell 1988);
- a carefully elicited theory of an Apache man of wisdom, the precision of his teachings, and how they can be obscured by current standards; for the Apache, learning comes most tellingly to those who do not ask too much (Basso 1996);
- an autobiographical account of learning in a contemporary Buddhist temple enlivened by a unique theory of how learning is organized, encouraged, and discouraged; Buddhist learning comes most insightfully to those who do not ask and then punished for not asking (Hori 1994);
- a loose account of Jacotot, on the run from French authorities in 1818, settling in Belgium to "teach" in a language he did not speak, discovering his students could learn well from French texts as long as he did not force his teaching on them (Ranciere 1991).

These examples complement decades of scholarship documenting native systems of know-how in botany and agriculture (e.g., Conklin, in press) or navigation and astronomy (e.g., Lewis 1972; Frake 1985). Together they offer a picture of prodigious learning without teachers and schools. In contrast, any proposed learning theory today enters an institutional field filled with pressures only loosely and perhaps invidiously tuned to the needs of the population—from discourse to discourse without regard to practice.[3]

So far, a useful account of learning requires three considerations: individuals putting information and skills in their heads; situations making specific information and skills relevant to ongoing affairs; and institutional functions to which either learning or its attribution are applied. A next consideration, a potent subset of the portrayal theory of learning, is difficult to describe, but necessary. Beyond the details of how individuals learn, the settings in which they learn, and the institutions that keep track, one further tension is ever poised to interpolate a kind of learner! Successful learning can make a person more adaptive and skilled, yes, and more marked. A person can be noticed, monitored, targeted, and crushed for learning too much. Looking learned in a cultural portrayal can make a person the mark in a cultural betrayal.

Accessment systems should be condemned if they are unfair, if they leave perfectly able people shut out from participation and acceptability. Inside an unfair portrayal, theories of learning can label and disable, shut out and shut down. This is standard fare in many societies, and complaints are standard across the social sciences. Betrayal involves a deeper misuse of accessment. Compliments can have invidious consequences. People left in the system when others were unfairly cut can have their roles reversed. Geniuses successful at school when others were cut as failures can have their roles reversed. A great compliment in a competitive school system, a genius label can be perversely productive in divided societies in search of a public enemy. Colossal learning in the head and hand, both hard won display sites for a portrayal of genius, can be made fodder for deeper cultural tensions: what more dangerous an enemy than an ingenious one? Being called a genius is as lethal as it is promising. Genius, as a least ingenius American president might say, leads to "an access of evil."

People use theories of genius as they use theories of kinship, sickness, sexuality, self, and moral worth. A new theory is not just a latest way to describe and explain, but a new tool in a division of labor. If dichotomies between teacher/learner, smart/dumb, and genius/talent make easy sense as differentials of learning, then any new theory enters a social field demanding the explanation of individuals on one or another side of each dichotomy. The cultural function of school-based theories of learning, development, disability, and genius has been to establish and negotiate mutually exclusive relations—successful/failing, smart/dumb—between those with and those seemingly without knowledge.

APPRECIATING, SITUATING, AND PORTRAYING GENIUS

Genius inside the Head

Current biases are coded in the concept of genius, the rare person smart enough to solve problems others cannot imagine. Talent is not enough. Talent is a currency (literally so in ancient Rome), a value inside a predefined game. Genius is more than talent and goes beyond predefined targets. Genius redefines the game. A genius is less a person with a focus, than one with brainpower across a wide range of foci, less a person with a system for discerning received patterns, than one who sees new patterns where others see mayhem. Genius cannot be confused with education. Galton defined the genius as "a man endowed with superior faculties" excluding "the effects of education" (1892: 26).[4]

By current usage, the term *genius* is devalued. From American examples of decay, we find:

- employees at testing companies create mundane targets for measuring potential geniuses;
- the top of the IQ range has a genius slot;
- college admission officers fight over recruiting a few geniuses to their schools;

- yearly awards are given out to high achieving academic geniuses;
- corporate advertisers for Apple Computers cozy up to those who "think different" and name their customer service personnel the "geniuses"; and
- popular movies (e.g., *Searching for Bobby Fischer, Good Will Hunting, A Beautiful Mind*) and staged dramas (*Genius, Proof*) celebrate individuals of mysterious accomplishment.

Now add hundreds of volumes about this or that genius, mostly people to be admired (Leonardo, Pascal, Beethoven, Nietzsche, Rodin, Ellington, with two or more biographies each), but not a few surprising (of six genius books on Newton: five for Isaac, one for Huey). There are hundreds of books with advice to "awaken" and "unlock" the genius in the family: self-help guides for genius written by people yet to score. Even after devaluation in the self-help market, genius is still treated as a mystical entity. Learning is still in the head, and the head of a genius learns better. By current use, genius is a real object ripe for discovery, and—because "second inventors count for nothing" (White 2001)—only one genius can be discovered at a time. By such terms, it is natural to see geniuses at each other's throats in competition, and wars between scientific geniuses are reported—without justification—as naturally occurring: "it may be argued that there was insufficient room for two such geniuses [Leibniz and Newton on calculus] living simultaneously, in view of which a conflict was quite inevitable" (White 2001: 37). Why not room for two? Why not count second inventors? Why such focus on the individual? Because genius is in the head, other considerations are irrelevant.

Situating the Genius

A situated theory focuses on interactive more than hierarchical steps to knowing and has no way to represent a single person generally smart at everything. By situated theory, the brainy genius is reduced to a nexus that fosters connections that allow for new information to develop cumulatively. Traditional learning theorists have ignored the whole population it takes to produce, recognize, and celebrate smart individuals. *By the situated theory of genius, there is no immaculate conception, not even in the mind.* The genius has usually spent years recombining particulars that others with less experience cannot handle. That's all, folks, that's the whole thing: people working with people and sometimes making progress.

How then can we think about exceptional achievement? There is such a thing. We turn consistently to some thinkers/artists/scientists for guidance we could never imagine coming from others. Isaac, not Huey, for most anything called genius. Shakespeare is never to be lessened by comparison with Neil Simon, nor Mozart with Paul Simon, Maria Callas with Carly Simon,

Wittgenstein with Herbert Simon. I appreciate all that Simon says, but their great achievements seem small, ordinary, conceivable, and all too predictable by comparison with Shakespeare, Mozart, Callas, and Wittgenstein. The "great man," warned William James, is not a piece of coal: it is justified that "in calculating the impetus of a locomotive we neglect the extra impetus given by a single piece of better coal," but the same claim cannot account for the impact of individuals on human affairs (1897: 255–56). A situated theory—coal is coal, all the way down—flattens genius and emphasizes the gray in what could be shining and brilliant. The cognitive fact, in contrast, taken one isolated person at a time, seems to conform to the commonsense theory of genius: "Not everyone can be Einstein."

A half-century of work situating genius in local contexts gives better, i.e., more situated, facts. Genius is fine tuned to circumstance. Michael Howe puts it nicely: "The exceptional individual goes further, and may move ahead faster, but always there is a route to be traced" (1999: 18). Analysis removes the mystery. Most societies have done well without an explicit theory of genius (Lavie et al. 1993). There are always prior developments, always others involved (Merton 1996; Chadwick and de Courtivron 1993; Stillinger 1991). Behind every lone inventor, there are others: helpful and essential, but uncelebrated and hidden.

Two examples and one famous account of genius envy illustrate the selectra complex that hides the communities of participation behind any acclaimed genius.

Genius Overtime: John Hayes (1985) makes a case for musical genius entrenched in collective perspiration. How much practice is necessary for a budding genius to create great music? Since Galton, we have been told that it springs from nowhere: "there is no career in which eminence is achieved so early in life as in that of music" (1892: 291). To locate a composer's best work, Hayes counts the recordings made of various pieces. Then he counts the years between first efforts, marked often by a single recording, and a composer's most popular period, with many recordings. Usually a decade separates early works and a full flowering of the composer's music. Even a child prodigy must devote a decade of training to the nuanced expectations of an audience. Early Mozart is only interesting because of his later work. No great audience, no great music. No long engagement, no genius. If great composers learn from participation and engagement, the model genius shifts from smartest to the person with the most relentless practice schedule and attentive friends. Great music should be celebrated: we should play it, listen to it, and then figure out how to support the environments composers need.

Genius over Time: To the same point at a different level of analysis, anthropologist A. L. Kroeber described periods of creativity that have inspired major civilizations. For Kroeber, the difference between great and small achievements is less about brainpower required and more about situation. Genius clusters: Socrates, Plato, and Aristotle follow each other in three generations; Confucius, Lao-tzu, Chuang-tzu, Mencius, and Han fei-tzu follow quickly in succession; and Darwin and Wallace state a theory of evolution in the same year:

> Lawgivers, statesmen, religious leaders, discoverers, inventors, therefore only seem to shape civilization. The deep-seated, blind, and intricate forces that shape culture, also mold the so-called creative leaders of society as essentially as they mold the mass of humanity. Progress . . . is something that makes itself. We do not make it. (Kroeber 1944: 839)

Cognition is not the locus of genius. The locus is people organizing collective problems well defined enough for a solution to be advanced and noticed. A situated theory of genius answers the "who learned how much how fast" question with an account not of a single person but of a long line of persons standing on each other's shoulders. Genius in a situational analysis is *ordinary* in the best sense of the term: people doing what has to be done with the materials at hand. Genius is best understood as everywhere, whenever necessary, wherever possible, whether directed to fixing cars (Harper 1987) or curing cancer (Fujimura 1998). Any unevenness in its distribution is symptomatic of systemic inequalities. Symptoms should not be touted. People making breakthroughs should be seen as moments in a sequence and not isolated by praise. Geniuses should be celebrated by our continuing their work.

Genius Envy: The facts of genius are so heavily weighted in circumstance and cooperation that celebration of lone accomplishment seems misplaced, a difficult problem for societies anxious to celebrate one person at a time. When awards are given to individuals, cooperation drops from sight, and collaborators get to complain. This sequence repeats itself endlessly in most modern societies. A famous line from three centuries ago shows the basic alternation between accomplishment and accusation. Isaac Newton is famous for acknowledging the work of others:

> If I have seen further it is by standing on the shoulders of others.

This sounds properly modest, the stuff of an awards dinner, but Merton (1965) has shown the phrase was borrowed from others centuries before. He traced one version to Bernard of Chartres, who left no surviving works when he died in 1126, but whose student, John of Salisbury, recorded his teacher's thoughts in his *Metalogicon* in 1159:

> In comparison with the ancients, we stand like dwarfs on the shoulders of giants.

Jeauneau (1967) has pushed the sentiment further to the sixth-century grammarian Priscian:

The more recent the scholars, the more sharp sighted.

The point of this detail is large. Just as the attribution of genius has to be in the air for a person to be counted as one, so even the mode of acceptance of genius is borrowed. As a sudden flash of genius requires shared labor, so the modesty of standing on the shoulders of others is borrowed. Who can really tell a Leibniz from a Newton? Why do we care? Could Newton tell? He did care, but was it worth it? Newton was not modest when he invoked the giants who came before. Robert Hooke had accused Newton of using Hooke's ideas without credit, and Newton defended himself by citing their predecessors (Koyré 1952). By a polite reading of Newton's letter to Hooke, many had come before them both, and Hooke was not Newton's only giant. A less polite reading hinges on a fact: Hooke was dwarf-like in stature (White 2001). Whoever were Newton's giants, Hooke could not have been one. Scientists work on shared problems with shared materials and pander solutions to a shared public. A traditional theory of genius requires us to calculate how much is done by whom, and a cycle of celebration and accusation is the result. A limited situated theory snickers at the fuss. A situated theory of situated genius reveals the political intrigue behind the hegemony of giants and the ridicule of dwarfs.

Genius as Portrayal and Betrayal

Common sense maintains genius in the brain, and situated theory offers genius in many people building right tasks for one person to make right moves in right places at the right time. Individually, says Leslie White, geniuses are only "the neurological loci of important cultural events" (1949: 280). Culturally, no individual genius is required for someone to be celebrated. Neurology is overrated. Only attribution is necessary. This fact makes an exciting social fabric: everyone is possibly a genius, institutions are built for its discovery, and, when no great ingenius work can be found, a genius is designated nonetheless. Each generation serves up its young to be consumed. The acquisition of persons by genius is part of the materials members use to shape each other. Genius has become a goal, a way of life separate from and even repellent to the learning and accomplishment that should mark its designation.

Anthropologists have generally seen genius as portrayal and staging. People create problems and tools for eventual solutions. Someone solves a problem, and sometimes others remember who solved what first. Sometimes the wrong problem or the wrong solution is identified, but genius can be staged nonetheless. Those remembered are geniuses even if their actual advance was small or simply the last to occur before a solution was noticed. Genius is always in retrospect. *When it comes to being recognized as a genius, there is no immaculate reception, not even for the most extraordinary mind.*

Leslie White (1949) minimized the highest achievements of genius. Everyone solves problems. There is no difference between what scientists do in laboratories and what housewives [*sic*] do in kitchens. Everyone solves problems defined by others. Anyone lucky enough to notice a breakthrough while reconceiving the heavens or reshaping a meatloaf is simply making one move that counts: Wallace as well as Darwin for a theory of evolution, or Apple as well as Xerox for a menu-based operating system. Others make equally coherent and interesting moves, but only one makes the last move, and that person, even the wrong person, gets called the genius:

> As for attributing "genius" to men who have "changed the course of history," we have seen that an idiot or a goose can accomplish it just as well. It is not high or low levels of ability that is significant in such contexts; it is being strategically situated in a moving constellation of events. (1949: 232)

With modes of inscription in view, individual genius becomes a production, a public relations mock-up more than an actual person. The genius is not just an object, nor just a symptom of inequalities, but a charged category to be filled regardless of the accomplishments or potentials of individuals. Seneca told Emperor Nero to stop killing those who wanted his job: no matter how many he would kill, he could not slay his successor! If a system for inscribing an emperor, hero, genius, or LD child is in place, someone will be emperor, hero, genius, or LD child.

Most cultures have done well without a notion of genius. Great ideas can emerge and hold sway without a pivot person being identified and celebrated. Conversely, a focus on individual genius can be ridiculous and harmful. Champagne (1992) has described a popular advice literature from China in the 1980s on how to have a genius child. There are better and worse times for conception, a panoply of techniques for in vitro stimulation of intelligence, and a mass of pamphlets and books telling parents how to handle the early years with a guarantee of genius. The procedures are foolish, but popular, and operate perhaps on a nostalgia for a China in which learning serves a hierarchy of smart and rich individuals who lord over the masses.

There are three reasons why a portrayal of the lone cognitive genius is a dangerous model. The first two are easy, the third more difficult. The first is obvious: celebrating lone genius is not true to the process of creation. It leaves everyone out and denies complexities and other potentials. It limits reality to retrospective simplification. Teachers, competitors, and helpers fall to the side. Latour situates Pasteur's genius with a helpful analogy:

> The Pasteurians were to arrive on the scene like players in a game of Scrabble. The "triple" words and "double" words were already marked and laid down. The Pasteurians translated these stakes and rules into their own terms, but without the hygienists [their predecessors], it is clear that very little would have been heard about them. The Pasteurians would have done something else. (1988: 25; also Latour 1998)

Latour does not describe Pasteur as less than he was. He does not reduce Pasteur to cognitive robot or a confluence of social forces. We should celebrate Pasteur and the Pasteurians in the detail of their situation as it was lived. In the nineteenth-century game of French science and health policy, Pasteur was a great player. To describe the microbe warrior without an account of the game board and the moves of other players would hide what is crucial. It would be unfair to Pasteur to ignore the ingenuity he spent organizing others. Pasteur did not do what he did because he was a genius. He was called a genius for what he did *and* for how he convinced others of its importance. He was more than a functionary for the category genius. He is distorted by a learning theory that simply names him and hides his struggles. If learning theory is a resource for people in their interpretations of others, a descriptively inadequate theory of inherent genius distorts the materials we bequeath a next generation.

The second negative side to the mock-up genius is less obvious. Endemic to situations institutionally ascribed for learning is a management problem: it takes hard work to learn and even harder work to look like a learner. A display of learning can take so much work, it can leave no time for learning. To have to learn quickly enough to look like a genius leaves a learner driven by display work. To look the genius takes so much effort that even Nietzsche (Pletsch 1991) and Joyce (Kershner 1993) could have done more if not tortured by the promise. In the U.S., the mark of a natural learner is to do well in school without trying. School is a display board for individuals to show how much they instinctively know or, in a pinch, have learned elsewhere. To look really bright, one must learn a great deal, hide how it developed, and then display it as instinctively known.

The third drawback to the easy acquisition of individuals by genius is difficult to critique and confront, but more revealing. The attribution of genius does worse than exclude some and manipulate others. It is alienating for everyone in the wider system.[5] It promises so much good, it can be bad. Its distortions are so attractive, it can fit the most invidious institutional arrangements.

Sander Gilman on the *image* of superior Jewish intelligence states the third case well. For centuries, people of African descent have been so stigmatized by measures of low intelligence, it has been easy to forget the opposite case: the attribution of genius to European Jews (and lately to Asians in the U.S.) has also served ugly purposes. Theories of Jewish genius offer "a case study in how praise becomes blame" (Gilman 1996: 30). A theory of learning serving a society with a misfit between, first, how and why people learn and, second, how learning is inscribed and made institutionally consequential, can be lethal. Any theory of the person as a source of great achievement can be turned against the same person as a source of evil. Superior intelligence in a moral person can be theorized as a gift, but the same trait in a bad erson can be theorized as a curse. Cultural pedestals built for the genius have a trap door. The ascription of genius is as dangerous in a divided society as beneficial in a benign society. It is bad to have enemies, but far worse to have ingenious enemies.

Having built a category for genius throughout the nineteenth century, and having long before built a negative place for Jewish people in Christian societies, Europe was ripe to measure the categories side by side. High profile success of Jewish persons in the arts and sciences had to be explained. The first step was easy. Jewish people were simply smarter, and this could be accounted for by the eugenic logic of late nineteenth-century evolutionary theory. Cleansed by persecution and slaughter across centuries, Jews should be the most adaptive and intelligent population. And so the pedestal was occupied by Jewish geniuses, but did this lead to constant celebration? Of course not. What of blame? What of the forces that made anti-Semitism in the first place? Cultural categories give, and they take away. Accounts of the dysfunctional side of genius help to situate the original function of the category. If Jews were entered onto the genius pedestal by one reading, they were taken off by a next. Gilman shows the European "yes, but" hand-wringing over the question of Jewish genius: "Yes, they are," "No, they are not," "They are a little, but not completely." We can list a few of the counter claims to Jewish genius:

- genius, yes, but more in poetry and self-expression than in drama, which demands a reciprocity of perspective (Russian semiticist Daniel Abromovich Khvol'son, 1870s);
- genius, yes, but in practical activity, not in higher quality pursuits (Italian Jewish forensic psychiatrist Cesare Lombroso, 1894);
- genius, yes, but at the price of great nervousness and mental instability (French historian Anatole Leroy-Beaulieu, 1893);
- genius, yes, but at the price of avoiding physical labor (German historian Werner Sombart, turn of the century);
- genius, yes, but with more variability in the population; more geniuses perhaps, but lower average intelligence (Canadian psychologist Carl Brigham, 1923).

For every myth, a counter myth. For every distinction made, another distinction unmaking it. The myth of genius makes individuals special, and, once special, new distinctions can counter that specialty. The simple story about the category genius celebrating the quickest minds cannot be maintained. *There is no immaculate deception, and even the finest minds can be equally well defined by illusions of success and counter illusions of being evil.*

The concept of genius serves well capitalist institutions that, in the name of equal opportunity, force people to compete so fiercely that the same cultural categories can be used either positively or negatively depending on the political demands of the moment. One mechanism for this trick is a theory that puts learning and achievement in individual heads far from their conditions of use. This way, individuals and groups can be celebrated for learning more than enough, degraded for not learning enough, and, the key to the system, destroyed for learning too much. A theory of situated genius forces a countercultural account of learning as people standing on the shoulders of others. It demands that conditions of practice become the focus for any ascription of learning; if there is genius, it is in the community of practice. A more situated theory of situated genius confronts procedures for ascribing genius and its use. It forces a worry: with every mention of the term *genius*, are we doing more harm than good? The conditions under which we develop and use a theory of genius must be confronted.

Theories of genius have been treated as a resource in the explanation of different kinds of children. This paper offers an opposite take. **Theories of genius are not in our lives to help us explain differential learning; they are part of what must be explained, accounted for, and confronted**. They and the demands they answer to are part of what must be changed.

ACKNOWLEDGMENTS

This paper began in talks with Naoki Ueno and Yasuko Kawatoko and was written because Zvi Bekerman insisted. An early version included a comparison of theories of learning with theories of genius. It offered too many boxes for easy clarity and too few boxes for any precision. Eric Bredo, Dorothy Holland, Jean Lave, and David Tyack all complained, and I have narrowed the discussion to just genius. A paper by DeNora and Mehan (1992) was a great stimulus. Bredo, Tyack, and Eamonn Callan all put a copy of the *Atlantic Monthly* in my mailbox. Vicky Webber, Dan Levitin, and Nathaniel Klemp directed me to sources.

NOTES

1. The brief history offered in this paper is based on the European genius (Nahm 1956; Engell 1979; Frieden 1985; Murray 1989). The term has a smaller history in the U.S. For example, letters between John Adams and Benjamin Rush (Schutz and Adair 1966) on the topic of fame make little use of the term (Adams uses it as a contrast term for prudence!). Ralph Waldo Emerson (1850) wrote demandingly of genius and the culture that might nurture one. In twentieth-century America, genius is dominated by splash inventors, from Thomas Edison to Bill Gates, and IQ measures, from Lewis Terman to Arthur Jensen. The European tradition is more nuanced, better contested, and, as we shall see, more violent.

Predating Addison by over a century, a discussion by Huarte (1594) was widely read in seventeenth-century Europe, but does not figure in recent histories of genius. Using a humoral biology, Huarte proposed a theory of inherent genius. With a different sense of humor, Robert Merton calls him a "sixteenth century master of educational tests and measurements" (1965: 282). Genius and copyright laws co-ocurred in early eighteenth-century England and then again almost a century late in Germany (Woodmansee 1984).

3. In the Meno, says Bourdieu (1977: 200), Plato claims learning is not a unique activity, but part of any practical situation. Learning through discourse serving an institution that in turn supervises learning is a unique and overly theorized case: "The emergence of institutionalized education is accompanied by a crisis in diffuse education, which goes directly from practice to practice without passing through discourse. Excellence has ceased to exist once people start asking whether it can be taught, i.e., as soon as the objective confrontation of different styles of excellence makes it necessary to say what goes without saying, justify what is taken for granted, make an ought-to-be and an ought-to-do out of what had up to then been regarded as the only way to be and do."
4. His faculties being both superior and filled with superiority, Galton focused on white, male, English, and upper-class genius. On bias for male genius, see Alaya (1977) and Battersby (1989).
5. As a commodity in a market for prestige, genius is an alienating fetish similar to money. For Marx money is useless on its own; it lives in exchange and promises what we do not have, that which, no sooner than we have it, loses its promise. Money points always to an absence: the more our money, the greater the undelivered promise. Genius also puts promise over action and suffers the same critique:

   > Money is not the same as production, and wanting money only serves to identify what is not owned. (1867)

   Marx could say of genius and genius envy:

   > Being called genius is not the same as good work, and wanting to be a genius only serves to identify what is not accomplished.

   The genius category orients people to what they have not been able to do; the ascription of genius to others offers an alienated account of production in lieu of the real thing (Plekanov 1908; Lave and McDermott 2002).

REFERENCES

Addison, J. (1711) [untitled]. *The Spectator*, 160 (3 September).

Alaya, F. (1977) Victorian Science and the "Genius" of Woman. *Journal of the History of Ideas* 38: 261–80.

Barfield, O. (1967) *History in English Words.* Second edition. Great Barrington: Lindisfarne Press, 1985.

Basso, K. (1996) *Wisdom Sits in Places.* Albuquerque: University of New Mexico Press.

Battersby, C. (1989) *Gender and Genius: Toward a Feminist Aesthetics.* Bloomington: Indiana University Press.

Bone, D. (1989) The Emptiness of Genius: Aspects of Romanticism. In P. Murray (ed.), *Genius: The History of an Idea*. London: Blackwell.
Bourdieu, P. (1977) *Outline of a Theory of Practice*. New York: Cambridge University Press.
Carlyle, T. (1841) *One's Heroes, Hero-Worship, and the Heroic in History*. Lincoln: University of Nebraska Press, 1966.
Chadwick, W., and de Courtivron, I. (eds.) (1993) *Significant Others: Creativity and Intimate Partnership*. London: Thames and Hudson.
Champagne, S. (1992) Producing the Intelligent Child: Intelligence and the Child Rearing Discourse in the People's Republic in China. Unpublished doctoral dissertation, Stanford University.
Conklin, H.C. (in press) *Fine Description: Ethnographic and Linguistic Essays*. J. Kuipers and R. McDermott (eds.). New Haven: Center for Southeast Asian Studies.
DeNora, T. (1995) *Beethoven and the Construction of Genius: Musical Politics in Vienna, 1792–1803*. Berkeley: University of California Press.
DeNora, T., and Mehan, H. (1993) Genius: A Social Construction. In J. Kitsuse and T. Sarbin (eds), *Constructing the Social*. Pp. 157–73. Thousand Oaks: Sage.
Emerson, R.W. (1850) *Representative Men*. New York: Marsilio, 1995.
Elfenbein, A. (1999) *Romantic Genius: The Prehistory of a Homosexual Role*. Berkeley: University of California Press.
Engell, J. (1981) *The Creative Imagination: Enlightenment to Romanticism*. Cambridge: Harvard University Press.
Fara, P. (2000) Faces of Genius: Images of Isaac Newton in Eighteenth-Century England. In G. Cubitt and A. Warren (eds.), *Heroic Reputations and Exemplary Lives*. Pp. 57–81. New York: Cambridge University Press.
Frake, C.O. (1983) Notes on the Formal. *TEXT* 3: 299–304.
Frake, C.O. (1985) Time and Tide in the Cognitive Maps of Medieval Seafarers. *Man* 20: 254–70.
Frieden, K. (1985) *Genius and Monologue*. Ithaca: Cornell University Press.
Fujimura, J. (1998) *Crafting Science*. Cambridge: Harvard University Press.
Galton, F. (1892) *Hereditary Genius*. Gloucester: Peter Smith, 1972.
Gilman, S.L. (1996) *Smart Jews: The Construction of the Image of Jewish Superior Intelligence*. Lincoln: University of Nebraska Press.
Harper, D. (1987) *Working Knowledge*. Chicago: University of California Press.
Hayes, J.R. (1985) Three Problems in Teaching General Skills. In J. Segal, S. Chipman, and R. Glaser (eds.), *Thinking and Learning*, vol. 2. Pp. 391–405. Hillsdale: Erlbaum.
Hori, V. (1994) Learning in a Rinzai Zen Monastery. *Journal of Japanese Studies* 20: 5–36.
Howe, M. (1999) *Genius Explained*. New York: Cambridge University Press.
Huarte, Juan. (1594) *Examen de Ingenios para Las Ciencias. Segunda edicion*. Buenos Aires: Espasa-Calpe Argentina, S.A., 1946.
James, W. (1897) *The Will to Believe and Other Essays in Popular Philosophy*. New York: Dover.
Jeauneau, E. (1967) Nani gigantum humeris insidentes: Essai d'interprétation de Bernard of Chartres. *Vivarium* 5: 79–99.
Kershner, R. (1993) Genius, degeneration, and the panopticon. In R. Kershner (ed.), *Portrait of the Artist as a Young Man*. Pp. 373–90. New York: St. Martin's.

Koyré, A. (1952) An Unpublished Letter of Robert Hooke to Issac Newton. *Isis* 43: 312–37.

Kroeber, A.L. (1944) *Configurations of Cultural Growth*. Berkeley: University of California Press.

Latour, B. (1988) *The Pasteurization of France*. Cambridge: Harvard University Press.

Latour, B. (1998) *Pandora's Hope*. Cambridge: Harvard University Press.

Lave, J., and McDermott, R. (2002) Estranged labor learning. *Outlines* 4: 19–48.

Lavie, S., Narayan, K., and Rosaldo, R. (eds.) (1993) *Creativity/Anthropology*. Ithaca: Cornell University Press.

Lewis, D. (1972) *We, the Navigators*. Honolulu: University of Hawaii.

Marx, K. (1867) *Capital*. Vol. 1. London: Penguin, 1973.

McDermott, R.P. (1988) Inarticulateness. In D. Tannen (ed.), *Linguistics in Context*. Pp. 37–68. Norwood: Ablex.

McDermott, R.P. (1993) Acquisition of a Child by a Learning Disability. In S. Chaiklin and J. Lave (eds.), *Understanding Practice*. Pp. 269–305. New York: Cambridge University Press.

Merton, R.K. (1965) *On the Shoulders of Giants: A Shandian Postscript*. New York: Free Press.

Merton, R.K. (1996) *On Social Structure and Science*. Chicago: University of Chicago Press.

Mitchell, T. (1988) *Colonizing Egypt*. New York: Cambridge University Press.

Mosely, W. (ed.) (2000) *Black Genius*. New York: Norton.

Murray, P. (ed.) (1989) *Genius: The History of an Idea*. London: Blackwell.

Nahm, M. (1956) *Genius and Creativity: An Essay in the History of Ideas*. New York: Harper.

Nietzsche, F. (1884) *Beyond Good and Evil*. London: Penguin.

Plekanov, G. (1908) *Fundamental Problems of Marxism*. New York: International, 1969.

Pletsch, C. (1991) *Young Nietzsche: Becoming a Genius*. New York: Free Press.

Ranciere, J. (1991) *The Ignorant Schoolmaster*. Stanford: Stanford University Press.

Schutz, J., and Adair, D. (Eds.). (2001). *The Spur of Fame: Dialogues of John Adams and Benjamin Rush 1805–13*. Indianapolis: Liberty Fund.

Screech, M.A. (1983) *Montaigne and Melancholy*. London: Penguin.

Stillinger, J. (1991). *Multiple Authorship and the Myth of Solitary Genius*. London: Oxford University Press.

Varenne, H., and McDermott, R. (1998) *Successful Failure: The School America Builds*. Boulder: Westview.

White, L.A. (1949) *The Science of Culture*. New York: Free Press.

White, M. (2001) *Acid Tongues and Tranquil Dreamers*. New York: William Morrow.

Woodmansee, M. (1984) The genius and the copyright. *Eighteenth Century Studies* 17: 425–48.

CONTRIBUTORS

Doris Ash is an Assistant Professor at the University of California Santa Cruz in the Education Department. Her research, in museums, aquariums, and other informal settings, has centered on analyzing dialogic interactions at life science exhibits, emphasizing the negotiation of thematic biological content, and dialogic inquiry. Her most recent research focuses on providing long-term cross-cultural comparisons of family dialogue within a cohort of bilingual Spanish/English families.

Zvi Bekerman teaches anthropology of education at the School of Education and at The Melton Center, Hebrew University of Jerusalem. His main research interests and publications are in the study of identity processes and negotiation during intercultural encounters and in informal learning contexts. He has recently become involved as well in the study of identity construction and development in educational computer-mediated environments.

Gregory Braswell is a Postdoctoral Researcher in the Department of Psychology at the University of California, Santa Cruz. His research interests entail the social and cultural contexts in which children learn to use symbols, with a focus on the development of drawing skills.

Nicholas C. Burbules is professor of Educational Policy Studies at the University of Illinois, Urbana/Champaign. He has published widely in the areas of philosophy of education, technology and education, and critical social and political theory. He is also current editor of *Educational Theory.* His most recent books include: Nicholas C. Burbules and Thomas A. Callister, Jr., *Watch IT: The Promises and Risks of New Information Technologies for Education* (Boulder, Colorado: Westview Press, 2000) and Nicholas C. Burbules and Carlos Torres, eds., *Globalization and Education: Critical Perspectives* (New York: Routledge, 2000).

Maureen A. Callanan is Professor of Psychology at the University of California, Santa Cruz. She studies cognitive and language development, with a focus on how development unfolds in everyday social contexts such as family conversations.

Michael Cole, is University Professor of Communication, Psychology, and Human Development at the University of California, San Diego. His research focuses on the role of culture in human development, with a special emphasis on the role of formal and informal educational practices in developmental processes.

Sally Duensing, is on leave from the Exploratorium in San Francisco, California, to direct the new Center for Informal Learning and Schools at UC Santa Cruz. Presently she is a visiting professor at Kings College London, Department of Education and Professional Studies. Prior to this she held the Collier Chair, a one-year professorship in the Public Understanding of Science at the University of Bristol, England. In her twenty-five years at the Exploratorium she has worked in different facets of informal science learning, ranging from exhibit development to directing professional development programs for museum staff from around the world. Her most recent publication is "The Object of Experience," in the book *Perspectives on Object-Centered Learning in Museums,* S. Paris, ed. LEA, 2002.

Shelley Goldman is still learning as she makes her way through the worlds of home, family, and work. A confirmed informal learner, she interacts with teachers and students in schools and parents and kids at home. She's making sense of these environments for learning, and is hoping to find ways to legitimate them all. She has a doctorate from Teachers College, Columbia University and works as an associate professor at the Stanford University School of Education.

Patricia M. Greenfield received her Ph.D. from Harvard University and is currently Professor of Psychology at UCLA, where she is a member of the developmental psychology group. Her central theoretical and research interest is in the relationship between culture and human development. She is a past recipient of the American Association for the Advancement of Science Award for Behavioral Science Research, and has received teaching awards from UCLA and the American Psychological Association. Her books include *Mind and Media: The Effects of Television, Video Games, and Computers* (Harvard, 1984), which has been translated into nine languages. In the1990s she coedited (with R. R. Cocking) *Interacting with Video* (Elsevier, 1996) and *Cross-Cultural Roots of Minority Child Development* (Erlbaum, 1994).

James G. Greeno is a professor of Education at Stanford University. He studies conceptual understanding, reasoning, and learning, especially as an aspect of students' discourse in classroom activities where the concepts students are to learn are implicit in project activities, rather than being taught explicitly. His publications include *Thinking Practices in Mathematics and Sci-*

ence Learning (edited with S. Goldman, 1998) and "The Situativity of Knowing, learning, and research" (with the Middle-school Mathematics through Applications Group, *American Psychologist,* 1998).

Glynda A. Hull is an associate professor of Education in Language, Literacy, and Culture at the University of California, Berkeley. She studies literacy teaching and practice in a range of settings—workplaces, schools, and communities—and the ways in which writing and reading intersect with new technologies. Her books include *School's Out! Bridging Out-of-School Literacies with Classroom Practice* (with K. Schultz, 2002) and *The New Work Order* (with J. P. Gee & C. Lankshear, 1996).

D. W. Livingstone is head of the Centre for the Study of Education and Work at OISE/UT. He directed the first Canadian national survey of informal learning practices. His recent publications include: *Public Attitudes towards Education in Ontario 2000; Down-to-Earth People;* The *Education-Jobs Gap; Working and Learning in the Information Age;* and *Hidden Dimensions of the Knowledge Society,* which extends the activity theory of learning based on case studies with unionized workers and their families.

Ashley E. Maynard received her Ph.D. from UCLA and is currently Assistant Professor of Psychology at the University of Hawaii. Her research interests include the development of teaching skills in young children, sibling socialization, and the impact of the family daily routine on development. She was awarded the James McKeen Cattell Award from the New York Academy of Sciences and the APA Division 7 (Developmental Psychology) Award for her dissertation work.

Ray McDermott teaches cultural anthropology at the School of Education, Stanford University. He is interested in the history and cultural analysis of theories of the mind, because he cannot believe the foolishness of the measures used to hold schoolchildren accountable around the world. He teaches courses on urban education, the political economy of the mind, and the analysis of social interaction.

Honorine Nocon is Assistant Professor of Teacher Education, Bilingual Education, and English as a Second Language at the School of Education, University of Colorado at Denver. Her research focuses on the development of collaboration and community among diverse partners as well as formal and informal learning contexts that link schools, universities, and community organizations.

Daniel Schugurensky is assistant professor at the Ontario Institute for Studies in Education of the University of Toronto (OISE/UT), in the Department of Adult Education, Community Development and Counselling Psychology. He is the Chair of Practices in Citizenship Education of the Citizenship Education Research Network (CERN). His current research interests focus on the intersection between informal citizenship learning and participatory democracy, particularly in Latin America.

Diana Silberman-Keller is the Dean of the School of Multidisciplinary Studies, Beit Berl College, Israel, and was previously head of the Non-Formal Education Department at the same institution. She has written widely in the areas of: Ideologies in Education, Literary Theory and Semiotics in Education, and Non-formal Education and Learning.

Mark K. Smith is the Rank Research Fellow and Tutor, YMCA George Williams College, London, and visiting Professor in Community Education, University of Strathclyde, Glasgow. His books include *Developing Youth Work* (1988), *Local Education* (1994), and *Informal Education* (1999) (with Tony Jeffs). He edits *informal education* (<www.infed.org>).

Gordon Wells is a Professor in the Department of Education at the University of California, Santa Cruz. He has a strong interest in cultural historical activity theory, developed on the basis of the seminal ideas of Vygotsky and Bakhtin. He relies on Halliday's work on systemic functional linguistics and on Dewey. The influence of these writers, together with what he has learned from teacher colleagues, is clearly seen in *Dialogic Inquiry: Towards a Sociocultural Practice and Theory of Education* (1999).

INDEX

A

B

D

E

F

G

H

I

J

K

N

O

P

R

S

T

W

X

Y

Z

Studies in the Postmodern Theory of Education

General Editors
Joe L. Kincheloe & Shirley R. Steinberg

Counterpoints publishes the most compelling and imaginative books being written in education today. Grounded on the theoretical advances in criticalism, feminism, and postmodernism in the last two decades of the twentieth century, Counterpoints engages the meaning of these innovations in various forms of educational expression. Committed to the proposition that theoretical literature should be accessible to a variety of audiences, the series insists that its authors avoid esoteric and jargonistic languages that transform educational scholarship into an elite discourse for the initiated. Scholarly work matters only to the degree it affects consciousness and practice at multiple sites. Counterpoints' editorial policy is based on these principles and the ability of scholars to break new ground, to open new conversations, to go where educators have never gone before.

For additional information about this series or for the submission of manuscripts, please contact:

Joe L. Kincheloe & Shirley R. Steinberg
c/o Peter Lang Publishing, Inc.
275 Seventh Avenue, 28th floor
New York, New York 10001

To order other books in this series, please contact our Customer Service Department:

(800) 770-LANG (within the U.S.)
(212) 647-7706 (outside the U.S.)
(212) 647-7707 FAX

Or browse online by series:

www.peterlangusa.com